Ius Gentium: Comparative Perspectives on Law and Justice

Volume 49

More information about this series at http://www.springer.com/series/7888

Ulla Liukkunen • Yifeng Chen
Editors

Fundamental Labour Rights in China — Legal Implementation and Cultural Logic

Springer

Editors
Ulla Liukkunen
Faculty of Law
University of Helsinki
Helsinki, Finland

Yifeng Chen
Peking University Law School
Beijing, China

ISSN 1534-6781 ISSN 2214-9902 (electronic)
Ius Gentium: Comparative Perspectives on Law and Justice
ISBN 978-3-319-23155-6 ISBN 978-3-319-23156-3 (eBook)
DOI 10.1007/978-3-319-23156-3

Library of Congress Control Number: 2015955556

Springer Cham Heidelberg New York Dordrecht London

Printed on acid-free paper

Springer International Publishing AG Switzerland is part of Springer Science+Business Media (www.springer.com)

Preface

This volume was born in the framework of the Academy of Finland funded international research project 'ILO Core Labour Standards Implementation in China: Legal Architecture and Cultural Logic' and its second international research seminar held at the University of Helsinki in January 2014. The seminar discussed how the fundamental labour rights conventions of the International Labour Organization (ILO) have influenced the development of labour law and labour law regulation in China and to what extent the international labour standards in these conventions have been implemented in Chinese law and practice. This volume also analyzes the cultural logic that informs implementation of fundamental labour rights and maps the roles of different actors in this process, paying heed to existing societal and normative structures, mandates and resources for implementing fundamental principles and rights at work. Simultaneously, we seek to map the wider role of international labour standards' influence in developing Chinese law and society.

We are grateful to authors from three different continents for their willingness to cooperate in this demanding research project and seek fresh comparative approaches to questions of labour standards implementation which are relevant not only in terms of China but also globally. The entity of individual contributions in this volume has enabled consideration of fundamental labour rights implementation in China from remarkably varied methodological and comparative perspectives. The views and opinions expressed in the chapters of this volume are those of the individual contributors.

We are indebted to a number of people for their invaluable help with the preparation of this book, in particular project coordinator Alice Neffe and research assistant Stuart Mooney for their unfailing and generous support and assistance. Several other persons have also greatly assisted the preparation, especially Wu Yixuan, Wei Qian, Zhang Yihong, Laura Salokangas and Huang Yiyin. We would like to extend our heartfelt thanks to Christopher Goddard, who has provided an excellent language review for this volume. We are also grateful to the staff of Springer for smooth co-operation.

Helsinki, Finland
Beijing, China
November 2015

Ulla Liukkunen
Yifeng Chen

Contents

About the Authors

Ronald C. Brown is Professor of Law at the University of Hawaii Law School, served as the University's Director of the Center for Chinese Studies, as an Attorney with the National Labor Relations Board, and as an Arbitrator in labour-management disputes. Professor Brown teaches labour and employment law and Asian international and comparative labour law. He has authored numerous articles, lately on labour provisions of free trade agreements. Professor Brown has served as a Consultant with the World Bank and the ILO and has taught at Beijing University and Tsinghua Law Schools as a Fulbright Distinguished Scholar.

Yifeng Chen is Assistant Professor at Peking University Law School, as well as a docent in international law, University of Helsinki. He is also Assistant Director of the Peking University Institute of International Law. Dr. Chen is a Senior Researcher on the Academy of Finland funded project 'ILO Core Labour Standards Implementation in China: Legal Architecture and Cultural Logic'. Dr. Chen's fields of interest include legal theory, international organizations, history of international law, and Chinese law.

Ulla Liukkunen is Professor of Labour Law and Private International Law at the University of Helsinki. She is also the Director of the Finnish Center of Chinese Law and Chinese Legal Culture. Professor Liukkunen has published on labour law, private international law, comparative law, and governance of the social dimension of globalization. Professor Liukkunen is leading two Academy of Finland research projects, 'ILO Core Labour Standards Implementation in China: Legal Architecture and Cultural Logic' and 'Employee Participation and Collective Bargaining in the Era of Globalization – Nordic and Chinese Perspectives', the latter in cooperation with the Chinese Academy of Social Sciences. In addition to her academic activities, Professor Liukkunen has wide experience in national and EU legal drafting and has acted as an expert in several EU projects on labour law. Her current research interests include Chinese labour law issues and transnational labour law.

Alan C. Neal is Professor of Law at the University of Warwick. He holds the position of a standing high-level independent expert at the Labour Law and Social Security Law Institute, Peking University, and is a visiting professor at the Zhejiang University and the Beijing Jiao Tong University. Since 1995 he has held judicial office in the United Kingdom as an Employment Judge in the London (Central) Employment Tribunal and he is the Convenor of the European Association of Labour Court Judges.

Teemu Ruskola is Professor of Law at Emory University. Professor Ruskola is an elected member of the International Academy of Comparative Law and a member of the executive editorial board of the *American Journal of Comparative Law*. Previously Professor of Law at the American University in Washington, Professor Ruskola has been a visiting professor at Cornell Law School, Georgetown University Law Center, and Princeton University. An expert in Chinese law and legal theory, Professor Ruskola has published on the socio-historical and epistemological foundations of Chinese political orders, the intersection of corporate and family law in China, the history and politics of Euro-American conceptions of sovereignty in the Asia-Pacific region, and China's historical status as an international legal subject.

Kari Tapiola is a Special Adviser to the Director-General of the ILO. His long association with the ILO began in 1974, when he attended his first International Labour Conference as a Worker Delegate. Since then, Mr Tapiola has served in a variety of capacities with and in the ILO, including as Deputy Director-General and Executive Director. Other professional appointments include Political Secretary of the Finnish Minister for Foreign Affairs (1972), Special Assistant to the Executive Director of the United Nations Centre on Transnational Corporations (1976–1978), General Secretary of the Trade Union Advisory Committee to the OECD (1978–1985), and Information Director and International Affairs Director of the Central Organization of Trade Unions (1985–1988).

Zengyi Xie is Professor of Law at the Institute of Law, Chinese Academy of Social Sciences. He has been a visiting scholar at the University of Oxford, Columbia University and Harvard University. He has published books and articles in both Chinese and English relating to labour, corporate, and social law issues. Professor Xie is also a member of the Academic Committee of the Chinese Labour and Social Law Association and Deputy Secretary-General of the Association. In 2014, he was the recipient of the Nomination Award of the 7th National Ten Outstanding Young Jurists sponsored by the China Law Society.

Ninglan Xue is Professor and Director of Social Law Office at the Institute of Law, Chinese Academy of Social Sciences. Her main research areas are family law and women's rights law. In 2001, she was a visiting scholar at the Human Rights Research Institute of the University of Oslo and conducted research on Norwegian anti-domestic violence legislation and practice. She has attended a number of academic exchanges in Finland, Denmark, Sweden, Switzerland, the United States,

Thailand, and South Korea. She is also Deputy Director of the Family Law Association of the China Law Society, a standing member of both the Marriage and Family Association and the China Women's Association.

Dong Yan is Assistant Professor at Beijing Foreign Study University. He received his doctoral degree from Warwick University. His interest area is employment law. Dr Yan has participated in a number of Chinese labour law drafting processes, such as the Labour Contract Law and the Labour Dispute Mediation and Conciliation Law. Dr Yan is a researcher at Peking University Labour Law and Social Security Law Institute and a standing member of the Chinese Labour and Social Law Association.

Jingyi Ye is Professor of law and Director of the Labour and Social Security Law Institute at Peking University Law School. Professor Ye has published extensively in the fields of labour law and social law. She also serves as Vice-Chair and Secretary-General of the Chinese Labour and Social Law Association. Professor Ye is a member of the Experts Committee for Consultation under the Chinese Ministry of Human Resources and Social Security. At the moment, Professor Ye is leading the research project 'Creating a Legal Framework for Harmonious Labour Relations in China' funded by the National Planning Office of Philosophy and Social Science of China.

Chapter 1
Developing Fundamental Labour Rights in China – A New Approach to Implementation

Ulla Liukkunen and Yifeng Chen

1.1 Fundamental Labour Rights as a Vantage Point

Since the turn of the millennium, labour law has been an increasingly notable and rapidly expanding field in China. Development of a labour law infrastructure in China, the impact of which involves a broad economic and social dimension, is attracting much attention both at home and abroad. In this phase of development the legal framework shows itself as a complex and fragmented entity. Recently enacted laws have significantly strengthened the rights and interests of workers. Increasing labour costs put economic pressure on enterprises, which in turn generates considerable repercussions for changes in the mode of economic growth. Various challenges facing China lie not only in improving and enforcing labour laws, but also in creating and managing labour welfare and social security systems, the development of which might gradually open the way towards transforming China into a welfare state. Labour law development in China has broad bearings on China's economic, social and political development.

This book is a continuation of the volume "China and ILO Fundamental Principles and Rights at Work".[1] While the latter elaborates more on the International Labour Organization (ILO) and its Declaration of Fundamental Principles and Rights at Work (1998 Declaration), the present book chooses to focus on fundamental labour rights and examine their domestic implementation in China more closely.

[1] See Liukkunen and Chen 2014.

U. Liukkunen (✉)
Faculty of Law, University of Helsinki, Helsinki, Finland
e-mail: ulla.liukkunen@helsinki.fi

Y. Chen
Peking University Law School, Beijing, China
e-mail: yifeng.chen@pku.edu.cn

U. Liukkunen, Y. Chen (eds.), *Fundamental Labour Rights in China — Legal Implementation and Cultural Logic*, Ius Gentium: Comparative Perspectives on Law and Justice 49, DOI 10.1007/978-3-319-23156-3_1

Table 1.1 ILO Core Conventions and Ratifications by China

ILO core conventions	Entry into force	Date of ratification by China
Forced Labour Convention, (No. 29) adopted on 28 June 1930	1 May 1932	Not ratified
Freedom of Association and Protection of the Right to Organise Convention, (No. 87) adopted on 9 July 1948	4 July 1950	Not ratified
Right to Organise and Collective Bargaining Convention, (No. 98) adopted on 1 July 1949	18 July 1951	Not ratified
Equal Remuneration Convention, (No. 100) adopted on 29 June 1951	23 May 1953	2 November 1990
Abolition of Forced Labour Convention, (No. 105) adopted on 25 June 1957	17 January 1959	Not ratified
Discrimination (Employment and Occupation) Convention, (No. 111) adopted on 25 June 1958	15 June 1960	12 January 2006
Minimum Age Convention, (No. 138) adopted on 26 June 1973	19 June 1976	28 April 1999
Worst Forms of Child Labour Convention, (No. 182) adopted on 17 June 1999	19 November 2000	8 August 2002

The following table includes a list of core Conventions[2] as defined by the 1998 Declaration and the status of ratifications by China (Table 1.1).

Fundamental labour rights are essential for an operational labour law system. They also provide a useful basis for comparative study on labour law and practice in China. Of course, caution is called for in any comparative exercise on the implementation of fundamental labour rights. We are aware of the weaknesses and risks associated with such a particular spectrum. At the outset, we would like to make it clear that we try to avoid an exercise in "orientalism",[3] or to impose cultural and legal experiences specific to the West as the only universal truth. The aim is not to position the Western/Chinese legal experience as normal/abnormal, or treat the former as the only source of universal standards and the latter as backward. To the contrary, we aim at a better understanding of the Chinese experience in the first place. Involving scholars from three continents in this joint endeavour will hopefully enlarge our perspective, as each author not only offers a particular approach to fundamental labour rights implementation but also enriches the research agenda. The diversity of perspectives seeks to contribute to a better knowledge and understanding of the Chinese situation.

[2]The eight ILO 'core' or 'fundamental' Conventions are: the Forced Labour Convention No. 29, the Freedom of Association and Protection of the Right to Organise Convention No. 87, the Right to Organise and Collective Bargaining Convention No. 98, the Equal Remuneration Convention No. 100, the Abolition of Forced Labour Convention No. 105, the Discrimination (Employment and Occupation) Convention No. 111, the Minimum Age Convention No. 138, and the Worst Forms of Child Labour Convention No. 182.

[3]For exposure and critique of legal orientalism, see Ruskola 2002 and 2013.

Other intellectual traps may also lie in wait. Singling out and focusing on "fundamental" labour rights may already have distorted identification of labour questions in the first place. It may fail to give an authentic voice and interpretation to the Chinese labour question by prioritizing certain issues and values over some other alternatives, by excluding certain matters from investigation, or by qualifying usable vocabularies of discourse. As the solution depends on formulation of the question, false identification of the question can hardly be conducive to a constructive understanding of labour matters in China. Even if fundamental labour rights are a useful point of departure, the parochialism of the concept of fundamental labour rights may not do justice to the diversity of labour law development in China and to the role that the international labour standards of the ILO have played in that development.

Indeed, the idea of fundamental labour rights is a concept with deeply European roots, at least historically, so that globally speaking it can be claimed to have sidelined cultural particularities.[4] The idea and content of fundamental labour rights rests squarely in the Western liberal tradition focusing on general participatory rights of workers. Even in the West, the fundamental labour rights approach itself is not without controversy.[5] And in practice, domestic implementation of fundamental labour rights in European countries also meets various difficulties and challenges, so that their realization among different countries is uneven.[6]

With the regulatory approach of the ILO, fundamental labour rights have gained a new foothold as a key pillar in managing the social dimension of globalization. This has brought a new global dimension to the idea of fundamental labour rights. Examining them in the Chinese context may highlight essential elements of the current developmental stage of the Chinese legal system, also revealing conflicting pressures caused by different interests that accompany further development of the system.

Various challenges in such a comparative undertaking notwithstanding, focusing on fundamental labour rights in China offers several research advantages. First of all, the concept of fundamental labour rights enables Western researchers to engage with profound labour issues and labour law development in China from a comparative perspective. When approaching and comparing legal phenomena of different jurisdictions, the cultural assumptions and conceptual framework stemming from the legal system of an individual researcher are relevant. In this regard, the idea of fundamental labour rights provides an analytical framework if this is taken as a starting point instead of as a natural axiom. It also carries within itself a set of Western legal doctrines, laws and practices that offers useful references in approaching the Chinese law question.

---

[4] See also Perry 1997, at pp. 508–509.

[5] See e.g., a strong critique voiced by Alston 2004. For a response from a former legal advisor to the ILO, see Maupain 2005.

[6] See e.g., the Annual Reports on Fundamental Labour Rights published by the European Union Agency for Fundamental Labour Rights.

Second, focus on fundamental labour rights offers an analytical framework against which to appraise the evolving Chinese labour law framework. Efforts invested by China since the 2000s on law-making in the field of labour law are significant. In addition to notable examples such as enactment of the Labour Contract Law,[7] the Employment Promotion Law[8] and the Labour Dispute Mediation and Arbitration Law in 2007,[9] more pervasive law-making is observed: by state councils, ministries and local people's congresses and governments. Any attempt to accomplish a general evaluation of such rapid legal development is a highly challenging task. To focus on fundamental labour rights allows one to measure legal development in China against a set of standards.

Indeed we consider fundamental labour rights paramount for the legal protection of workers. We seek to offer a broad perspective that allows a better understanding of China's legal development and related stage of labour rights. The vocabulary of fundamental labour rights offers a useful angle from which China may consider its possible direction in future legal development.

Third, China itself has subscribed to various international undertakings relating to protection of fundamental labour rights. Implementing those conventions in the domestic setting has been an effort of several years. In this sense, fundamental labour rights today are no longer so particular to Europe or the West. Many of these rights have already been translated into China's legal system. However, Chinese experience of fundamental labour rights implementation has not been completely successful or positive. Yet, even symptoms or difficulties experienced by China during implementation also provide good research material for further reflecting both on fundamental labour rights and the Chinese legal system.

Fourth, research on fundamental labour rights implementation not only tells of experience in China, but also offers insights that may be globally relevant. Fundamental labour rights gain particular significance in the era of globalization.[10] Globalization has posed many challenges to the protection of labour rights and made the ILO reassess its approach to promoting better labour standards. It is noteworthy that fundamental labour rights as defined by the ILO are also included in major public codes on corporate social responsibility directed to multinational companies.[11] Formulation of a list of fundamental labour rights belongs to the heart of efforts by the ILO to combat the challenges of the global labour market. However, the refocusing of the ILO in the 1998 Declaration has been widely debated and has also prompted concerns and criticism of the usefulness and effectiveness of the

[7] [Labour Contract Law of the People's Republic of China] 中华人民共和国劳动合同法 (zhōng huá rén mín gòng hé guó láo dòng hé tóng fǎ), 2007.

[8] [Employment Promotion Law of the People's Republic of China] 中华人民共和国就业促进法 (zhōng huá rén mín gòng hé guó jiù yè cù jìn fǎ), 2007.

[9] [Labour Dispute Mediation and Arbitration Law of the People's Republic of China] 中华人民共和国劳动争议调解仲裁法 (zhōng huá rén mín gòng hé guó láo dòng zhēng yì tiáo jiě zhòng cái fǎ), 2007.

[10] See e.g., Sengenberger 2005.

[11] See also Liukkunen 2014.

chosen strategy as well as the institutional capacity of the ILO itself.[12] Delineating some rights as fundamental has remarkably shaped the way efforts are directed in order to extend social justice and fair labour standards in the turbulence of global market forces. The status of fundamental labour rights can be understood as a point of reference when assessing the achievements of a single country in terms of governance of the social dimension of globalization. The trajectory of labour law development in China could be especially relevant to those transitional, industrializing, or developing economies in strengthening their paths towards more sustainable development in the long run. China's experience is thus relevant to the Chinese people, but could also be useful globally.

1.2 Bringing Cultural Logic to the Forefront of Legal Research

Law as a social phenomenon is deeply embedded in the culture and tradition of a particular nation, or community. Yet often comparatists focus on the normative structure and system and stay at the surface of the legal system, while treating any extra-legal cultural and social factors either as irrelevant, or as something to overcome. To talk about legal culture is sometimes considered an excuse for deviation from what is understood to be the usual understanding of law, or a symbol of a less developed, problematic society. From this perspective, culture is something outside the law, and indeed antagonistic to law. Our research project challenges that approach and seeks to bring the cultural aspect with its multidimensionality to the forefront of research.

Our research approach assumes the following propositions about law. First of all, the autonomy of law is understood to be relative, with the legal system in constant interaction with other sub-systems of a society. Secondly, we adopt a social concept of law, looking at law both as a sovereign command as well as law in action. Thirdly, law is an anthropological phenomenon. It constructs an interpretative framework. The concept of workers as defined in a legal system affects the self-identity of those workers in real life and possibly also the conception of their relationship with other groups in a society. In all these mirrored conceptions of law, culture is an essential component which affects the actual operation of law.

Of course, reference to culture should not be understood as an attempt to create or reinforce any stereotype. Moreover, the idea of culture is not to be viewed as something static, but rather involving dynamic, evolving factors. Therefore, when talking about culture, we are not searching for the history or traditions of China, but emphasize their importance to the development of law. At the same time, various economic, social and political elements are looked upon as relevant not only to legal

[12] See e.g., Maupain 2013. For an assessment of the ILO as an international organization marginalized in global governance and not capable of fulfilling its mandate, see Klabbers 2014.

development in China but also as essential for a better understanding of how law functions in China.[13]

As our research focus is on fundamental labour rights in China, the following cultural aspects of China in particular are relevant. As China practices a socialist system, one wonders how a proletarian dictatorship and Marxist ideology could contribute to labour governance. It is equally important to bear in mind that China has been developing a market economy since the 1990s. The state has retreated considerably from economic sectors compared to the degree of its involvement in the earlier planned economy phase. Developing a balanced approach between marketization and proactive regulation in labour governance poses specific challenges to the role and functions of the state itself. In addition, the rule of law and human rights developments are increasingly relevant parts of the new political and social discourse, which opens new possibilities to address labour issues in new normative frameworks and vocabularies. The scale of the country and its developmental phase need to be viewed through this broad frame.[14]

Even when a legal system is embedded with seemingly conflicting elements, it may function according to its particular logic. We need to identify and analyse that logic in order to understand the role that fundamental labour rights play in the legal system. Here, methods of comparison which take into account the cultural context of law are needed and even challenged. We may ask whether the viewpoints raised in Western comparative law sufficiently address the challenges and problems of a developing giant country like China. In particular, existing comparative law theories with their Western-loaded vocabulary seem unable to catch the peculiarities of culturally loaded legal questions related to the implementation of law in China. This volume seeks to contribute to filling that gap in research by offering an analysis of cultural factors and dynamics at play in the implementation of international legal instruments in China. By so doing, the volume aims at further extending the present comparative labour law research agenda.

1.3 A Broader Perspective on Implementation

The notion of legal implementation is often used in a rather specific and narrow manner. In the field of international law, implementation typically refers to mechanisms for incorporating or transforming international legal norms into the domestic legal order.[15] This approach pays attention to inter-system compatibility and to

---

[13] See also Chen at Chap. 4 in this volume.

[14] For example, Jean-Michel Servais observes that "the level of economic development plays however a key role in the process of integrating international labour law into the domestic legal order". See Servais 2011, at p. 344.

[15] This subject is often dealt with under the theme of "the relation of municipal and international law" in textbooks of international law. See e.g. Brownlie 2008, at chapter 2; Cassese 2005, at chapter 12; Wang 1998, at chapter 6.

interaction between different levels of law. At the same time, in the domestic context, legal implementation often looks at judicial practice and how norms are interpreted and enforced by the courts. The court system is given the key role in legal implementation. However, neither approach is adequate from the perspective of the current research project. When the perspective is shifted to labour law, assessing implementation requires placing emphasis on the characteristics of the individual labour law system and related industrial relations system as well as authorities and mechanisms specifically targeted at ensuring compliance with labour standards.

For the purposes of our research project, we adopt a much broader understanding of implementation than usual. First of all, our understanding of implementation does not limit itself to examining how ratified international labour conventions are implemented in China through various laws, regulations and rules enacted by the National People's Congress and its Standing Committee, or by the State Council and its constituent ministries. Our research project highlights the importance of regulations and rules enacted at the local level, and the relevance of varied administrative practice in different localities. This is in particular relevant in the field of labour law where various nuances of implementation appear, given the enormous developmental, economic and social differences within China.

Secondly, while the court system is essential for examining implementation of fundamental labour rights, the project does not turn a blind eye to the abundant administrative practice which is much richer, often more diverse and also more problematic. An essential feature of legal development in China is seen to be administrative dominance.[16] The State Council and local governments at various levels are much more powerful than local authorities often tend to be. Labour inspections exercise growing importance in the implementation of labour laws in China. This is particularly noteworthy because an effective labour inspectorate is characteristic of the requirements set generally for efficient labour standards implementation. Moreover, in practice mediation conducted by administrative bodies or social groups is important in settling collective disputes.

Thirdly, when looking at fundamental labour rights implementation, the question how fundamental labour rights affect the international performance of the Chinese government in negotiating and concluding free trade agreements and investment agreements also deserves close attention.[17] Besides, the overseas investment of Chinese multinational companies also generates new needs and concerns as to how Chinese companies might respect and promote labour rights abroad. These aspects are also particularly relevant to China's growth into a world power.

Fourthly, our research approach takes into account the roles of different institutions and actors in applying the law, especially the activities of para-state or social actors, including enterprises and individuals. In the Chinese context, the role and function of the trade unions deserves special attention. According to the Trade Union Law, the All-China Federation of Trade Unions (ACFTU) is characterized as

[16] See Chen 2014, at pp. 29–39.

[17] See e.g., Brown at Chap. 7 in this volume.

"a mass organization formed by the Chinese working class on a voluntary basis".[18] It is not an administrative authority but is recognized with the status of a *de facto* parastatal authority. Not infrequently it releases important policy documents on labour issues capable of influencing administrative practice.[19] The ACFTU and its local chapters are also often consulted or directly involved in the formulation of national and local labour policies.[20] Local trade unions at various levels often play an essential role in settlement of specific labour disputes or labour conflicts.

In addition, various other actors should also be taken into account. This includes the practice of enterprises, non-governmental organisations, and even the media, as well as naturally individual employers and employees. These are all relevant to an in-depth understanding of the framework of the implementation of fundamental labour rights in China. This actor-oriented approach will provide a highly useful supplement to an authority-centred approach to legal implementation. This leads us from a purely normative exercise to a more sociological and anthropological investigation into how fundamental labour rights might affect the power relationship between different actors, including that between employers and employees in concrete circumstances.

Fifthly, implementation is also a matter closely connected to the nature of the rights in question. Two different clusters of labour rights exist under the title of fundamental labour rights. Freedom from forced labour, prevention of child labour and anti-discrimination belong to the category of individual labour rights while, in contrast, freedom of association and the right to collective bargaining are labelled as collective labour rights. The study of implementation should be carried out with due regard to the specific features of substantive labour rights.

[18] [Trade Union Law of the People's Republic of China] 中华人民共和国工会法 (zhōng huá rén mín gòng hé guó gōng huì fǎ), 1992 (as revised in 2001), Article 5 provides that: "Trade unions shall organize and educate employees to exercise their democratic rights pursuant to the provisions of Chinese Constitution and laws, to play their role as the nation's master, to participate through various channels and forms in the management of state affairs, economic, cultural and social affairs. It shall also assist the people's governments in performing their duties, and uphold the people's democratic dictatorship of socialist state power, which is under the leadership of the working classes and based on worker-peasant alliance".

[19] An outstanding example is the [Provisions on the Democratic Management of Enterprises] 企业民主管理规定 (qǐ yè mín zhǔ guǎn lǐ guī dìng), 2012. This has been one of the most important sources for promoting employee participation in company administration in private enterprises.

[20] [Trade Union Law of the People's Republic of China] 中华人民共和国工会法 (zhōng huá rén mín gòng hé guó gōng huì fǎ), 1992 (as revised in 2001), Article 33 expressly confirms the trade unions' right to be consulted. "The state organs shall listen to the view of the trade unions when drafting or amending laws, statutory rules and regulations directly involving the rights and interests of employees. The people's governments at the level of county or above shall, when formulating national economic and social development plans, listen to the views of the equivalent level trade unions on important issues involving the rights and interests of employees. When the people's governments at the county level or above and their relevant authorities formulate important policies or measures on employment, wages, labour safety and hygiene, social insurance, etc., the equivalent level trade unions shall be invited to participate in the research work and the views of the said trade unions shall be taken into consideration."

In terms of terminology, the concept of implementation is used as a generic term, broadly covering adoption, interpretation, application, compliance, enforcement and promotion of fundamental labour rights at work in China. These elements can have related yet distinguishable meanings in specific contexts and in different legal systems. Nevertheless, they can also be viewed as different aspects of implementation and can thus be studied under the general theme of implementation.

Meanwhile, the term implementation itself calls for some clarification. Implementation often connotes the transmission of a certain normative imperative from an authoritative text into actual practice, in a typical situation being a top-down perspective. This approach often presumes the existence and availability of a clear-cut, hard-core normativity of a legal norm. However, we highlight here that possible meanings of fundamental labour rights are something which is approached and interpreted by various actors in different contexts. These actors may appropriate and interpret, use or misuse the concept of fundamental labour rights for their own purposes. The use of fundamental labour rights by various actors should be treated as authentic and as such we seek to include their experience in our reflection. This allows us to better understand the possibility offered by the legal framework of fundamental labour rights as well as its structural limits.

The broad perspective of implementation thus covers legislative implementation by national and local legislatures, monitoring by labour protection inspectorates, judicial implementation by labour arbitration committees and courts, mediation by administrative bodies and social groups, as well as implementation and application of fundamental labour rights by enterprises and other non-state actors. In addition, the realization of fundamental labour rights and labour protection in China needs to be studied in relation to China's domestic economic and social transition as well as China's integration into the global economic system.

1.4 Identifying Normative Layers and Structure

The emergence of the notion of fundamental labour rights, sometimes used interchangeably with "core labour standards", has been a rather recent phenomenon. Several different levels of normative layers can be identified. First of all, the 1998 Declaration defines as fundamental rights freedom of association and effective recognition of the right to collective bargaining, the elimination of forced or compulsory labour, the abolition of child labour and the elimination of discrimination in respect of employment and occupation. These four categories of labour rights are considered to be fundamental. The idea of fundamental labour rights came as an international response to the need to address the social dimension of globalization.[21] The wording of the Declaration asserts the obligations of ILO member states in relation to those fundamental labour rights. The Declaration pronounces "that all Members, even if they have not ratified the Conventions in

[21] See Tapiola 2014.

question, have an obligation arising from the very fact of membership in the Organization to respect, to promote and to realize, in good faith and in accordance with the Constitution, the principles concerning the fundamental rights which are the subject of those Conventions". First of all, these principles and rights are considered to be universally applicable, irrespective of political systems, developmental phases or cultural traditions, and irrespective of whether or not states have ratified the relevant conventions. In addition, the ILO has established a follow-up procedure that aims at constantly tackling with non-ratification or non-compliance by states.

Secondly, under the 1998 Declaration, the eight conventions comprise the "hard core". These conventions create normative obligations for those states that have ratified them. State parties have the obligation to implement the conventions in their domestic legal systems. States may incur international responsibility for failing to perform their international obligations, and a series of investigation and sanction procedures as envisaged in the ILO Constitution may follow in case of default.[22]

Thirdly, fundamental labour rights form part of international human rights. We can also find their roots or legal bases in human rights treaties. Notable examples include recognition of the right to form trade unions in Article 8 of the International Covenant on Economic, Social and Cultural Rights (ICESCR), freedom from forced labour in Article 8 of the International Covenant on Civil and Political Rights (ICCPR), and the general principle of non-discrimination in Article 2 of both the ICESCR and ICCPR. The 1998 Declaration can be viewed as emphasizing recognition of labour rights as human rights. The Declaration highlights fundamental labour rights as universal rights applicable to all human beings in all states, regardless of their level of economic development. It can be seen as embodying a significant change in the policy approach of the ILO, caused by demands raised by globalization, endorsing the fundamental nature of certain labour rights and their utmost importance in the global search for social justice and sustainable development.

China has become an active participant in the international human rights system since the 1990s.[23] China signed the ICCPR in 1998, pending domestic ratification. China ratified, *inter alia*, the ICESCR in 2001. In its second periodic report to the UN Committee on Economic, Cultural and Social Rights on 6 July, 2012, China expressed its commitment to a series of policies to enhance labour protection.[24] Chinese labour law scholars tend to relate protection of labour rights to China's commitment and efforts to deliver human rights protection in the domestic setting.[25]

[22] It was reported in 2000 for the first time in ILO history that Article 33 of the ILO Constitution was activated against Myanmar's persistent violation of its obligations under the Forced Labour Convention. See Maupain 2005, at p. 441.

[23] China has adopted two National Human Rights Action Plans: [National Human Rights Action Plan of China] 国家人权行动计划 (guó jiā rén quán xíng dòng jì huà) respectively 2009–2010 and 2012–2015.

[24] See UN Committee on Economic, Cultural and Social Rights 2012.

[25] [Xie] 谢增毅 2011, at p. 2.

Fourthly, fundamental rights in the constitutional framework of a country are often highly relevant to the realization and promotion of labour rights. The constitutional right of freedom of association provides powerful justification for reinforcing freedom of association on labour issues and the right to collective bargaining; the elimination of discrimination in respect of employment and occupation can be inferred from the constitutional guarantee of equality; and the elimination of forced or compulsory labour are part of freedom from coercion. In China, the development of constitutionalism also provides a frame of reference which is useful for assessing the stage of development in terms of adoption of fundamental labour rights.

Fifthly, detailed regulations and protection of fundamental labour rights are mostly governed through domestic laws and regulations. In terms of normative hierarchy, they are often inferior to international conventions and national constitutions. Yet they are not the least important and are often key to labour rights protection. For example, a general rule on the prohibition of child labour in China is prescribed in the Law on the Protection of Minors (1991)[26] and the Labour Law (1994).[27] Yet more comprehensive regulation on this matter is an administrative regulation enacted by the State Council in 1991, updated by a 2002 regulation soon after the Standing Committee of the National People's Congress ratified the Worst Forms of Child Labour Convention No. 182.[28] Freedom of association in China is also to be exercised only in accordance with approval procedures as defined in the Trade Union Law (1992, revised in 2001).[29] These regulations provide a much more nuanced picture of how fundamental labour rights are defined and implemented in the national context.

As can be seen, recognition of fundamental labour rights can be found at different layers of legal normativity and are connected in a hybrid structure. Interaction, dialogue and mutual enforcement among different layers of normativity also constitute an important aspect of research.

1.5 Normative Effects of Fundamental Labour Rights

As a legal institution, fundamental labour rights are capable of producing normative effects upon a national legal system, although their actual operation hinges upon political and legal traditions and various other factors. Systematic elucidation on this would be conducive to a better understanding of the institution of fundamental labour rights itself as well as their relevance to China.

---

[26] [Protection of Minors Law of the People's Republic of China] 中华人民共和国未成年人保护法 (zhōng huá rén mín gòng hé guó wèi chéng nián rén bǎo hù fǎ), 1991, Article 38.

[27] [Labour Law of the People's Republic of China] 中华人民共和国劳动法 (zhōng huá rén mín gòng hé guó láo dòng fǎ), 1994, Article 15.

[28] See also Liukkunen at Chap. 6 in this volume.

[29] [Trade Union Law of the People's Republic of China] 中华人民共和国工会法 (zhōng huá rén mín gòng hé guó gōng huì fǎ), 1992.

First of all, fundamental labour rights provide workers with a normative floor of rights protection. The globalization progress has led to increasing economic competition at the global level. This raises the concern of a "race to the bottom", as the cost of labour is rather sensitive, especially in labour-intensive industries. At the end of 2012 the total number of employed persons in China was reported to be around 767 million. Of these, roughly 232 million worked in secondary industry and 277 million in tertiary (or service) industry.[30] The structure and distribution of the labour force between coastal areas and inland areas are rather different. Most high technology industry and educated labour forces are in economically relatively developed areas. Protection of migrant workers from rural areas has become a perennial concern. Workers who are vulnerable to poverty may often suffer from lack of labour rights. The global economic and financial crisis brought into the spotlight structural problems of the labour market that relate not only to employment but also to the ability of states to guarantee the fundamental labour rights of workers. Examining the implementation of fundamental labour rights can lead to identification of the most persistent labour market problems and highlight the right approach to labour protection.

It is important to analyse the legal situation of fundamental labour rights in terms of further developing Chinese labour market regulation and in order to increase understanding of elements that can contribute to providing better protection for workers. It should be noted that lack of sufficient protection is not only affected by the content of existing labour standards but has much to do with their weak enforcement, which businesses can take advantage of.

Secondly, fundamental labour rights have the potential to contribute to systematizing the labour law system. Fundamental labour rights cover only specific rights out of a broad array of labour rights. Yet, in so far as those rights are defined as fundamental, they project and reinforce a particular legal image of "workers" possessing a bundle of liberal rights. As such, the notion of fundamental labour rights is capable of generating a new systemic understanding of labour protection on this liberal conception of workers.

Thirdly, fundamental labour rights possess a transformative capacity to contribute to developing a labour protection system from a regulatory, administration-centred institution towards a rights-centred institution. Labour protection often relies on an administrative system based on labour inspectorates' monitoring activities. This is particularly relevant in matters such as safety at work, working hours, minimum wages, and so on. At the same time, in essence the idea of fundamental labour rights stresses the importance of empowering workers as rights-holders. This can also be seen as a requirement for effective implementation of rules which create rights of a human rights nature.

Fourthly, fundamental labour rights have a radiative effect upon labour protection and other social issues. The labour issue is unavoidably mingled with other social issues. Moreover, given the enormous size of the workforce in China its practical implications often go beyond the field of labour protection. A high-profile

[30] National Bureau of Statistics of the People's Republic of China 2014, at p. 121.

example is the development of anti-discrimination in employment in China bringing about considerable public debate on social equality beyond employment as such.[31] The development of freedom of trade unions might further strengthen democratic elements not only in the workplace but also in society at large.

Fifth, fundamental labour rights have a relating and developing function as they introduce the language of fundamental rights and international human rights into the labour protection discourse. Labour protection and human rights approaches can work so as to mutually reinforce each other. The importance of developing labour protection in relation to human rights cannot be overstated. This perspective is of much significance and full of potential. Labour rights can and do benefit from the fundamental rights and human rights discourses.

1.6 Towards an Open Discourse on Fundamental Labour Rights in China

In Chinese scholarship on labour law and labour protection, attention to fundamental labour rights as defined by the ILO is less outspoken.[32] Most legal scholarship still focuses on the right to work.[33] The two notions have different historical roots in their development and focus on rather different aspects.

We might summarize by saying that more discourse on fundamental labour rights in China would be desirable. Promoting fundamental labour rights and an efficient economy need not be conflicting aims of society. Developing labour rights increases means of participation in the labour market and hence also contributes to maintaining the stability of the labour market as well as the adaptability of society in times of change. It appears to us that the landscape is gradually changing, not least due to the challenges posed by labour unrest and the present legal situation, which emphasize a need to improve labour market stability.[34]

The rule of law discourse is growing in importance and this can be expected also to have a bearing on fundamental labour rights discourse. With the recent opening of the rule of law discussion by the Chinese Communist Party (CCP), promotion of fundamental labour rights might gain new dynamics. In October 2014, the 4th Plenum of the 18th Central Committee of the CCP promulgated the CCP Central Committee Decision concerning Some Major Issues in Comprehensively Promoting Governing the Country According to Law.[35] The Decision emphasizes several

[31] For a thorough discussion on legal development on anti-discrimination in employment, see Xie 2014.

[32] For an exception see, however, [Yang and Xuan] 杨帅 and 宣海林 2013.

[33] See e.g., [Qin] 秦国荣 2012.

[34] See also an analysis provided by Ye at Chap. 10 in this volume.

[35] [CCP Central Committee Decision concerning Some Major Issues in Comprehensively Promoting Governing the Country According to Law] 中共中央关于全面推进依法治国若干重大问题的决定 (zhōng gòng zhōng yāng guān yú quán miàn tuī jìn yī fǎ zhì guó ruò gān zhòng dà wèn tí de jué dìng), 2014.

factors that are important to promotion of fundamental labour rights and provides a reform plan with a focus on issues such as implementation and enforcement.[36] The Decision represented the first occasion when the Central Committee addressed the rule of law in China as the main theme of its plenary session. Although the Decision does not explicitly address the role of fundamental labour rights or labour standards in advancing the rule of law, it contains important elements in terms of developing further realization of fundamental labour rights and related legal infrastructure.

References

Literature

Alston, Philip. 2004. 'Core Labour Standards' and the transformation of the international labour rights regime. *European Journal of International Law* 15: 457–521.

Brown, Ronald C. 2016. China – U.S. Implementation of ILO standards by BITs and pieces (FTAs). In *Fundamental labour rights in China – Legal implementation and cultural logic*, ed. Ulla Liukkunen and Chen Yifeng, 169–202. Dordrecht: Springer.

Brownlie, Ian. 2008. *Principles of international law*. Oxford: Oxford University Press.

Cassese, Antonio. 2005. *International law*. Oxford: Oxford University Press.

Chen, Yifeng. 2014. Legal formalism, justice and judicial independence in China. In *Oikeuden historiasta tulevaisuuden Eurooppaan. Pia Letto-Vanamo 60 vuotta*, ed. Olli Mäenpää, Dan Frände, and Päivi Korpisaari, 29–39. Helsinki: Suomalainen Lakimiesyhdistys.

Chen, Yifeng. 2016. ILO, Extraterritoriality and labour protection in Republican Shanghai. In *Fundamental labour rights in China – Legal implementation and cultural logic*, ed. Ulla Liukkunen and Chen Yifeng, 83–116. Dordrecht: Springer.

Klabbers, Jan. 2014. Marginalized International Organizations: Three hypotheses concerning the ILO. In *China and ILO fundamental principles and rights at work*, ed. Roger Blanpain, vol. eds. Ulla Liukkunen and Chen Yifeng. Bulletin of Comparative Labour Relations 86: 181–196. Alphen aan den Rijn: Kluwer Law International.

Liukkunen, Ulla. 2014. Transnational labour law and fundamental labour rights: Making Chinese workers matter? In *China and ILO fundamental principles and rights at work*, ed. Roger Blanpain, vol. eds. Ulla Liukkunen and Chen Yifeng. Bulletin of Comparative Labour Relations 86: 163–180. Alphen aan den Rijn: Kluwer Law International.

Liukkunen, Ulla. 2016. Child labour regulation in China – Prospects and complexities. In *Fundamental labour rights in China – Legal implementation and cultural logic*, ed. Ulla Liukkunen and Chen Yifeng, 139–168. Dordrecht: Springer.

Liukkunen, Ulla and Chen Yifeng vol. eds. 2014. *China and ILO fundamental principles and rights at work*. In 86 Bulletin of Comparative Labour Relations, ed. Roger Blanpain. Alphen aan den Rijn: Kluwer Law International.

Maupain, Francis. 2005. Revitalization not retreat: The real potential of the 1998 ILO Declaration for the Universal Protection of Workers' Rights. *European Journal of International Law* 16: 439–465.

Maupain, Francis. 2013. *The future of the International Labour Organization in the global economy*. Oxford: Hart Publishing Ltd.

[36] See also Peerenboom 2014.

Peerenboom, Randall. 2014. *Fly high the banner of socialist rule of law with Chinese characteristics! What does the 4th plenum decision mean for legal reforms in China?* Available at: http://papers.ssrn.com/sol3/papers.cfm?abstract_id=2519917. Last accessed 19 Jun 2015.
Perry, Michael. 1997. Are human rights Universal? *Human Rights Quarterly* 19(3): 508–509.
[Qin, Guorong] 秦国荣. 2012. [*Protection of the right to work and the labour law revision*] 劳动权保障与《劳动法》的修改 (láo dòng quán bǎao zhàng yǔ "láo dòng fǎ" de xiū gǎi). Beijing: [People's Press] 人民出版社.
Ruskola, Teemu. 2002. Legal orientalism. *Michigan Law Review* 101: 179–234.
Ruskola, Teemu. 2013. *Legal orientalism: China, the United States and modern law*. Cambridge, MA: Harvard University Press.
Sengenberger, Werner. 2005. *Globalization and social progress: The role and impact of international labour standards*. Bonn: Friedrich-Ebert-Stiftung. Available at: http://www.uni-kassel.de/~tduermei/iksa/readerengl/addtext%2022%20Sengenberg%20Globalization%20and%20Social%20Progress.pdf. Last accessed 19 Jun 2015.
Servais, Jean-Michel. 2011. *International labour law*. Dordrecht: Kluwer Law International.
Tapiola, Kari. 2014. The ILO declaration on fundamental principles and rights at work and its implementation in China. In *China and ILO fundamental principles and rights at work*, ed. Roger Blanpain, vol. eds. Ulla Liukkunen and Chen Yifeng. Bulletin of Comparative Labour Relations 86: 9–17. Alphen aan den Rijn: Kluwer Law International.
[Wang, Tieya] 王铁崖. 1998. [*Introduction to international law*] 国际法引论 (guó jì fǎ yǐn lùn). Beijing: [Peking University Press] 北京大学出版社.
[Xie, Zengyi] 谢增毅. 2011. [*Labour law: Comparison and reflections*] 劳动法的比较与反思 (láo dòng fǎ de bǐ jiào yǔ fǎn sī). [*Social Sciences Academic Press*] 社会科学文献出版社.
Xie, Zengyi. 2014. New developments in anti-discrimination in the workplace in China: Law and practice. In *China and ILO fundamental principles and rights at work*, ed. Roger Blanpain, vol. eds. Ulla Liukkunen and Chen Yifeng. Bulletin of Comparative Labour Relations 86: 143–162. Alphen aan den Rijn: Kluwer Law International.
[Yang, Shuai] 杨帅 and [Hailin Xuan] 宣海林. 2013. [*International labour standards and their implementation in China*] 国际劳动标准及其在中国的适用 (guó jì láo dòng biāo zhǔn jí qí zài zhōng guó de shì yòng). Beijing: [Law Press] 法律出版社.
Ye, Jingyi. 2016. Reforming the collective labour relationship governance in China: Possible direction of future legislation. In *Fundamental labour rights in China – Legal implementation and cultural logic*, ed. Ulla Liukkunen and Chen Yifeng, 243–264. Dordrecht: Springer.

Documents and Official Publications

ILO Documents

Constitution of the International Labour Organisation, adopted 1 April 1919. Entry into force 28 June 1919.
Convention concerning Forced or Compulsory Labour, adopted 28 June 1930, ILO C029. Entry into force 1 May 1932. (Forced Labour Convention).
Convention concerning Freedom of Association and Protection of the Right to Organise, adopted 9 July 1948, ILO C087. Entry into force 4 July 1950. (Freedom of Association and Protection of the Right to Organise Convention).
Convention concerning the Application of the Principles of the Right to Organise and to Bargain Collectively, adopted 1 July 1949, ILO C098. Entry into force 18 July 1951. (Right to Organise and Collective Bargaining Convention).
Convention concerning the Abolition of Forced Labour, adopted 25 June 1957, ILO C105. Entry into force 17 January 1959. (Abolition of Forced Labour Convention).

Convention concerning Discrimination in Respect of Employment and Occupation, adopted 25 June 1958, ILO C111. Entry into force 15 June 1960. (Discrimination (Employment and Occupation) Convention).

Convention concerning Minimum Age for Admission to Employment, adopted 26 June 1973, ILO C138. Entry into force 19 June 1976. (Minimum Age Convention).

Convention concerning the Prohibition and Immediate Action for the Elimination of the Worst Forms of Child Labour, adopted 17 June 1999, ILO C182. Entry into force 19 November 2000. (Worst Forms of Child Labour Convention).

Declaration on Fundamental Principles and Rights at Work, adopted 18 June 1998 (Annex revised 15 June 2010). (1998 Declaration).

Equal Remuneration Convention, adopted 29 June 1951, ILO C100. Entry into force 23 May 1953.

Other International Law Sources

International Covenant on Economic, Social and Cultural Rights, adopted 16 December 1966, 993 U.N.T.S. 3. Entry into force 3 January 1976. (ICESCR).

International Covenant on Civil and Political Rights, adopted 16 December 1966, 999 U.N.T.S. 171. Entry into force 23 March 1976. (ICCPR).

UN Committee on Economic, Social and Cultural Rights. Implementation of the International Covenant on Economic, Social and Cultural Rights: 2nd periodic reports submitted by States parties under articles 16 and 17 of the Covenant: China, 6 July 2012, U.N. Doc. E/C.12/CHN/2.

Chinese Regulation

Laws by the National People's Congress

[Trade Union Law of the People's Republic of China] 中华人民共和国工会法 (zhōng huá rén mín gòng hé guó gōng huì fǎ), National People's Congress, adopted and effective 3 April 1992. Revised and effective 27 October 2001.

Laws by the Standing Committee of the National People's Congress

[Employment Promotion Law of the People's Republic of China] 中华人民共和国就业促进法 (zhōng huá rén mín gòng hé guó jiù yè cù jìn fǎ), Standing Committee of the National People's Congress, adopted 30 August 2007, effective 1 January 2008. Revised and effective 24 April 2015.

[Labour Contract Law of the People's Republic of China] 中华人民共和国劳动合同法 (zhōng huá rén mín gòng hé guó láo dòng hé tóng fǎ), Standing Committee of the National People's Congress, adopted 29 June 2007, effective 1 January 2008. Revised 28 December 2012, effective 1 July 2013.

[Labour Dispute Mediation and Arbitration Law of the People's Republic of China] 中华人民共和国劳动争议调解仲裁法 (zhōng huá rén mín gòng hé guó láo dòng zhēng yì tiáo jiě zhòng cái fǎ), Standing Committee of the National People's Congress, adopted 29 December 2007, effective 1 May 2008.

[Labour Law of the People's Republic of China] 中华人民共和国劳动法 (zhōng huá rén mín gòng hé guó láo dòng fǎ), Standing Committee of the National People's Congress, adopted 5 July 1994, effective 1 January 1995.

[Protection of Minors Law of the People's Republic of China] 中华人民共和国未成年人保护法 (zhōng huá rén mín gòng hé guó wèi chéng nián rén bǎo hù fǎ), Standing Committee of the National People's Congress, adopted 4 September 1991, effective 1 January 1992. Revised 26 October 2012, effective 1 January 2013.

Other Chinese Official Documents

[CCP Central Committee Decision concerning Some Major Issues in Comprehensively Promoting Governing the Country According to Law] 中共中央关于全面推进依法治国若干重大问题的决定 (zhōng gòng zhōng yāng guān yú quán miàn tuī jìn yī fǎ zhì guó ruò gān zhòng dà wèn tí de jué dìng), Central Committee of the Chinese Communist Party, adopted and effective 23 October 2014.

[National Human Rights Action Plan (2009–2010)] 国家人权行动计划 (2009－2010年) (guó jiā rén quán xíng dòng jì huà (2009–2010)), State Council, 13 April 2009.

[National Human Rights Action Plan (2012–2015)] 国家人权行动计划 (2012－2015年) (guó jiā rén quán xīng dòng jì huá (2012–2015)), 11 June 2012.

[Provisions on the Democratic Management of Enterprises] 企业民主管理规定 (qǐ yè mín zhǔ guǎn lǐ guī dìng), promulgated jointly by the CCP Central Commission for Discipline Inspection, Organization Department of the CCP Central Committee, State-owned Asset Supervision and Administration Commission of the State Council, Ministry of Supervision, All-China Federation of Trade Unions and the All-China Federation of Industry and Commerce, 13 February 2012.

Other Sources

[*China Statistical Yearbook* 2013] 中国统计年鉴-2013 (zhōng guó tǒng jì nián jiàn-2013), National Bureau of Statistics of the People's Republic of China. 2014. Beijing: China Statistics Press.

Chapter 2
Implementing ILO Fundamental Labour Rights in China: A Sensitive Meeting of Form and Substance?

Alan C. Neal

2.1 Introduction

A dramatic development of labour law in the People's Republic of China (PRC) has been witnessed over the past two decades. The framework of individual employment protection rights established by the Labour Law of 1994 has been consolidated to provide a basic "floor of rights" for Chinese workers in relation to working hours, payment of wages, dismissal, and a variety of related matters.[1]

More recently, that 1994 framework has been further developed through a combination of enactments – including the "centrepiece" Labour Contract Law of 2007, which came into force on 1 January 2008.[2] In parallel with this "individual employment rights" development, a clear route has also been mapped out for "employment promotion" – particularly through the Employment Promotion Law of 2007 – drawing largely upon experience in the European Union at the end of the twentieth century.[3] Meanwhile, the foundations have been laid for a universal system of social insurance arrangements. Alongside these regulatory strides forward, the associated enforcement regime for the modern framework of employment rights has been updated and streamlined – not least through important legislative revisions which took effect in 2008.

[1] [Labour Law of the People's Republic of China] 中华人民共和国劳动法 (zhōng huá rén mín gòng hé guó láo dòng fǎ), 1994.

[2] [Labour Contract Law of the People's Republic of China] 中华人民共和国劳动合同法 (zhōng huá rén mín gòng hé guó láo dòng hé tóng fǎ), 2007.

[3] [Employment Promotion Law of the People's Republic of China] 中华人民共和国就业促进法 (zhōng huá rén mín gòng hé guó jiù yè cù jìn fǎ), 2007.

A.C. Neal (✉)
University of Warwick, Coventry CV4 7AL, UK
e-mail: Alan.Neal@warwick.ac.uk

U. Liukkunen, Y. Chen (eds.), *Fundamental Labour Rights in China — Legal Implementation and Cultural Logic*, Ius Gentium: Comparative Perspectives on Law and Justice 49, DOI 10.1007/978-3-319-23156-3_2

The focus for this presentation is upon the implementation of "fundamental labour rights" within the framework of the International Labour Organization's (ILO) international standard-setting activities. Consideration is given to the developments which have led to the modern framework of regulation for "the world of work" in China, with some comment on areas where provisions "in the books" appear to reflect commitments at the international standard-setting level. This is accompanied by consideration of historical developments in Chinese labour dispute resolution, and an evaluation of the extent to which the modern PRC possesses appropriate and adequate arrangements and mechanisms for delivering, in practice, the values enshrined in those "fundamental labour rights".

While "headline" concern is addressed to the implementation of "fundamental" labour rights, the treatment here is not limited only to China's position in respect of the ILO's "core" standards and instruments. Attention is regularly drawn to the formal position of the PRC in relation to "core" instruments highlighted by the Declaration on Fundamental Principles and Rights at Work (1998 Declaration) and its Follow-up. However, an approach which confines itself to four specific areas of standard-setting through eight instruments carries with it a temptation to ignore, or downplay, numerous other significant areas of regulation.[4] This is particularly the case in relation to technical standards reflecting concern for the physical health, safety and hygiene of workers at work. It may well also serve to under-emphasize important areas of particular concern to transition and developing economies – and not only in the South-East Asian context.

It also has to be borne in mind that mere noting of the "rate of ratifications" for a particular country in relation to ILO Conventions and Recommendations does not necessarily carry with it any guarantee that the words in those instruments will not remain just that – words rather than actions, or "law in the books" rather than "law in action". The same is true of declarations expressing adherence to the international standards established by ILO instruments – whether implicit, as with the consequences of ILO membership for the obligations in respect of the eight "core" Conventions, or explicit in any number of political statements, official reports, or memoranda of understanding. The spotlight has, therefore, been placed upon the position in China as regards mechanisms designed, expressly or impliedly, to deliver the rights and values embedded in those standard-setting instruments.

This has given rise to some reflections upon both what may be described as "socialized" labour dispute resolution mechanisms in China, and more formalized institutionally "juridified" mechanisms intended or expected to perform that role. This extends to consideration of post-1949 institutional arrangements for labour dispute resolution through the bodies known as "labour arbitration committees". It also covers modern arrangements designed to deal with the delivery and enforcement

[4]Thus, for example, it is important – as is indicated below – to bear in mind that, within the historical context for China's relationship with the ILO, pre-PRC China was a founding member of the ILO, while ratification of a variety of international standard-setting instruments was undertaken during the 1930s, at a time when nationalist China was developing a strengthening engagement with representatives of the ILO in Geneva.

of labour rights through administrative means – such as "labour inspection" – and judicial activity within the framework of the People's Courts. Such consideration is not confined only to ILO-inspired "fundamental" labour rights. Rather, it concerns the whole range of modern frameworks for "access to justice" and the effective resolution of disputes in the Chinese world of work at large.

Finally, some brief observations are made in relation to the "cultural logic" of the arrangements to be found in the PRC. This is a particularly sensitive area upon which to embark for a Western "outsider" such as the present author. Nevertheless, within the framework for delivering such rights to workers it has been suggested that there may be discerned reflections of specifically "Chinese", or, possibly, even "Oriental", approaches to disputes and dispute resolution. Some of these tend to be addressed by "Western" commentators in terms of a strong implicit desire not to take disputes outside relatively narrow localized circumstances. Where, however, matters do metamorphose into more "formalistic" confrontations, it is sometimes suggested that there is a strong urge to avoid direct apportionment of "blame", and a pervasive desire to enable all protagonists to "save face". Whether such perceptions are over-stereotypical may be a matter for debate. However, it is interesting to note that modern declarations by Chinese leaders and policy-makers stress the importance, in the course of adoption by the PRC of "global values", of ensuring that where rules, "models", or institutions are inspired by external experiences the eventual introduction into the PRC of any such foreign-inspired phenomena is properly imbued "with Chinese characteristics".

The following comments, therefore, offer some thoughts on the exciting blend of historical, political, social, and institutional drivers which make up the "cross-currents" in modern Chinese labour law for the twenty-first century.[5]

2.2 Labour Law in China (1): Volatile Pre-1949 Roots

The framework of arrangements for regulating work in pre-1949 China reflected a period following the ending of a 2,000-year imperial era on the conclusion of the Qing dynasty in 1912. Ushered in by the Xinhai revolution of 1911, the Republic of China was established in highly volatile circumstances. A second revolution in 1913 underlined just how precarious was the situation, and the weakened position of China was further emphasized by the terms extracted from the government in return for recognition by the major international powers. Eventually, after more than a decade of what is often described as the "warlord era", a so-called "Nanjing decade" was brought into effect from 1928 onwards. It was largely during this period of relative stability and consolidation for post-imperial China that the earliest phase of activity in relation to the ILO and its standard-setting activities was witnessed. However, the outbreak of the second Sino-Japanese war in 1936 marked the

[5] For consideration of a number of current debates in relation to regulation of the world of work in the PRC, see the contributions in Neal ed. 2014b.

beginning of a period which was eventually to end with Japan's surrender in North China, in August 1945, to the US-supported nationalist government. Mention should also be made here of the brief period (1931–1934) of the Chinese Soviet Republic, which, although short-lived, provided a foretaste of some of the underlying arrangements which were to find their way into the modern regulation of working relationships in the post-1949 PRC.

Throughout this period, and immediately following the ending of World War II, tension and hostilities between the nationalist government, led by Chiang Kai-shek, and the Communist Red Army forces, headed by Mao Zedong, intensified, and the outbreak of full-scale civil war saw what had now become the People's Liberation Army achieve a position of rapidly increasing military supremacy by early 1949. By the time of the declaration of the People's Republic of China on 1 October 1949, the nationalist government had lost any semblance of influence in mainland China, and a withdrawal to Taiwan by Chiang Kai-shek and remaining Republic of China troops resulted in a declaration that Taipei, Taiwan, would henceforth be the temporary capital of the Republic of China.

Given the volatile context of the developments in mainland China between the late 1920s and the proclamation of the PRC in 1949, it is rather difficult to ascertain the extent to which engagement with the ILO by the Chinese nationalist government during the 1930s can justifiably be said to have constituted a commitment to "real implementation" of the international standards embedded in the ILO Conventions of the time or simply to have reflected one of a number of endeavours by the government of the day to raise and maintain a profile on the international level. This is particularly the case for a period in history marked by invasion by Japanese forces and civil war until the end of the 1940s. Whatever the position, however, any line of development which might be discerned in the first three decades of the ILO's existence was swiftly and dramatically overtaken by the chain of events which led to the establishment of the People's Republic of China on 1 October 1949.

2.3 Labour Law in China (2): 1949–1978

In evaluating the situation at the time of the launching of the PRC in 1949 a sense of the historical events leading up to that moment swiftly confirms the need to take into consideration the influence of experience in the Union of Soviet Socialist Republics (USSR) after the 1917 Revolution.[6] Some of that significance is relatively obvious and direct, as with the particular influence of the Labour Code of the Russian Soviet Federative Socialist Republic (RSFSR) of 1922 (1922 Labour Code) in relation to regulatory innovations such as the PRC Trade Union Law of 1950.[7]

---

[6] For specific comparisons between some of the Soviet and the Chinese provisions, see van den Berg 1983.

[7] The Labour Code of the RSFSR of 9 November 1922 (*Kodeks Zakonov o Trude RSFSR 1922 goda*) – together with its subsequent amendments (LS 1936 – Russ. 1, 1958 – USSR 1) – remained

However, some of the historical legacy is less well-known, as in the case of Soviet support for the Chinese Communist Party (CCP) after its formation in Shanghai in 1921.

The debt owed to USSR experience in the field of socialist labour relations can, for example, be clearly found in the Chinese arrangements concerning the role of the trade union, the phenomenon referred to as the "collective agreement", and arrangements for labour dispute resolution. Indeed, much of that debt continues even today. The historical USSR time-line runs, effectively, from the 1917 Russian revolution, through an early "labour code" drawn up in 1918,[8] and thereafter to the 1922 Labour Code.

Introduction into China of the experience from those early days of the Soviet Union was first witnessed in the context of the establishment of the Chinese Soviet Republic, which operated from 1931 until 1934, before being formally abolished in 1937.[9] Thus, a Labour Law of the Chinese Soviet Republic was adopted in November 1931, together with a Resolution on implementing the Labour Law, the following month, and a set of "Provisional Organisational Principles for Labour Sections of Chinese Soviets".[10] Chapter 9 of the Labour Law also formalized the position of the "All-Chinese Labour Federation", along with local-level organizations.[11] In addition, the Labour Law included provisions on "collective contracts", as well as setting out arrangements for dealing with violations of the Labour Law and for the settlement of labour disputes between workers and employers.[12] Meanwhile, the Resolution on implementing the Labour Law provided that violation of any provision in that instrument should be dealt with as a matter of labour law by the appropriate labour tribunal, even if the matter in question was attended with criminal liability for the person or persons responsible for such violation.

In relation to the standing and role of the trade union, a starting point, once again, may be taken in the experience of the Soviet Union. Thus, the approach to the trade

in force until the Decree of the Presidium of the Supreme Soviet of the RSFSR to repeal certain legislative texts of the RSFSR consequent upon the entry into force of the Labour Code of the RSFSR [LS 1971 – USSR 1]. The 1922 Labour Code itself included a number of provisions originally to be found in the 1918 Labour Code of the RSFSR. For clear evidence of this influence upon China, see the [Trade Union Law of the People's Republic of China] 中华人民共和国工会法 (zhōng huá rén mín gòng hé guó gōng huì fǎ), 1950.

[8] *Kodeks Zakonov o Trude 1918.*

[9] For an introductory survey of that period, see Butler 1983.

[10] [Labour Law of the Chinese Soviet Republic] 中华苏维埃共和国劳动法 (zhōng huá sū wéi āi gòng hé guó láo dòng fǎ), 1931; [Resolution on Implementing the Labour Law] 关于实施劳动法的决议案 (guān yú shí shī láo dòng fǎ de jué yì àn), 1931 and [Provisional Organisational Principles for Labour Sections of Chinese Soviets] 中华苏维埃共和国劳动感化院暂行章程 (zhōng huá sū wéi āi gòng hé guó láo dòng gǎn huà yuàn zàn xíng zhāng chéng), 1932.

[11] That body had been established on 1 May 1925 during the Second National Labour Congress, convened in Guangzhou (following the First Congress held in the same city in May 1922). With the adoption of a "Constitution of the All-China Federation of Trade Unions" and election of a first "Executive Committee", the forerunner to what is now the modern All-China Federation of Trade Unions (ACFTU) was thus launched. See Lee 1986, at pp. xi–xii and Traub-Merz 2011.

[12] [Labour Law of the Chinese Soviet Republic] 中华苏维埃共和国劳动法 (zhōng huá sū wéi āi gòng hé guó láo dòng fǎ), 1931, Article 72 and 73.

union in the post-revolutionary USSR treated that institution as a worker representative body with powers,[13] through its workers' committee,[14] to undertake five main functions.[15] The first of these encompassed the duty to represent and safeguard the interests of the workers belonging to it, in relation to the management of the undertaking, in respect of matters connected with the conditions of employment and life of the workers. This was accompanied by the duty to represent the workers before the Government and other public authorities. Those "representative" functions were coupled with the duty to ensure that the legislative provisions concerning the protection of workers, social insurance, payment of wages, regulations for hygiene and safety, and the like, are faithfully carried out by the management of the undertaking, and to co-operate with the state authorities concerned with the protection of workers. Thereafter, the trade union was tasked with the duty to take steps to improve the social and material situation of workers, as well as to co-operate in the regular carrying on of production in state undertakings, and participate in the regulation and organization of economic activities through the competent trade union.

Drawing strongly upon that Soviet Union frame of reference for its post-1949 inspiration, therefore, the 1950 Trade Union Law of the PRC, in its turn, provided for trade union organizations to be established as "mass organizations formed by the working classes of their own will".[16] As with the USSR arrangements, those trade union organizations were to be set up on the basis of the principles of "democratic centralism", and a number of particular "rights and duties" were spelled out for those bodies in Part II of the Trade Union Law. Thus, they were granted the right "to take part in production management and to sign collective contracts with the administrations of state and collectively-owned enterprises on behalf of workers".[17] Article 6 of the Trade Union Law, in similar vein, provided rights for trade union organizations to negotiate and conclude collective contracts on behalf of workers in relation to privately-owned enterprises.

As with Article 158 of the USSR's 1922 Labour Code, the Trade Union Law of the PRC stipulated that:

> Trade unions have the duty to protect the interests of the workers and employees, to supervise the implementation, by the administration or employer, of labour protection, labour insurance, standards of wage payments, rules on sanitation and technical security in factories, and other related rules and mandates provided by government laws, and to improve facilities in relation to the material and cultural life of the workers and employees.[18]

---

[13] Labour Code of the RSFSR, 1922, Article 151.

[14] Labour Code of the RSFSR, 1922, Article 156.

[15] Labour Code of the RSFSR, 1922, Article 158, (a)–(e). The provisions in the Labour Code themselves came under the umbrella of the 1918 Constitution of the RSFSR, which, for example, set out, in Article 16, various rights to be granted to these trade unions. See, for a brief historical context, Ashwin and Clarke 2002, at Chapter 2.

[16] [Trade Union Law of the People's Republic of China] 中华人民共和国工会法 (zhōng huá rén mín gòng hé guó gōng huì fǎ), 1950, Article 1.

[17] Ibid., Article 5.

[18] Ibid., Article 7.

Meanwhile, Article 8 of the Trade Union Law provided Chinese trade unions established in state-run or collective enterprises with the right to require managements to report on their work and activities, as well as "the right to attend meetings of the management committees or administrations of the enterprises of the same level on behalf of the workers and employees". These rights were complemented by duties for the Chinese trade union to:

> ...(1) educate and organize workers in upholding the laws and implementing the policies of the People's Government so as to strengthen the people's regime under the leadership of the working class; (2) educate and organize workers and employees in cultivating a new attitude toward labour and in observing labour discipline, and to organize production emulation drives or other production movements so as to guarantee the fulfilment of their production targets; (3) protect public properties, combat corruption, waste and bureaucracy, and struggle against saboteurs in state and collectively-owned enterprises, government organs and schools; and (4) carry out the policy of promoting production and benefiting both labour and employer, and to fight against all deeds which run counter to the government's laws or hamper the growth of production in private enterprises.[19]

Similar inspiration drawn from the USSR experience can be seen in relation to regulatory treatment of "collective agreements" in the socialist context.[20] Such agreements (generally described as "collective contracts") had existed under the Tsarist regime, although they then went into abeyance in the wake of the 1917 revolution, until their reintroduction by Articles 15-26 of the 1922 Labour Code of the RSFSR.[21] Thus, Article 15 of the 1922 Labour Code provided for the conclusion of collective contracts, which were defined as:

> an agreement concluded between a trade union, as representative of the workers, on the one hand, and an employer, on the other hand, laying down the conditions of work and employment for individual undertakings, institutions, and businesses or groups thereof, and specifying the contents of future individual contracts of employment.

Any terms included in such a "collective contract" had to be in written form and registered,[22] and were expressed to apply to "all persons employed in a specified undertaking or institution, whether they are members of the trade union which has concluded the contract or not".[23] This framework for "collective contracts" subsequently found some mirroring in the post-1949 Chinese situation, where the

[19] [Trade Union Law of the People's Republic of China] 中华人民共和国工会法 (zhōng huá rén mín gòng hé guó gōng huì fǎ), 1950, Article 9.

[20] For discussion of the institution of the "collective agreement" in the former socialist legal systems of Eastern Europe, see Schmidt and Neal 1984 and, in particular, the material derived from memoranda prepared by Professor Karel Witz and Professor Marie Kalenska (University of Prague, Czechoslovakia), at pp. 84 and following. An early post-war presentation of the phenomenon in a specific USSR setting (with historical references) is to be found in International Labour Review, 1952.

[21] See International Labour Review, 1952.

[22] Labour Code of the RSFSR, 1922, Article 21.

[23] Labour Code of the RSFSR, 1922, Article 16.

PRC Trade Union Law expressly provided for powers to enter into such arrangements with the employer.[24]

More generally, the economic organization of the new PRC followed the Soviet model of "5-Year Plans" from 1953 onwards. Already, in institutional terms, the basic policies and direction for a post-revolutionary China had been set out in a declaration at the Second Plenary Session of the Seventh Central Committee of the Chinese Communist Party.[25] This included, in particular, the "route-map" for the transformation of China from an agricultural country to a socialist industrial nation. By the time the First Plenary Session of the Chinese People's Political Consultative Conference (CPPCC) was convened in Beijing,[26] the "Common Programme" of that body had been agreed and the institutional trappings for the new "People's Republic of China" had been put in place, establishing "a New Democratic or a People's Democratic state" which:

> …carries out the people's democratic dictatorship led by the working class, based on the alliance of workers and peasants, and uniting all democratic classes and all nationalities in China. It opposes imperialism, feudalism and bureaucratic capitalism and strives for independence, democracy, peace, unity, prosperity and strength of China.[27]

This vision of the new nation, subsequently set out formally in Article 1 of the 1954 Constitution in terms that "The People's Republic of China is a people's democratic state led by the working class and based on the alliance of workers and peasants", now finds voice in Article 1 of the 1982 Constitution, which provides that:

> The People's Republic of China is a socialist state under the people's democratic dictatorship led by the working class and based on the alliance of workers and peasants....

Although a number of normative instruments were issued in the years immediately following the establishment of the PRC in 1949, this was quickly followed by a long period of "darkness" for such regulation, including the so-called decade of the "cultural revolution" between 1966 and 1976.[28] Only after the death of Mao Zedong in 1976 was the way opened for coherent modern development of a regulatory framework for working life in China, and the declaration by Deng Xiaoping of the so-called "open door policy" in 1978 provided a particularly significant boost in the same direction.[29]

---

[24] [Trade Union Law of the People's Republic of China] 中华人民共和国工会法 (zhōng huá rén mín gòng hé guó gōng huì fǎ), 1950, Articles 5 and 6.

[25] Which took place in Xibaipo (Hebei) between 5 and 13 March 1949.

[26] Between 21 and 30 September 1949.

[27] [Common Programme of the Chinese People's Political Consultative Conference] 中国人民政治协商会议共同纲领 (zhōng guó rén mín zhèng zhì xié shāng huì yì gòng tóng gāng lǐng), 1949, Article 1.

[28] The "Cultural Revolution" was formally declared ended at the 11th Party Congress in 1977.

[29] Announced at the Third Plenary Session of the 11th Central Committee of the Communist Party of China (18–22 December 1978). That policy marked a dramatic shift from the formerly "closed" relationships which the PRC had enjoyed with (primarily) the former USSR and its associated "satellite" states and heralded the beginning of a period for intense reform and the "opening up" of the PRC to markets around the world.

Yet, it should not go unnoticed that even the decade of the 'Cultural Revolution', between 1966 and 1976, was by no means devoid of regulatory activity in relation to the world of work in China.[30] Thus, the period 1949–1976 was characterized by the early enactment of certain key "basic building-block" provisions, as has already been described above, followed by enactments which began to take on a much more "administrative" tone – particularly from the late 1950s onwards.[31] However, there was no sense in which this period could be regarded as laying stable foundations for a modern system of labour law regulation. At best, as has been suggested by this author elsewhere,[32] labour law, at least in any modern sense, was largely consigned to a state of inertia.

Yet, it also has to be borne in mind that, in the opinions of some commentators, the Mao Zedong era had reflected contradictory stances in relation to the desirability and value of formalized "juridified" arrangements for regulating social activity – arguably, including the world of work. Thus, on the one hand, there was the call to "Depend on the rule of man, not the rule of law".[33] Yet, as early as at the time of the Chinese Socialist Republic, Mao had reported to the 2nd All-Chinese Congress of Soviets how the Labour Law of the Chinese Soviet Republic was being implemented and had resulted in a better standard of living.[34] Subsequently, the perceived dichotomy between a "jural (formal) model", and a "societal (informal) model" has seen the latter characterized as "a distinctly Maoist approach to law".[35]

Early moves in the wake of Mao's death included a variety of administrative provisions in relation to the organization of Chinese arrangements to deal with workers who had been dealt with under provisions current in the earlier "dark"

---

[30] See e.g., [Circular on Adjusting Wages for Certain Type of Workers] 国务院关于调整部分工人和工作人员工资的通知 (guó wù yuàn guān yú tiǎo zhěng bù fèn gōng rén hé gōng zuò rén yuán gōng zī de tōng zhī), 1971, and measures such as thc [Circular on Wage Levels for Demobilized Soldiers with Higher Education Degrees] 国家计划委员会劳动局关于复员退伍军人中的大专院校学生工资待遇的通知 (guó jiā jì huà wěi yuán huì láo dòng jú guān yú fù yuán tuì wǔ jūn rén zhōng de dà zhuān yuàn xiào xué shēng gōng zī dài yù de tōng zhī), 1975.

[31] See e.g., [Provisions on the Qualifying Period of Seniority and Wage Issues relating to Anti-Revolutionary or Other 'Bad' Individuals who have been indentified in the Counter Anti-Revolutionary Movement] 关于处理国家机关、企业、学校在肃反运动中查出的反革命分子和其他坏分子的工龄和工资问题的规定 (guān yú chǔ lǐ guó jiā jī guān, qǐ yè, xué xiào zài sù fǎn yùn dòng zhōng chá chū de fǎn gé mìng fèn zǐ hé qí tā huài fèn zǐ de gōng líng hé gōng zī wèn tí de guī dìng), 1957, as well as [Opinion as to whether the Children of Capitalist Bourgeois are Eligible to Replace their Parent when they Retire or are on Long-Term Absence] 劳动部、中央工商行政管理局关于资产阶级工商业者退休或请长假后可否由子女顶替工作的意见 (láo dòng bù, zhōng yāng gōng shāng xíng zhèng guǎn lǐ jú guān yú zī chǎn jiē jí gōng shāng yè zhě tuì xiū huò qǐng cháng jià hòu kě fǒu yóu zǐ nǚ dǐng tì gōng zuò de yì jiàn), 1963.

[32] Neal 2011.

[33] See the attribution by Rodearmel 1988, at p. 43.

[34] See van der Sprenkel 1983, at p. 113.

[35] See Leng 1977, at pp. 356–357. The discussion is taken as a prelude to discussion focused upon penal law, and not addressed specifically to regulation of the world of work. Thus, consideration of regulation in relation to labour is only undertaken by the author in the context of the Chinese notion of "education and rehabilitation through labour".

period – including, for example, a Circular on resolving issues for those who have been mistreated and wish to return to the city to work 1979.[36] They also included provisions aimed at deterring the temptation to exploit a rapidly-changing situation, such as a 1982 Circular on prohibiting workers gaining extra profits from unreasonable economic activities.[37]

The enactment of a new PRC Constitution in 1982[38] also served to hasten this development, and important State Council measures – the Provisions on Mining Safety and the Provisions on Mining Safety Inspection – followed in the same year.[39] This "first-stage" reform and innovation in the development of normative "rights" through legislation also began to deal directly with areas of concern to what are now regarded as the ILO's "core" Conventions, with a Circular on Strictly Prohibiting the Use of Child Labour of 1987, being complemented shortly afterwards by the State Council's Provisions on the Prohibition of Using Child Labour of 1991.[40] Meanwhile, the Provisions on Protecting Female Workers of 1988 had heralded enactment of the highly significant Protection of Women's Rights and Interests Law, eventually adopted by the NPC in 1992.[41] These years also saw the introduction, at the initiation of the NPC Standing Committee, of the Disabled Persons Protection Law of 1991.[42]

With the coming into force of the revised PRC Trade Union Law in 1992 – a measure which has subsequently been further amended by provisions introduced in 2001 – and the Ministry of Labour's Provisions on Collective Contracts of 1994, it was clear also that reform was not being confined to new normative rights for individual workers.[43] These important provisions were introduced along with the

---

[36] [Circular on Resolving Issues for Those who have been Mistreated and Wish to Return to the City to Work] 中共中央、国务院关于处理当前部分人员要求复职复工回城就业等问题的通知 (zhōng gòng zhōng yāng guó wù yuàn guān yú chǔ lǐ dāng qián bù fèn rén yuán yāo qiú fù zhí fù gōng huí chéng jiù yè děng wèn tí de tōng zhī), 1979.

[37] [Circular on Prohibiting Workers Gaining Extra Profits from Unreasonable Economic Activities] 关于制止企业职工从事不正当经济活动牟取额外收入问题的通知 (guān yú zhì zhǐ qǐ yè zhí gōng cóng shì bù zhèng dāng jīng jì huó dòng móu qǔ é wài shōu rù wèn tí de tōng zhī), 1982.

[38] [Constitution of the People's Republic of China] 中华人民共和国宪法 (zhōng huá rén mín gòng hé guó xiàn fǎ), 1982.

[39] [Provisions on Mining Safety] 矿山安全条例 (kuàng shān ān quán tiáo lì) and [Provisions on Mining Safety Inspection] 矿山安全监察条例 (kuàng shān ān quán jiān chá tiáo lì), 1982.

[40] [Circular on Strictly Prohibiting the Use of Child Labour] 劳动人事部关于严格禁止招用童工的通知 (láo dòng rén shì bù guān yú yán gé jìn zhǐ zhāo yòng tóng gōng de tōng zhī), 1987; [Provisions on the Prohibition of Using Child Labour] 禁止使用童工规定 (jìn zhǐ shǐ yòng tóng gōng guī dìng), 1991.

[41] [Provisions on Protecting Female Workers] 女职工劳动保护规定 (nǚ zhí gōng láo dòng bǎo hù guī dìng), 1988; [Law on the Protection of Rights and Interests of Women] 中华人民共和国妇女权益保障法 (zhōng huá rén mín gòng hé guó fù nǚ quán yì bǎo zhàng fǎ), 1992.

[42] [Disabled Persons Protection Law of the People's Republic of China] 中华人民共和国残疾人保障法 (zhōng huá rén mín gòng hé guó cán jí rén bǎo zhàng fǎ), 1991.

[43] [Trade Union Law of the People's Republic of China] 中华人民共和国工会法 (zhōng huá rén mín gòng hé guó gōng huì fǎ), 1992; [Provisions on Collective Contracts] 集体合同规定 (jí tǐ hé tóng guī dìng), 1994.

Mining Safety Law in 1992 and the important Provisions on Workers' Working Time in 1994, as well as an Occupational Training Law in 1996.[44] The overall effect of these initiatives, therefore, provided confirmation that many of the pieces had been brought together to construct a jigsaw designed to deliver a basic "floor of rights" to Chinese workers.

There was also a reorganization of the governmental supervisory framework for this area – including gradual expansion during the 1990s of the functions of the re-constituted Ministry of Labour to include a variety of social matters. That Ministry was eventually re-designated in 1998 as the Ministry of Labour and Social Security (MoLSS),[45] whose successor is nowadays known as the Ministry of Human Resources and Social Security (MoHRSS) following a change introduced in 2008.

By the mid-1980s, however, matters had already been moving swiftly forward – in particular following enactment of the important Interim Regulations on the Practice of the Labour Contract System in State-Owned Enterprises (SOEs),[46] and the Sino-Foreign Co-operative Joint Venture Law of 13 April 1988.[47] It was also noteworthy that a relatively large volume of technical "labour rights" measures had been introduced during this period, including Interim Measures for the State Council on an Employee's Retirement and Withdrawal from Post,[48] and Provisions of the State Council on Employees' Family Leave,[49] as well as Regulations on Rewarding and Disciplining Employees in Enterprises.[50]

It was the process which eventually led to the introduction of the PRC's Labour Law of 1994,[51] however, which really set the modern ball rolling, and which continues to define the framework for regulation of labour relationships in modern China.

---

[44] [Mining Safety Law of the People's Republic of China] 中华人民共和国矿山安全法 (zhōng huá rén mín gòng hé guó kuàng shān ān quán fǎ), 1992; [Provisions on Workers' Working Time] 国务院关于职工工作时间的规定 (guó wù yuàn guān yú zhí gōng gōng zuò shí jiān de guī dìng), 1994; [Occupational Training Law of the People's Republic of China] 中华人民共和国职业教育法 (zhōng huá rén mín gòng hé guó zhí yè jiào yù fǎ), 1996.

[45] See the brief note in Taylor et al. 2003, at p. 28, fn. 15.

[46] [Interim Regulations on the Practice of the Labour Contract System in State-Owned Enterprises] 国营企业实行劳动合同制暂行规定 (guó yíng qǐ yè shí xíng láo dòng hé tóng zhì zàn xíng guī dìng), 1986.

[47] [Sino-Foreign Co-operative Joint Venture Law of the People's Republic of China] 中华人民共和国中外合作经营企业法 (zhōng huá rén mín gòng hé guó zhōng wài hé zuò jīng yíng qǐ yè fǎ), 1988.

[48] [Interim Measures for the State Council on an Employee's Retirement and Withdrawal from Post] 国务院关于工人退休、退职的暂行办法 (guó wù yuàn guān yú gōng rén tuì xiū tuì zhí de zàn xíng bàn fǎ), 1978.

[49] [Provisions of the State Council on Employees' Family Leave] 国务院关于职工探亲待遇的规定 (guó wù yuàn guān yú zhí gōng tàn qīn dài yù de guī dìng), 1981.

[50] [Regulations on Rewarding and Disciplining Employees in Enterprises] 企业职工奖惩条例 (qǐ yè zhí gōng jiǎng chéng tiáo lì), 1982.

[51] [Labour Law of the People's Republic of China] 中华人民共和国劳动法 (zhōng huá rén mín gòng hé guó láo dòng fǎ), 1994.

2.4 Labour Law in China (3): Post-1994

For most commentators on modern developments of labour law in China the Labour Law of 1994 constitutes the foundation and template for the current system of individual employment rights and their enforcement. However, what is often overlooked is that the historical lead-up to the adoption of the Labour Law in 1994 had been long and tortuous.

As described by Jia and Wei,[52] even after the fundamental question of whether there should be a "Labour Law" at all – reflecting, in turn, the recognition of an independent labour law sphere for legal regulation, separate from "economic law" within the Chinese legal system – had been answered in the affirmative, it took a decade and a half from the production of a first draft of the proposed Law in July 1979 until adoption of the final measure in July 1994.[53]

From the time when a drafting committee had first been established by the Ministry of Labour at the beginning of 1979, there were two distinct periods in the Law's development. The first extended from 1979 to 1984, at which point a 5-year period of inertia ensued. However, the re-appointment of a drafting task force heralded the onset of a second developmental phase from February 1989 to eventual adoption in 1994.

A particularly noteworthy feature of the second period for development of the eventual Labour Law was the "comparative experience" basis upon which research and debate over the basic principles to be espoused by the new instrument was conducted. For this purpose, translation of almost 50 foreign labour laws had been undertaken for the benefit of the group established at the beginning of 1989. Nor were these limited to Eastern European (socialist) legislation – extending also to laws from *inter alia* Taiwan, the United Kingdom, and the United States of America.

From an international perspective, therefore, while direct or indirect influence from some of the ILO's established international labour standards can arguably be discerned in the text of the Labour Law, the very fact of "opening up" the Chinese legislative drafting process to international experience must inevitably have played a significant part. In the first place, a channel was thereby opened up through which the values underlying international standards were able to flow, and merge with, the developing "principles" characterizing a "floor of rights" for working citizens of the PRC. In addition, exposure to foreign experience of various technical forms through

[52] Jia and Wei 2014.

[53] On the way, the original draft underwent no less than 17 revisions in its first developmental period, before being "put on the shelf" in the wake of consideration by the Standing Committee of the National People's Congress, in 1983, and further consideration and revision by the Legislative Affairs Office of the NPC in February 1984. Thereafter, following the establishment of a new "Task Force" in February 1989, a fresh draft emerged in June 1989, and – by now, in the context of China seeking to establish a modern "socialist market economy", with labour relationships based upon a "labour contract system" – the final version was eventually agreed after a total of more than 30 revisions.

which those values could be delivered will also have opened Chinese eyes to a range of "less-traditional" non-administrative enforcement techniques.

Jia and Wei report[54] that the issue of how to bring China into line with international labour standards was expressly included in discussions between the lawmakers of the time, and particular mention is made by those authors of the fields of minimum wages, rest periods, and holiday entitlement. Stress is also placed upon the importance of "new phenomena" for a system developing as part of the establishment of the "socialist market economy" – the most significant of which were the notion of the "collective agreement", the phenomenon of the "labour contract", and arrangements for the provision of "social insurance".

The eventual Labour Law of the PRC established what is still the modern framework for individual rights of workers, based upon a "labour contract" relationship. That Law was also notable in providing for a very broad scope of application.[55] At the heart of the structures introduced in 1994 are the basic rules on establishing and terminating labour contracts. These are combined with a wide range of provisions dealing with the "terms and conditions" making up the content of those labour contracts. The catalogue of detailed provisions has been said to constitute a legal recognition of "fundamental labour rights" – involving employment equality and employment freedom; the right to payment; the right to rest and vacation; the right to occupational health and safety; the right to vocational training; the right to social insurance and benefits; and the right to legal relief in labour disputes.[56] Summing up the significance of that piece of legislation, it is suggested that:

> …[i]n short, the Labour Law of 1994 stimulated the social transformation of China from arrangements based upon social status (workers in State-owned enterprises, collective ownership enterprises, or private enterprises) to relationships based on contract…[57]

at the same time as:

> …the nature of labour relations in China was also structurally changed from relations between the State and workers, to relationships between employing units and workers.[58]

Equally important, it may be suggested, was the reality that the Law included a clear indication of the trajectory for future modern labour law development – which has subsequently given rise to a substantial number of specific pieces of legislation, based upon the powers set out in the Labour Law.[59]

---

[54] Jia and Wei 2014.

[55] For a detailed presentation of the 1994 Labour Law at the time of its enactment, see Josephs 1995.

[56] Jia and Wei, 2014, citing [Jia] 贾俊玲, 1994, at p. 14. These authors go further and claim that "… the Law could also be said to have promoted human rights protection in China", citing Ling and Li, 1995, at pp. 7–12.

[57] [Jia] 贾俊玲 1994.

[58] Jia 1999, at p. 12.

[59] Of particular importance in this regard was the Ministry of Labour's "blueprint" for labour laws, set out in its [Opinions on the Implementation of Labour Law] 劳动部关于贯彻实施《劳动法》的意见 (láo dòng bù guān yú guàn chè shí shī "láo dòng fǎ" de yì jiàn), 1994. Amongst the numer-

However, although that "framework" Labour Law continues to provide the basic point of reference for legal and administrative regulation of working relations in China, the regulatory picture has not remained in a "1990s time-warp". Against a background of rapid industrial development, dramatic economic growth, and increasing sensitivity to global social and market pressures, the socialist market economy developed for the PRC has been posing a series of challenges to the 1994 framework. This, in turn, has given rise to loud calls for both substantive and institutional reform – in the light of which a new phase of development has been witnessed in the opening decade of the twenty-first century.[60]

The most recent period of development has witnessed a group of post-Millennium reforms, which have served, in the eyes of many commentators, to move the "floor of rights" well beyond the scope of the arrangements regulated under the Labour Law. Four key instruments have emerged in that process, at the centre of which has been the Labour Contract Law of 2007.[61] While a discrete area of that law, dealing with what are referred to as "dispatched workers", was the subject of amendment in 2013, otherwise, the original 2007 provisions remain in force. Those provisions have, however, been subject to clarification (and, arguably, amplification) by the Implementing Measures for the Labour Contract Law in 2008,[62] as well as by judicial guidance contained in the *Fourth Interpretation of the Supreme People's Court on Certain Issues Concerning the Application of Law in Trials of Labour Disputes*.[63]

ous instruments introduced under this "blueprint" have been [Regulations providing for Revision of Rules on Working Hours] 国务院关于职工工作时间的规定 (guó wù yuàn guān yú zhí gōng gōng zuò shí jiān de guī dìng), 1995; [Temporary Rules on Wage Payment] 工资支付暂行规定 (gōng zī zhī fù zàn xíng guī dìng), 1994; [Economic Compensation Measures for Violation or Illegal Termination of Labour Contracts] 违反和解除劳动合同的经济补偿办法 (wéi fǎn hé jiě chú láo dòng hé tóng de jīng jì bǔ cháng bàn fǎ), 1994; [Rules on Vocational Training] 职业培训实体管理规定 (zhí yè péi xùn shí tǐ guǎn lǐ guī dìng), 1994; [Rules on Labour Inspection Procedures] 劳动监察程序规定 (láo dòng jiān chá chéng xù guī dìng), 1995; [Regulations on the Implementation of the Mine Safety Law of the People's Republic of China] 中华人民共和国矿山安全法实施条例 (zhōng huá rén mín gòng hé guó kuàng shān ān quán fǎ shí shī tiáo lì), 1996; [Rules on Minimum Wages] 最低工资规定 (zuì dī gōng zī guī dìng), 2004; and [Regulations on Unemployment Insurance] 失业保险条例 (shī yè bǎo xiǎn tiáo lì), 1999. Other significant measures in this period have included [Trial Measures on Collective Negotiation of Wages] 工资集体协商试行办法 (gōng zī jí tǐ xié shāng shì xíng bàn fǎ), 2000 and [Rules on Collective Contracts] 集体合同规定 (jí tǐ hé tóng guī dìng), 2004; while the important [Occupational Disease Prevention and Control Law of the People's Republic of China] 中华人民共和国职业病防治法 (zhōng huá rén mín gòng hé guó zhí yè bìng fáng zhì fǎ), 2001; and [Occupational Safety Law of the People's Republic of China] 中华人民共和国安全生产法 (zhōng huá rén mín gòng hé guó ān quán shēng chǎn fǎ), 2002 were also introduced at this time.

[60] See, *inter alia*, the assessment of this author in Neal 2007 and Neal 2011.

[61] [Labour Contract Law of the People's Republic of China] 中华人民共和国劳动合同法 (zhōng huá rén mín gòng hé guó láo dòng hé tóng fǎ), 2007.

[62] [Regulations on the Implementation of the Labour Contract Law of the People's Republic of China] 中华人民共和国劳动合同法实施条例 (zhōng huá rén mín gòng hé guó láo dòng hé tóng fǎ shí shī tiáo lì), 2008.

[63] [Fourth Interpretation of the Supreme People's Court on Certain Issues Concerning the Application of Law in Trial of Labour Disputes] 最高人民法院关于审理劳动争议案件适用法

Alongside that Labour Contract Law in 2007, an Employment Promotion Law was brought into force on the same date,[64] while a Labour Dispute Mediation and Arbitration Law has endeavoured to deal with issues concerning access to justice and enforcement of the substantive provisions making up the modern Chinese "floor of rights".[65] Finally, a wide-ranging Social Insurance Law of 2010 came into effect on 1 July 2011 and administrative arrangements to complement that statute have been developed over the last two and a half years.[66]

Nor should it be overlooked that further development had been taking place in relation to areas such as protection of the health, safety and hygiene of workers, through the Occupational Disease Prevention and Control Law of 2001 and the Occupational Safety Law of 2002.[67] So, too, had there been important underpinning of the prohibitions concerning one of the ILO's "core" convention areas, with introduction of the State Council Provisions on the Prohibition of Using Child Labour in 2002.[68]

The eventual introduction of the 2007 Labour Dispute Mediation and Arbitration Law, and the sometimes controversial political debate which preceded it, highlights what is probably the most challenging issue in modern Chinese labour law – the extent to which the provisions "in the books" which make up the labour law floor of rights are, in practice, susceptible to effective delivery and enforcement. Before turning, however, to the practical arrangements for supervising, monitoring, and enforcing the normative provisions making up that "floor of rights", a brief comment will be offered in respect of the historical and developing relationship between the PRC and the ILO.

2.5 China and the ILO

The relationship between the ILO and what is now the People's Republic of China reflects significant "swings" over the best part of a century. In particular, it is often overlooked that post-imperial China was a founder member of the organization in

律若干问题的解释(四) (zuì gāo rén mín fǎ yuàn guān yú shěn lǐ láo dòng zhēng yì àn jiàn shì yòng fǎ lǜ ruò gān wèn tí de jiě shì (sì)), 2012.

[64] [Employment Promotion Law of the People's Republic of China] 中华人民共和国就业促进法 (zhōng huá rén mín gòng hé guó jiù yè cù jìn fǎ), 2007.

[65] [Labour Dispute Mediation and Arbitration Law of the People's Republic of China] 中华人民共和国劳动争议调解仲裁法 (zhōng huá rén mín gòng hé guó láo dòng zhēng yì tiáo jiě zhòng cái fǎ), 2007.

[66] [Social Insurance Law of the People's Republic of China] 中华人民共和国社会保险法 (zhōng huá rén mín gòng hé guó shè huì bǎo xiǎn fǎ), 2011.

[67] [Occupational Disease Prevention and Control Law of the People's Republic of China] 中华人民共和国职业病防治法 (zhōng huá rén mín gòng hé guó zhí yè bìng fáng zhì fǎ), 2001; [Occupational Safety Law of the People's Republic of China] 中华人民共和国安全生产法 (zhōng huá rén mín gòng hé guó ān quán shēng chǎn fǎ), 2002.

[68] [Provisions on the Prohibition of Using Child Labour] 禁止使用童工规定 (jìn zhǐ shǐ yòng tóng gōng guī dìng), 2002.

1919 – at that time constituted under the umbrella of the League of Nations – and that a period of steady engagement with the ILO's standard-setting and implementation arrangements in the wake of the First World War was developed throughout the 1920s and 1930s.[69] By 1934, indeed, China had been elected as a member of the ILO Governing Body, and the years preceding the outbreak of the Second World War saw the continuation of a process of ratification of a wide range of ILO standard-setting instruments by the Chinese nationalist government.[70]

As already suggested, however, it is rather difficult to ascertain the extent to which the engagement with the ILO of the Chinese nationalist government during the 1930s constituted a commitment to "real implementation" of international standards or simply reflected efforts by the government of the day to maintain a profile on the international level. Whatever view is taken of that period, however, any line of development which might be discerned in the first three decades of the ILO's existence was swiftly and dramatically overtaken by the chain of events which led to the establishment of the People's Republic of China on 1 October 1949.

In passing, it may be observed that the establishment of the "New Democratic" or "People's Democratic state", underpinning the declaration of "a people's democratic state" in the 1954 Constitution, raises an interesting issue as to the historical response of the ILO more generally to "socialist system" developments amongst its member states. Indeed, one might go so far as to suggest that the ILO's stance in the face of, first, Bolshevism, and then, successively, the consolidation of the pre-war

[69] Article 23 of the original Covenant of the League of Nations provided that the Members of the League "…will endeavour to secure and maintain fair and humane conditions of labour for men, women, and children, both in their own countries and in all countries to which their commercial and industrial relations extend, and for that purpose will establish and maintain the necessary international organisations…". Part XIII of the Treaty of Peace of Versailles, 1919, included provisions on "Labour" (Articles 387–426), which established the International Labour Office and set out the basis upon which the modern constitution of the ILO has been developed. The first meeting of the Annual Labour Conference took place in Washington in October 1919.

[70] In particular, a number of technical Conventions were ratified during the 1930s, beginning in May 1930 with the Minimum Wage-Fixing Machinery Convention No. 26, 1928, and in June of the following year, the Marking of Weight (Packages Transported by Vessels) Convention No. 27, 1929. Then followed ratification of the Right of Association (Agriculture) Convention No. 11, 1921, and the Equality of Treatment (Accident Compensation) Convention No. 19, 1925, in April 1934, together with the Weekly Rest (Industry) Convention No. 14, 1921, only weeks later. At the end of November 1935 the Protection against Accidents (Dockers) Convention (Revised) No. 32, 1932, was ratified, paving the way for a further group of six Conventions to be ratified on 2 December 1936. This important "volume" step involved the Minimum Age (Sea) Convention No. 7, 1920; the Minimum Age (Trimmers and Stokers) Convention No. 15, 1921; the Medical Examination of Young Persons (Sea) Convention No. 16, 1921; the Seamen's Articles of Agreement Convention No. 22, 1926; the Repatriation of Seamen Convention, No. 23, 1926; and the Underground Work (Women) Convention No. 45, 1935. Finally, 1940 saw ratification of the Minimum Age (Industry) Convention (Revised) No. 59, 1937; while the ending of the Second World War saw ratification in 1947 of one final pre-PRC instrument, in the shape of the Final Articles Revision Convention No. 80, 1946. While the ratifications of the majority of those instruments remain in force, three of them – Conventions No. 7, No. 15 and No. 59 – were subject to automatic denunciation in 2000 by reason of the adoption of the Minimum Age Convention No. 138, 1973 – one of the ILO's "core" Conventions, which the PRC ratified on 28 April 1999.

USSR, the re-emergence of the USSR post-war, and the arrival of the PRC, was, at the very lowest, "uneasy". As an international organization operating on the basis of "diplomatic relations", it certainly appeared to reflect an uneasy combination of "pragmatic acquiescence" accompanied by quite a "deep-seated unease" at an ambition such as that set out in Article 4 of the 1954 Constitution of the PRC to the effect that:

> The People's Republic of China, by relying on the organs of state and the social forces, and by means of socialist industrialisation and socialist transformation, ensures the gradual abolition of systems of exploitation and the building of a socialist society.

Nor is this a stance which was confined to experience with socialist systems in the post-Second World War era. Looking back to the period immediately after the Russian revolution of 1917, one finds, for example, highly critical observations from the first Director of the ILO, Albert Thomas, when he questioned[71]:

> Has Bolshevism, which exercises a powerful fascination for the masses, shown itself capable of doing anything more than organising a Jacobin dictatorship on the one hand, and of causing discontent and poverty on the other? To what constructive work can it point? Has it really secured for men, women and children the hours, wages and hygiene conditions provided for in the labour charter, or even the conditions of life which the traditions of labour legislation promise to the world?

Nor does that inherent scepticism appear ameliorated to any extent in the author's further propositions that:

> ...As a result of Bolshevism the former socialist International has been broken up. Its numerous fragments spend their time in discussions of principle, while most of the various national groups of which it is composed have not sufficient influence to affect legislation or state policy...Even if from the point of view of policy they are thinking rightly, what immediate hopes of betterment do they offer to the wage-earners?[72]

It was, of course, Albert Thomas whose efforts to draw in the nationalist government of China at the end of the 1920s helped to promote the initiation of closer ties with the ILO, and a rich period of formal ratification for ILO instruments in the decade and a half before the establishment of the PRC in 1949.[73]

History has demonstrated that some of the more extreme proposals propounded in the wake of the 1917 Russian revolution – for example, that the USSR should not even be admitted to the newly-instituted ILO – never eventually came to pass. However, it may be suggested that, throughout the history of the organization (both in its League of Nations guise and in the post-Philadelphia Declaration era) there have been delicate paths to be trodden when dealing with established socialist systems. The underlying values of a "socialist system", in particular, that operating in the USSR itself,[74] have presented major challenges to the coherence of values

[71] Thomas 1921, at pp. 20–21.

[72] Ibid., at p. 21.

[73] See the study and presentation of this period by Chen in Chap. 4 of this volume, and earlier scholarship by the same author in Chen 2014.

[74] See, for example, the contributions by a group of leading Soviet scholars to Butler et al. 1987.

espoused by the ILO in the course of its international standard-setting activities – something which can be seen particularly sharply in the context of dealing with the socialist countries of Eastern Europe prior to the fall of the Berlin Wall in 1989.[75]

Nevertheless, so far as the PRC is concerned, this problematic relationship between ILO standard-setting values and certain of the underlying principles to be found within major socialist systems of labour law and regulation had been of little or no relevance until China's shift to a much more active participation in the ILO's activities towards the end of the Millennium. Indeed, even by the time the PRC had been established in October 1949, the ILO itself had already undergone dramatic reform and (it was hoped) reinvigoration at the end of the Second World War. In particular, the key "Declaration of Philadelphia", promulgated in 1944, had reaffirmed "the fundamental principles on which the Organisation is based", and set out the now-famous principles that:

(a) Labour is not a commodity;
(b) Freedom of expression and of association are essential to sustained progress;
(c) Poverty anywhere constitutes a danger to prosperity everywhere;
(d) The war against want requires to be carried on with unrelenting vigour within each nation, and by continuous and concerted international effort in which the representatives of workers and employers, enjoying equal status with those of governments, join with them in free discussion and democratic decision with a view to the promotion of the common welfare.[76]

Since then, following the ILO's Declaration on Fundamental Principles and Rights at Work (1998 Declaration), attention at the global standard-setting level has been focused upon a group of eight so-called "core" Conventions, covering four distinct areas: (i) freedom of association and the effective recognition of the right to collective bargaining; (ii) elimination of all forms of forced or compulsory labour; (iii) effective elimination of child labour; and (iv) elimination of discrimination in respect of employment and occupation.[77] This emphasis upon specific Conventions

---

[75] Thus, simply to provide a flavour of this continuing discomfort, it is instructive to select – and this represents only one of many possible selections which could be made to the same end – observations in relation to the report on Freedom of Association and Protection of the Right to Organise Convention No. 87, which include the following: "The Government states that Soviet law and practice afford the trade unions more favourable conditions of existence, operation and independence than those prescribed by the Convention. It adds that the provisions laid down in the Convention were put into effect in the Soviet Union long before their adoption by the I.L.O. It therefore considers that there is no need for any amendment to its legislation, which meets and even surpasses the standards set by the Convention…"; and "…In conclusion the Government states that, as a result of the structure and philosophy of the régime, the workers, and hence the unions, play an active part in all aspects of the country's economic, social and cultural life. Evidence of this participation can be seen in their association in the drafting and subsequent enforcement of labour legislation". See ILC, USSR Government report, 1957, at p. 83.

[76] ILO Declaration of Philadelphia 1944, at Part I.

[77] That focus has also to be seen in the context of the ILO's "Decent Work" programme, flowing from the initiatives outlined in the Report of the Director-General, 1999, and the later submission by the Director-General to the Third WTO Ministerial Conference in Seattle (30 November–3

has been the hallmark of ILO activity and priorities throughout the twenty-first century.[78]

Of particular significance within that post-1998 approach has been the emphasis upon the principle that:

> ...all Members, even if they have not ratified the Conventions in question, have an obligation arising from the very fact of membership in the Organisation, to respect, to promote and to realise, in good faith and in accordance with the Constitution, the principles concerning the fundamental rights which are the subject of those Conventions...[79]

As has already been noted, China had been a founding member of the ILO on its inception in 1919. However, the period following the establishment of the People's Republic in 1949 was marked by non-engagement in the activities of that organization, which effectively ended any meaningful participation by the PRC. In large part this came about in the context of broad non-recognition for the newly-established People's Republic on the part of the international community. It was also the case that the government of Taiwan (the Republic of China) was active within the ILO for much of the post-1949 period until the adoption of a United Nations General Assembly resolution in October 1971 to recognize the government of the People's Republic of China as the representative government of China. That UN Resolution was followed, in November 1971, by a decision on the part of the Governing Body of the ILO also to recognize the PRC as the representative government of China.[80]

December 1999). Attention should also be had to the "labour principles" of the UN Global Compact, which was formulated in 2000 as a voluntary partnership between UN agencies and businesses. See e.g., ILO, Labour Principles of the United Nations Global Compact, 2008, and the comments of Bellace 2013, 2014.

[78] The eight key instruments are: the Forced Labour Convention No. 29, the Freedom of Association and Protection of the Right to Organise Convention No. 87, the Right to Organise and Collective Bargaining Convention No. 98, the Equal Remuneration Convention No. 100, the Abolition of Forced Labour Convention No. 105, the Discrimination (Employment and Occupation) Convention No. 111, the Minimum Age Convention No. 138, and the Worst Forms of Child Labour Convention No. 182. There is also a 'Follow-up procedure' to the 1998 Declaration, involving annual reporting arrangements in relation to countries which have not yet ratified all of the "core" instruments, as well as the production of a Global Report (dealing, in turn, with the four designated areas of concern).

[79] ILO 1998 Declaration, at para 2. It is also important to note the 2008 Declaration to the effect that: "The Conference further recognises that, in a globalised economy: The implementation of Part I of this Declaration requires that the ILO effectively assist its Members in their efforts. To that end, the Organisation should review and adapt its institutional practices to enhance governance and capacity building in order to make the best use of its human and financial resources and of the unique advantage of its tri-partite structure and standards system...". See ILO 2008 Declaration, at Part 2(A).

[80] The modern sensitivities still raised by the existence of the PRC and Taiwan are well illustrated by the ILO's document ILO Country and Areas Designations and Rules for their Use, replacing ILO Circular 12/19 (Rev. 9) of 9 March 1992 and its addenda. That document sets out "the standard office nomenclature relating to country and area designations which must be used in *all* ILO publications and documents", and provides that: "*Taiwan* should not be treated as a country, since its status is that of a province of the People's Republic of China. If in exceptional cases it has to be mentioned in an ILO publication or document it should be referred to as *Taiwan, China*." For an

Thereafter, little by way of tangible progress was made in the immediate aftermath of this shift in position as regards the standing of China in the ILO, until eventually, in 1981,[81] the PRC announced its intention to resume participation in the ILO. Soon afterwards China returned to being an active member of the organization when its first post-1949 delegation attended the 69th session of the International Labour Conference in 1983.

The early period of renewed ILO participation saw a declaration by the PRC government that it considered itself bound by only 14 of the 37 international labour Conventions which were registered in the name of China – effectively excluding those instruments which had been ratified in the period between the establishment of the PRC and the ILO's 1971 decision. However, China resumed its seat on the Governing Body, and within 2 years the ILO had opened a branch office in Beijing, while Chinese experts were participating in their first ILO technical co-operation project.[82] Thereafter, a significant "Memorandum of Understanding for future co-operation between the PRC and the ILO" entered into force in 2001, marking an intensification of collaboration at the level of international standard-setting, and there has been a notable raising of China's profile in that context since the turn of the Millennium.[83]

Quite apart from a strong focus upon institutional pressures associated with the commitment of the PRC, as a member state of the ILO, to the principles set out in the eight "core" Conventions, co-operation between the ILO and the Chinese government has not been confined to technical support and co-operation.[84] There has also been a steady deepening of the relationship between the ILO's Beijing office and the PRC Ministry of Human Resources and Social Security, even to the extent of the ILO office contributing feedback in the context of legislative consultations over areas such as the Labour Contract Law, the Employment Promotion Law, and the Social Insurance Law. In complementary manner, it has also become evident that, in recent years, the PRC government has been endeavouring to play an increasingly high-profile role within the framework of activities of the ILO – and, in particular, has demonstrated a willingness to ratify a number of key instruments.

If one simply looks at the "ratification balance-sheet", it can be seen that the PRC has committed itself to the "equal treatment/non-discrimination" obligations, having ratified the Discrimination (Employment and Occupation) Convention No. 111 in 2006, while ratification of the Equal Remuneration Convention No. 100 had

account of the political divisions at the time of the UN and ILO resolutions, see Ghebali, Ago and Valticos 1989.

[81] After the National Trade Union Federation had been reconstituted in 1978 following the ending of the period of the "cultural revolution" and the death of Mao Zedong.

[82] See Ghebali et al. 1989, at pp. 124–125.

[83] Memorandum of Understanding for co-operation between the ILO and the Ministry of Labour and Social Security of China 2000.

[84] As, for example, in relation to various Conventions covering the physical security of workers (especially in the construction and mining sectors), or protection against the dangers posed by working with chemical and other hazardous agents.

already taken place in 1990. In this context, a broad raft of domestic provisions dealing with equal treatment and non-discrimination (particularly in relation to women in the labour market) has been introduced by the Chinese legislator, although it is evident that many of these have enjoyed a long pedigree, and can hardly be said to have derived their primary inspiration from particular ILO instruments. Thus, as far back as in the 1954 Constitution of the PRC, Article 96 declared the equal rights of women – a fundamental principle which has transferred through amendments to the Chinese Constitution in 1975 and 1978, and now finds expression in the current 1982 Constitution. Beneath that constitutional umbrella, the Law on the Protection of Rights and Interests of Women of 1992 introduced specific provisions relating to work and social security rights, and the Labour Law of 1994 incorporated much of that 1992 framework of protective rights. More recently, the prohibition of discrimination on the basis of differences in ethnic group, race, sex or religious belief, as well as protection for groups such as disabled workers, have been supplemented by provisions designed to ensure non-discrimination against *inter alia* migrant workers.[85]

As regards the area of child labour, the PRC can also be seen to have ratified the Minimum Age Convention No. 138 on 28 April 1999, as well as, on 8 August 2002, the Worst Forms of Child Labour Convention No. 182. Even before those ratifications, however, domestic provisions outlawing the employment of children under the age of 16 were already to be found – as, for example, in Article 15 of the Labour Law. Thereafter, following ratification of the Worst Forms of Child Labour Convention No. 182, further domestic provisions were forthcoming. Thus, a Provision on the Prohibition of Using Child Labour was issued by the State Council in 2002, and a supplementary Circular on implementing that measure was issued by the Ministry of Labour and Social Security in the following year.[86]

In the field of forced labour, by contrast, there has to date been no ratification by the PRC of the Forced Labour Convention No. 29 or of the Abolition of Forced Labour Convention No. 105. Nevertheless, in September 2008, the PRC government indicated that co-operation with the ILO was continuing with regard to ratification of those Conventions,[87] and more recently that process has been confirmed as continuing.[88] Since then, a vote by the Standing Committee of the National

[85] In particular, basic provisions to this effect contained in the [Labour Law of the People's Republic of China] 中华人民共和国劳动法 (zhōng huá rén mín gòng hé guó láo dòng fǎ), 1994 have been complemented by stipulations in the [Employment Promotion Law of the People's Republic of China] 中华人民共和国就业促进法 (zhōng huá rén mín gòng hé guó jiù yè cù jìn fǎ), 2007.

[86] [Provisions on the Prohibition of Using Child Labour] 禁止使用童工规定 (jìn zhǐ shǐ yòng tóng gōng guī dìng), 2002; [Circular on Implementing the Provisions on the Prohibition of Child Labour] 关于贯彻落实《禁止使用童工规定》的通知 (guān yú guàn chè luò shí "jìn zhǐ shǐ yòng tóng gōng guī dìng" de tōng zhī), 2003.

[87] See ILO, Committee on Legal Issues and International Labour Standards, 2008, at para. 20. For recent evaluation of activity in the PRC concerning ILO initiatives in this field, see ILO, Contributing to Realising Decent Work: ILO Decent Work Country Programme in the People's Republic of China 2006–2010, 2010.

[88] See ILO, Decent Work Country Programme in the People's Republic of China 2013–2015.

People's Congress to abolish China's long-criticized system of "re-education through labour" is regarded by some observers as "opening a door" to eventual ratification of the ILO's two forced labour Conventions.[89]

Controversially, however, this leaves unaddressed the ILO Conventions dealing with freedom of association and collective bargaining: the Freedom of Association and Protection of the Right to Organise Convention No. 87 and the Right to Organise and Collective Bargaining Convention No. 98. The matters encompassed by those two instruments have tended to be the areas most commonly commented upon by non-Chinese observers – and, indeed, there has been an increasing concern for issues such as "the right to strike" amongst PRC scholars and policy-makers.[90] However, despite such attention, there has been little tangible progress towards the creation of any enhanced "collective labour rights" in respect of trade union activities, the establishment of representative channels for workers other than through the All-China Federation of Trade Unions (ACFTU), or that elusive "right to strike".

In addition to the ratification of four "core" Conventions, the PRC has also ratified two of the ILO's "priority governance" Conventions.[91] Alongside this, there has been ratification of a total of 19 "technical" Conventions over the period of China's (pre- and post-1949) ILO membership.[92] However, it is to be noted that no new ratifications have taken place since 2007.

---

[89] On 28 December 2013. For some background on this issue, see [Prison Law of the People's Republic of China] 中华人民共和国监狱法 (zhōng huá rén mín gòng hé guó jiān yù fǎ), 1994, especially in Chapter V. See also the [Supplementary Provisions of the State Council for Rehabilitation Through Labour] 国务院关于劳动教养的补充规定 (guó wù yuàn guān yú láo dòng jiào yǎng de bǔ chōng guī ding), 1979.

[90] See, for example, the policy debates over "social management", and, specifically in relation to "collective" labour market disputes, the discussions at the "Conflict and Co-operation: International Symposium on Collective Labour Dispute Resolution and Regulation", hosted at the Remnin University, Beijing, on 17–18 December 2011. A selection of the contributions to that symposium can be found in a special edition of *The International Journal of Comparative Labour Law and Industrial* Relations: see Issue 2 of Volume 29, 2013. Some scholars – including, in particular, Professor Chang Kai – have gone so far as to suggest that the Chinese position is beginning to take on "Western-style" collectivized features. However, it may be suggested that, on the basis of the evidence so far, such predictions remain largely in the realms of "wishful thinking" on the parts of those who would see modern developments in China progress along the "classical" lines of the model espoused by ILO Conventions No. 87 and No. 98. See e.g., Chang 2014.

[91] Namely, the Employment Policy Convention No. 122, 1964, and the Tripartite Consultation (International Labour Standards) Convention No. 144, 1976. Convention No. 144 was ratified on 2 November 1990 and Convention No. 122 on 17 December 1997.

[92] Thus, as well as the pre-1949 ratifications already alluded to, 1988 saw ratification of the Vocational Rehabilitation and Employment (Disabled Persons) Convention No. 159, 1983, followed by the Chemicals Convention No. 170, 1990, in 1995. China ratified two instruments in 2002: the Labour Administration Convention No. 150, 1978, and the Safety and Health in Construction Convention No. 167, 1988, and the Occupational Safety and Health Convention No. 155, 1981, in 2007.

2.6 Labour Rights Enforcement

It is only, however, by looking at the institutions and procedures for delivering labour rights in the PRC that any real assessment of the "effectiveness", or otherwise, of those rights can be made. So, too, if one is to offer any view at all in respect of the "implementation" of ILO fundamental, or indeed any, labour rights in China, it is necessary to identify the mechanisms for monitoring, supervision, and enforcement of the instruments and provisions which are supposed to deliver those rights. Having once identified them, an attempt to assess their functional efficacy may be in order.

The institutional arrangements for labour dispute resolution in the PRC have a long genealogy, and, once again, reflect initial inspiration derived from experience in the post-1917 Russian revolution period for USSR labour law. Thus, Article 126 of the 1918 Labour Code of the RSFSR provided that "self-governing bodies of the workers" were given the task of ensuring the observance of labour discipline within factories. The eventual 1922 Labour Code of the RSFSR provisions on this matter were also supplemented by further instruments, such as the Decision of the Council of People's Commissars of the USSR of 6 March 1929, on measures to strengthen labour discipline in state enterprises.[93] More generally, the basic normative provisions on the procedures to be used in examining labour disputes were set out in Articles 168 and following of the 1922 Labour Code, with primary reliance being placed upon "labour disputes boards" set up in undertakings, institutions and organizations.[94] In the absence of such organs, examination of disputes relating to labour fell to the People's Courts[95] – the same instance as was competent to deal with applications from workers who disagreed with the outcome of a consideration by a labour disputes board.[96]

It has already been mentioned that the brief period of the Chinese Soviet Republic, in the early 1930s,[97] included the enactment of a Labour Law of the Chinese Soviet Republic, which was adopted in November 1931. That instrument included, in its Articles 72 and 73, arrangements for dealing with violations of the Labour Law and for the settlement of labour disputes between workers and employers. Here, the inspiration of the 1922 Labour Code of the USSR can clearly be seen – as was also the case in relation to the contemporaneous "Resolution on implementing the Labour Law".[98]

---

[93] For a limited consideration of the evolution of labour codification in the USSR, see van den Berg 1975, at pp. 23–38.

[94] Labour Code of the RSFSR, 1922, Article 169.

[95] Labour Code of the RSFSR, 1922, Article 169–2.

[96] Labour Code of the RSFSR, 1922, Article 171.

[97] For an introductory survey of that period, see Butler 1983.

[98] [Resolution on Implementing the Labour Law] 关于实施劳动法的决议案 (guān yú shí shī láo dòng fǎ de jué yì àn), 1931.

Prior to the establishment of the PRC in 1949, however, labour disputes within the areas of China under the control of the nationalist government were dealt with in accordance with fragmented arrangements introduced during the late 1920s and early 1930s. Early on in the development of such regulation came a 1924 resolution to introduce a Labour Law, which was passed at the first National Convention of Delegations of the Chinese nationalist party held in that year.[99] A subsequent "trade union-related platform" announced at the end of 1924, included, amongst its 21 points, provisions guaranteeing the right for trade unions to represent workers in negotiations with an employer, as well as investing the trade union with the role of mediator in the event of a dispute between workers and the employer. There was also commitment to express provision of a "right to strike", subject to majority approval by the members of the trade union. Of particular significance thereafter was the enactment of a Factory Law in 1929,[100] which provided *inter alia* for "…the establishment of a "Joint Factory Council" in every factory employing more than 30 workers, with responsibility for dealing with employer-employee disputes".[101] Thereafter, however, issues arising in the context of labour disputes tended increasingly to be addressed in terms of "the government maintaining control of labour",[102] and, as a combination of foreign occupation and civil war came to dominate the decade leading up to 1949, concern for "labour law" regulation within a framework of effective laws and enforcement mechanisms became less and less the reality.

From what limited evidence is available, that somewhat incoherent state of affairs continued until the effective collapse of the nationalist government's ability to govern the economy in the aftermath of the Second World War. Indeed, the period following Japan's surrender in 1945 rapidly developed into one in which the officially established procedures for resolution of labour-management disputes were widely "flouted" by workers seeking pay increases to off-set the effects of the hyper-inflation which developed dramatically during the period of civil war.[103]

Once the People's Republic had been declared in October 1949, however, institutional arrangements for dealing with disputes and contraventions in the context of labour regulation were quickly established. Normative provisions constituted the essential method of establishing those arrangements, and, indeed, it is noteworthy

---

[99] However, no instrument to that effect was actually adopted at the National Convention – this being at a time when the Kuomintang (Chinese Nationalist Party) had still to establish itself as a ruling "nationalist government".

[100] [Factory Law] 工厂法 (gōng chǎng fǎ), 1929.

[101] Edles 1969, discussing the content of the 1929 Factory Law, at p. 398. A detailed account of the Factory Law is provided by Kim 2009. "In June 1928, the Nationalist Government drew up the bill for the Labour Dispute Resolution Act (the Factory Act) and sent it to the Parliament in January 1929. The Parliament passed the Act in December 1929 at its 67th session, and it was promulgated forthwith. In December 1930, the Enforcement Ordinance of the Factory Act was promulgated." See Kim 2009, at p. 230.

[102] See e.g., Edles 1969, at p. 400.

[103] See e.g., the account in Eastman et al. 1991; in that volume see especially Pepper, Chapter 5, at pp. 309–311. According to the sources cited in Pepper, 1946 witnessed "…a total of 1,716 strikes and labour disputes recorded in Shanghai alone. In 1947 the number for that city reached 2,538".

that this has remained the case over the 60 years of the PRC. In addition to "legislation" – which may be introduced and piloted through the legislative process by a variety of bodies – it is also important to have regard to the existence of "secondary" regulations (again, emanating from a variety of institutions) and "guidance" which may derive from Ministries, from the People's Courts, or from high-level organs such as the NPC.[104]

Thus, setting out the normative framework for delivering and safeguarding labour rights, the Trade Union Law, which was introduced by the PRC Central Government Committee, was followed by a Regulations on Labour Insurance in 1951 and a Measure on Registering Unemployed Persons in 1952 – both emanating from the State Council.[105] These important "rights-bearing" instruments were accompanied by specific procedural measures, in the form of the Provisions regarding the Procedure for Settling Labour Disputes in 1950, and, in the same year, a Directive on Establishing Congresses for Worker-Employer Conciliation inside Private Enterprises[106] – both introduced by the Ministry of Labour.[107]

Following the chaotic experiences of the "Cultural Revolution" period, before it was formally declared at an end in 1977, the arrangements designed to make existing labour-related rights "effective" took some time to coalesce as the PRC embarked upon its journey towards establishing a modern "socialist market economy". In the early stages of this period the focus was upon labour dispute resolution in SOEs, with Regulations on Workers' Congresses in State-Owned Enterprises, introduced at the initiative of the ACFTU in 1986, and the Interim Provisions on Dealing with Labour Disputes in State-Owned Enterprises, introduced by the Ministry of Labour and Personnel in the following year.[108]

---

[104] For an overview of the multiple layers and sources of regulation, see the presentation in Yan 2014.

[105] [Labour Insurance Regulations of the People's Republic of China] 中华人民共和国劳动保险条例 (zhōng huá rén mín gòng hé guó láo dòng bǎo xiǎn tiáo lì), 1951; [Measure on Registering Unemployed Persons] 关于失业人员统一登记办法 (guān yú shī yè rén yuán tǒng yī dēng jì bàn fǎ), 1952.

[106] [Provisions regarding the Procedure for Settling Labour Disputes] 关于劳动争议解决程序的规定 (guān yú láo dòng zhēng yì jiě jué chéng xù de guī dìng) and [Directive on Establishing Congresses for Worker-Employer Conciliation Inside Private Enterprises] 关于在私营企业中设立劳资协商会议的指示 (guān yú zài sī yíng qǐ yè zhōng shè lì láo zī xié shāng huì yì de zhǐ shì), 1950.

[107] This is described by Wang et al. 2003, at p. 6 in terms that: "Labour dispute settlement system was initiated in 1950, which was symbolised by the [Rules on Organisational Structure and Working Procedures of Municipal Labour Dispute Arbitration Committees] 劳动争议仲裁委员会组织及工作规则 (láo dòng zhēng yì zhòng cái wěi yuán huì zǔ zhī jí gōng zuò guī zé), enacted by the Ministry of Labour in June 1950, and [Regulations on Labour Dispute Settlement Procedure] 关于劳动争议解决程序的规定 (guān yú láo dòng zhēng yì jiě jué chéng xù de guī dìng) issued by the Ministry of Labour with approval of the State Administrative Council in November 1950."

[108] [Regulations on Workers' Congresses in State-Owned Enterprises] 全民所有制工业企业职工代表大会条例 (quán mín suǒ yǒu zhì gōng yè qǐ yè zhí gōng dài biǎo dà huì tiáo lì), 1986; [Interim Provisions on Dealing with Labour Dispute in State-Owned Enterprises] 国营企业劳动争议处理暂行规定 (guó yíng qǐ yè láo dòng zhēng yì chǔ lǐ zàn xíng guī dìng), 1987.

Central to much of the dispute resolution processes to be found both at that time and throughout modern times is what is known in the Chinese system as "labour arbitration".[109] This, it should be stressed, has little or nothing to do with what many Western commentators recognize as "arbitration" in commercial transaction spheres, but reflects, rather, a pattern of socialized dispute resolution developed with Russian post-revolutionary roots throughout a wide range of Eastern European and other socialist states.[110] Shortly thereafter, a fundamental formulation of the relevant procedures to be utilized in the emerging "socialist market economy" was set out in the State Council's Regulations on Settlement of Labour Disputes in Enterprises (1993 Regulations).[111] Those 1993 Regulations[112] repealed the Provisional Regulations of 1987, and have formed the basis for the Chinese labour arbitration dispute-resolution system for the last two decades. Further clarification and amplification was forthcoming in a Circular on Further Perfecting the Labour Dispute Settlement System,[113] and a Circular on Perfecting the Tripartite Labour Arbitration Mechanism.[114] Thereafter, with the exception of a Trial Measure for Collective Conciliation, issued in 2000 by the MoLSS,[115] and a Circular on Promoting Equal Conciliation and a Collective Contract System,[116] which emanated from the same Ministry in 2001, the formal 1993 framework for labour dispute resolution has remained intact until, and in large measure since, enactment of the most recent initiative in this area – the Labour Dispute Mediation and Arbitration Law, which came into force on 1 May 2008.[117]

[109] For one of the few studies of labour arbitration arrangements in China, see Ho 2003.

[110] Thus, a set of Provisional Regulations on Settlement of Labour Disputes in State-Owned Enterprises was promulgated by the State Council on 31 July 1987, while a [Circular on Reinforcing Labour Arbitration Activities] 关于加强劳动仲裁工作的通知 (guān yú jiā qiáng láo dòng zhòng cái gōng zuò de tōng zhī) was issued in 1989 by the Ministry of Labour.

[111] [Regulations of the People's Republic of China on Settlement of Labour Disputes in Enterprises] 中华人民共和国企业劳动争议处理条例 (zhōng huá rén mín gòng hé guó qǐ yè láo dòng zhēng yì chǔ lǐ tiáo lì), 1993. This key instrument was accompanied by a Code of Conduct and Organisation of Labour Arbitration Committees 1993, drawn up by the Ministry of Labour.

[112] Which came into force on 1 August 1993.

[113] [Circular on Further Perfecting the Labour Dispute Settlement System] 劳动部关于进一步完善劳动争议处理工作的通知 (láo dòng bù guān yú jìn yī bù wán shàn láo dòng zhēng yì chǔ lǐ gōng zuò de tōng zhī), 1995.

[114] [Circular on Perfecting the Tripartite Labour Arbitration Mechanism] 关于进一步完善劳动争议仲裁三方机制的通知 (guān yú jìn yī bù wán shàn láo dòng zhēng yì zhòng cái sān fāng jī zhì de tōng zhī), 1996.

[115] [Trial Measures for Collective Salary Negotiation] 工资集体协商试行办法 (gōng zī jí tǐ xié shāng shì xíng bàn fǎ), 2000.

[116] [Circular on Promoting Equal Conciliation and a Collective Contract System] 关于进一步推行平等协商和集体合同制度的通知 (guān yú jìn yī bù tuī xíng píng děng xié shāng hé jí tǐ hé tóng zhì dù de tōng zhī), 2001.

[117] [Labour Dispute Mediation and Arbitration Law of the People's Republic of China] 中华人民共和国劳动争议调解仲裁法 (zhōng huá rén mín gòng hé guó láo dòng zhēng yì tiào jiě zhòng cái fǎ), 2007.

The current modern system for labour dispute resolution has thus now developed into a primary framework which is often described in terms of "one mediation, one arbitration and two lawsuits".[118] The "mediation" component is designed to operate at the enterprise level, and aims to prevent disputes taking on an increasingly rigid formalistic character, eventually becoming subject to intervention outside the enterprise. This is then supplemented by arrangements for "labour arbitration", undertaken by Labour Arbitration Committees at local, city, and provincial levels, and organized and administered through the Ministry of Human Resources and Social Security. That "administrative" justice tier is then backed-up by judicial arrangements organized under the supervision of the Supreme People's Court.[119] These judicial arrangements are, themselves, operative at two levels – with a first instance, effectively providing for an "appeal" by way of re-hearing from a Labour Arbitration Committee decision, by way of a hearing before the relevant regional People's Court, and a further opportunity for re-hearing of the same matter by the relevant Intermediate People's Court.

The structure for providing labour dispute resolution through the Labour Arbitration Committees has been the subject of criticism since the turn of the Millennium, with concern expressed that the composition, competence and capacity of these bodies were increasingly proving "unfit for purpose" in the new "socialist market economy". Indeed, it was very much this concern – particularly at a time when the official statistics for cases dealt with by labour arbitration were indicating a dramatic increase in work-load – which led, eventually, to the enforcement provisions of the draft Labour Contract Law being taken out of that instrument and dealt with separately through what was to become the Labour Dispute Mediation and Arbitration Law of 2007.[120] At the same time, a variety of experimental schemes were being developed in an attempt to address both the need for greatly enhanced capacity to deal with the rising case-load and what was fast becoming realized to be a pressing need for greater "professionalization" of the personnel and procedures

---

[118] However, it should be noted that the "one mediation" phase is not mandatory, so that, in practice, this initial component may fall away from the procedure. Indeed, it has been suggested in some quarters that, in the context of SOE privatization and restructuring at the turn of the Millennium (and, possibly, with increasing complexity of disputes arising), the importance of "first phase" mediation committees gradually faded. On the other hand, even if that proposition holds good, it appears that the more recent regulatory policy focus upon encouraging early mediation in labour disputes may have begun to reverse that trend.

[119] It should be noted that this is distinct from the provisions for mediation during court proceedings to be found under the [Civil Procedure Law of the People's Republic of China] 中华人民共和国民事诉讼法 (zhōng huá rén mín gòng hé guó mín shì sù sòng fǎ), 1991 (as revised in 2012), [Criminal Procedure Law of the People's Republic of China] 中华人民共和国刑事诉讼法 (zhōng huá rén mín gòng hé guó xíng shì sù sòng fǎ), 1979 (as revised in 2012) and [Administrative Litigation Law of the People's Republic of China] 中华人民共和国行政诉讼法 (zhōng huá rén mín gòng hé guó xíng zhèng sù sòng fǎ), 1989 (revised 2014). For an early discussion of those procedural arrangements, see Woo 1999 along with contributions by Turner et al. 2000.

[120] This followed consideration and feedback in relation to an early 2005 draft of the proposed Law (revised on 25 April of that year) – in which the enforcement and sanctioning provisions had been included as Chapters 6 and 7.

for labour arbitration.[121] While adjustments were eventually made to the system by the Labour Dispute Mediation and Arbitration Law – including the introduction of "fast track" treatment for certain categories of dispute – there continues to be concern that even the reformed system is struggling to deal with the issue of ever-rising numbers of labour disputes, with all of the attendant problems which those disputes might carry for social stability and "the harmonious society".

While a fairly broad range of issues fall within the jurisdiction of the labour arbitration arrangements,[122] a wide variety of matters are dealt with by way of "labour inspection".[123] These include, in particular, areas of regulation relating to the health, safety and hygiene of workers,[124] together with matters concerning observance of minimum wage provisions[125] and the timely payment of wages due.[126] This mechanism of administrative inspection – again organized through the Ministry of Human Resources and Social Security – is also utilized in relation to various components of the newly-introduced social security net, established by the Social Insurance Law of 2010.[127]

---

[121] Particular progress was made in Shenzhen, where a pilot so-called "Labour Arbitration Court" was established (with technical co-operation from the Foreign and Commonwealth Office of the United Kingdom government) – providing for a pattern which has subsequently been taken up in more than half of the provinces of the PRC. The same city also witnessed experimentation within the system of People's Courts – notably with the designation of one division of the first instance People's Court to deal exclusively with labour dispute matters.

[122] The scope of jurisdiction of Labour Arbitration Committees extends to cover wages, issues affecting the labour relationship (including termination of employment), social insurance issues (e.g. payment of social dues by the employer) and cases concerning occupational injuries.

[123] In particular, the [Labour Law of the People's Republic of China] 中华人民共和国劳动法 (zhōng huá rén mín gòng hé guó láo dòng fǎ), 1994, Chapter 11 sets out fundamental supervision and inspection duties in this regard, extending across the whole spectrum of rights and duties established by that instrument.

[124] For a recent evaluation of the modern Chinese situation in relation to state-owned enterprises, see Chen and Chan 2010. An overview of the general framework for health, safety and hygiene protection at work is to be found in Guo 2014. Mention should also be made of the biennial "China International Fora on Work Safety", organized between the ILO and the PRC's State Administration of Work Safety. The 6th such Forum took place in 2012, and the 7th Forum took place in Beijing in September 2014.

[125] See e.g., [Regulations concerning Minimum Wages in Enterprises] 企业最低工资规定 (qǐ yè zuì dī gōng zī guī dìng), 1993, Article 22 placing responsibility for inspection in this field upon the departments of labour administration under the People's Governments at various levels.

[126] One of the various areas for which the Labour Inspectorate (part of the Provincial and Area Labour Bureaux) is responsible for enforcing employment rights – particularly those deriving from the [Labour Law of the People's Republic of China] 中华人民共和国劳动法 (zhōng huá rén mín gòng hé guó láo dòng fǎ), 1994. See, for an external perspective and overview of the general labour inspection arrangements, OECD 2005.

[127] Thus, primary supervision of the rights and duties under this Law is entrusted to social insurance administrative departments of the People's Governments at and above the county level. See [Social Insurance Law of the People's Republic of China] 中华人民共和国社会保险法 (zhōng huá rén mín gòng hé guó shè huì bǎo xiǎn fǎ), 2010, Chapter X for the administrative and inspection arrangements, and see Chapter XI for the relevant sanctions attaching to failures to observe the Law. For a brief general overview of the Social Insurance Law, see Lin 2014.

The normal arrangements providing for the activities of the relevant inspectorates also make use of criminal sanctions to back up inspection activities. A wide range of sanctions is included in all of the relevant statutes to ensure both that the designated administrative organs, at various levels, discharge their supervisory and enforcement duties fully and effectively, and that individuals who fail to meet the obligations imposed upon them, or who act dishonestly or in a manner inappropriate to their "public official" status, are also made subject to individual administrative and criminal sanctions.[128] Such powers are also combined with various powers to order rectification where non-compliance has been identified, as well as to order payment of "fines" by way of financial penalties.

While, on the face of the statutory provisions, wide-ranging powers appear to have been provided for the effective enforcement of labour law rights in the modern PRC world of work, it does not necessarily follow that true "access to justice" is always achieved through those provisions. One area, for example, in which shortcomings are perceived relates to situations where inspection activities identify shortcomings or non-compliance in the delivery of statute-based rights, but eventual enforcement is then left to be pursued by or on behalf of the individual worker affected – normally, by way of recourse to the system for "labour arbitration".[129] There is, however, some evidence that a number of factors tend towards dissuading individual workers in China from taking advantage of such arrangements for "access to justice".[130] This would suggest that – without institutional support from either the ACFTU or from some variant upon a publicly-funded system of "legal aid" – the individual who may be entitled to the right in question, e.g. payment of due wages or social insurance entitlements, may not eventually go through with the procedure intended to ensure delivery of that right.[131]

---

[128] See e.g., the criminal sanctions provided for by the [Labour Law of the People's Republic of China] 中华人民共和国劳动法 (zhōng huá rén mín gòng hé guó láo dòng fǎ), 1994, Articles 92 and 93, in relation to health, safety and hygiene – which represent the creation by that Law of specific criminal offences. Elsewhere, use of criminal law tends to be invoked in terms such as: "Any person who violates this Law shall be subject to criminal liability if the violation constitutes a crime", [Social Insurance Law of the People's Republic of China] 中华人民共和国社会保险法 (zhōng huá rén mín gòng hé guó shè huì bǎo xiǎn fǎ), 2010, Article 94. Such an approach is to be found *inter alia* in Article 95 of the [Labour Contract Law of the People's Republic of China] 中华人民共和国劳动合同法 (zhōng huá rén mín gòng hé guó láo dòng hé tóng fǎ), 2007.

[129] Something which may arise in the context of payment in accordance with minimum wage rates, or, more significantly, in the context of protective arrangements set out in the [Social Insurance Law of the People's Republic of China] 中华人民共和国社会保险法 (zhōng huá rén mín gòng hé guó shè huì bǎo xiǎn fǎ), 2010.

[130] These may include lack of adequate knowledge on the part of the worker, lack of resources to proceed with a claim, the absence of any accessible form of "legal aid" (whether from general State social provision or through the ACFTU), or, simply, an unwillingness to engage in a public confrontation for cultural reasons reflecting the long Chinese traditions of mediation and conciliation in relation to social disputes.

[131] See e.g., the discussion in Neal 2013. A particular such problem might be envisaged in the context of Article 83(3) of the [Social Insurance Law of the People's Republic of China] 中华人民共和国社会保险法 (zhōng huá rén mín gòng hé guó shè huì bǎo xiǎn fǎ), 2010.

By way of final comment, a word should also be added in relation to the role of the People's Courts other than in their capacity of re-hearing matters which have been subject to a decision by a Labour Arbitration Committee. The historical debates which preceded the drafting of the Labour Law included theoretical discussion as to whether, and if so how, the labour relationship could be differentiated from "economic law" within the Chinese legal system.[132] While "labour law" eventually established an independent niche in the regulatory framework of Chinese civil law, it has to be borne in mind that disputes relating to "the labour contract", such as those over payment of due wages or rights to "overtime" remuneration, may fall to be treated as a "normal" matter of contract interpretation and compliance – without the need for any "special regime" such as that provided by labour arbitration. The jurisdictional borderline between the field of activity of the administratively-constituted Labour Arbitration Committees and the judicial instances established with the system of People's Courts has thus given rise to some matters of controversy in recent years. For the time being, such issues – several of which came to light in the context of implementing the Labour Contract Law – have been resolved through the issuing of "Guidance" by the Supreme People's Court.[133] However, whether this approach will serve adequately to deal with what has become a growing problem of labour dispute cases finding their way before the People's Courts must be open to question. A sharp increase has been noted, for example, in cases concerning "overtime" payment being brought directly to the People's Courts, while a much larger volume of cases arising out of the new social insurance arrangements introduced by the 2010 Social Insurance Law can also be anticipated.

[132] See the observations of Jia and Wei 2014, especially at p. 50.

[133] The most recent of these has been the [Fourth Interpretation of the Supreme People's Court on Certain Issues Concerning the Application of Law in the Trial of Labour Dispute Cases] 最高人民法院关于审理劳动争议案件适用法律若干问题的解释(四) (zuì gāo rén mín fǎ yuàn guān yú shěn lǐ láo dòng zhēng yì àn jiàn shì yòng fǎ lǜ ruò gān wèn tí de jiě shì (sì)), 2013. That Fourth Interpretation followed the earlier [First Interpretation of the Supreme People's Court of Several Issues on the Application of Law in the Trial of Labour Dispute Cases] 最高人民法院关于审理劳动争议案件适用法律若干问题的解释(一) (zuì gāo rén mín fǎ yuàn guān yú shěn lǐ láo dòng zhēng yì àn jiàn shì yòng fǎ lǜ ruò gān wèn tí de jiě shì (yī)), 2001; the [Second Interpretation of the Supreme People's Court of Several Issues on the Application of Law in the Trial of Labour Dispute Cases] 最高人民法院关于审理劳动争议案件适用法律若干问题的解释(二) (zuì gāo rén mín fǎ yuàn guān yú shěn lǐ láo dòng zhēng yì àn jiàn shì yòng fǎ lǜ ruò gān wèn tí de jiě shì (èr)), 2006; and the [Third Interpretation of the Supreme People's Court of Several Issues on the Application of Law in the Trial of Labour Dispute Cases] 最高人民法院关于审理劳动争议案件适用法律若干问题的解释(三) (zuì gāo rén mín fǎ yuàn guān yú shěn lǐ láo dòng zhēng yì àn jiàn shì yòng fǎ lǜ ruò gān wèn tí de jiě shì (sān)), 2010.

2.7 Comment

The foregoing offers a historical overview of the development of labour law provisions establishing the modern framework for regulating the world of work in China. It also highlights the trend towards increasingly formalized supervisory and monitoring arrangements in relation to that normative "floor of rights", and considers the evolution of modern labour dispute resolution mechanisms in the PRC.

So far as the place of international, and in particular, ILO-initiated, standards in China is concerned, what swiftly emerges is that, while evidence is not hard to find of direct and indirect influence upon the Chinese "law in the books" which has derived from the international standard-setting regime, there is no specific formalized mechanism whereby the values and norms encapsulated within that international-level regime are infused into the regulatory arrangements of the PRC. Thus, in order to address the question whether, and to what extent, China has implemented ILO standards at the national level, it is necessary to go through a number of stages:

1. First, it is helpful to consider the extent to which China has ratified particular ILO Conventions and Recommendations. Such a consideration includes, of course, recognition of the fact that, as a member of the ILO, China is subject to the expectation that ratification of the ILO's eight "core" Conventions will be achieved. This preliminary "scoping exercise" may assist, in particular, in identifying areas in which the PRC has committed itself to implementation, and lead to direct comparisons between the content of those ratified instruments and the content of domestic Chinese law. It also serves to identify areas where concern for international standards is *not* present in modern Chinese labour law and labour market regulatory arrangements.[134]
2. Having identified areas in which China has entered into commitments to implement particular international standards, it is then necessary to investigate the extent to which the content of those standards has found its way into current Chinese regulatory provisions. That challenging exercise, which includes evaluation not only of the "law in the books" but also of "the law in action", has not been the province of what has been considered in this presentation, although a number of areas in which it is suggested that shortcomings in implementation can be identified have been mentioned from time to time.
3. Where international standards, or some parts of them, have – whether formally or indirectly – found their way into Chinese regulatory arrangements, the important practical question then arises as to what might be the monitoring, supervisory, and enforcement regimes associated with those arrangements. Mention has been made of a variety of institutions and mechanisms which might be regarded

[134] An important comparative methodology point regularly emphasized by the late Tore Sigeman. See Sigeman 1984. Sigeman uses an example from Horrebow 1758, at p. 91, where, describing the island of Iceland, Horrebow states: "*Concerning snakes*. No snakes of any kind are to be met with throughout the whole island." See Sigeman 1984, at p. 291.

as having a role to play in this context. These include varieties of "labour inspection", for example, in relation to payment of wages or to the health, safety and hygiene of workers at work. They also include what has been described as "socialized" dispute resolution mechanisms, such as the various layers of "conciliation", "mediation" or "arbitration" – in the Chinese senses – which are regularly to be found throughout the social fabric of modern Chinese society. Inevitably, given the trajectory of modern development towards a "labour contract system" for Chinese labour law, this also includes varieties of "judicial" or "quasi-judicial" dispute resolution, including both the "administrative" procedures for "labour arbitration" organized through the Ministry of Human Resources and Social Security, and the activities of the People's Courts organized under the auspices of the Supreme People's Court.

In what follows, a few concluding observations are offered in respect of these matters. These include consideration of the extent to which "access to justice" is afforded to Chinese workers who are the intended addressees of the protective cover which those international standards seek to establish. It also includes a contemporary evaluation of the adequacy of modern Chinese arrangements in providing "effective implementation" of the values and protections enshrined in those international standards.

2.7.1 "Core" Conventions Ratified by the PRC

At the formal level of "law in the books", it is not difficult to describe the position of the PRC in relation to the implicit obligation, as a member of the ILO, to ratify, and thereafter to implement, the so-called "core" Conventions highlighted by the 1998 Declaration.

Thus, on the "positive" side of the formal balance-sheet, the Equal Remuneration Convention No. 100 was ratified on 2 November 1990, while the Discrimination (Employment and Occupation) Convention No. 111 was ratified on 12 January 2006. The Minimum Age Convention No. 138 was ratified on 28 April 1999 (establishing 16 years of age as the minimum age), and the Worst Forms of Child Labour Convention No. 182 was ratified on 8 August 2002. As a matter of formality, therefore, the "core" concerns of the ILO for "equal treatment and non-discrimination" and "child labour" are reflected in modern domestic Chinese labour law. Indeed, these both constitute areas in relation to which domestic normative provisions had been introduced well before the PRC embarked upon the modern programme of ratifications in 1990.

The third area of concern for the "core" Conventions – "forced labour" – is currently in a state of flux, and constitutes "one to watch". In terms of the formal position, neither the Forced Labour Convention No. 29 nor the Abolition of Forced Labour Convention No. 105 has been ratified by the PRC. One particular problem constituting an obstacle to ratification of these instruments has been the Chinese system commonly known as "re-education through labour" (*láo jiào*), the existence of which has been consistently regarded as standing in the way even of formalistic commitment to international standards dealing with forced labour. Significantly, however, the Standing Committee of the National People's Congress, through a vote at its bi-monthly session on 28 December 2013, adopted a motion to abolish legal documents on "re-education through labour".[135] One therefore awaits indications as to what effect, if any, this may have upon the position of the PRC in relation to ILO Forced Labour Convention No. 29 and Abolition of Forced Labour Convention No. 105.

By contrast, in relation to the remaining two instruments making up the ILO's "core" Conventions, the message undoubtedly has to be "Don't hold your breath!" Neither the Freedom of Association and Protection of the Right to Organise Convention No. 87 nor the Right to Organise and Collective Bargaining Convention No. 98 would appear to have any realistic prospect of finding reflection in Chinese regulatory arrangements for the foreseeable future. Controversies over, in particular, issues of "freedom of expression" and "freedom of association" continue to rage not only in the field of work-related regulation but also much more widely within the arrangements for governing Chinese society in the modern twenty-first century. At the same time, the "monopoly role" of the ACFTU, and associated obstacles to any alternative form of representation for workers – which might be regarded with great disfavour in "pluralist trade union" systems elsewhere – remains a matter in relation to which sharply contrasting views are maintained by Beijing and Geneva.

A fundamental "clash of cultures" appears to have given rise to sharp differences between the predominantly "European" and "North American" values discernible in ILO instruments of the immediate post-war era and systems such as that which operated in the post-war Soviet Union until 1989 and that to be found in the PRC. In particular, it has proved almost impossible for international standards developed on the basis of values such as those enshrined in the ILO Freedom of Association and Protection of the Right to Organise Convention No. 87 and the Right to Organise and Collective Bargaining Convention No. 98 to accommodate arrangements in countries where the role of the trade union, the influence of "the Party" – in this case, the Chinese Communist Party – and the institutional extent of "the State" are very different from those commonly found, for example, in "(Western) parliamentary democracies". Once one then proceeds further to engage with issues such as "the right to strike" against a background of such fundamentally divided perspectives, the reason for the fervour which so often accompanies discourse in this area of international regulatory standards is not hard to identify.

[135] "The Standing Committee of the National People's Congress (NPC) adopted a resolution to abolish legal documents on re-education through labour, commonly known as 'laojiao', through a vote at its bi-monthly session on Saturday." China Daily (Europe), 'China abolishes re-education through labour', 28 December 2013.

2.7.2 China and Non-"Core" Standards

However, once one begins the search for evidence of Chinese implementation of a broader range of ILO standards than those enshrined in the "core" Conventions, a somewhat more optimistic view emerges – particularly when one considers the extent of the "influence", especially at the stage of drafting protective labour legislation, which such international standards appear to exert upon those responsible for regulation of the world of work in China.

Thus, while it would be too easy to dismiss commitment to the group of Conventions ratified by the nationalist Chinese government during, predominantly, the 1930s as attempts to ingratiate China with the broader international community at that time, the fact remains that there has never been any wholesale condemnation of the instruments ratified before the inception of the People's Republic in 1949. Nor – even taking into account the long period during which the PRC was disengaged from the standard-setting work of the ILO prior to 1983 – would it necessarily be fair to suggest that there was an active resiling during the first three decades of the People's Republic from the, albeit limited, commitments made to fundamental standards for workers on the part of the former pre-1949 government. In reality, involvement with the international standard-setting and enforcement framework of the ILO was simply not an issue for China of the Mao era – while the effective "freezing-out" of the People's Republic from the international community until the hugely important resolutions of the United Nations and the ILO in 1971 goes a long way to explaining why active participation at this level was not a realistic option, in any event, for the PRC.

Consequently, once the "opening-up" process began to take hold after 1978, it was not so surprising to find China engaging with fields of standard-setting such as the areas covered by the Vocational Rehabilitation and Employment (Disabled Persons) Convention No. 159, which was ratified on 2 February 1988 – as one of the first "high-profile" acts confirming a "new approach". Nor did adherence to the Chemicals Convention No. 170 give rise to particular astonishment, once it had been ratified on 11 January 1995. However, once the 2001 MOU had been agreed, the real significance of careful engagement began to become apparent – particularly with ratification of the Labour Administration Convention, No. 150 in 2002. The PRC formally ratified that instrument at the same time as committing itself to the Safety and Health in Construction Convention, No. 167 – a significant collaborative trend which saw further fruit with the ratification of the Occupational Safety and Health Convention, No. 155 in 2007.

The importance of this new era of technical collaboration and development – particularly through the PRC's re-established permanent delegation in Geneva and the ILO's office established in Beijing – cannot be under-estimated. This is particularly so in relation to fields of activity concerned with the inspection and enforcement of protective measures in major sectors such as construction and mining, where there continue to be all-too-frequent reports of deaths and serious injuries sustained at work. However, the impact of an ILO presence has not just been limited to such areas of "physical security" for workers. The involvement of the Chinese labour inspectorate within the Ministry of Human Resources and Social Security in the wake of well-publicized incidents of "slave labour" discovered in the Shanxi Province brickyards in 2007 or in a construction materials facility in Xinjiang Province in 2010 has also facilitated a close presence for technical assistance from the ILO in relation to forced labour. As policy development moves away from the pattern witnessed to date, this may well be an area in which the ILO can assist the Chinese authorities in their efforts to develop arrangements which no longer rely upon the problematic regime of "re-education through labour".

2.7.3 Delivering Compliance with International Labour Standards

Mention of "labour inspection" serves to underline the importance of this particular approach to monitoring, supervision and enforcement of labour standards in a country such as the PRC, where the socialist tradition has also tended to regard such matters as being largely a concern for "administrative" regulation. Indeed, while frequent complaint is heard of the Chinese authorities' alleged shortcomings on the enforcement front, it is important to recognize that wide-ranging provision has been made for inspection activity – whether in relation to payment of wages, the health, safety and hygiene of workers, or compliance with more recent arrangements within China's modern system of social insurance provision.

That underlying inspection regime has, over the last quarter of a century, been complemented by the combination of "administrative" and judicial dispute resolution arrangements furnished through the Labour Arbitration Committees and the People's Courts. Major challenges remain in relation to both of those channels for "industrial justice", particularly in terms of the need for capacity-building and the provision of public resources to facilitate the activities of those mechanisms. Yet, when one has regard to the very size of the PRC – with a population of some 1.3 billion citizens and a labour market of over 800 million workers – and to the continuing contrasts to be found across the "many Chinas" constituting the People's Republic, the progress made during the last two decades does suggest genuine attempts to facilitate access for workers to their formal rights at work.

So far as ILO-derived labour rights are concerned, there is no specific mechanism through which these find their way into the body of Chinese labour law and regulation. The PRC does not provide for automatic incorporation of internationally-agreed commitments – any more than do the majority of European legal systems. Nor is there any developed mechanism for directly incorporating values based upon internationally-recognized "human rights" into Chinese labour law – such as may exist for member states of the Council of Europe in relation to instruments such as the 1950 European Convention on Human Rights, or any of a myriad of UN and other international treaties and declarations.

Consequently, when one embarks upon the enquiry into whether, how, and to what extent the PRC implements ILO-inspired, or indeed any other, labour rights, that enquiry has to be directed to the domestic framework for monitoring, supervising, and enforcing labour law rights in general. Such an approach raises, inevitably, the many criticisms and alleged shortcomings which are commonly recited by external commentators on the developing Chinese labour relations scene. At the same time, however, it serves to identify the significant progress which has been made over the last quarter of a century in relation to delivering individual employment rights – if not in relation to "collective labour rights" in the "Western" sense.

Where, then, do we go from here? Perhaps the developing future for China's labour law and social policy may be discerned from an observation contained in the "Implementation Report on the 2011 Plan for National Economic and Social Development",[136] to the effect that:

> We will enhance and make innovations in social management. We will improve the community service system, improve the training of professional social workers, and help urban and rural communities better provide public services and conduct social management. We will properly deal with people's legitimate and reasonable complaints; work harder on public order, workplace safety, food and drug safety oversight, and emergency response management; and resolutely set right all actions that harm people's interests so as to safeguard social harmony and stability.

As this author has observed elsewhere,[137] that apparent recognition of the need to be able to deal with "people's legitimate and reasonable complaints" is set in the framework of what has, in recent times, come to be described as "social management". However, whether that eye-catching label encapsulates the germ of a way forward in relation to the effective delivery of social rights in the PRC is something which only time will tell. In the meantime, the need remains for international co-operation and technical support in order to enable China to continue with its development of a modern "floor of rights" for workers; to ensure that, where rights are provided for, there is effective "access to justice" for those workers who suffer from non-compliance; and to promote the infusion into domestic Chinese labour law of the values which underpin the ILO's post-Philadelphia Declaration framework for international labour standard-setting.

---

[136] Second follow-up [Report on the Implementation of the 2012 Plan for National Economic and Social Development and on the 2013 Draft Plan for National Economic and Social Development] 关于 2012 年国民经济和社会发展计划执行情况与 2013 年国民经济和社会发展计划草案的报告 (guān yú 2012 nián guó mín jīng jì hé shè huì fā zhǎn jì huà zhí xíng qíng kuàng yǔ 2013 nián guó mín jīng jì hé shè huì fā zhǎn jì huà cǎo àn de bào gào), 2013, building upon the earlier [Report on the Implementation of the 2011 Plan for National Economic and Social Development and on the 2012 Draft Plan for National Economic and Social Development] 关于 2011 年国民经济和社会发展计划执行情况与 2012 年国民经济和社会发展计划草案的报告 (guān yú 2011 nián guó mín jīng jì hé shè huì fā zhǎn jì huà zhí xíng qíng kuàng yǔ 2012 nián guó mín jīng jì hé shè huì fā zhǎn jì huà cǎo àn de bào gào), 2012.

[137] Neal 2014a, at p. 19.

References

Literature

Ashwin, Sarah, and Simon Clarke. 2002. *Russian trade unions and industrial relations in transition*. Basingstoke/New York: Palgrave. Available at: http://web.warwick.ac.uk/russia/tubook.pdf. Last accessed 19 June 2015.

Bellace, Janice R. 2014. Human rights at work: The need for definitional coherence in the global governance system. *The International Journal of Comparative Labour Law and Industrial Relations* 30: 175–198.

Butler, William (ed.). 1983. *The legal system of the Chinese Soviet Republic 1931–1934*. New York: Transnational.

Butler, William E., B.A. Hepple, and Alan C. Neal (eds.). 1987. *Comparative labour law: Anglo-Soviet perspectives*. Aldershot: Gower Publishing Company.

Chang, Kai. 2014. Reconsideration of the subject-matter of labour law and the reconstruction of labour law. In *Cross-currents in modern Chinese labour law*, ed. Alan C. Neal, 63–72. Alphen aan den Rijn: Kluwer Law International.

Chen, Yifeng. 2014. The International Labour Organisation and labour governance in China 1919–1949. In *China and ILO fundamental principles and rights at work*, eds. Roger Blanpain, Ulla Liukkunen, and Chen Yifeng. Bulletin of Comparative Labour Relations 86: 19–54. Dordrecht: Kluwer Law International.

Chen, Yifeng. 2016. ILO, extraterritoriality and labour protection in Republican Shanghai. In *Fundamental labour rights in China – Legal implementation and cultural logic*, ed. Ulla Liukkunen and Chen Yifeng, 83–116. Dordrecht: Springer.

Chen, Meei-shia, and Anita Chan. 2010. Occupational health and safety in China: The case of state-managed enterprises. *International Journal of Health Services* 40: 43–60. Available at: http://www.ncbi.nlm.nih.gov/pubmed/20198803. Last accessed 19 June 2015.

Eastman, Lloyd, Jerome Ch'en, Suzanne Pepper, and Lyman van Slyke. 1991. *The nationalist era in China, 1927–1949*. Cambridge: Cambridge University Press.

Edles, Gary. 1969. Mobilization of the masses: A survey of Communist Chinese labor law. *Washington University Law Quarterly* 1969: 395–422.

Ghebali, Victor-Yves, Robert Ago, and Nicolas Valticos (eds.). 1989. *The International Labour Organisation: A case study on the evolution of U.N. specialised agencies*. Dordrecht: Martinus Nijhoff.

Guo, Jie. 2014. Occupational health and safety rights and legal protection at work. In *Cross-currents in modern Chinese labour law*, ed. Alan C. Neal, 133–145. Alphen aan den Rijn: Kluwer Law International.

Ho, Virginia H. 2003. *Labor dispute resolution in China: Implications for labor rights and legal reform*. Berkeley: Institute of East Asian Studies, University of California.

Horrebow, Niels. 1758. *The natural history of Iceland*. London: Printed for A. Linde.

[Jia, Junling] 贾俊玲. 1994. [Legal basis, aim, scope and principles, understanding on the labour law from Article 1 to Article 5] 立法依据、宗旨、适用范围、基本原则—对"总则"一至五条的理解 (lì fǎ yī jù, zōng zhǐ, shì yòng fàn wéi, jī běn yuán zé—duì "zǒng zé" yī zhì wǔ tiáo de lǐ jiě). [*China Labour Science*] 中国劳动科学.

[Jia, Junling] 贾俊玲. 1999. [New development of labour law system] 劳动法制建设的新历程 (láo dòng fǎ zhì jiàn shè de xīn lì chéng). [*Labour Protection Report*] 劳动保障通讯. 7: 12.

Jia, Junling, and Qian Wei. 2014. The evolution and development of China's Labour Law 1994. In *Cross-currents in modern Chinese labour law*, ed. Alan C. Neal, 47–62. Alphen aan den Rijn: Kluwer Law International.

Josephs, Hilary. 1995. Labor law in a 'socialist market economy': The case of China. *Columbia Journal of Transnational Law* 33: 559–582.

Kim, Jihwans. 2009. The Factory Act of the Nanjing Nationalist Government of China, and the response of local and foreign-invested enterprises (FIEs') to the Said Act. *Journal of Northeast Asian History* 6: 219–262.

Lee, Lai to. 1986. *Trade unions in China 1949 to the present: The organization and leadership of the All-China Federation of Trade Unions*. Singapore: Singapore University Press.

Leng, Shao-Chuan. 1977. The role of law in the People's Republic of China as reflecting Mao Tse-Tung's influence. *The Journal of Criminal Law and Criminology* 68: 356–373.

Lin, Jia. 2014. The significance of, and innovation in, China's Social Insurance Law. In *Cross-currents in modern Chinese labour law*, ed. Alan C. Neal, 147–159. Alphen aan den Rijn: Kluwer Law International.

Ling X., and Q. Li. 1995. Human rights protection in labour law. *Law Review* (April): 7–12.

Neal, Alan C. 2011. Towards a functioning framework for individual labour law rights: Challenges for China in a changing world of work. *The International Journal of Comparative Labour Law and Industrial Relations* 27: 365–385.

Neal, Alan C. 2014a. Cross-currents in modern Chinese labour law. In *Cross-currents in modern Chinese labour law*, ed. Alan C. Neal, 1–20. Alphen aan den Rijn: Kluwer Law International.

Neal, Alan C. (ed.). 2014b. *Cross-currents in modern Chinese labour law*. Alphen aan den Rijn: Kluwer Law International.

Rodearmel, David. 1988. Military law in Communist China: Development, structure and function. *Military Law Review* 119: 1–43.

Schmidt, Folke, and Alan C. Neal. 1984. *Collective agreements and collective bargaining*. Tübingen: Mohr.

Sigeman, Tore. 1984. A Nordic method of labour law comparison. *Comparative Labour Law* 6: 291–292.

Taylor, Bill, Kai Chang, and Qi Li. 2003. *Industrial relations in China*. Cheltenham: Edward Elgar Publishing.

Thomas, Albert. 1921. The International Labour Organisation – Its origins, development and future. *International Labour Review* 1(1): 5–22.

Traub-Merz, Rudolf. 2011. *All-China Federation of Trade Unions: Structure, functions and the challenge of collective bargaining*, Global Labour University working paper no. 13. Geneva: International Labour Office.

Turner, Karen, James Feinerman and R. Kent Guy (eds.). 2000. *The limits of the rule of law in China*. Washington, DC: University of Washington Press.

van den Berg, Godfried. 1975. Codification of Soviet labour law – A case study on the influence of expert opinion. In *Codification in the communist world*, ed. Ferdinand Feldbrugge, 23–38. Leiden: Documentation Office for East European Law University of Leiden.

van den Berg, Godfried. 1983. Affinities between USSR and Chinese Soviet labor legislation. In *The legal system of the Chinese Soviet Republic 1931–1934*, ed. Butler William. New York: Transnational.

van der Sprenkel, Sybille. 1983. Labor legislation of the Chinese Soviet Republic. In *The legal system of the Chinese Soviet Republic 1931–1934*, ed. Butler William. New York: Transnational.

Wang, Zhenqi, Changshuo Wang and Shangyuan Zheng. 2003. Labour disputes settlement system in China: Past and perspective. *Institute of Developing Economies Asian Law Series* 22: 1–55. Available at: http://www.ide.go.jp/English/Publish/Download/Als/pdf/22.pdf. Last accessed 19 June 2015.

Woo, Margaret. 1999. Law and discretion in the contemporary Chinese courts. *Pacific Rim Law & Policy Journal* 8: 581–616.

Yan, Dong. 2014. In search of Chinese labour law. In *Cross-currents in modern Chinese labour law*, ed. Alan C. Neal, 21–46. Alphen aan den Rijn: Kluwer Law International.

Documents and Official Publications

ILO Documents

Convention fixing the Minimum Age for Admission of Children to Employment at Sea, adopted 9 July 1920, ILO C007. Entry into force 27 September 1921. (Minimum Age (Sea) Convention).

Convention concerning the Rights of Association and Combination of Agricultural Workers, adopted 25 October 1921, ILO C011. Entry into force 11 May 1923. (Right of Association (Agriculture) Convention).

Convention concerning the Application of the Weekly Rest in Industrial Undertakings, adopted 17 November 1921, ILO C014. Entry into force 19 June 1923. (Weekly Rest (Industry) Convention).

Convention fixing the Minimum Age for the Admission of Young Persons to Employment as Trimmers or Stokers, adopted 11 November 1921, ILO C015. Entry into force 20 November 1922. (Minimum Age (Trimmers and Stokers) Convention).

Convention concerning the Compulsory Medical Examination of Children and Young Persons Employed at Sea, adopted 11 November 1921, ILO C016. Entry into force 22 November 1922. (Medical Examination of Young Persons (Sea) Convention).

Convention concerning Equality of Treatment for National and Foreign Workers as regards Workmen's Compensation for Accidents, adopted 9 June 1925, ILO C019. Entry into force 8 September 1926. (Equality of Treatment (Accident Compensation) Convention).

Convention concerning Seamen's Articles of Agreement, adopted 24 June 1926, ILO C022. Entry into force 4 April 1928. (Seamen's Articles of Agreement Convention).

Convention concerning the Repatriation of Seamen, adopted 23 June 1926, ILO C023. Entry into force 16 April 1928. (Repatriation of Seamen Convention).

Convention concerning the Creation of Minimum Wage-Fixing Machinery, adopted 16 June 1928, ILO C026. Entry into force 14 June 1930. (Minimum Wage-Fixing Machinery Convention).

Convention concerning the Marking of the Weight on Heavy Packages Transported by Vessels, adopted 21 June 1929, ILO C027. Entry into force 9 March 1932. (Marking of Weight (Packages Transported by Vessels) Convention).

Convention concerning Forced or Compulsory Labour, adopted 28 June 1930, ILO C029. Entry into force 1 May 1932. (Forced Labour Convention).

Convention concerning the Protection against Accidents of Workers Employed in Loading or Unloading Ships (Revised), adopted 27 April 1932, ILO C032. Entry into force 30 October 1934. (Protection against Accidents (Dockers) Convention (Revised)).

Convention concerning the Employment of Women on Underground Work in Mines of all Kinds, adopted 21 June 1935, ILO C045. Entry into force 30 May 1937. (Underground Work (Women) Convention).

Convention Fixing the Minimum Age for Admission of Children to Industrial Employment (Revised 1937), adopted 22 June 1937, ILO C059. Entry into force 21 February 1941. (Minimum Age (Industry) Convention (Revised)).

Convention for the Partial Revision of the Conventions Adopted by the General Conference of the International Labour Organisation at Its First Twenty-eight Sessions for the Purpose of Making Provision for the Future Discharge of Certain Chancery Functions Entrusted by the Said Conventions to the Secretary-General of the League of Nations and Introducing therein Certain Further Amendments Consequential upon the Dissolution of the League of Nations and the Amendment of the Constitution of the International Labour Organisation, adopted 9 October 1946, ILO C080. Entry into force 28 May 1947. (Final Articles Revision Convention).

Convention concerning Freedom of Association and Protection of the Right to Organise, adopted 9 July 1948, ILO C087. Entry into force 4 July 1950. (Freedom of Association and Protection of the Right to Organise Convention).

Convention concerning the Application of the Principles of the Right to Organise and to Bargain Collectively, adopted 1 July 1949, ILO C098. Entry into force 18 July 1951. (Right to Organise and Collective Bargaining Convention).

Convention concerning Equal Remuneration, adopted 29 June 1951, ILO C100. Entry into force 23 May 1953.

Convention concerning the Abolition of Forced Labour, adopted 25 June 1957, ILO C105. Entry into force 17 January 1959. (Abolition of Forced Labour Convention).

Convention concerning Discrimination in Respect of Employment and Occupation, adopted 25 June 1958, ILO C111. Entry into force 15 June 1960. (Discrimination (Employment and Occupation) Convention).

Convention concerning Employment Policy, adopted 9 July 1964, ILO C122. Entry into force 15 July 1966. (Employment Policy Convention).

Convention concerning Minimum Age for Admission to Employment, adopted 26 June 1973, ILO C138. Entry into force 19 June 1976. (Minimum Age Convention).

Convention concerning Tripartite Consultations to Promote the Implementation of International Labour Standards, adopted 16 May 1978, ILO C144. Entry into force 16 May 1978 (Tripartite Consultation (International Labour Standards) Convention).

Convention concerning Labour Administration: Role, Functions and Organisation, adopted 26 June 1978, ILO C150. Entry into force 11 October 1980. (Labour Administration Convention).

Convention concerning Occupational Safety and Health and the Working Environment, adopted 22 June 1981, ILO C155. Entry into force 11 August 1983. (Safety and Health in Construction Convention).

Convention concerning Vocational Rehabilitation and Employment (Disabled Persons), adopted 20 June 1983, ILO C159. Entry into force 20 June 1985. (Vocational Rehabilitation and Employment (Disabled Persons) Convention).

Convention concerning Safety and Health in Construction, adopted 20 June 1988, ILO C167. Entry into force 11 January 1991. (Safety and Health in Construction Convention).

Convention concerning Safety in the Use of Chemicals at Work, adopted 25 June 1990, ILO C170. (Chemicals Convention).

Convention concerning the Prohibition and Immediate Action for the Elimination of the Worst Forms of Child Labour, adopted 17 June 1999, ILO C182. Entry into force 19 November 2000. (Worst Forms of Child Labour Convention).

Declaration concerning the Aims and Purposes of the International Labour Organisation, adopted 10 May 1944. (Declaration of Philadelphia).

Declaration on Fundamental Principles and Rights at Work, adopted by the International Labour Conference at its 86th Session, Geneva, 18 June 1998. (1998 Declaration).

Declaration on Social Justice for a Fair Globalization, adopted by the International Labour Conference at its 97th Session, Geneva, 10 June 2008. (2008 Declaration).

Other ILO Documentation

Committee on Legal Issues and International Labour Standards, *Ratification and promotion of fundamental ILO Conventions*, GB.303/LILS/5. 7 November 2008.

Contributing to Realising Decent Work: ILO Decent Work Country Programme in the People's Republic of China 2006–2010. 2010. Geneva: International Labour Office.

Decent Work. Report of the Director-General to the 87th Session of the International Labour Conference. 1999. Available at: http://www.ilo.org/public/english/standards/relm/ilc/ilc87/rep-i.htm. Last accessed 19 June 2015.

Decent Work for All in a Global Economy: An ILO Perspective. Speech of the Director-General to the Third WTO Ministerial Conference. 30 November to 3 December 1999. Seattle. Available at: http://www.ilo.org/public/english/bureau/dgo/speeches/somavia/1999/seattle.htm. Last accessed 19 June 2015.

Decent Work Country Programme in the People's Republic of China 2013–2015. Available at: http://www.ilo.org/public/english/bureau/program/dwcp/download/china.pdf. Last accessed 19 June 2015.
Defending Values, Promoting Change. Report of the Director-General to the 81st Session of the International Labour Conference. 1994. Available at: http://www.ilo.org/public/english/standards/relm/ilc/ilc86/rep-vii.htm. Last accessed 19 June 2015.
ILO Country and Areas Designations and Rules for their Use (replacing ILO Circular 12/19 (Rev. 9) of 9 March 1992). 2013. Available at: http://www.ilo.org/public/english/standards/relm/ctry-ndx.htm. Last accessed 19 June 2015.
Labour Principles of the United Nations Global Compact: A Guide for Business. 2008. Geneva: International Labour Office.
Memorandum of Understanding for co-operation between the ILO and the Ministry of Labour and Social Security of China. 2000. Available at: http://www.ilo.org/beijing/countries-covered/WCMS_144733/lang--en/index.htm. Last accessed 19 June 2015.
USSR Government Report on Convention 87 (Freedom of Association and Protection of the Right to Organise) 1948. 40th Session of the International Labour Conference. 1957. Available at: http://www.ilo.org/public/libdoc/ilo/P/09661/09661(1957-40).pdf. Last accessed 19 June 2015.

Other International Law Sources

League of Nations, Covenant of the League of Nations, adopted 28 April 1919. Entry into force 10 January 1920.
Organisation for Economic Co-operation and Development. 2005. *Governance in China: China in the global economy*. Paris: OECD Publishing.
Treaty of Versailles, signed on 28 June 1919. Entry into force 10 January 1920.
UN General Assembly. Resolution on the Restoration of the lawful rights of the People's Republic of China in the United Nation. GA Res. 2758, U.N. Doc. A7RES/2758(XXVI), 25 October 1971.

Chinese Regulation

Laws by the National People's Congress

[Administrative Litigation Law of the People's Republic of China] 中华人民共和国行政诉讼法 (zhōng huá rén mín gòng hé guó xíng zhèng sù sòng fǎ), National People's Congress, adopted 4 April 1989, effective 1 October 1990. Revised and effective 1 November 2014.
[Civil Procedure Law of the People's Republic of China] 中华人民共和国民事诉讼法 (zhōng huá rén mín gòng hé guó mín shì sù sòng fǎ), National People's Congress, adopted and effective 9 April 1991. Revised and effective 31 August 2012.
[Constitution of the People's Republic of China] 中华人民共和国宪法 (zhōng huá rén mín gòng hé guó xiàn fǎ), National People's Congress, adopted and effective 20 September 1954.
[Constitution of the People's Republic of China] 中华人民共和国宪法 (zhōng huá rén mín gòng hé guó xiàn fǎ), National People's Congress, adopted and effective 17 January 1975.
[Constitution of the People's Republic of China] 中华人民共和国宪法 (zhōng huá rén mín gòng hé guó xiàn fǎ), National People's Congress, adopted and effective 5 March 1978.
[Constitution of the People's Republic of China] 中华人民共和国宪法 (zhōng huá rén mín gòng hé guó xiàn fǎ), National People's Congress, adopted and effective 4 December 1982. Available at: http://english.people.com.cn/constitution/constitution.html. Last accessed 19 June 2015.

[Criminal Procedure Law of the People's Republic of China] 中华人民共和国刑事诉讼法 (zhōng huá rén mín gòng hé guó xíng shì sù sòng fǎ), National People's Congress, adopted 1 July 1979, effective 1 January 1980. Revised 15 March 2012, effective 1 January 2013.

[Law on the Protection of Rights and Interests of Women] 中华人民共和国妇女权益保障法 (zhōng huá rén mín gòng hé guó fù nǚ quán yì bǎo zhàng fǎ), National People's Congress, adopted 3 April 1992, effective 1 October 1992. Revised and effective 18 August 2005.

[Trade Union Law of the People's Republic of China] 中华人民共和国工会法 (zhōng huá rén mín gòng hé guó gōng huì fǎ), Central People's Government Commission, adopted 28 June 1950, effective 29 June 1950.

[Trade Union Law of the People's Republic of China] 中华人民共和国工会法 (zhōng huá rén mín gòng hé guó gōng huì fǎ), National People's Congress, adopted and effective 3 April 1992. Revised and effective 27 October 2001.

Laws by the Standing Committee of the National People's Congress

[Disabled Persons Protection Law of the People's Republic of China] 中华人民共和国残疾人保障法 (zhōng huá rén mín gòng hé guó cán jí rén bǎo zhàng fǎ), Standing Committee of the National People's Congress, adopted 28 December 1991, effective 15 May 1991. Revised 24 April 2008, effective 1 July 2008.

[Employment Promotion Law of the People's Republic of China] 中华人民共和国就业促进法 (zhōng huá rén mín gòng hé guó jiù yè cù jìn fǎ), Standing Committee of the National People's Congress, adopted 30 August 2007, effective 1 January 2008. Revised and effective 24 April 2015.

[Labour Contract Law of the People's Republic of China] 中华人民共和国劳动合同法 (zhōng huá rén mín gòng hé guó láo dòng hé tóng fǎ), Standing Committee of the National People's Congress, adopted 29 June 2007, effective 1 January 2008. Revised 28 December 2012, effective 1 July 2013.

[Labour Dispute Mediation and Arbitration Law of the People's Republic of China] 中华人民共和国劳动争议调解仲裁法 (zhōng huá rén mín gòng hé guó láo dòng zhēng yì tiáo jiě zhòng cái fǎ), Standing Committee of the National People's Congress, adopted 29 December 2007, effective 1 May 2008.

[Labour Law of the People's Republic of China] 中华人民共和国劳动法 (zhōng huá rén mín gòng hé guó láo dòng fǎ), Standing Committee of the National People's Congress, adopted 5 July 1994, effective 1 January 1995.

[Mining Safety Law of the People's Republic of China] 中华人民共和国矿山安全法 (zhōng huá rén mín gòng hé guó kuàng shān ān quán fǎ), Standing Committee of the National People's Congress, adopted 7 November 1992, effective 1 May 1993.

[Occupational Disease Prevention and Control Law of the People's Republic of China] 中华人民共和国职业病防治法 (zhōng huá rén mín gòng hé guó zhí yè bìng fáng zhì fǎ), Standing Committee of the National People's Congress, adopted 27 October 2001, effective 1 May 2002. Revised and effective 31 December 2011.

[Occupational Training Law of the People's Republic of China] 中华人民共和国职业教育法 (zhōng huá rén mín gòng hé guó zhí yè jiào yù fǎ), Standing Committee of the National People's Congress, adopted 15 May 1996, effective 1 September 1996.

[Occupational Safety Law of the People's Republic of China] 中华人民共和国安全生产法 (zhōng huá rén mín gòng hé guó ān quán shēng chǎn fǎ), Standing Committee of the National People's Congress, adopted 29 June 2002, effective 1 November 2002. Revised 31 August 2014, effective 1 December 2014.

[Prison Law of the People's Republic of China] 中华人民共和国监狱法 (zhōng huá rén mín gòng hé guó jiān yù fǎ), Standing Committee of the Eighth National People's Congress, adopted and effective 29 December 1994.

[Sino-Foreign Co-operative Joint Venture Law of the People's Republic of China] 中华人民共和国中外合作经营企业法 (zhōng huá rén mín gòng hé guó zhōng wài hé zuò jīng yíng qǐ yè fǎ), Standing Committee of the National People's Congress, adopted 13 April 1988, effective 13 April 1988.

[Social Insurance Law of the People's Republic of China] 中华人民共和国社会保险法 (zhōng huá rén mín gòng hé guó shè huì bǎo xiǎn fǎ), Standing Committee of the National People's Congress, adopted 28 October 2010, effective 1 July 2011.

Regulations by the State Council

[Circular on Adjusting Wages for Certain Types of Workers] 国务院关于调整部分工人和工作人员工资的通知 (guó wù yuàn guān yú tiào zhěng bù fēn gōng rén hé gōng zuò rén yuán gōng zī de tōng zhī), State Council, adopted and effective 30 November 1971.

[Circular on Prohibiting Workers Gaining Extra Profits from Unreasonable Economic Activities] 关于制止企业职工从事不正当经济活动牟取额外收入问题的通知 (guān yú zhì zhǐ qǐ yè zhí gōng cóng shì bù zhèng dāng jīng jì huó dòng móu qǔ é wài shōu rù wèn tí de tōng zhī), State Council, adopted and effective 28 April 1982.

[Circular on Resolving Issues for Those Who have been Mistreated and Wish to Return to the City to Work] 中共中央、国务院关于处理当前部分人员要求复职复工回城就业等问题的通知 (zhōng gòng zhōng yāng, guó wù yuàn guān yú chǔ lǐ dāng qián bù fèn rén yuán yāo qiú fù zhí fù gōng huí chéng jiù yè děng wèn tí de tōng zhī), CCP Central Committee and State Council, adopted and effective 4 June 1979.

[Interim Measures for the State Council on an Employee's Retirement and Withdrawal from Post] 国务院关于工人退休、退职的暂行办法 (guó wù yuàn guān yú gōng rén tuì xiū tuì zhí de zàn xíng bàn fǎ), State Council, adopted 24 May 1978, effective 2 June 1978.

[Interim Provisions on Dealing with Labour Disputes in State-Owned Enterprises] 国营企业劳动争议处理暂行规定 (guó yíng qǐ yè láo dòng zhēng yì chǔ lǐ zàn xíng guī dìng) State Council, adopted 31 July 1987, effective 15 August 1987.

[Interim Regulations on the Practice of the Labour Contract System in State-Owned Enterprises] 国营企业实行劳动合同制暂行规定 (guó yíng qǐ yè shí xíng láo dòng hé tóng zhì zàn xíng guī dìng), State Council, 12 July 1986, effective 1 October 1986.

[Labour Insurance Regulations of the People's Republic of China] 中华人民共和国劳动保险条例 (zhōng huá rén mín gòng hé guó láo dòng bǎo xiǎn tiáo lì), Government Affairs Council, adopted 23 February 1951 and effective 1 March 1951.

[Provisions on Employees' Family Leave] 国务院关于职工探亲待遇的规定 (guó wù yuàn guān yú zhí gōng tàn qīn dài yù de guī dìng). State Council, 6 March 1981, effective 14 March 1981.

[Provisions on Mining Safety] 矿山安全条例 (kuàng shān ān quán tiáo lì), State Council, adopted 13 February 1982, effective 1 July 1982. Abolished 15 January 2008.

[Provisions on Mining Safety Inspection] 矿山安全监察条例 (kuàng shān ān quán jiān chá tiáo lì), State Council, 13 February 1982, effective 1 July 1982. Abolished 15 January 2008.

[Provisions on the Prohibition of Using Child Labour] 禁止使用童工规定 (jìn zhǐ shǐ yòng tóng gōng guī dìng), State Council, adopted and effective 15 April 1991. Abolished 1 December 2002.

[Provisions on the Prohibition of Using Child Labour] 禁止使用童工规定 (jìn zhǐ shǐ yòng tóng gōng guī dìng), State Council, adopted 1 October 2002, effective 1 December 2002.

[Provisions on Protecting Female Workers] 女职工劳动保护规定 (nǚ zhí gōng láo dòng bǎo hù guī dìng), State Council, adopted 21 July 1988, effective 1 September 1988. Abolished 28 April 2012.

[Provisions on Qualifying Period of Seniority and Wage Issues relating to Anti-Revolutionary or Other 'Bad' Individuals who have been identified in the Counter Anti-Revolutionary Movement] 关于处理国家机关、企业、学校在肃反运动中查出的反革命分子和其他坏分子的工龄和工资问题的规定 (guān yú chǔ lǐ guó jiā jī guān, qǐ yè, xué xiào zài sù fǎn yùn dòng zhōng chá chū de fǎn gé mìng fèn zǐ hé qí tā huài fèn zǐ de gōng líng hé gōng zī wèn tí de guī dìng), State Council, adopted and effective 9 August 1957.

[Provisions on Workers' Working Time] 国务院关于职工工作时间的规定 (guó wù yuàn guān yú zhí gōng gōng zuò shí jiān de guī dìng), State Council, adopted 17 February 1995, effective 1 May 1995.

[Regulations of the People's Republic of China on Settlement of Labour Disputes in Enterprises] 中华人民共和国企业劳动争议处理条例 (zhōng huá rén mín gòng hé guó qǐ yè láo dòng zhēng yì chǔ lǐ tiáo lì), State Council, adopted 11 June 1993, effective 1 August 1993. Abolished 8 January 2011.

[Regulations on the Implementation of the Labour Contract Law of the People's Republic of China] 中华人民共和国劳动合同法实施条例 (zhōng huá rén mín gòng hé guó láo dòng hé tóng fǎ shí shī tiáo lì), State Council, adopted and effective 18 September 2008.

[Regulations on the Implementation of the Mine Safety Law of the People's Republic of China] 中华人民共和国矿山安全法实施条例 (zhōng huá rén mín gòng hé guó kuàng shān ān quán fǎ shí shī tiáo lì), State Council, adopted 11 October 1996, effective 30 October 1996.

[Regulations on Rewarding and Disciplining Employees in Enterprises] 企业职工奖惩条例 (qǐ yè zhí gōng jiǎng chéng tiáo lì), State Council, adopted and effective 10 April 1982. Abolished 15 January 2008.

[Regulations on Unemployment Insurance] 失业保险条例 (shī yè bǎo xiǎn tiáo lì), State Council, adopted and effective 22 January 1999.

[Regulations on Workers' Congresses in State-Owned Enterprises] 全民所有制工业企业职工代表大会条例 (quán mín suǒ yǒu zhì gōng yè qǐ yè zhí gōng dài biǎo dà huì tiáo lì), CCP Central Committee and State Council, adopted 15 September 1986, effective 1 October 1986.

[Supplementary Provisions of the State Council for Re-education through Labour] 国务院关于劳动教养的补充规定 (guó wù yuàn guān yú láo dòng jiào yǎng de bǔ chōng guī dìng), State Council, adopted and effective 29 November 1979. Abolished 28 December 2013.

Administrative Regulations

[Circular on Further Perfecting the Labour Dispute Settlement System] 劳动部关于进一步完善劳动争议处理工作的通知 (láo dòng bù guān yú jìn yī bù wán shàn láo dòng zhēng yì chǔ lǐ gōng zuò de tōng zhī), Ministry of Labour, adopted and effective 9 May 1995.

[Circular on Implementing the Provisions on the Prohibition of Using Child Labour] 关于贯彻落实《禁止使用童工规定》的通知 (guān yú guàn chè luò shí "jìn zhǐ shǐ yòng tóng gōng guī dìng" de tōng zhī), promulgated jointly by Ministry of Labour and Social Security, Ministry of Public Security, State Administration for Industry and Commerce, Ministry of Education, Ministry of Health, All-China Federation of Trade Unions, Central Committee of the Communist Youth League and All-China Women's Federation, adopted and effective 18 April 2003.

[Circular on Perfecting the Tripartite Labour Arbitration Mechanism] 关于进一步完善劳动争议仲裁三方机制的通知 (guān yú jìn yī bù wán shàn láo dòng zhēng yì zhòng cái sān fāng jī zhì de tōng zhī), promulgated jointly by the Ministry of Labour, All-China Federation of Trade Unions and the State Economic and Trade Commission, adopted and effective 18 March 1996.

[Circular on Promoting Equal Conciliation and a Collective Contract System] 关于进一步推行平等协商和集体合同制度的通知 (guān yú jìn yī bù tuī xíng píng děng xié shāng hé jí tǐ hé tóng zhì dù de tōng zhī), Ministry of Labour and Social Security, adopted and effective 14 November 2001.

[Circular on Reinforcing Labour Arbitration Activities] 关于加强劳动仲裁工作的通知 (guān yú jiā qiáng láo dòng zhòng cái gōng zuò de tōng zhī), Ministry of Labour and Social Security, adopted and effective 26 May 1989.

[Circular on Strictly Prohibiting the Use of Child Labour] 劳动人事部关于严格禁止招用童工的通知 (láo dòng rén shì bù guān yú yán gé jìn zhǐ zhāo yòng tóng gōng de tōng zhī), Ministry of Labour and Personnel, adopted and effective 23 June 1987.

[Circular on Wage Levels for Demobilized Soldiers with Higher Education Degrees] 国家计划委员会劳动局关于复员退伍军人中的大专院校学生工资待遇的通知 (guó jiā jì huà wěi yuán huì láo dòng jú guān yú fù yuán tuì wǔ jūn rén zhōng de dà zhuān yuàn xiào xué shēng gōng zī dài yù de tōng zhī), Labour Bureau of State Planning and Revolutionary Committee, adopted and effective 22 August 1975. Abolished 10 December 1986.

[Directive on Establishing Congresses for Worker-Employer Conciliation Inside Private Enterprises] 关于在私营企业中设立劳资协商会议的指示 (guān yú zài sī yíng qǐ yè zhōng shè lì láo zī xié shāng huì yì de zhǐ shì), Ministry of Labour, adopted 21 April 1950, effective 29 April 1950.

[Economic Compensation Measures for Violation or Illegal Termination of Labour Contracts] 违反和解除劳动合同的经济补偿办法 (wéi fǎn hé jiě chú láo dòng hé tóng de jīng jì bǔ cháng bàn fǎ), Ministry of Labour, adopted 3 December 1994, effective 1 January 1995.

[Measure on Registering Unemployed Persons] 关于失业人员统一登记办法 (guān yú shī yè rén yuán tǒng yī dēng jì bàn fǎ), Government Affairs Council, adopted and effective 27 August 1952.

[Opinion as to whether the Children of Capitalist Bourgeois are Eligible to Replace their Parent when they Retire or are on Long-Term Absence] 劳动部、中央工商行政管理局关于资产阶级工商业者退休或请长假后可否由子女顶替工作的意见 (láo dòng bù, zhōng yāng gōng shāng xíng zhèng guǎn lǐ jú guān yú zī chǎn jiē jí gōng shāng yè zhě tuì xiū huò qǐng cháng jiǎ hòu kě fǒu yóu zǐ nǚ dǐng tì gōng zuò de yì jiàn), Ministry of Labour and Central Administrative Bureau of Industry and Commerce, adopted and effective 9 February 1963.

[Opinions on the Implementation of Labour Law] 劳动部关于贯彻实施《劳动法》的意见 (láo dòng bù guān yú guàn chè shí shī "láo dòng fǎ" de yì jiàn), Ministry of Labour, adopted and effective 22 August 1994.

[Provisions regarding the Procedure for Settling Labour Disputes] 关于劳动争议解决程序的规定 (guān yú láo dòng zhēng yì jiě jué chéng xù de guī dìng), Ministry of Labour, adopted 16 November 1950, effective 26 November 1950.

[Provisions on Collective Contracts] 集体合同规定 (jí tǐ hé tóng guī dìng), Ministry of Labour, adopted 5 December 1994, effective 1 January 1995. Abolished 20 May 2004.

[Regulations concerning Minimum Wages in Enterprises] 企业最低工资规定 (qǐ yè zuì dī gōng zī guī dìng), Ministry of Labour, adopted and effective 24 November 1993. Abolished 1 March 2004.

[Rules on Collective Contracts] 集体合同规定 (jí tǐ hé tóng guī dìng), Ministry of Labour and Social Security, adopted 30 December 2003, effective 1 May 2004.

[Rules on Labour Inspection Procedures] 劳动监察程序规定 (láo dòng jiān chá chéng xù guī dìng), Ministry of Labour, adopted and effective 20 December 1995. Abolished 1 February 2005.

[Rules on Minimum Wages] 最低工资规定 (zuì dī gōng zī guī dìng), Ministry of Labour and Social Security, adopted 20 January 2004, effective 1 March 2004.

[Rules on Organization Structure and Working Procedures of Municipal Labour Dispute Arbitration Committees] 劳动争议仲裁委员会组织及工作规则 (láo dòng zhēng yì zhòng cái wěi yuán huì zǔ zhī jí gōng zuò guī zé), Ministry of Labour, adopted and effective 16 June 1950.

[Rules on Vocational Training] 职业培训实体管理规定 (zhí yè péi xùn shí tǐ guǎn lǐ guī dìng), Ministry of Labour, adopted 14 December 1994, effective 1 January 1995. Abolished 9 November 2007.

[Temporary Rules on Wage Payment] 工资支付暂行规定 (gōng zī zhī fù zàn xíng guī dìng), Ministry of Labour, adopted 6 December 1994, effective 1 January 1995.

[Trial Measures on Collective Negotiation of Wages] 工资集体协商试行办法 (gōng zī jí tǐ xié shāng shì xíng bàn fǎ), Ministry of Labour and Social Security, adopted and effective 8 November 2000.

Regulations of the Chinese Soviet Republic

[Labour Law of the Chinese Soviet Republic] 中华苏维埃共和国劳动法 (zhōng huá sū wéi āi gòng hé guó láo dòng fǎ), People's Commissariat of Labour, adopted and effective 7 November 1931.
[Provisional Organisational Principles for Labour Sections of Chinese Soviets] 中华苏维埃共和国劳动感化院暂行章程 (zhōng huá sū wéi āi gòng hé guó láo dòng gǎn huà yuàn zàn xíng zhāng chéng), People's Commissariat of Labour, adopted 10 August 1932, effective 15 August 1932.
[Resolution on Implementing the Labour Law] 关于实施劳动法的决议案 (guān yú shí shī láo dòng fǎ de jué yì àn), Chinese Soviet Republic Interim Central Government, adopted 21 December 1931, effective 1 June 1932.

Other Chinese Official Documents

[Common Programme of the Chinese People's Political Consultative Conference] 中国人民政治协商会议共同纲领 (zhōng guó rén mín zhèng zhì xié shāng huì yì gòng tóng gāng lǐng), adopted and effective 29 September 1949.
[Declaration of the Third Plenary Session of the 11th Central Committee of the Chinese Communist Party] 第十一届中央委员会第三次全体会议制报 (dì shí yī jiè zhōng yāng wěi yuán huì dì sān cì quán tǐ huì yì gōng bào), adopted 22 December 1978.
[Factory Law] 工厂法 (gōng chǎng fǎ), Nationalist Government, adopted and effective 21 December 1929.
[First Interpretation of the Supreme People's Court of Several Issues on the Application of Law in the Trial of Labour Dispute Cases] 最高人民法院关于审理劳动争议案件适用法律若干问题的解释(一) (zuì gāo rén mín fǎ yuàn guān yú shěn lǐ láo dòng zhēng yì àn jiàn shì yòng fǎ lǜ ruò gān wèn tí de jiě shì (yī)), adopted 22 March 2001, effective 30 April 2001.
[Fourth Interpretation of the Supreme People's Court on Certain Issues Concerning the Application of Law in the Trial of Labour Dispute Cases] 最高人民法院关于审理劳动争议案件适用法律若干问题的解释(四) (zuì gāo rén mín fǎ yuàn guān yú shěn lǐ láo dòng zhēng yì àn jiàn shì yòng fǎ lǜ ruò gān wèn tí de jiě shì (sì)), adopted 31 December 2012, effective 1 February 2013.
[Second Interpretation of the Supreme People's Court of Several Issues on the Application of Law in the Trial of Labour Dispute Cases] 最高人民法院关于审理劳动争议案件适用法律若干问题的解释(二) (zuì gāo rén mín fǎ yuàn guān yú shěn lǐ láo dòng zhēng yì àn jiàn shì yòng fǎ lǜ ruò gān wèn tí de jiě shì (èr)), adopted 10 July 2006, effective 1 October 2006.
[Third Interpretation of the Supreme People's Court of Several Issues on the Application of Law in the Trial of Labour Dispute Cases] 最高人民法院关于审理劳动争议案件适用法律若干问题的解释(三) (zuì gāo rén mín fǎ yuàn guān yú shěn lǐ láo dòng zhēng yì àn jiàn shì yòng fǎ lǜ ruò gān wèn tí de jiě shì (sān)), adopted 12 July 2010, effective 14 September 2010.

RSFSR Regulation

Constitution of the Russian Soviet Federated Socialist Republic, adopted on 10 July 1918.
Decree of the Presidium of the Supreme Soviet of the RSFSR to repeal certain legislative texts of the RSFSR consequent upon the entry into force of the Labour Code of the RSFSR [LS 1971 – USSR 1].
Labour Code of the RSFSR. Kodeks Zakonov o Trude 1918, adopted and effective 10 December 1918.
Labour Code of the RSFSR. Kodeks Zakonov o Trude RSFSR 1922 goda, adopted 9 November 1922, effective 15 November 1922. (1922 Labour Code of the RSFSR).

Other Sources

Bellace, Janice R. 2013. *Who defines the meaning of human rights at work? The UN global compact and the ILO declaration of fundamental rights*. Paper presented to the European Regional Congress of the International Labour and Employment Relations Association, 20–22 June 2013, Amsterdam.

China Daily (Europe), 'China abolishes reeducation through labor', 28 December 2013. Available at: http://europe.chinadaily.com.cn/china/2013-12/28/content_17202297.htm. Last accessed 19 June 2015.

First Plenary Session of the Chinese People's Political Consultative Conference (CPPCC). 21–30 September 1949. Beijing.

Neal, Alan C. 2007. *China's future labor market and the impact of new (globally inspired) labor laws*. Zurich: Adecco Institute White Paper No. 3.

Neal, Alan C. 2013. *Making rights effective: Social security disputes resolution and rights enforcement in China.* Paper presented to an international symposium. Peking University, Beijing. 6 December 2013.

Reports and Inquiries: Collective Agreements in the U.S.S.R. 1952. *International Labour Review* 5–6: 477–484. Available at: http://www.heinonline.org/HOL/Page?handle=hein.journals/intlr66&id=491&collection=journals&index=#498. Last accessed 19 June 2015.

[Report on the Implementation of the 2011 Plan for National Economic and Social Development and on the 2012 Draft Plan for National Economic and Social Development] 关于 2011 年国民经济和社会发展计划执行情况与 2012 年国民经济和社会发展计划草案的报告 (guān yú 2011 nián guó mín jīng jì hé shè huì fā zhǎn jì huà zhí xíng qíng kuàng yǔ 2012 nián guó mín jīng jì hé shè huì fā zhǎn jì huà cǎo àn de bào gào), 5 March 2012.

[Report on the Implementation of the 2012 Plan for National Economic and Social Development and on the 2013 Draft Plan for National Economic and Social Development] 关于2012年国民经济和社会发展计划执行情况与2013年国民经济和社会发展计划草案的报告 (guān yú 2012 nián guó mín jīng jì hé shè huì fā zhǎn jì huà zhí xíng qíng kuàng yǔ 2013 nián guó mín jīng jì hé shè huì fā zhǎn jì huà cǎo àn de bào gào), adopted at the 1st Session of the 12th National People's Congress, 5 March 2013.

Second Plenary Session of the Seventh Central Committee of the Chinese Communist Party. 5–13 March 1949. Xibaipo (Hebei).

Chapter 3
Economic, Social, Political and Legal Transition in China

Kari Tapiola

3.1 Introduction

Although this article is mainly about China, it is set against the patterns of systemic transition in several countries over the last quarter century. Some of the obvious comparisons are with the former socialist states of Central and Eastern Europe. Yet I have tried to stress that simplistic parallels should not be drawn. I attempt to draw some conclusions on, in particular, the relationship between economic and social transition. The transition of labour markets and labour relations is a crucial part of social transition. Possible conclusions on political transition are more difficult to draw. In many ways this is the 800-pound gorilla in the room. My positive working hypothesis is that the success of economic, legal and social transition is a precondition for dealing with this gorilla. In any case, while gorillas are sizeable animals, there is no inherent reason to believe that their intentions could not be benign.

The Oxford Dictionaries define transition as the process or a period of changing from one state or condition to another. Over the last two decades transition has become a notion generally used for countries undergoing nonviolent systemic change towards a market economy and greater democracy. Transition is assumed to be positive, signifying improvement, as opposed to stagnation or deterioration. Transition is politically a more neutral word than "modernization", as it does not contain a value judgement on the situation from which transition is taking place. At the same time it avoids distinguishing between different levels of industrial and other development. While in practice the respective logics of development and transition may not fundamentally differ from one another, in political terms they belong to different worlds.

K. Tapiola (✉)
International Labour Organization, Geneva, Switzerland
e-mail: tapiola@ilo.org

U. Liukkunen, Y. Chen (eds.), *Fundamental Labour Rights in China — Legal Implementation and Cultural Logic*, Ius Gentium: Comparative Perspectives on Law and Justice 49, DOI 10.1007/978-3-319-23156-3_3

The transition of national economic, political and social systems has had varying degrees of success. In Europe since 1989 the notion of "countries in transition" has signified the change from single-party rule in Central and Eastern Europe to democratic economies, in most cases with multiparty systems and an expanding market economy. In other parts of the world, transition has taken place from minority rule (South Africa), dictatorships (Latin America) or authoritarian military rule (Indonesia, Myanmar) without an overhaul of the economic or the social system.

For more than three decades, China has been a significant example of managed transition which has embraced all aspects, starting with the economic, moving to the legal, social and eventually the political spheres. Each of these stages poses the question of the way in which transition is managed as well as its direction and speed.

Social transition reaches deep into the infrastructure of societies and touches upon traditions, culture and popular beliefs. Management of this transition is a complex issue. It generally takes place as a result of political and economic advances, including changes in communications and technology. In certain situations pressures for political, economic and legal changes arise out of social aspirations, which in turn are affected by the information and means of communication available.

3.2 The Shortcomings of Shock Therapy

Democratization in Central and Eastern Europe was forced by rising discontent with the ossified structures of control over societies. This was increasingly affected by the growing technological gap with the rapidly developing Western world and an increased awareness through means of mass communication. Once started, political and economic changes were remarkably rapid. This process became characterized as "shock therapy".[1] It focused on economic and structural change through privatisation and a rapid introduction of market mechanisms. Social change was expected to take place more or less automatically, but measures promoting it were allowed to lag behind. The secondary effect of successful change was disillusionment and cynicism among one part of the population which felt that its expectations and basic safety concerns were not met.

As the "Arab Spring" has most recently shown, while social pressures are a strong and possibly decisive factor behind political and economic change, failure to address and manage their underlying reasons can seriously weaken the sustainability of change. This may be a general rule of revolutions, which are slow in producing promised and expected results beyond immediate political change. Also, instant information produced by social media contributes to the expectation of immediate tangible results. The instability in North Africa and the Middle East reminds us that

[1] The term "shock therapy" was coined by the economist Jeffrey Sachs. Its most prominent example was the Balcerowicz Plan in Poland 1990, named after the then Deputy Prime Minister and Finance Minister Leszek Balcerowicz.

no transition is successful unless – and until – it addresses in a credible way the social issues which have provided a key basis for its legitimacy.

The current phase of economic transition in China started in 1978. As with earlier stages of transition, modernization has involved adoption of new technologies, industrialization and the application of "Western" methods. The roots of different versions of Marxism, including Leninist or Chinese Communism, lie in a critical analysis of the effects of European industrialization but do not deny the aims of industrial and social development. China was actually an early recipient of technical assistance from the International Labour Organization (ILO) for the development of labour legislation.[2]

The economic transition phase in China from the late 1970s involved controlled entry of foreign direct investment. This happened at a time of growing global concern about the political and social consequences of activities by transnational corporations. In the late 1970s and early 1980s the debate was on between, on the one hand, the desire to obtain foreign direct investment and, on the other hand, the need to minimize the negative effects of activities by transnational corporations. These corporations had become the most visible non-state agents at that stage of globalization, and the question of their social responsibility had started to be raised. China wished to make use of foreign direct investment in its new economic development phase while maintaining control over the effects of transnational corporations. It became a prominent example of a programme which the United Nations Commission and Centre on Transnational Corporations was implementing at the time: strengthening the bargaining position of host countries *vis-à-vis* transnational corporations.[3] Whereas in pre-transition Central and Eastern Europe the limits of joint ventures had become evident – as the "Vodka-Cola" model[4] failed to contribute significantly to the development of host countries – in China, investment through special economic zones was an engine of growth which set the course towards future prosperity.

Comparisons between Russia and China on the outcomes of transition clearly favour the outcome in China in economic terms. The argument can be made that Russian transition could have been significantly more beneficial if it had relied on a more managed opening to market mechanisms instead of an initial shock therapy approach.[5] This conclusion does not take into account either the political dimension of transition or the weight of tradition. What worked relatively quickly in Poland was not transferable to the different entities of the former Soviet Union, excluding the Baltic states. After a rather chaotic and oligarch-led rush to create a market, the Russian political elite (and especially the power elite) opted for a more restricted approach to economic and democratic liberties than other countries which had belonged to the Eastern European group.

[2] Chen 2014, at pp. 19–54.

[3] UN Economic and Social Council, 1974, at p. 100.

[4] Levinson 1978.

[5] Kotz 2000.

3.3 The Market as a Pragmatic Approach

Development of a "socialist market economy" in China was a pragmatic solution which significantly deideologized economic activity and ownership relations. That a market economy and socialist beliefs are not by themselves incompatible should not be surprising. Their mutual interaction is demonstrated by various success stories of democratic socialism, or social democracy, in the industrialized part of the world. As Deng Xiaoping famously noted, what was important was not the colour of the cat but the fact that it caught mice.[6] No doubt there might have been more second thoughts if the new cats had, in fact, failed in this supreme task. In addition, Deng Xiaoping's cat theory was far from being acceptable at the time when he first expressed it. It was only some decades later that both private economic activity and Deng Xiaoping himself made their way into the Chinese Constitution. Varying degrees of private entrepreneurship were not only recognized but also encouraged, although formally they, too, remained in constitutional terms subject to the leading role of the Chinese Communist Party (CCP).[7] The effect was to give them a growing degree of autonomy, as a key element of the socialist market economy.

The social and employment consequences of economic transition started gradually pushing the social agenda to the forefront. One of them was large-scale displacement, or the threat of it, of employment and activity in the state-owned enterprise (SOE) sector. Another was internal large-scale migration to where labour was needed. The transition from state-owned entities to a socialist market economy signified the end of a system where the main role of enterprises had been to employ and meet the basic needs of society; not to create growth and profits for redistribution. This could not fail to have a considerable effect on the security of the industrial, organized labour force.

As most states with a labour-oriented (Marxist) philosophy, China had not only a strong foundation of labour and social legislation but also a high degree of administrative regulations setting out the labour practices of SOEs. Chinese legislation has been to a considerable extent influenced by international labour standards,[8] but its application has varied regionally and locally. The role of labour legislation setting national benchmarks started developing after adoption of the first new labour laws in 1994.[9] With the end of a system effectively based on SOEs, labour law, labour market institutions and collective bargaining have developed through legislative action. Given that international labour standards are historically a means for formalization of the economy, it is only natural that they have provided higher levels of protection for workers with permanent or long-term work contracts. Yet protection

[6] Deng Xiaoping expressed this "cat theory" for the first time in a speech at a Communist Youth League Conference in July 1962.

[7] [Amendment to the Constitution of the People's Republic of China] 中华人民共和国宪法修正案 (zhōng huá rén mín gòng hé guó xiàn fǎ xiū zhèng àn), 2004.

[8] Cooney et al. 2013.

[9] [Labour Law of the People's Republic of China] 中华人民共和国劳动法 (zhōng huá rén mín gòng hé guó láo dòng fǎ), 1994.

remained weak for very large segments of the non-industrial labour force, which with the new economic developments provided the bulk of the migrant working population.

3.4 The Political Limits of Transition

In different countries, political transition has moved at a different pace for several reasons. In China this was at a certain stage affected by observing the consequences of perestroika in the Soviet Union, coinciding with the events of Tiananmen Square in May – June 1989. This reinforced the political limits of transition by setting certain "red lines", one of which is the leading role of the CCP. The example of, first, Central and Eastern Europe and then the break-up of the Soviet Union could not be ignored by a state which had shared with them the same principles, if not the actual practice, of a certain political ideology. With or without the stance taken by President Putin in Russia, namely that the collapse of the Soviet Union was a major catastrophe of the last century, we can recall that periods of internal strife and break-up are no strangers to Chinese history.

It should not be a big surprise if the Chinese leadership was wary of such processes of transition, which in Central and Eastern Europe and the former Soviet Union and Yugoslavia led to fragmentation so that altogether 22 independent states now occupy the space where 24 years ago there were only nine. To make a comparison, throughout this period in Africa, there have been only two adjustments to its colonially drawn borders, with Eritrea emerging out of Northern Ethiopia and the recent independence of South Sudan. In Asia, changes in the composition and borders of countries for the last six decades have seen the separation of Singapore from Malaysia, the emergence of Bangladesh from East Pakistan in 1971, the formal unification of Vietnam, and the separation of Timor Leste from Indonesia.

For the foreseeable future, the question of the leading role of the CCP is bound to remain a central feature of the Chinese political system. The centralized model in countries with a Marxist-Leninist ideology was developed on the basis of the leading role of the Communist Party. The Party, and not formal state bodies, is ultimately in control. There is merit in recalling how all-embracing this model has been in the history of socialist countries in the twentieth century, and how closely it has been tied, for example, to basic security arrangements. This notion emerged as a key element of early Soviet rule and was notably written into the Soviet Constitution adopted in 1936. In this system, the Communist Party was not "above" the institutions of the state and political, economic and social life. It formed the nucleus inside each of the institutions – including such mass institutions as trade unions and other significant social bodies. In different forms, it survived in all subsequent constitutions of socialist countries; in the Soviet Union, abandoning this vanguard role was one of the final steps before the break-up of the country at the end of 1991.

The question of the leading role of the Communist Party in a socialist country has not been one of power or control alone; it concerns both unity and cohesion.

It was a prominent feature of the 1936 Constitution of the Soviet Union.[10] This made the Party the unquestioned leading power not only in governmental decisions but also for all economic and social activity. The Party can be described as being the central nervous system of society, including all key social institutions and actors, civilian and military alike. Little space was left for an autonomous civil society, and legal non-state economic activity did not exist on any large scale. There were no independent employers, while the trade unions were among the social organizations whose work was specifically to be directed by the Communist Party.

This model, developed by Stalin and maintained by his successors, extended during the Cold War era to the whole group of socialist countries. Its importance was driven home by the Prague Spring and the subsequent occupation of Czechoslovakia in 1968. A few weeks before the invasion, the future occupiers jointly reminded the Czechoslovak leaders that while it was otherwise up to them to decide how to run their economy and organize social life, their desire to abandon the leading role of the Communist Party was not a sovereign issue for them alone. Undermining it would also undermine the structure of relations between the socialist countries.[11]

Political transition in the European sphere, including the former Soviet Union, led to rejection of the leading role – i.e. monopoly position – of the ruling Party. For now, in China, as well as in Viet Nam or Cuba, its key features remain. The alternatives would appear to be either pluralism, which shakes the roots of the system, or managed pluralism within the system. In any transition, the autonomy of actors plays an important role. The issue may be more immediate in regional developments than in the evolution of institutions. Increasing the autonomy of both regional and local actors, and empowering institutions – especially those of civil society – would seem to be both desirable and necessary for transition. Yet neither of them is without dangers.

Against the background of what happened to the Soviet Union and in Yugoslavia in the early 1990s, the question can be asked: when political transition amounts to a fundamental departure from hitherto existing power structures, how big is the risk that it ends not only with the collapse of the system but also the disintegration of large geographical entities? Of course this is determined among other things by the size of those entities, their homogeneity, and their historical background. While no simple answer is possible, and comparisons tend to be misleading, any enlightened political leadership will wish to be aware of where transition may run the risk of crossing into something which threatens the viability and survival of the entity itself.

---

[10] The essence of the power structure of the Soviet Union was discreetly contained in Article 126 of the 1936 Constitution, which said: "...the most active and politically most conscious citizens in the ranks of the working class and other sections of the working people unite in the Communist Party of the Soviet Union (Bolsheviks), *which is the vanguard of the working people in their struggle to strengthen and develop the socialist system and is the leading core of all organizations of the working people, both public and state.*" Later the leading role of the Communist Party was raised to more prominent and visible articles of the Constitutions of the Soviet Union and other socialist countries.

[11] This position was explained by the leaders of the Soviet Union, the German Democratic Republic, Hungary and Bulgaria in their "Warsaw letter" of 19 July 1968 to the Czechoslovak leaders, a month before the armed forced of these countries occupied Czechoslovakia.

3.5 The Economic Imperative of Transition

In addition to territorial integrity and the capacity to maintain sufficient authority and public order, the economic security of societies and their members is one key determinant of transition. If transition can produce economic goods and ensure decent living standards for a majority of the population and promise for the future, naturally the outlook is significantly improved. But can this be compatible with a high degree of central rule? Anyone who would rush to conclusions would be well advised to remember that economic success, political democracy and relative stability are not by themselves guarantees against centrifugal tendencies, as is shown by such European regions as Scotland or Catalonia, with their distinct national identities.

Political and economic transition invariably raises the question of central control compared with decentralized development. Especially in large countries, the question of national cohesion is always present. Over-centralization can impede the emergence of manageable and dynamic growth centres with a capacity for initiative and innovation. The ensuing stifling of regional and local potential was no doubt a factor in the dysfunctionality of the Soviet Union and could still be a threat to development in Russia today. The United States again is historically both a decentralized and a growth-oriented economy. Growth in Germany following World War II embraced several centres throughout the country with a degree of political decentralization which would be unthinkable, say, in France. Yet a lack of central support can lead to large and ultimately non-functional entities, such as the Austro-Hungarian or Ottoman empires. Ultimately, the success of political and economic transition is dependent on how central and decentralized forces balance one another off.

This does not mean to say that China could be threatened by a break-up of the country. But it should be fair to expect that any large and diverse country with a recent or longer-term centralized structure would weigh the effects of different scenarios, including potential threats. In Europe, revisiting the borders established at various times, be it 1848, 1919–1920 or 1945, has let the genie out of the bottle. This is most recently to be seen in the southern regions of the former Soviet Union. Yet the territorial scope of China has in recent historical times basically not been created through adding different national components, and parts of China itself have been subject to foreign annexation. The scope of decentralization is different, especially when it can be seen extending to the "one country, two systems" approach regarding Hong Kong and Macao. One can but hope that the different kinds of current tensions involving Hong Kong or Tibet and Xingkiang will be accommodated through dialogue and respect for fundamental rights.

Social transition has often been associated with conflict – either acute conflict or development of an understanding that the diverse interests of different groups in society and the economy need to be reconciled through negotiation. Two examples of social and labour conflict in the transition phase of the late 1980s in Europe appear in the shape of the Soviet Union and Poland. An important event in the Soviet Union was the 1988 miners' strike. This conflict can more appropriately be called a protest by the mining communities against the centre of power (Moscow), as the interests of the strikers and their managers at the time were largely identical. The strike was not against the system; it was for a fairer deal, a bigger share and a greater say in matters of direct concern to the mining communities. One of the notable by-products of the strike was to demonstrate that the old trade union movement was suffering a systemic identity crisis, as it did not know on which side of the bargaining table it belonged. The miners' strike thus became a factor in the internal transformation of the trade union structure and a reassessment of its role towards government.

In Poland, the strike by Solidarność in 1989 was for a fairer deal – but it was also for a change in the system. On this count, Solidarność proved to be politically successful. It was not equally successful as a trade union movement, as up to this day it has not become the majority organization among the workers. In many respects it actually had more features of a political liberation movement than of a trade union organization. In practice, it took over much of the dissipated leading role of the Communist Party.[12]

Yet Solidarność was not a political party or a centrally led organization. Its strength arose out of the capacity to mobilise large numbers of people so that at a given stage anything up to a quarter of the Polish population saw themselves as members of it. But movements have their own logic, which is different from that of organizations with management structures, rules and systems of accountability.

3.6 From Administrative Control to Contractual Labour Relations

In China, the restructuring of SOEs and the introduction of new labour contracts in the 1990s brought fundamental changes to the employment relations regime. Employment was no longer guaranteed for life, and it increasingly became conditioned by performance on the job. The new conditions and demands altered workers' relations both with enterprises and the state. This posed a challenge to the existing social security and welfare systems as well. Over a short period of time new forms of labour contract (fixed-term) were introduced as norms of employment practice, while many other countries have taken decades to work out such diversification. The levels of protection provided by this diversification of forms of contract were lower than earlier, and they were also lower compared with other countries.

The dismantling of the old socialist employment system changed traditional relationships on two fundamental counts. For workers in SOEs, working under new contracts became more insecure; jobs threatened to disappear; and new contracts tended to become of shorter duration and more precarious. Where new investments

[12] This was driven home to me when visiting a factory in Warsaw in March 1990. The representative of the traditional trade union had remained in his old office while the Solidarność representative had been installed in the former office of the local Communist Party Secretary.

were made – such as in the opportunities opened by foreign direct investment and associated activities – the labour that migrated to them did not obtain the security offered by the traditional labour relations model. In many cases they got no contracts and minimal security. Yet this process made rural migrant workers, with their challenges and aspirations, into significant new social actors, thus further transforming the nature and scope of the labour market in China.

Earlier top-down administrative industrial relations practices were being shaken, and trade union bodies, which in the old system had been little more than an extension of management, were not capable of exercising a protective function. Higher-level union organizations did not get involved in enterprise problems, and the government's drive for industrialization initially had limited space for social concerns. The system had little space for initiatives from the rank-and-file level, and consequently workers found themselves in a situation where the old authoritarian model was ill-equipped to deal with the challenges that workers were asked to cope with.

Greater concern for labour protection has manifested itself since the beginning of the last decade. Several factors account for this. With increased growth, development and diversity, the quality of labour grew in importance. It is one thing to have at your disposal a large pool of labour, migrants or surplus labour from non-productive and closed down entities; it is another thing to secure a sufficient supply of qualified labour in whose skills investments have to be made. Also, discontent arising out of closures or reductions of activity of large state-owned entities had consequences, in numerous cases leading to strikes. Due to the traditional close links between enterprise management and local bureaucracies, strike action blurred the dividing line between social and political issues; yet not all protest could be labelled anti-social or treason.

At least in some regions and provinces, there have been consistent efforts to build industrial relations processes at both regional and sectoral levels – beyond individual enterprises. Higher-level union organizations have also demonstrated more concern about workplace relations and reflected on their role in the transition process. One indicator is the overall growth of trade union membership, from 123.4 million in 2003 to 240 million in 2010.[13] During the same period, the number of unionized workplaces with wage agreements increased from 293,000 to 1,116,000, representing 25.9 % of the total. The share of workers covered by either regional or sectoral wage agreements has also been on the rise. Regional and sectoral bargaining appears to be due to the campaign by Chinese trade unions to expand collective bargaining, which in turn was supported by local employers' concerns about high turnover. Another important factor was the desire to avoid or at least manage local conflicts.

On the workers' side, contributing factors have been higher rates of organization and an expanding realization that various methods of collective bargaining are needed for workers to protect their interests. It is difficult to assess what the impact has been from increased attention from foreign trade union organizations in China. On their side, the need for greater interaction across borders was driven by shifts of

[13] Lee and Liu 2011.

production and jobs towards subsidiaries and subcontractors of foreign enterprises. This international trade union reaction has been expressed through sometimes vocal criticism, but it has also led to a significant increase in international study visits and other interaction with workers and existing trade union structures at local enterprise level.

In Europe and North America, 2008 was the year of the beginning of the financial crisis. In China it was a year of social and labour legislation, notably the Labour Contract Law, the Employment Promotion Law, the Labour Dispute Mediation and Arbitration Law and, later on, the Social Insurance Law.[14]

3.7 Voice, Representation and Organization of Workers

The evolution of industrial relations has been evident above all in some provinces, particularly around the Pearl River delta and the Yangtze River delta. In Guangdong, which has the longest history of transition of labour-management relations, modernization of the industrial relations system has been part of the industrial upgrading strategy of the province. Such modernization addresses questions of increased voice by workers and their organizations, collective bargaining and codetermination in the production process. The relative proximity of local Non-Governmental Organisations, and support from Hong Kong, has also played a role.

In May 2010 a 2-week strike by 1,900 workers at a Honda plant in Foshan soon paralyzed the company's production throughout China. It secured a 24 % pay rise for the workers after negotiations between the leaders of the action and management. The official trade union bodies tried to intervene but were sidelined in the process. This highlighted the issue of union democracy at the workplace, including the legitimacy of workers' representatives and the introduction of genuine collective bargaining. As a significant difference to the protest strikes of the earlier phase, when action was taken in response to a threat to jobs, this strike was "classically" for wages and working conditions. It was not against local or central political leaders. It was directed against management, thus corresponding to the true logic of industrial relations systems.

In such a situation, the response by management is crucial. In the Honda strike, management responded and a settlement was reached. This was not a simple process, but the higher-level trade union bodies also accommodated themselves to it, while the local authorities did not resort to disruptive interference. If in this kind of

[14] Respectively, these are [Labour Contract Law of the People's Republic of China] 中华人民共和国劳动合同法 (zhōng huá rén mín gòng hé guó láo dòng hé tóng fǎ), 2007; [Employment Promotion Law of the People's Republic of China] 中华人民共和国就业促进法 (zhōng huá rén mín gòng hé guó jiù yè cù jìn fǎ), 2007; [Labour Dispute Mediation and Arbitration Law of the People's Republic of China] 中华人民共和国劳动争议调解仲裁法 (zhōng huá rén mín gòng hé guó láo dòng zhēng yì tiáo jiě zhòng cái fǎ), 2007; and [Social Insurance Law of the People's Republic of China] 中华人民共和国社会保险法 (zhōng huá rén mín gòng hé guó shè huì bǎo xiǎn fǎ), 2010.

case management took early recourse to local political and law enforcement powers, then it – and not the workers – would effectively politicize the conflict. Management thus has a responsibility to correctly assess the nature of the discontent it is facing.

Equally, if a higher-level trade union organization interprets such discontent as a political protest against it, and by extension, although not primarily, against the political system, it also contributes to politicization of an interest conflict. It is to be noted, however, that in China, as in any other country, a considerable degree of both political and internal union elements may be at play in any given conflict. A similar phenomenon has been evident in wildcat strikes and other local union protests in Europe, especially when Labour parties have been in government. In China, the link between trade unions and the CCP remains prominent, as witnessed by a very high proportion of Party members among enterprise union leaders.[15]

Blue-collar workers' pay has grown ninefold in the past decade while China has still been able to maintain its comparative advantage.[16] This has been due to higher productivity, rising skills of the workforce and developed supply chains to and from factories. China is no longer a low-wage country where imported components are assembled; indeed, China is increasingly a producer of these components. While globally the growth of wages remains under the level it was before the current financial crisis, among Asian countries, wages in China amount to most of the growth. Chinese wages today are roughly three times those of Indonesia; four times those of Vietnam; five times those of Cambodia; and ten times more than workers in Bangladesh earn. This shows that growth is being translated into better incomes for a considerable number of workers, paving the way for a situation where collective bargaining can play the stabilizing and supportive economic role it is designed to have. Genuine collective bargaining should lead to compromises which are informed by a realistic assessment of the economic prospects of the enterprise and the real short and medium term income and employment expectations of the workers.

While the emergence of several economic power centres in China does raise questions of coherence, this does not necessarily mean fragmentation. The way in which they interact can have an overall stabilizing effect as they give room for experimenting and solutions, some of which will be better than others. The firm belief of this author is that in the interaction between different regions and growth centres, those with a sufficiently strong social component will fare better. There could well be more success stories in the better off, more exposed areas. However, sometimes balanced growth can also take place in areas which are not necessarily very visible on the central radar screen.

At the same time strengthened legal guarantees and collective bargaining action are important for those in greatest need. This is particularly true for hitherto unprotected workers and those whose contractual relationships are precarious. Also,

[15] J. Qiao's research conducted in 2010 shows a percentage of 90.3 %, according to a survey of 1,811 enterprise union leaders, as quoted in Lee and Liu 2011, at p. 209.

[16] National Bureau of Statistics of the People's Republic of China, China Statistical Yearbook, 2012. See also ILO Global Wage Database.

while decentralization works to the advantage of some groups, for others it can weaken or impede the protection which universal and solidaristic systems are designed to give. Outcomes can also be thwarted by bureaucratic inertia or the resistance of vested interests, and they can succumb to corruption.

3.8 The Role of Actors at All Levels

All too often in the context of transition, the centre is the slowest to adjust, although the need for a central-level push – through campaigns, policy instructions, enforceable and respected laws – remains evident. The Soviet transition also started at the central level when the *perestroika* of Mikhail Gorbachev questioned the way in which the system was working. Both the centre and different sub-centres can make use of a whole range of tools for managed transition. This starts with information flows, experiments and analysis of their consequences, necessary clarification of the role and responsibility of different actors. When more responsibility is transferred from above, it should be matched by more representation and participation from below.

One way of ensuring that the local industrial relations system is made functional is to develop and strengthen a consensus regarding the respective roles of each of the actors. Workers' representatives are elected to represent workers *vis-à-vis* management; they are not part of management – not even in participatory systems for corporate governance. Neither workers nor employers should have a political agenda, and state and local authorities should retain their neutrality when conflicts of interest are solved.

Successful transition helps in proving that social empowerment does not lead to chaos or revolt. This calls for the strengthening of trust and confidence-building measures. In this context, opposition by employers – including foreign employers – to collective bargaining and labour contracts is not helpful. Such resistance is actually counterproductive and also politically unwise. Such opposition, which was voiced during preparation of the Labour Contract Law,[17] damages the prospects for a successful transition of labour relations. It is actually a significant and unwarranted interference in the internal Chinese process.

In transition of labour practices, care and understanding are needed from all sides. The dismantling and replacement of top-down patterns is a process which can, and will, take many different forms. There is a need for an inclusive process whereby the primary level finds agreement on aims and means of action – but then trusts in the negotiating capacity of its authorized representatives. This calls for solidarity, which can build both confidence and capacity. Transitions can be undone or seriously weakened by the failure of a newly-empowered basic level to establish a balanced interaction with those it entrusts to act on its behalf. Indeed, one pitfall of transitions of trade union structures (which is also true of political and other

[17] [Labour Contract Law of the People's Republic of China] 中华人民共和国劳动合同法 (zhōng huá rén mín gòng hé guó láo dòng hé tóng fǎ), 2007.

elected structures) is that if a "consensus" imposed from above is removed, the result tends to be chaotic unless it is replaced by a legitimate delegation of authority from below.[18]

3.9 The Search for Win-Win Outcomes

What then could be a successful formula for continued transition at the current and future stages in China? This question can be answered only by the Chinese leadership and economic, social and academic actors in China itself. An outsider cannot suggest a blueprint. Yet in the light of experience of processes of transition, and bearing in mind the complex framework, certain principles would seem to be clear, although they need to find their rightful Chinese characters.

An obvious issue is establishing the optimal geographical and institutional balance between the centre on the one hand and both regional and national cross-cutting authorities on the other hand. It should be possible to deideologize and depoliticize the issue of central versus decentralized decisions and authority. Assuring an effective level of subsidiarity is not in contradiction with centrally debated, agreed and implemented aims and policies.

Another issue which helps to build both capacity and confidence is addressing the transparency of decision-making and actions as well as the accountability of each of the actors. This means developing further representative systems, with delegation of authority and accountability by those to whom authority has been delegated.

Legal underpinning of the system calls for efficient implementation, in particular at local levels. Issues of both the will and the capacity for action need to be addressed. In the social and labour field, the framework is given by international labour standards, especially the agreed fundamental principles and rights at work of the ILO, together with the need to ensure a basic social floor for the whole population. The exact way in which labour law and collective bargaining interact is bound to vary over time; negotiated arrangements may be more advantageous than the legal minimum framework, but especially for the more disadvantaged parts of the actual or potential labour force, minimum standards are likely to remain part of the necessary social safety net.

Campaigns would appear to work best when they are truly awareness-raising processes and participatory, involving economic and social actors at each of the different levels.[19] Studying local and regional initiatives, to assess "best practices", further increases the alternatives available to primary and higher-level actors.

How far then can transition be managed so that it will produce optimal outcomes for everyone? In principle, nothing is impossible if, together with economic considerations, social and human factors are also taken into account early on. Many transition processes have been less than successful because they have been either overtly

[18]Tapiola 1995.

[19]Cooney et al. 2013.

political or exclusively economic. Once a process driven by economic aims achieves a degree of success, to be sustainable it needs to lead to beneficial social transition. This raises questions of income and wealth distribution, including the need to share positive outcomes within a larger labour market and avoid polarization, marginalization or growth where the fruits are restricted to a limited number of centres, regions or professions. This is why in China measures to deal with the rights of informal and precarious workers are an important item on the social agenda.

There is the human factor, too. The prospects of transition are limited if there is not a generally shared feeling that not only the collective but also individuals within the collective have a promise of prosperity. Joint action – such as collective bargaining and labour-management negotiations – is undertaken for the purpose of legitimately achieving something that individual members of society cannot obtain if they act alone. Progress in the social and labour field generally means that the scope is increased for people to achieve their fair share. This calls for conceiving and applying fair rules so that the prosperity of some individuals is not reached at the cost of many others.

The stated aim of China is to develop a harmonious society, which implies that transition should continue to yield beneficial results for a growing number of members of that society. Transition in China started as an economic process, and its success made legal and social transition necessary. An unavoidable question for the future is the way in which political transition is shaped. In the light of the experience of the European former socialist countries, it is understandable that there is fear of the kind of political transition which can lead to disruption and uncontrolled systemic change. In this light abandoning the vanguard role of the CCP can still appear to be inviting chaos.

According to its Constitution, China will "stay in the primary stage of socialism for a long period of time". The text of the preamble was amended in 1999 by, among other things, adding Deng Xiaoping Theory to Mao Zedong thought, Marxism-Leninism and the leadership of the CCP.[20] To these the 2004 revision added "the important thought of "Three Represents".[21] The Constitution itself notes that evolution will be of a step-by-step nature, underlining the desire to maintain a high degree of stability. The promise of turning China into a powerful and prosperous socialist country has been vindicated to a considerable degree at the international economic and political level. The rest of this sentence in the Constitution refers to a high level of culture and democracy. It may be appropriate to think that this is an invitation, in due time, to further develop and qualify the thoughts and practices according to which China's society and its vast and dynamic labour market are to be governed.

[20] [Amendment to the Constitution of the People's Republic of China] 中华人民共和国宪法修正案 (zhōng huá rén mín gòng hé guó xiàn fǎ xiū zhèng àn), adopted at the 2nd plenary session of the 9th National People's Congress on 15 March 1999.

[21] The "Three Represents" were laid out by former President Jiang Zemin for the first time in 2000, of what the Chinese Communist Party should stand for: advanced social productive forces, advanced culture and the interests of the overwhelming majority.

References

Literature

Chen, Yifeng. 2014. The international labour organisation and labour governance in China 1919–1949. In *China and ILO fundamental principles and rights at work*, ed. Roger Blanpain, vol. eds. Ulla Liukkunen and Chen Yifeng. Bulletin of Comparative Labour Relations 86: 19–54. Alphen aan den Rijn: Kluwer Law International.

Cooney, Sean, Sarah Biddulph, and Ying Zhu. 2013. *Law and fair work in China*. London: Routledge.

Kotz, David M. 2000. Lessons of economic transition in Russia and China. In *Political economy and contemporary capitalism: Radical perspectives on economic theory and policy*, ed. Ron Raiman, Heather Boushey, and Dawn Saunders, 210–217. New York: M.E. Sharpe.

Lee, Chang-Hee, and Mingwei Liu. 2011. Collective bargaining in transition: Measuring the effects of collective voice in China. In *The role of collective bargaining in the global economy – Negotiating for social justice*, ed. Susan Hayter, 205–226. Geneva: Edward Elgar.

Levinson, Charles. 1978. *Vodka-Cola*. New York: Gordon and Cremonesi.

Tapiola, Kari. 1995. Trade union development in the CEECs. *Transfer: European Review of Labour and Research* 1(3): 360–377.

Documents and Official Publications

ILO Documents

ILO Global Wage Database. Available at: www.ilo.org/ilostat/GWR. (Last accessed 19 June 2015).

Other International Law Sources

UN Economic and Social Council. Report of the Secretary-General on the Impact of Multinational Corporations on Development and on International Relations U.N. Doc. E.74.II.A.5. (E/5500/Re4v.1 ST/ESA/6), 14 June 1974.

Chinese Regulation

Laws by the National People's Congress

[Amendment to the Constitution of the People's Republic of China] 中华人民共和国宪法修正案 (zhōng huá rén mín gòng hé guó xiàn fǎ xiū zhèng àn), adopted at the 2nd plenary session of the 9th National People's Congress on 15 March 1999.

[Amendment to the Constitution of the People's Republic of China] 中华人民共和国宪法修正案 (zhōng huá rén mín gòng hé guó xiàn fǎ xiū zhèng àn), adopted at the 2nd plenary session of the 10th National People's Congress on 14 March 2004.

Laws by the Standing Committee of the National People's Congress

[Employment Promotion Law of the People's Republic of China] 中华人民共和国就业促进法 (zhōng huá rén mín gòng hé guó jiù yè cù jìn fǎ), Standing Committee of the National People's Congress, adopted 30 August 2007, effective 1 January 2008. Revised and effective 24 April 2015.

[Labour Contract Law of the People's Republic of China] 中华人民共和国劳动合同法 (zhōng huá rén mín gòng hé guó láo dòng hé tóng fǎ), Standing Committee of the National People's Congress, adopted 29 June 2007, effective 1 January 2008. Revised 28 December 2012, effective 1 July 2013.

[Labour Dispute Mediation and Arbitration Law of the People's Republic of China] 中华人民共和国劳动争议调解仲裁法 (zhōng huá rén mín gòng hé guó láo dòng zhēng yì tiáo jiě zhòng cái fǎ), Standing Committee of the National People's Congress, adopted 29 December 2007, effective 1 May 2008.

[Labour Law of the People's Republic of China] 中华人民共和国劳动法 (zhōng huá rén mín gòng hé guó láo dòng fǎ), Standing Committee of the National People's Congress, adopted 5 July 1994, effective 1 January 1995.

[Social Insurance Law of the People's Republic of China] 中华人民共和国社会保险法 (zhōng huá rén mín gòng hé guó shè huì bǎo xiǎn fǎ), Standing Committee of the National People's Congress, adopted 28 October 2010, effective 1 July 2011.

Other Sources

China Internet Information Center. 2015. What is "Three Represents" CPC Theory? Available at: http://www.china.org.cn/english/zhuanti/3represents/68735.htm. Last accessed 19 June 2015.

[*China statistical yearbook* 2012] 中国统计年鉴-2012 (zhōng guó tǒng jì nián jiàn-2012), National Bureau of Statistics of the People's Republic of China. 2013. Beijing: China Statistics Press.

Constitution of the Soviet Union, adopted on 5 December 1936.

Deng Xiaoping. 1962. Speech at the Seventh Plenary Session of the Third Central Committee, 7 July 1962.

Lee, Chang-Hee. 2013. *Evolution of labour market institutions and industrial relations, and their labour market effects in China*. Presentation at the Conference on Regulating for Decent Work: Regulating for Equitable and Job-Rich Growth (3–5 July 2013) on 4 July 2013 at the ILO.

The "Warsaw letter" sent by the Party leaders of the Soviet Union, the German Democratic Republic, Hungary and Bulgaria after their meeting in Warsaw, Poland, on 14–15 July 1968. Available at: www.dhr.history.vt.edu/modules/eu/mod05_1968/evidence_detail_14.html. Last accessed 19 June 2015.

Chapter 4
ILO, Extraterritoriality and Labour Protection in Republican Shanghai

Yifeng Chen

4.1 Introduction

A close examination of Chinese experience of labour protection during the Republican era highlights the multiple dimensions of a noble cause. Besides a humanitarian face, labour protection is also amenable to be conceived and conceptualized prominently as a political issue, the characterization of which hinges upon the context of its operation. The implementation of Factory Law[1] in Republican China became a focal point of dispute between China and the Western powers, for the significance of the matter lies in its implications pointing to the abolition of extraterritoriality as a whole. The disagreement between China and the West was not at all about whether or not protection of labour was a desirable cause, nor so much about the level or standard of protection. Rather, it was primarily a struggle over authority to exercise jurisdiction over labour regulation, a contestation as to who was ultimately the legitimate sovereign entitled to administer labour issues.

The politicization of labour protection in Republican China was largely owing to an intense interplay between various factors. These included, among others, the political struggle between imperialistic expansion and nationalistic resistance, the ideological contest between the Chinese Communist Party (CCP) and the Kuomintang Party, economic competition between Chinese and Western enterprises, and legal contestation over administrative jurisdiction between foreign and Chinese authorities – all find their footings in labour issues. The intensity of such politicization culminated in Shanghai, where all those factors were present and made strongly felt.

[1] [Factory Law] 工厂法 (gōng chǎng fǎ), 1929.

Y. Chen (✉)
Peking University Law School, Beijing, China
e-mail: yifeng.chen@pku.edu.cn

U. Liukkunen, Y. Chen (eds.), *Fundamental Labour Rights in China — Legal Implementation and Cultural Logic*, Ius Gentium: Comparative Perspectives on Law and Justice 49, DOI 10.1007/978-3-319-23156-3_4

By the 1920s Shanghai was not only the principal industrial center of China,[2] but also a city of international importance where the Western powers had a vested stake, conspicuously in the areas of the International Settlement and the French Concession. The industrial workers in Shanghai, while not enormous in number, were noted for their distinctive class consciousness.[3] The increasing radicalization of the labour movement from 1919 onwards gave workers a visible political profile in Shanghai. At the same time, anti-imperialistic sentiment in Shanghai was in particular fuelled by the May Thirtieth Incident of 1925 when the Shanghai Municipal Police shot at Chinese students and workers protesting in the street. The Kuomintang Party, with its consolidation as a national ruling power in 1927, also gathered more resolve to strengthen its control over Shanghai and abolish the extraterritoriality system, in the course of which labour protection in foreign settlements became highly relevant. All these factors made labour protection in Shanghai a deeply important yet complex issue.

This article aims for a more accurate account of the origin and trajectory of labour law development in Republican China as well as a better understanding of the role which the International Labour Organisation (ILO) played in that development.[4] At the same time, the article also endeavours to shed light on the interplay between a political conception of labour and a humanitarian one. The enactment and implementation of labour law, as the research will illustrate, are closely intermingled with China's efforts towards national liberation from colonialism and imperialism, in particular the persistent struggle for abolition of the extraterritoriality system and unequal treaties as a whole. The ILO, in delivering its commitment to global social justice, not only aspired to the making of labour laws in China, but also lent considerable political legitimacy, internationally and domestically, to China's claim to and exercise of sovereignty in relation to labour protection. Meanwhile, it is also noted that engaging in the humanitarian cause of labour protection reinforced the political process of state building in China.

The article is structured as follows. As background the system of extraterritoriality practiced by the treaty powers in China 1843–1943 and structure of the administration in Shanghai with special emphasis on that of the International Settlement and the French Concession is briefly recounted (Sect. 4.2). This is followed by an in-depth examination of the legislative history of the Provisional Factory Regulations promulgated by the Beijing government in 1923.[5] The connection between the enactment and the movement to ban child labour in Shanghai was extensively documented, which unveiled the underlying rationale of Regulations aiming to curtail expansion of the colonial powers in Shanghai (Sect. 4.3). Then special attention is given to disputes between the Chinese government and the International Settlement

[2] See Lieu 1936.

[3] It is estimated that in 1933 Shanghai had up to 350,000 industrial workers. See Ibid., at pp. 112–115. In contrast, the total population in Shanghai amounted to 3,391,909 in the same year, at p. 396.

[4] This article is a continuation of previous research in the same direction, see Chen 2014.

[5] [Provisional Factory Regulations] 暂行工厂通则 (zàn xíng gōng chǎng tōng zé), 1923.

arising from implementation of the Factory Law of 1929 (Sect. 4.4). Detailed accounts are given of ILO assistance with implementation of the Factory Law in China (Sect. 4.5). This continues with an exposure of various efforts by the Chinese government at the International Labour Conference to address the injustice caused by the inability to enforce the Factory Law in foreign settlements (Sect. 4.6). The regulation of industrial conditions by the City government of Greater Shanghai as well as exercise by the International Settlement through its own licensing system are also documented (Sect. 4.7).

4.2 Extraterritoriality and the Administration of Foreign Settlements in Shanghai

At the core of the various arrangements under the unequal treaty system between China and the colonial powers sat the notorious system of extraterritoriality.[6] This system was introduced by the Western powers along with their global expansion in the nineteenth century into East Asian countries such as China, Japan, Korea and Burma to remove their nationals from local jurisdictions. It was usually justified on the grounds of the backwardness of the legal system in those countries, the cruelty of punishments, lack of judicial independence or a combination of all these elements.[7] The extraterritoriality system, as designed, was to exempt the subjects of the treaty powers from local jurisdiction when accused of a criminal offence or sued as a defendant in a civil case. In practice, this meant that the operation of jurisdiction depended on the nationality of the defendant. Put succinctly, in civil and criminal cases where a foreign defendant enjoyed extraterritorial rights, it was the sole prerogative of the consulate or court of the country of the defendant's nationality to hear or try these cases.[8] Thus the system of extraterritoriality was also often referred to as consular jurisdiction. For disputes where the defendant was Chinese, jurisdiction fell within the jurisdiction of a Chinese magistrate or court irrespective of the nationality of the plaintiff, although in practice it was not uncommon for foreign consuls to observe or even intervene in Chinese proceedings when a foreign plaintiff was involved.

The extraterritoriality system was forced upon China through a series of coerced treaties after China's defeat in the First Opium War, with the first recognition of

[6] See generally Keeton 1969, Willoughby 1927, and Fishel 1952. It is, however, to be noted that outside the context of the unequal treaties system the term "extraterritoriality" can also be used in a neutural manner, referring to, for example, the immunity enjoyed by foreign diplomats from local jurisdiction, or the application of statutes of a certain country outside its territorial jurisdiction on matters such as anti-trust and human rights.

[7] See Woodhead 1929, at pp. 1–3.

[8] Great Britain and the United States had established special judicial bodies for exercising extraterritorial power. The British Supreme Court for China and Japan was established as early as 1865, and the United States Court for China was established in 1906. For a discussion on the United States Court for China, see Ruskola 2013, at pp. 152–185.

extraterritoriality codified in the Treaty of Bogue between the British and Chinese Empires on 8 October 1843.[9] The same course was immediately pursued by the United States and France in 1844 as well as by a number of other European and American powers and Japan in the years that followed. By 13 June 1918, when the last concession of consular jurisdiction was made (to Switzerland), altogether 19 states enjoyed extraterritorial privileges in China, albeit for longer or shorter periods. In 1930, the holding of extraterritorial privileges remained with 14 countries: Great Britain, the United States, France, Belgium, Brazil, Denmark, Italy, Japan, the Netherlands, Norway, Portugal, Spain, Sweden, and Switzerland.[10]

Yet the administration of justice by foreign consuls was also highly problematic in practice. It led to a multiplicity of courts and diversity of legal regimes in China. A Chinese plaintiff who intended to appeal against the decision of a consul was often prevented by the fact that the appeal could only be handled in the home country of the defendant, which meant Europe or America.[11] The consuls were diplomats, in most cases not having received legal training at all, and were unfamiliar with legal terms and reasoning. As a result, the administration of justice by consuls was not even satisfactory to their own nationals. In practice it was not rare for foreign consuls to rule with bias against Chinese plaintiffs. On one occasion, the Chinese Minister of Justice even in a governmental circular openly denounced foreign consuls for being open to corruption, an accusation incurring an immediate formal protest from the diplomatic representatives of the treaty powers.[12] The existence of the system of extraterritoriality on the Chinese side was a constant concern for the political elites, dating back to the late Qing Dynasty. In the Republican era, the continuation of the system generated increasing feelings of humiliation and resentment among the public, especially with awakening nationalism. In the Treaty between Great Britain and China concluded on 5 September 1902, Great Britain pledged that it was "prepared to relinquish extraterritorial rights when satisfied that the state of Chinese laws, the arrangements for their administration and other

---

[9] In promulgating the "General Regulations under which British Trade is to be conducted at the Five Ports of Canton, Amoy, Foochow, Ningpo, and Shanghai" on 22 July 1843, China for the first time had to concede consular jurisdiction to the British Empire on a unilateral basis. The "General Regulations" was later incorporated in the Treaty of Bogue concluded by the British and Chinese Empires in Hong Kong on 8 October 1843.

[10] Having declared war against Germany and Austro-Hungary, China promulgated regulations in accordance with international law and abrogated the extraterritorial rights of German and Austro-Hungarian subjects in 1917. Russia formally renounced its extraterritorial privileges in 1924. In 1927 Peru confirmed the renunciation of its extraterritorial rights, as a result of the expiration of the Treaty of Friendship, Commerce, and Navigation between Peru and China of 1874. In an exchange of notes with the Chinese government in 1929, Mexico also confirmed the termination of its extraterritorial right, brought about by the expiration on 30 November 1928 of the Treaty of Amity, Commerce, and Navigation between Mexico and China of 1899. After the Paris Peace Conference of 1919, the Beijing government pursued a policy of seeking revision of unequal treaties with foreign powers with limited success. See [Tang] 唐启华 2010.

[11] Report of the Commission on Extraterritoriality in China 1926, at pp. 20–21.

[12] See Letter from Mr. Palairet to Mr. Austen Chamberlain, dated 10 October 1925, in Jarman 2008a, at pp. 275–276.

considerations" warranted so doing. A similar position was expressed by the United States in its treaty with China for the extension of commercial relations between them dated 8 October 1903 and by Japan in the supplementary treaty of commerce and navigation with China on the same date.

In parallel to the system of extraterritoriality operated the foreign settlements and concessions in China. In 1842 Shanghai, Ningbo, Xiamen, Fuzhou and Guangzhou were opened as trade ports after China's defeat in the First Opium War. As a practical aspect of operationalizing free trade, Chinese officials authorized the construction of foreign settlements in treaty ports. In Shanghai this began with the delineation of a British settlement in 1845. The Land Regulations, as promulgated in 1845 by the Chinese Daotai of Shanghai, Gong Mujiu, demarcated a specific area, outside the old Shanghai city wall, where subjects of the British Empire were allowed to rent land in perpetuity and build residences. This was followed by delineation of an American settlement in 1848, and a French one in 1849. In 1863 the American settlement joined the British one and the whole area was named the Foreign Settlement (later the International Settlement).[13]

The International Settlement and the French Concession developed their own *de facto* administrative structure, the legality of which was constantly questioned and challenged throughout the time of its existence.[14] The administration of the International Settlement evolved over time and consolidated itself significantly by taking advantage of the political disintegration of China and the weakness of its central government. The regulatory structure of the British Settlement started with activities of self-regulation delegated by Chinese officials on limited civil matters such as building and repairing bridges, maintaining and cleaning roads, installing fire engines and hiring watchmen.[15] However, in 1854 an Executive Committee was established by foreign residents under the revised Land Regulations. The Committee extended its authority to self-asserted police power and other administrative issues, leading to a transition from delegated civil autonomy to self-asserted administrative power *proper* in nature.[16] However, the revision had never been submitted to the

[13] For a comprehensive and authoritative record, in Chinese, of the International Settlement and French Concession in Shanghai, see [Shi] 史梅定 2001; documentation for the development and practice of the International Settlement can also be found in Feetham 1931.

[14] Its legality was viewed suspiciously even from a western perspective. After careful examination, Johnstone concludes with the observation that the Land Regulations rested on "an indefinite and decidedly vague legal basis." Johnstone 1937, at p. 53. Even the British government was sceptical of the foundational basis of the Shanghai Municipal Council and the legal force of the rules and regulations issued by the SMC. See Memorandum on the International Municipal Government of Shanghai by the British Foreign Office, dated 27 July 1925, in Jarman 2008a, at p. 182.

[15] The Committee on Roads and Jetties, established in 1846, was charged with a limited duty of self-regulation on civil matters that was authorized by the Chinese government in the Land Regulations of 1845.

[16] The revision of Land Regulations in 1854 by ratepayers without seeking consent from the Chinese government was a critical step for the maturing of an "administrative structure". The Executive Committee, replacing the Committee on Roads and Jetties, was later renamed the Shanghai Municipal Council. In the same year, the Municipal Police Force was established. These intrusive institutional reforms were backed up politically by the metropolitan centres of the colo-

Chinese authorities for approval, and therefore the "administrative" authority of the International Settlement fell short of a constitutional basis. Thus the whole structure and authority was developed in practice, with the omission of a clearly chartered mandate.[17] In reality, the assumption of administrative power by the International Settlement was criticized as an encroachment on China's sovereignty and met with constant opposition from the Chinese authorities, businessmen, workers, students, and common Chinese.

In practice, the administration of the International Settlement was run by the Shanghai Municipal Council (SMC).[18] A privileged group of foreign residents, known as ratepayers, was entrusted with the right to elect board members to the SMC. The ratepayers were also authorized to adopt or modify bylaws of the Land Regulations for the International Settlement, although any change required the sanction of the Consular Body in Shanghai and the Diplomatic Body in Beijing. The Chinese were completely deprived of representation on the Council until 1928, when three Chinese members, chosen by the Chinese community through the Chinese Ratepayers' Association, took their seats on the Council. The number of Chinese members increased to five from 1930 onwards with a corresponding increase in the overall size of the Council from nine to fourteen members.[19] The Council performed dual functions, acting as the administrative agency for local ratepayers as well as the channel through which the diplomatic bodies of the Western powers coordinated their policies.[20]

The system of administration in the French Concession was different from the International Settlement, in that the former was solely under the supreme authority of the Consul-General of France in Shanghai. It had a municipal council, but of an advisory nature, consisting of members appointed by the Consul-General. As early as 1912, two Chinese members were appointed to the council. It was observed that, while the International Settlement was more under the influence of British liberalism, the French Concession operated more under the French bureaucratic style.

In practice, the system of extraterritoriality extended from a personal concept to a territorial one when operated in combination with foreign concessions such as in the case of Shanghai. By virtue of extraterritoriality, foreign nationals were exempt not only from the jurisdiction of the Chinese courts but also from the administrative authorities of the Chinese government. The Chinese police were not allowed to operate in the foreign settlements and concessions. Nor were other administrative

nial powers. The revised Land Regulations of 1869 were approved by the diplomatic corps in Beijing and then sent to the Chinese government for the record. In addition, a military force, called the "Shanghai Volunteer Corps", existing between 1853 and 1942, was placed under the Shanghai Municipal Council from 1870.

[17] See Hinder 1944, at pp. 21–23.

[18] Only foreigners who owned property worth 500 taels or more or who paid rent of an equivalent value were eligible to vote, according to the Land Regulations.

[19] Although Chinese residents made up more than 98 % of the local population and were the most important source of tax contribution, only by 1926 did the International Settlement adopt a resolution to allow for Chinese representation.

[20] On this point, see Barnett 1941, at p. 23.

authorities such as tax collectors admitted to the International Settlement.[21] As a consequence, exemption from compliance with Chinese laws was not only applied to foreign nationals personally, but territorially, to the settlement as a whole (to any persons or properties within it). Thus the Chinese authorities were barred from enforcing their own laws against Chinese nationals in the foreign settlements, despite the sovereignty of those localities remaining with the Chinese government, at least nominally.[22] It was exactly on this point that fundamental disagreements arose between the foreign powers and China.

The abrogation of unequal treaties and of extraterritoriality became a perennial obsession and the first priority for successive governments in China after 1919. Upon establishment of the Shanghai Special City by the Nationalist Government in 1927,[23] the whole of Shanghai in terms of administration was divided into three distinct zones: the International Settlement, in practice administered by the Shanghai Municipal Council, the French Concession under the rule of the French Consul-General, and Shanghai Municipality under the City Government of Greater Shanghai, the Republic of China. Each area had its own administrative system. While the foreign powers conceived the two Settlements as being out of the reach of Chinese administration, the Chinese government nevertheless considered the two Settlements as no more than special districts under the Greater Shanghai Municipality. To restore the whole of Shanghai was an important, yet the most sensitive, part of the political project of the Nationalist Government owing to the political, industrial and financial importance of the city.

4.3 Child Labour and the 1923 Factory Regulations Reconsidered

China was a founding member of the ILO in 1919 and was actively engaged in the activities of the ILO until the withdrawal of the Nationalist Government to Taiwan in 1949.[24] As early as 1919 at the inaugural session of the International Labour Conference, the Chinese government was advised by the Commission of Special

---

[21] Tax collection activities in the Settlement by Chinese authorities were prosecuted as a criminal offence. See Kotenev 1927.

[22] It was correctly observed that "the existence of foreign 'Settlements' and 'Concession' in various of her Treaty Ports, operate as a limitation upon her local administrative powers". Willoughby 1922, at p. 52.

[23] Shanghai Special City was established in 1927 by incorporating 17 adjacent counties and towns into its administration. Having ceded from Jiangsu Province, Shanghai was put under direct control of the Nationalist Government as a special administrative area. The Kuomintang Central Executive Committee approved the Provisional Regulations of Shanghai Special City on 7 May 1927. The Shanghai Special City Government was inaugurated on 7 July 1927.

[24] For an account of the three decades of dynamics between the ILO and China 1919–1949, see generally Chen 2014; useful information can also be found in Wagner 1938, at pp. 175–200; Porter 1994, at pp. 145–159.

Countries established under Article 405 of the Treaty of Versailles "to adhere to the principle of the protection of labour by factory legislation" and to apply certain regulatory measures on working hours and rest.[25] Yet, due to the underdeveloped stage of industrialization and very limited number of modern factories in China, labour law, as developed by the Western industrialized countries, was not considered suitable for or particularly relevant to China at that time.

In 1923, however, the Provisional Factory Regulations were promulgated by the Beijing government, the very first comprehensive regulation on industrial conditions and labour protection at national level. Very naturally outside observers tended to stress the influence of the ILO on adoption of the Regulations. For example, the *International Labour Review* offered an optimistic reading of the Regulations that "they represent the first direct effect of the work of the Conference in the great Chinese Empire, and signify the first introduction into that country of modern principles of labour protection".[26] The moral influence exercised by the ILO should not be overlooked. However, a close examination of various sources reveals a more complicated and nuanced story. Promulgation of the Regulations by the Chinese government was largely motivated by its desire to resist imperial expansion by the Western powers in Shanghai.

The movement towards outlawing child labour was launched by some Christian organizations in Shanghai from 1921.[27] The child labour problem was already under review by the Young Women's Christian Association of China by the autumn of 1921. Its general sectary, Ms. Agatha Harrison, was particularly active in the promotion and improvement of labour conditions in China. Her efforts had aroused attention from the bourgeois groups in Shanghai and a joint committee of the Women's Club in Shanghai was created with the specific aim of abolishing child labour in Shanghai. Meanwhile, in May 1922 the National Christian Conference was held in Shanghai, where 1200 delegates gathered and recommendations were adopted on regulation of industrial conditions, including the principle of no employment for children under 12 years of age. The National Christian Council established the Commission on Church and Industry, later known as the Industrial Commission, to promote the application of Christian principles to industrial conditions, among its other aims.[28]

[25] See ILC, First Annual Meeting 1920, at p. 231.

[26] Unsigned author 1924, at p. 1009. The Director, Albert Thomas, reported this news to the Governing Body of the ILO with barely concealed excitement: "This Decree is an illustration of the influence which the decisions of the Conference may exercise in a country where social legislation is comparatively new. The Decree is inspired by the Washington Draft Conventions (…) In issuing this Decree, the government has given evidence of its desire to give effect to the proposals made with regard to China by the Commission on Special Countries appointed by the Conference at the Washington Session in 1919." Governing Body of the International Labour Office 1923, at p. 588.

[27] This movement was particularly encouraged by developments in Hong Kong, the latter resulting in approval by the Hong Kong governor of the Ordinance on Industrial Employment of Children on 29 September 1922. For a useful discussion of the involvement of Christian organizations leading to establishment of the Child Labour Commission, see Anderson 1928, at pp. 102–124.

[28] See Porter 1994, at pp. 74–80.

In November 1922, Ms. Harrison approached Mr. H. G. Simms, Chairman of the SMC, and urged the Council to regulate the issue of child labour. The board of the Council met and decided to approach employers for a possible solution. The Employers' Federation and the Cotton Mill Owners' Association of China, both foreign associations, responded to the SMC "that legislation must first come in the first instance from the Chinese".[29] The SMC then also sent letters to the Chinese Chamber of Commerce and the Chinese Cotton Mill Owners' Association.

The response from the Chinese Chamber of Commerce,[30] dated 11 January 1923, signed by its Chairman, H. C. Sung, deserves close attention.

> We fully agree with you that legislation on the part of the Chinese Government is essential to the improvement of the conditions of child labour in factories. In this connection we have the pleasure of drawing your attention to the fact that already two bills have been introduced into the House of Representatives in Peking……

In the letter, Mr. Sung also mentioned that they had dispatched telegrams to the House of Representatives, the Ministry of the Interior and the Ministry of Agriculture and Commerce, urging that immediate steps be taken for the early passage of the bills in question.[31]

On 9 February 1923, the SMC was approached by the joint committee of the Women's Club in Shanghai requesting the Council to regulate the employment of child workers.[32] In the letter, the Council was advised to take necessary steps to ensure abolition of child labour. Specifically it was suggested that the powers of the Health Department under the SMC could be extended to "include the supervision of the factories in matters relating to ventilation, sanitation, and safety".[33] The move, with its strong implication of an unwarranted assumption of more administrative power, really raised the concern of the General Chamber of Commerce.

In March 1923 the Ministry of Agriculture and Commerce in Beijing received a telegram from the General Chamber of Commerce warning that the International Settlement would very likely enact its own factory regulations in Shanghai through its own bylaws. Should such unilateral action be pursued, in the opinion of the Chamber, it would seriously undermine the sovereignty and honour of China. The Ministry was advised to enact a factory law at the central government level as soon as possible.

As of October 1922, the drafting of factory regulations had stayed on the agenda of the Law Revision Committee under the Ministry of Agriculture and Commerce. The initial plan was that the factory regulations would be submitted to the National Parliament for deliberation only at a much later stage. The drafting of factory regulations was not considered an urgent matter and their completion within that session

[29] Full texts of the correspondence can be found in the Municipal Gazette of the Shanghai Municipal Council, 25 Jan 1923.

[30] For a historiographical study of the General Chamber of Commerce, see [Xu] 徐鼎新 and [Qian] 钱小明 1991.

[31] Quoted from Anderson 1928, at pp. 130–131.

[32] See Kotenev 1927, at pp. 108–109.

[33] See Municipal Gazette of the Shanghai Municipal Council, 5 Apr 1923.

was not even contemplated by the Law Revision Committee. However, in response to the warning from the General Chamber of Commerce, at its first meeting on 19 March 1923, the Law Revision Committee decided to finalize the text of the Regulations by 21 March 1923 and to promulgate the Regulations for provisional application before submitting them to the Parliament.[34] By Ministerial Order No. 223 the Regulations were formally promulgated on 29 March 1923,[35] shortly before the SMC announced in the *Municipal Gazette* of 5 April 1923 its intention to appoint a child labour commission. The substance of the Factory Regulations was clearly moulded on the basis of the recommendation of the Commission of Special Countries in 1919 and relevant ILO standards, despite the first accession of China to the ILO Covention (Minimum Wage-Fixing Machinery Convention, No. 26) only in 1930.

The aim of containing foreign expansion can be sensed even from the content of the Regulations. Article 3 of the Factory Regulations sets an age limit for employment in factories for female children under twelve and male children under ten. Article 2 expressly pronounced that foreign factories established on Chinese territory should also be governed by the Regulations. In an official response to an ILO enquiry, in June 1924 the Chinese government unambiguously reiterated its position that the newly promulgated provisional Factory Regulations would of course also apply to all factories in foreign settlements and concessions.[36] In September 1924, the Ministry of Commerce and Agriculture convened an industrial conference, where its constituent Labour Department introduced a resolution regarding enforcement of the Factory Regulations.[37]

The practical effect of the Regulations was limited due to the weakness of the Beijing government. The Regulations contain no provision for enforcement and no penalty is prescribed for their violation. It is noted that the Regulations were not enforced in most of China, not to mention foreign settlements and concessions.[38] Nevertheless, at least one case was reported in the China Year Book (1924–5), namely that the Shanghai Silk Reeling Guild decided to "to forbid the employment of children under twelve" in response to the Regulations.[39]

While probably failing in their legal enforcement, the Regulations did achieve the desired political results. They created a set of standards from which all subsequent debates on protection of child labour or regulation of industrial affairs in the foreign settlements would have to take reference. The enactment hardened into a symbol of affirmation of Chinese sovereignty on labour matters. Even if the legal

[34] [Morning Post] 晨报 1923.

[35] An English translation is provided in Woodhead 1926–7, at pp. 908–910.

[36] [China Office of the International Labour Organisation] 国际劳工组织中国分局编 (guó jì láo gōng zǔ zhī zhōng guó fēn jú biān), 1948, at p. 106.

[37] See Anderson 1928, at p. 21.

[38] The British position was clearly stated as follows: "So far as the British concessions and settlements are concerned, the regulation would be applied by the municipal authorities by means of new bye-laws and inspectors appointed thereunder." Great Britain Foreign Office 1925, at p. 5.

[39] See Woodhead 1924–5, at p. 657.

force stayed mostly on paper,[40] the Regulations had a constraining, delegitimizing, and deterrent effect upon the foreign powers from attempts to extend competing jurisdiction in this important field.

In June 1923 a Child Labour Commission was appointed by the SMC with a mandate to investigate the child labour issue and recommend appropriate regulatory measures to the Council. Members of the Child Labour Commission included, among others, Adelaide M. Anderson, formerly the Principal Lady Inspector of Factories in the UK, and Mayling Soong, who was to marry Chiang Kai-shek four years later.[41] The Commission was instructed by the then Chairman of the Council that in recommending any regulations, the Commission should take the Factory Regulations as a basis with a view to securing uniformity within and without the limits of the foreign Settlement.[42] The constraining effect of the 1923 Provisional Factory Regulations can be clearly detected from the message of the SMC.

On 9 July 1924, the Child Labour Commission submitted its report to the SMC.[43] Employment of children was found to be a pervasive practice in domestic services, apprenticeships, and many industrial factories. As the powers of the Council were limited to those enumerated in the Land Regulations, which did not cover authority over labour protection or industrial regulations, the SMC was advised to seek power to regulate use of child labour by adopting a new by-law.

The SMC acted accordingly. A Special Meeting of Ratepayers was convened on April 15, 1925 to consider several draft by-laws, including the one dealing with regulation of child labour. The legality as well as the desirability of such action was immediately challenged and protested by the Shanghai General Chamber of Commerce and other organizations on the ground that the SMC should simply enforce Chinese factory law in the settlement.[44] The Chinese considered that the action by the Council constituted "an *ultra vires* use of the power vested in it by virtue of the Land Regulations",[45] and "an encroachment upon China's sovereign rights".[46]

Even worse, the SMC at the same meeting tried to introduce other by-laws aiming at increasing wharfage fees and control of the press, so that regulation of child labour was felt by the Chinese to be no more than "a subterfuge to obtain a quorum

[40] It was commented that "the Regulations which marked such a great step forward, marked it on paper only". Wagner 1938, at p. 97.

[41] Ms. Mayling Song was active in the Young Women's Christian Association of China. See e.g., Song 1924.

[42] See Report of Child Labour Commission 1924, Municipal Gazette of the Shanghai Municipal Council, 19 July 1924, at pp. 259–282. A reprint of the Report can also be found in Woodhead 1925–6, and in Papers Respecting Labour Conditions in China 1925, at pp. 113–130.

[43] Municipal Gazette of the Shanghai Municipal Council, 19 July 1924, at pp. 259–282.

[44] See Henry 1927, at p. 32.

[45] Kotenev 1927, at p. 115.

[46] Ibid., at p. 113.

to pass the other amendments to which the Chinese objected".[47] Adelaide Anderson wrote with regret that, in her opinion, if the proposed bylaw on regulation of child labour had not been listed together with other unpopular measures, there would have been a good chance for the bylaw to be accepted.[48]

In the face of strong opposition from the Chinese community, the draft bylaw failed to secure the necessary quorum for its adoption, one third of qualified voters. Only 399 ratepayers, representing 622 votes, were present, falling short by 302 votes. The draft bylaw could not be put to the vote. The British consul in Shanghai tried to revitalize the draft bylaw and another special meeting of ratepayers was called for on 2 June 1925.[49]

On 29 May 1925 the Chinese opposition was again unequivocally stated in the "unanimous opposition of the General Chamber of Commerce of Shanghai and Commercial Bodies to Resolution III to VI submitted to the special meeting of ratepayers by the Shanghai Municipal Council" undersigned by the General Chamber of Commerce and 30 Chinese business organizations. The question was raised by the opposition "if the Shanghai Municipal Council is really guided by humanitarian consideration and at the same time pay due respect to China's sovereign rights, why not enforce the Chinese factory law in the Settlement?"[50] Here the Factory Regulations exerted a delegitimizing effect on the SMC's attempted assumption of regulatory power over industrial affairs. "On political grounds even socially minded Chinese leaders in the Settlement opposed the Council's assumption of control over labour conditions, notwithstanding that the issue was a humane one of preventing the exploitation of children."[51] Shadowed by the incident of May Thirtieth, the second ratepayers meeting again failed to reach the required quorum, although the number of votes represented increased to 725.[52]

A revisit to the Factory Regulations and the context of their enactment shows that concern over the hegemonic expansion of Western powers was thus decisive for the Ministry's issue of the Regulations. As rightly observed, the Regulations were "largely as the result of political agitation by its opponent and the attempts to regulate conditions of child labour in the International Settlement".[53] The Regulations resulted from competition with the colonial powers concerning regulatory authority over industrial conditions and labour protection. They were not made for purely humanitarian considerations or in response to an international request. The labour issue was conceptualized as a political issue rather than an economic or social issue, over which sovereignties compete for regulatory authorities in industrial affairs.

This was the first time that labour protection became a focal point of contestation between the foreign powers and the Chinese government, a prelude for a prolonged

[47] For documentation of the Chinese opposition, see Woodhead 1926–7, at pp. 907–908.

[48] Anderson 1928, at pp. 19–20.

[49] See Porter 1994, at pp. 5–6.

[50] For documentation of the Chinese opposition, see Woodhead 1926–7, at pp. 907–908.

[51] Hinder 1944, at p. 5.

[52] For an analysis of various underlying contributing factors, see Porter 1994, at pp. 111–114.

[53] Wagner 1938, at p. 95.

struggle between them. The Beijing government at that time was too weak to induce any real improvement of labour protection by the enactment of the Factory Regulations. Yet the contestation became more intense with the accession to power of the Nationalist Government, for which labour protection had become an important ideological vocabulary since the 1920s.[54] And the political and ideological competition with the CCP, and its revolutionary programme, made the protection and control of labour an imminent necessity and an urgent task for the Kuomintang.[55]

4.4 Implementing the Factory Law: Disputes over Jurisdiction

Having established itself as the national ruling power, the Kuomintang Party was immediately seized by the need to pledge on labour protection. The break-up with the CCP and suppression of labour activists brought immense pressure upon the Kuomintang Party to find an alternative vocabulary to endorse and promote labour welfare, so as to boost its political legitimacy. This started with the promulgation on 9 June 1928 of the Law Governing the Settlement of Disputes between Employers and Employees (later amended on 17 March 1930 and on 27 September 1932). Then followed the promulgation on 21 October of the Labour Union Law, through which the Kuomintang Party tightened its control over the organization and activities of trade unions. Throughout its period of rule, the Nationalist Government enacted a number of important laws concerning settlement of labour disputes and regulation of trade unions.[56]

The ambition of the Nationalist Government to promote labour protection was most obvious in its enactment of a new Factory Law on 27 December 1929. The Factory Law, consisting of seventy-seven articles as amended on 30 December 1932, deals with a broad range of issues including protection of juvenile and women workers, working time, rest and holidays, wages, allowances and compensation, termination of labour contracts, workers' welfare, factory safety and sanitation, factory council, apprenticeships, and so on. Compared with the Factory Regulations promulgated in 1923, the 1929 Factory Law was characteristically systemic and elaborate. As such the Factory Law is also notorious for its disconnection from actual industrial conditions in China. The Factory Law was initially scheduled to come into force on 1 February 1931, yet its application had to be postponed until 1 August 1931 in view of practical difficulties of implementation.

---

[54] It is however noteworthy that after 1927 the Kuomintang Party turned to a more conservative position towards the labour movement. For a study of the Kuomintang's early labour policy and labour law-making activities up to 1928, see Chan 1929.

[55] This is closely related to the Kuomintang official ideology of the Three Principles of Peoples, namely, nationalism, democracy, and the livelihood of the people.

[56] For the full texts of those laws, in both English and Chinese, see Yuen 1935.

In support of application of the Factory Law, the Factory Inspection Law was promulgated on 10 February 1931 and came into force as of 1 October 1931. On 29 September 1933 the Central Factory Inspection Bureau was established under the Ministry of Industries.[57] In April 1934, the Inspection Bureau issued a Program for the Enforcement of Factory Inspection, which draws a plan of five stages of step-by-step implementation of the Factory Law. The first period of implementation focused on regulation of apprentices, employment of children and women, compensation for industrial injuries or death, and the like.[58] Matters under inspection were considerably moderate compared to the extent of progressiveness and comprehensiveness of the Factory Law. On 13 October 1935 the Ministry of Industries promulgated a series of Health and Safety Regulations under Chapter 8 of the Factory Act, and at the same time declared that stage 2 of the enforcement had begun.[59]

Since implementation of the Factory Law necessarily involved the question of its applicability to foreign settlements in China, it was unavoidably connected with China's larger endeavours to abolish extraterritoriality and unequal treaties. As early as 1919 at the Paris Peace Conference, China formally requested international readjustment including, among other items, "abolition of the consular jurisdiction" and "restoration of foreign concessions and settlements".[60] A relatively sympathetic reception at the Washington Conference was countered by the report of the Commission on Extraterritoriality in China, submitted on 16 September 1926, which provided a rather pessimistic account of the situation of the Chinese legal and judicial system.[61] Limited progress was made, though, notably in restoring customs autonomy to China at the Tariff Conference of 1926, and rendition of the Shanghai Mixed Court back to Chinese authority in 1927.

The continuing existence of extraterritoriality was increasingly resented by political elites, intellectuals, students and common Chinese alike, becoming a source of arousing nationalism and anti-foreign sentiment. As soon as the Kuomintang Party brought about national unification and consolidated its rule, bringing an end to the system of unequal treaties became the party's priority agenda. Upon establishing itself in Nanjing, the Nationalist Government soon approached the treaty powers and urged negotiation for new treaties. In the following years, it spent laborious diplomatic efforts, which yielded only very limited progress.[62]

---

[57] For an overview of the work by the Factory Inspection Bureau, see Djang 1944.

[58] Program for the Enforcement of Factory Inspection, issued by the Central Factory Inspection Bureau and approved by the Ministry of Industries in April 1934. Full version available in Yuen 1935, at pp. 40–47.

[59] See Shanghai Municipal Council 1936, at p. 1.

[60] "Questions for Readjustment Submitted by China to the Peace Conference", a full text with selective appendixes, is reprinted in Chinese Social and Political Sciences Review, 1920, at pp. 116–161; the same reprint is also reproduced in Woodhead 1921–2, at pp. 719–739.

[61] The Commission on Extraterritoriality in China, composed of the representatives of the United States, Great Britain, France, Japan, Belgium, the Netherlands, Italy, Portugal, Spain, Denmark, Sweden, Norway and China, was established in 1926 in pursuance of Resolution V adopted at the Washington Conference 1921. For the full report of the Commission on Extraterritoriality in China, see Report of the Commission on Extraterritoriality in China, Peking, 1926.

[62] At the Washington Conference 1921 China again vigorously demanded abolition of extraterritoriality. An excellent exposure of China's involvement in the Washington Conference can be found

The efforts by the Nationalist Government to implement the Factory Law are better appreciated against its unremitting efforts to abrogate unequal treaties. Enforcement of the Factory Law would be a useful starting point to assert Chinese sovereignty over residual issues in foreign settlements and concessions.[63] The sensitivity of Factory Law enforcement lies in that it would "have an important bearing on the larger political issue of extra-territoriality".[64] Moreover, as regulation of labour significantly affects economic and regulatory cost, a nationwide uniform enforcement of the labour regulations, including in foreign settlements and concessions, was a highly desirable cause. In view of the fact that the Shanghai International Settlement and the French Concession had no power to regulate labour conditions, there was good cause to put the Chinese regulations into effect in the foreign settlements. One Western observer commented that the Factory Law "did, however, serve as a further stick with which to beat the foreign powers over the continued existence of the treaty port system".[65]

It should be noted at the outset that conflicts between the Chinese authorities and the SMC were not confined to implementation of the Factory Law labour regulations, but also occurred in other issues such as tax collection, police powers in extra-settlement roads, educational issues, and so on. For example, the Education Section of the Shanghai City Government disputed with the SMC concerning sovereignty over educational institutions in the International Settlement. After some lengthy negotiation, in 1931 the SMC conceded its recognition of the full sovereignty of the Education Bureau of the Shanghai Municipality over Chinese schools in the settlements.[66] On less political issues, the SMC also showed more flexibility in the application of Chinese law. For example, in April 1931, "the International Settlement reach[ed] an agreement with Chinese Authorities on the enforcement of a banking law in Shanghai".[67]

Indeed, the power of the SMC had been weakened by the rendition of the Mixed Court to China in 1927.[68] Chinese control over the court enabled the Chinese authorities to check and veto actions by the SMC police force against Chinese.[69] In addition, on 20 June 1927, the Chinese government imposed a rent tax on Chinese

---

in Willoughby 1922.

[63] Some Chinese sources offered useful discussion on the implementation of factory regulations and the problem of extraterritoriality. See generally [Cheng] 程海峰 1934; [Chen] 陈宗城 1933; [Zhu] 朱懋澄 1933.

[64] See Wagner 1938, at p. 143.

[65] Porter 1994, at p. xiv.

[66] See Henriot 1993, at p. 197. The concession was motivated by British indifference to Chinese education in the International Settlement. See a dispatch from the British Consul-general Mr. J. F. Brenan respecting Chinese education in the International Settlement dated 12 February 1931, in Jarman 2008c, at pp. 35–38.

[67] Coble 1980, at p. 19.

[68] For a discussion on this point, see Memorandum Respecting the Problem in Shanghai, dated 14 August 1929, authored by J. T. Pratt, in Jarman 2008b, at pp. 388–393. For useful documentation on the practice of the Mixed Court 1864–1924, see Kotenev 1925. For a Western assessment of its performance, see Stephens 1992.

[69] Coble 1980, at p. 40.

landlords in the International Settlement, and as a means of deterrence it announced that the Provisional Court would not hear cases brought by landlords for default of rent if the landlords had failed to pay the tax.[70] It was acknowledged that "the reconquest of Chinese national sovereignty was relatively successful", and in Shanghai itself, the regime of extraterritoriality began to melt as a result of the restrictive interpretation put by the Chinese on the powers of the foreign settlements.[71]

The foreign powers did not extend application of their national labour laws to the International Settlement,[72] irrespective of the general feeling that the colonial powers had responsibilities to do so.[73] Consul-General Barton reported on 18 June 1924 that "the British Factory Acts have not up to the present time been applied by Order-in-Council to China, and there is, so far as I am aware, no Imperial Legislation under which the local British authorities could take jurisdiction with regard to general conditions in British-owned factories in China."[74] Eleanor Hinder, chief of the Industrial Section of the SMC, also confirmed that "the authorities of the countries with extra-territorial rights held in general that the labour codes of their respective countries did not apply in their Shanghai courts".[75] In any case, the Shanghai International Settlement and the French Concession had not been authorized by the Land Regulations to regulate labour conditions. As a result, foreign enterprises in the International Settlement operated in a more or less legal vacuum except for the rules considered beneficial to them.[76]

The Chinese government asserted that the Chinese Factory Law should apply to all factories in China, regardless of whether they were situated in foreign concessions, and irrespective of being owned by foreign or Chinese nationals. As a corollary, the Chinese government asserted that the Chinese authorities were legally entitled to inspect implementation of the Factory Law in all establishments, including those in the International Settlement of Shanghai. The legal grounds of China's claim can be explained in two lines of argument. The first of these, as exposed in the following, focuses on the limits of powers conferred by the Land Regulations and

[70] See ibid., at p. 40; see also Wakeman 1995, at p. 71.

[71] See Bergere 2009, at pp. 167–168.

[72] To the contrary, it is noted that in 1881 the British Government authorized the extraterritorial application of the UK Companies Act of 1862 to China. Joint-stock companies in the International Settlement could be registered with the British Consular Court of Shanghai, and the shareholders were consequently protected by liability limited to the amount of their investment in the company, a system which is contrary to the customary practice in China of unlimited liability for investors. See Bergere 2009, at pp. 75–76.

[73] For example, during preparation of the ILO at the Paris Peace Conference in 1919, the matter of applying labour law to colonies was conceived. The commission responsible for drafting the ILO Constitution was of the opinion that "in the case of colonies which are not fully self-governing, the mother country undertakes the obligation to apply labour conventions to them, unless local conditions render it impossible to apply them either wholly or in part". The Commission on International Labour Legislation 1920, at p. 10. Of course, the status of the International Settlement was fundamentally different from a colony.

[74] Papers Respecting Labour Conditions in China 1925, at p. 18.

[75] Hinder 1944, at p. 9.

[76] See also Porter 1994, at p. xvii.

attributes the residual powers to China based on the principle of sovereignty. According to the terms of the various treaties relating to concessions in China, from that of 8 October 1843 with Great Britain to that of 19 October 1896 with Japan, the powers of the concessionary authorities were limited to municipal administration, and, in certain special cases, police measures. It was thus clear that in all other connections Chinese legislation must be enforced, the concessionary authorities merely confining themselves to seeing that this was done. There was no reason why this rule should not be observed in regard to labour legislation.[77]

The second line of argument is based on the principle of separation of powers. According to this view, the system of extraterritoriality only applied to judicial proceedings. It said nothing about administration. Thus foreigners were subject to administration by the Chinese government including Factory Law implementation.[78]

The Shanghai Municipal Council strongly disapproved of the Chinese position. While the SMC expressed its readiness to implement the principles of the Factory Law in the International Settlement, it firmly opposed its enforcement within the Settlement by any Chinese authorities by insisting on the principle of so called "administrative integrity" of the Settlement.[79] The SMC in fact took active measures to prevent Chinese inspectors from entering factories in the International Settlement.

The scenario of Factory Law implementation was extremely complicated because of the presence of different administrative zones in Shanghai. Six different situations could be distinguished in the case of Shanghai: (1) Chinese factories in the Shanghai Municipality; (2) foreign factories in the Shanghai Municipality; (3) Chinese factories in the International Settlement; (4) foreign factories in the International Settlement; (5) Chinese factories in the French Concession; and (6) foreign factories in the French Concession.[80] Legally speaking, a further distinction should be made between those foreign factories that enjoyed extraterritorial rights, because of the nationality of the owner, and those that did not. In the face of such a complex situation, implementation of the Factory Law would be a doomed fragmentation.

4.5 China's Request for ILO Assistance in Factory Law Implementation

Having anticipated the difficulty of implementing the Factory Inspection Law in foreign settlements, two weeks after its promulgation, the Chinese government approached the International Labour Office for assistance with implementation. In a letter to Albert Thomas, Director of the International Labour Office, dated 26 February 1931, the Chinese Minister of Industry, Mr. Kong, requested the

[77] Henry 1927, at p. 31.

[78] [Chen] 陈宗城 1933, at pp. 85–92.

[79] See Wagner 1938, at p. 158.

[80] See Pone 1932, at pp. 600–601.

International Labour Office to send an expert commission to assist with implementation of the Factory Law and the Factory Inspection Law in China. The Chinese government stated its resolve to fully implement the Factory Law and its plan to establish a factory inspectorate system. The letter openly identified the existence of extraterritoriality as a major obstacle to nationwide implementation of the Factory Law. "As the question of extraterritoriality is not settled, immediate uniform enforcement of the Laws throughout the land would have been faced with difficulties."[81] The Chinese government asked the ILO for "expert opinions and assistance" to clear these obstacles.

As a strategy to seize the ILO with the matter, the Chinese government further sought to align factory law implementation in China with the commitment of the ILO to universal social justice and humanity. Kong stated in the letter: "we are aware that enforcement of our Factory Law and the success of our inspectorate will not only affect Chinese labour, but also the aims and policy of your good Office. It is for the good of our mutual interest…"[82]

The request was hardly a random action by the Chinese government. When Thomas visited China in 1928, Chinese government officials had extensive discussion with him about the extraterritoriality issue in China. The existence of extraterritoriality was criticized as a major obstacle to improvement of labour conditions in China. Chinese officials hoped that the ILO could contribute to a solution of extraterritoriality in China. On several occasions during his visit, Thomas expressed a sympathetic position as to the desire of the Chinese government to enforce labour regulations in foreign settlements and concessions.[83]

Another noteworthy aspect was that the Chinese government specifically expressed its wish to include in the commission Dame Adelaide Anderson, who had earlier served as a member of the Child Labour Commission in Shanghai,[84] and who held a sympathetic view towards labour conditions in China.[85] An examination of the correspondence between Adelaide Anderson and Mr. M. T. Tchou, the then director of the labour department at the Ministry of Industries, showed that Adelaide Anderson had accepted the invitation to advise and assist the Chinese government with its factory law implementation, a plan approved and endorsed by the Minister of Industries himself.[86]

---

[81] Governing Body of the International Labour Office 1931, at p. 381.

[82] Ibid.

[83] Tian 2008, at pp. 101–106.

[84] For a report and self-account of the experience in China concerning labour improvement, see Anderson 1928.

[85] In response to Thomas Tchou concerning the question of foreign settlements, Adelaide Anderson replied: "I am immensely interested in the important question you refer to in the foreign industrial establishments and feel very sure that from my own countrymen we shall obtain ready sympathy and support for uniform, efficient methods of inspection. To win their co-operation we shall have simply to convince them that it is not only being aimed at but practically being secured in Chinese Factories." Letter from Adelaide Anderson to Thomas Tchou, 25 April 1930.

[86] See Letter from Thomas Tchou to Adelaide Anderson, 26 March 1930.

The Chinese request was warmly received by Director Albert Thomas. In his note to the Governing Body, Thomas expressed his understanding towards efforts undertaken by China on social reform and saw that "the Organisation would be failing in its duty if it did not respond to the request". The request from China was interpreted as an opportunity for the ILO to intervene more actively in the social progress of China.[87] However, Thomas was fully aware of the political dimension of the request. Thomas defined the request as a request for "technical collaboration" without being blind to the inevitable political implications of such "technical assistance". "Apart from the technical problems involved, organisation of the inspection service would probably raise certain political difficulties in a country where a not inconsiderable proportion of industrial undertakings were situated on the territory of foreign concessions. It would of course be for the Chinese government to settle any such difficulties by diplomatic means. Probably, however, the technical collaboration of the proposed small Commission would in itself tend to promote a settlement between the Chinese government and the Concessionary Powers on this question."[88] The ILO would engage the political aspect of the issue only from an indirect and measured manner and thus stay focused on the technical aspect.

Having being represented and reduced as a mainly technical matter, the request from the Chinese government was positively received by the Governing Body. The majority of the members regarded the request as a sign of confidence placed in the ILO and an opportunity for the ILO to render service to its member. The Governing Body decided unanimously to accede to the request of the Chinese government.[89]

In the autumn of 1931, the International Labour Office sent Mr. Camille Pone, Chief of the Section of Inspection, and Dame Adelaide Anderson to China to assist with implementation of the Factory Law in China. The whole mission lasted for about two months. Pone and Anderson were received by the Chinese Minister of Industry, Mr. Kong, and other senior officials from the Ministry of Industry and from Shanghai Municipality. During the mission, Pone and Anderson rendered useful technical assistance to China with establishment of a factory inspectorate system. They provided information on the practice of European countries and suggested a gradual enforcement of the Factory Law by three stages.[90]

Pone and Anderson soon realized the Chinese government had counted on them to mediate with the International Settlement and the French Concession in Shanghai to reach a practical solution for uniform application of labour regulations in Shanghai. Pone was also sympathetic to the position of the Chinese government. For him, "it is after all nothing but a practical illustration of the fundamental conception which underlies the constitution of the International Labour Organisation".[91] Being aware of the strong political connotation, he reported, "in any case, we had to

[87] Governing Body of the International Labour Office 1931, at p. 382.

[88] Ibid., at pp. 382–3.

[89] Ibid., at pp. 233–238.

[90] See the report by Pone to the Governing Body of the International Labour Office 1932, at pp. 183–189.

[91] Pone 1932, at pp. 591–604.

preserve the purely technical character of our mission, and avoid any action which might be construed as being of a political character".[92]

Two meetings were thus organized on 3 and 6 November 1931, right before Pone and Anderson's departure on 7 November. In addition to Pone and Anderson, the meeting was also attended by Brigadier General Macnaghten, Chairman of the Municipal Council of the International Settlement of Shanghai; Edgar Koechlin, Consul-General of France; Dr. Zau, Vice-Minister of Industries of China, and several others. During the negotiation all parties showed a commitment to labour protection and support for the work of factory inspection. An agreement on general principles was reached that there should be only one system of labour regulations for all parts of industrial districts of Shanghai and that the regulations should be applied by an inspectorate acting in a uniform way. It was further agreed that all the factory inspectors should be under the supervision of the Chinese government but also report regularly to the authorities of the International Settlement and the French Concession.[93]

However, shortly after the departure of Pone and Anderson for Europe, the Shanghai Municipal Council fundamentally reversed its position and opposed the idea of organizing the inspectorate under Chinese authority. In a letter dated 20 November 1931, Mr. Fessenden, General Secretary of the Shanghai Municipal Council, who attended the previous negotiations, claimed that their position as expressed at the meeting was that all factory inspection in the International Settlement could only be carried out by the Shanghai Municipal Council. Chinese inspectors could only be appointed by and affiliated to the police or sanitation department of Shanghai Municipal Council and acted solely under the instructions and supervision of the directors of the departments.[94]

The sudden change of position took Anderson by surprise. In response to Ms. Eleanor Hinder, who reported the latest news from the SMC, Anderson emphasized that:

> …Mr. Pone and I were assured by Mr. Fessenden and General MacNaghten that it was not a more hopeful line of action now. Because, on the contrary, it was definitely agreed by General Macnaghten and Mr. Fessenden that they would try to obtain the consent of the Council to accepting the visits of Chinese inspectors, paid by the Chinese authority, to the factories in the International Settlement, and that the following reports of these inspectors should be sent to both the Chinese authority, and to the Settlement official responsible for these matters.[95]

Anderson wrote to Pone and tried to repair the situation but to no avail. Pone wrote back in an equally disappointed tone. "I entirely share your view that it is an

[92] Governing Body of the International Labour Office 1932, at p. 183.

[93] See Woodhead 1932, at p. 276; see also Governing Body of the International Labour Office 1932, at pp. 187–188.

[94] Archive of the Shanghai Municipal Council at the Shanghai Archive Library, Numbered U1-6-111, quoted from [Ma] 马长林 2002, at p. 64.

[95] Letter from Adelaide Anderson to Eleanor M. Hinder, 22 January 1932.

absolute contradiction to the arrangement to which they seemed to agree in our presence last year."[96]

4.6 The Work Through the International Labour Conference

As early as 1919 at the first International Labour Conference, special attention was paid to the issue of extraterritoriality in China by the Commission of Special Countries when deliberating on the applicability to China of the Hours of Work (Industry) Convention No. 1. The existence of extraterritoriality was considered an obstacle to China's adoption of international labour standards. The Commission "suggests that the conference should make the necessary representations to the governments concerned (that is, to those governments which at present exercise jurisdiction in these settlements and territories under treaties and engagements with China) to enforce in their territories within China the same restrictions as the Chinese government has accepted; or, in the alternative, to decree that labour legislation adopted by the government of China shall be enforced by that government within those foreign settlements and territories where extraterritorial jurisdiction exists at present".[97] This encouraging statement had invigorated the Chinese government's unremitting efforts to work on the extraterritoriality issue through the ILO. In the years to come China made a series of efforts, domestically and internationally, to seek a solution to the problem but without success.

At the twelfth session of the International Labour Conference in 1929, the Chinese government delegate submitted a draft resolution urging that "States Members whose nationals now enjoy the privileges of extra-territorial jurisdiction or similar privileges in certain other countries should order their nationals to submit themselves and their industrial and commercial undertakings to the administration of the labour laws by the governments of these countries".[98] This was the first time that China started to use the ILO strategically as an international forum to challenge Western imperialism in China. In his speech the Chinese government delegate Thomas Tchou explained the draft resolution very tactically. First, the draft resolution was interpreted only to implement the resolution adopted by the ILO Commission of Special Countries in 1919. What the draft resolution intended was but to give effect to the earlier activities of the ILO itself. The resolution was drafted in light of the humanitarian aims of the ILO. Secondly, Tchou carefully characterized the resolution as a labour issue rather than a political issue. "I am not here to raise any question concerning international politics, but I am here to state before

[96] Letter from Camille Pone to Adelaide Anderson, 1 December 1932.

[97] ILC, First Annual Meeting 1920, at p. 231.

[98] Draft Resolution concerning the application of labour legislation to the nationals of certain States which enjoy the privilege of extra-territorial jurisdiction or similar privileges, see ILC, 1929, at pp. 709–711.

you a serious labour problem; a labour problem concerning more than one nation, in fact a labour problem concerning a large number of nations."[99]

The draft resolution received favourable support from the French and German governmental delegates at a debate during the Conference. However, it was strongly opposed by the Japanese and British governmental delegates, both characterizing it as a political issue. The proposed resolution was considered, from the perspective of the Japanese delegates, as beyond the competence of the International Labour Conference and, in the opinion of the British delegate, beyond his delegated competence.[100] The distinction between the humanitarian and the political was again critical. They were defined antagonistically so as to justify each excluding the other. The characterization of the matter thus involved and decided the distribution or re-distribution of rights, interests and duties among the colonial powers, the colonized, and workers. The characterization itself was a politically contested issue and was ultimately decided through the exercise of political muscle. British opposition at the International Labour Conference was decisive in defeating China's proposal. Many governmental delegates abstained from the vote. The resolution received 57 votes in favour and no objections, yet it failed to achieve the required quorum for its adoption.[101] The Chinese government delegate was deeply disappointed at the result and criticized the International Labour Conference for having stepped backwards from where it stood 10 years earlier.

In the same year, at the thirteenth session of the International Labour Conference (Marine), the issue of extraterritorial rights and privileges was again raised. In a proposed resolution, the Chinese government delegate criticized foreign ships for ignoring Chinese labour regulations and administration by taking advantage of extraterritoriality. China tried to extend the application of Chinese labour regulations to Chinese seamen working on vessels sailing in Chinese territorial waters and inland waterways. In the selection committee, the British and Italian delegates opposed inclusion of the proposal on the ground of its being political rather than social. Much owing to support from Director Albert Thomas in the Selection Committee, the British and Italian delegates softened their opposition.[102] As a compromise, the Chinese delegate revised the proposal and phrased it in more general terms without expressly mentioning China or extraterritoriality.[103] At the plenary meeting, the British and German delegates expressed their support and the resolution was finally adopted by 59 votes to 0.[104] Another proposed resolution from the Chinese employers' delegate, alleging that the extraterritorial rights and privileges

[99] ILC, 1929, at p. 620.

[100] See ILC, 1929, at pp. 619–627.

[101] For a record of the votes, see ibid., at p. 628.

[102] [Ministry of Industry Compilation Committee of the Chinese Labour Yearbook] 实业部中国劳动年鉴编纂委员会 (shí yè bù zhōng guó láo dòng nián jiàn biān zuǎ n wěi yuán huì) 1933, at pp. 13–15.

[103] See Draft Resolution concerning the equitable treatment of seamen, both the original text and revised text, in ILC, 1929, at p. 322.

[104] See ILC, 1929, at p. 232.

of foreign powers had prevented the development of Chinese navigation,[105] was withdrawn after some discussion in the Selection Committee.

In 1933, Chinese government delegates tried to revitalize the 1929 draft resolution.[106] The Chinese government delegate explained the draft to the International Labour Conference as follows:

> In submitting this resolution to the Conference, I should like to say at the outset, in order to avoid any misunderstanding, that I am dealing with the question purely from the labour point of view, which is the only one which concerns us here……These principles are identical to those of the Labour Charter embodied in the Treaty of Peace. We do not ask for any more than this.[107]

The draft resolution was again strongly resisted by the British and Japanese government delegates. With their political campaign, many government and employers' delegates absented themselves from the sitting. The resolution received 63 affirmative votes, yet failed to achieve the required quorum of 76 for its adoption.[108]

In April 1937, the ILO organized the World Textile Conference in Washington to survey problems in the textile industry as a result of over-production. The study report *The World Textile Industry, Economic and Social Problems* compiled by the International Labour Office, included a section on China.[109] Chinese delegates again pointed to the existence of foreign concessions as the reason for low standards of labour protection and appealed for a uniform application of labour regulations in the foreign settlements. This led to a recommendation from the General Committee on Social Problems, which requested the ILO to resume its efforts in bringing about even application of a single set of labour standards in the foreign settlements and in the rest of China.[110] This was the first time that China succeeded in using the labour issue to delegitimize the operation of foreign settlements.

This progress continued with a major success in June 1937 when the International Labour Conference at the twenty-third session passed a resolution entitled "uniformity of the protection of workers in China". The resolution affirmed the fundamental importance of uniform application of labour law to all industrial undertakings "irrespective of whether they are or are not situated in the foreign settlements or whether they do or do not enjoy extraterritoriality", and called for the Governing Body to facilitate an effective solution either by direct agreement between the governments concerned or an international convention.[111]

---

[105] See Draft Resolution concerning modification of the conditions which prevent development of Chinese navigation, in ibid., at p. 323.

[106] For the text of the draft resolution, see ILC, 1933, at p. 509.

[107] Ibid., at p. 199.

[108] See ILC, 1933, at pp. 197–200. The chair of the sitting Italian government delegate Giuseppe De Michelis even resisted taking a record of the vote. At the insistence of some delegates, a vote record was taken on the morning of the second day where 49 votes were recorded in favor. See ibid., at pp. 216–217.

[109] ILO, The World Textile Industry: Economic and Social Problems, 1937.

[110] See Wagner 1938, pp. 193–194.

[111] See ILC, 1937, at pp. 785–786.

The resolution was jointly submitted by Mr. Mertens, the Belgian Workers' Delegate, Mr. Chu, the Chinese Workers' Delegate, Mr. Koizumi, the Japanese Workers' Delegate, and Mr. Sen, the Indian Workers' Delegate. It was presented as a regional initiative from the workers' group. The resolution met with opposition from the employers' adviser of Japan, once again claiming that the question was political rather than economic or social.[112] The Chinese workers' advisor immediately responded by arguing that "the gist of the whole problem lies rather with the social and economic side than otherwise".[113] The Chinese government delegate also concurred on the non-political nature of the resolution. With strong support from various groups, the resolution was adopted by 103 votes to nil. This was the first time that China was able to have the extraterritoriality issue directly addressed by the International Labour Conference in a resolution.

However, the International Labour Conference was not entitled to impose any direct solution on states. What it could and did do in its resolution was to refer the issue to the Governing Body. At the request of the International Labour Conference, the Governing Body discussed the matter at a private sitting. It turned out that no concrete adjustment was made.

In 1937, Harold Butler, the succeeding Director of the International Labour Office, made a trip to Malaya, the Netherlands Indies, Ceylon and India. In the first place he had planned to visit China for a three-week stay to meet government officials, employers, and workers' groups.[114] Mediation on the application of labour law in foreign settlements and concessions was also part of the agenda. The Sino-Japanese war in 1937 prevented the director from discharging the planned visit. Suspension of work on factory inspection in China was regarded as "one of the first casualties of the war".[115]

Various endeavours by China through the ILO yielded very little concrete progress on implementing labour law in foreign settlements or concessions. Yet it was important for China that it had been able to publicly discuss and criticize the extraterritoriality system in China at the International Labour Conference. Public opinion was important. Through the work of the Conference, colonial imperialism, to a limited extent, was resisted and delegitimized. China won some understanding and sympathy at the International Labour Conference, but little more than that.

4.7 De Facto Administration of Labour Issues in Shanghai

As soon as conditions in Shanghai became stabilized after the Sino-Japanese conflict in 1931–1932, the Chinese authorities resumed their pursuit of factory inspection in the International Settlement. Beginning in January 1933, informal meetings

[112] Ibid., at p. 484.

[113] Ibid., at p. 485.

[114] See Porter 1994, at p. 151.

[115] Djang 1944, at p. 292.

were held between the representatives of the SMC and the Bureau of Social Affairs of Greater Shanghai.[116] The Chinese government offered a concession and proposed establishment of a joint factory inspectorate which would have jurisdiction over the whole Shanghai area. The Council opposed China's proposal and denounced it as being "chiefly intent on establishing their right to interfere in the settlement for political reasons quite unconnected with the welfare of labour".[117] The SMC instead proposed establishment of a separate inspectorate for each area, which meant that the International Settlement would revise the by-laws to further expand the scope of SMC administrative authority. Therefore the Chinese government rejected the counter-proposal, re-asserting that authority over factory inspection control wholly and solely rested with the Chinese government.[118]

Yet this time the SMC decided to pursue a unilateral cause on its own. "Since they cannot allow the Chinese authorities to take over the responsibility for factory supervision, they must assume it themselves, and… the only practical way of doing it is to amend bye-law 34 of the Land Regulations so as to bring factories and workshops within the scope of its licensing provisions."[119] The amendment to Bylaw XXXIV was tabled before and adopted by the Special Meeting of Ratepayers on 19 April 1933, which expressly authorized the SMC to regulate industrial conditions in the Settlement through operating a license system for factories and industrial establishments.[120] The amendment was subsequently approved by the Consular Body in Shanghai on May 10 and the Diplomatic Body in Beijing on 9 June. Consequently, the SMC "then felt it had a constitutional right to license factories and, by this means, to enforce certain conditions".[121] The Chinese government immediately protested the aggressive action of the SMC. From the Chinese perspective adoption of the bylaw was in the nature of an ultra vires act that undermined China's sovereignty.[122]

In order to resolve the stalemate, an unofficial meeting of government delegates of the countries concerned took place during the Nineteenth Session of the International Labour Conference in 1935. As the issue of jurisdictional difficulties in implementing the labour law in foreign concessions was raised by the Chinese

[116] See Woodhead 1932, at p. 276.

[117] See dispatch from the British Consul-General Mr. J. F. Brenan dated 1 March 1933, in Jarman, 2008c, at pp. 589–590.

[118] See Wagner 1938, at p. 19; see also Hinder 1944, at pp. 7–8.

[119] See dispatch from the British Consul-General Mr. J. F. Brenan dated 1 March 1933, in Jarman, 2008c, at p. 590.

[120] In commenting on the revision of Bylaw 34, Hinder said "I know this, that nothing will induce this Settlement to give way to its thesis of the administrative integrity within this area: and being a practical person I am ready for negotiations and compromise.... I therefore understood the viewpoint of the YWCA when it published a statement pointing out that the Council's action was a limitation on China's sovereignty." Letter from Eleanor M. Hinder, 20 April 1933.

[121] Hinder 1944, at p. 7. However, the change of the bylaw is considered to be "a pyrrhic victory", as the bylaw could not be enforced by the First Special District Court of Shanghai. See Porter 1994, at pp. 136–137.

[122] See Shanghai Municipal Council 1934, p. 36; also Kotenev 1927, at pp. 113–115.

government at the International Labour Conference, the Director of the International Labour Office offered his good offices in Geneva to meet the government delegates of Great Britain, the United States, Japan, France and Italy.[123] In 1935 the Director of the ILO China Office, Cheng Haifeng, took part in a further exchange of views between the Chinese and foreign authorities in Shanghai. Compromise was at first attempted, yet no concrete result was achieved.[124]

Negotiations then continued between the Shanghai Municipality of China and the Shanghai Municipal Council. A draft agreement was reached between the two parties on 15 June 1936. A factory inspectorate would be established within the SMC, consisting of equal numbers of inspectors nominated by the Chinese authorities and by the Council. The authority of the SMC on industrial regulation would derive from delegation by the Chinese authorities. The inspectorate would apply the Chinese Factory Law and Factory Inspection Law as well as applicable by-laws and regulations of the International Settlement to all factories in the Settlement regardless of nationality.[125] The draft agreement was approved by the Shanghai Municipal Council. But the Consular Body disapproved it, out of concern that the agreement would imply a partial abrogation of extraterritorial privileges.[126] The Consular Body stated that the inspectorate would have no authority over factory interests of foreign nationals enjoying extraterritorial rights. It would only have jurisdiction over factories owned by Chinese and by those foreign nationals who did not enjoy extraterritorial privilege.[127] This proposal reopened all the debates and rendered the whole agreement nonsense. It also brought to an end to whatever endeavours made to solve the matter through diplomatic channels.

At the same time, the SMC had developed its reach to industrial regulation through its licensing system. A licence system had already developed since the establishment of the Settlement to a stage of comprehensive coverage governing various business activities such as bakeries, food shops, hotels, restaurants, markets, entertainment, tailors, teashops, theatres, and wines and spirits, as well as vehicles including boats, motor vehicles, rickshas, and many others, including raising dogs. Often sanitary and health conditions and security conditions were the main requirement for applying for a license from the SMC.[128] With the new bylaw adopted in 1933, the SMC felt on a better footing to regulate industrial conditions.

---

[123] Ibid., at p. 10.

[124] See the speech by Mr. Li Pingheng the Chinese delegate to the Governing Body, Governing Body of the International Labour Office 1937, at p. 43.

[125] For the English text of the draft agreement, see Shanghai Municipal Council 1937, at pp. 1–2; see also Wagner 1938, at pp. 161–162; for the Chinese text, [Draft Agreement Respecting the Implementation of Factory Law in the International Settlement] 上海公共租界内施行工厂法之协定草案 (shàng hǎi gōng gòng zū jiè nèi shī xíng gōng chǎng fǎ zhī xié dìng cǎo àn), see Labour Monthly, 1935, pp. 7–8.

[126] See Shanghai Municipal Council 1937, at p. 2.

[127] See Shanghai Municipal Council 1937, at p. 2.

[128] See Shanghai Municipal Council 1928.

As early as 1932, an industrial section was established under the Secretariat of the SMC. Eleanor Hinder, an Australian, was appointed chief of a small section consisting of four persons. At the beginning, the Industrial Section worked in the field of hygiene and safety promotion.[129] In the field of safety, attention was given to such matters as safety in the generation and use of acetylene, use of hazardous goods, electricity safety, and machine safety. In 1936 the Council adopted rules governing vessels and systems under pressure, and for the registration of boiler yards.[130] In 1937 the invasion by the Japanese army in Shanghai met with tough resistance by the Chinese army, and the hostilities destroyed almost all the industrial enterprises in the Eastern district. When industrial buildings were rebuilt in mostly the Western district of the International Settlement, the Industrial Section took the opportunity to enforce the hygiene and security rules. "In July 1940 licence conditions under Byelaw 35 were instituted as a measure to control the use of celluloid and allied substances."[131] "From July 1941, all enterprises handling hazardous liquids such as alcohol, ether, amyl acetate, etc., also became subject to licence."[132]

Attention was also paid to improving the working conditions of young workers under apprenticeship.[133] Further efforts were made to address the grievances of young girls and boys working in factories under the "contractor system" and usually subject to heavy exploitation by contracting middlemen. In 1938 a small "Child Protection Section" was established by the Council, under the leadership of Eleanor Hinder, concurrently chief of the Industrial Section.[134] In 1939 an experimental programme of protection of young children was tested through using a standard "Young Workers' Employment Contract". Under this contract, employers were required to assume greater responsibility in terms of wages, food, accommodation and other issues for young children in employment.[135]

As for the Shanghai Municipality City Government, its activities were mostly involved in mediation of labour disputes.[136] Third party dispute settlement mechanisms were available, with resort to either the Labour and Capital Mediation Committee, or the Arbitration Committee, or the Bureau of Social Affairs. The two committees were semi-official as they were also appointed by the Shanghai City Government.[137] The efficiency of this mechanism was impressive. As reported by the Bureau of Social Affairs, out of 1491 disputes in 1928–1932, 394 were resolved through mediation by the Conciliation Board and 849 through mediation offered by

[129] See Shanghai Municipal Council 1935, at pp. 1–2, 6–7; see also Shanghai Municipal Council 1936, at pp. 6–9; also Porter 1994, pp. 118–120.

[130] See Shanghai Municipal Council 1937, at p. 8.

[131] Hinder 1944, at p. 38.

[132] Ibid.

[133] See Shanghai Municipal Council 1937, at pp. 11–12.

[134] See Shanghai Municipal Council 1939, at pp. 14–16.

[135] See Porter 1994, at pp. 125–127.

[136] Woodhead 1939, at p. 496.

[137] See Lieu 1936, at pp. 133–135.

the Bureau, in sum accounting for 83.37 % of all disputes.[138] It was also reported that in a labour dispute case in 1938, the First Special District Court of Shanghai applied the Factory Law in reasoning its judgment.[139]

In 1937 after the Japanese military occupation of the Chinese part of Shanghai City, Chinese government institutions had to withdraw from Shanghai. In practice, between 1937 and 1941 the Industrial section started to take over the power vacuum created by the absence of the Bureau of Social Affairs. Following the withdrawal of the City Government of Shanghai, the Industrial Section of the SMC started to become involved in mediation of industrial disputes.[140] While in 1938 only seven labour disputes were referred to the Industrial Section, in 1940 the section mediated 111 disputes.[141] Another important field of work undertaken by the Industrial Section was to continue with compilation of living statistics conducted by the City Government of the Greater Shanghai Bureau of Social Affairs. The statistics were published in the *Municipal Gazette* from October 1938 until 1942.[142]

Meanwhile, regulation of labour issues also involved responsibilities of other departments under the SMC. Useful support came from the Public Health Department on improving hygiene situations. Nevertheless, the Shanghai Municipal Police took a rather passive approach to trade unions. The Shanghai Municipal Police ordered that from 1937 onwards all organizations must be registered. Yet in practice the Police refused to register trade unions and were hostile to any group action by workers.[143]

The expansion of the work of the Industrial Section led to the decision of the Council on 16 October 1940 to upgrade the Industrial Section formerly under the Secretariat by establishing a separate Industrial and Social Division.[144] In April 1941, an Industrial and Social Affairs Committee of the Council was formed. The number of staff grew from four in 1934 to an impressive fifty-five in 1943, with mostly Chinese members on it.[145]

However, since the outbreak of Sino-Japanese war in 1937, the Japanese government aggressively pressed for control over management of the International Settlement. The foreign concessions in Shanghai were eventually occupied by the Japanese on 8 December 1941 as the Pacific War broke out. After that, the SMC gradually faded into an instrument of Japanese imperialism. An illustrative example can be seen from a notice issued by the Council Chamber on 29 October 1942 requiring that "no Association, Organization, Labour Union or Club (other than state organizations) shall operate in the International Settlement unless registered with and licensed by the Shanghai Municipal Council".[146]

---

[138] Ibid., at p. 394.

[139] See Shanghai Municipal Council 1939, at p. 34.

[140] Ibid.

[141] See Porter 1994, at pp. 124–125.

[142] Hinder 1944, at pp. 22–23.

[143] Hinder 1944, at p. 22.

[144] Hinder 1944, at p. 15.

[145] Ibid., at p. 24.

[146] Municipal Gazette of the Shanghai Municipal Council, 30 October 1942.

4.8 Conclusions

When assessing labour law development in Republican China, one can hardly disconnect the development of labour law in China from the political and social context of China's anti-colonial movement or its struggle for national independence in the early twentieth century. As discussed, the first factory regulations emanated from determination to curtail the intrusive expansion of colonial power into industrial regulations. In the Republican context, labour protection was distorted in that it primarily became a matter over which to compete for power and authority between the colonial institutions and the Chinese government.

The ILO played a fundamental role in modelling the development of labour law in Republican China. Much emphasis was also put by the Chinese government on collaboration with the ILO for the purpose of strengthening labour protection. Meanwhile, it is noted that the Nationalist Government also used the ILO for other purposes. The Chinese request for ILO assistance with Factory Law implementation is a prominent example that China used the labour issue to challenge the hegemonic assertion of foreign settlements in Shanghai. On a number of occasions, China tried to use the ILO and its universal commitment to social justice to expose the injustice created by the system of extraterritoriality. The Nationalist Government worked through the ILO and other forums to address the extraterritoriality issue in China. China learned to speak the vocabulary of European humanitarianism and universalism. China captured the social dimension of the problem of extraterritoriality and represented it as a social problem in relation to labour protection. European humanitarianism was used to challenge colonialism and imperialism. The commitment of the ILO to universal social justice created a limited political space for political struggle against colonialism and imperialism. It also tests the possibility and limits how a local, legal-technical approach could positively transform global, political-social contestations into discourse about humanity, equality and social justice. Although China did not make much progress on the problem of extraterritoriality through the ILO, the efforts by the Chinese government did attract greater international attention and delegitimized the system of extraterritoriality in China.

Implementation of the Factory Law of 1929 also presented additional challenges to the Chinese government. In view of the underdeveloped economic situation, the Chinese government could only plan for a five-stage gradual implementation, and had to engage in capacity building of its own, notably by training qualified personnel for factory inspectorates. The protection of labour opened a new dimension through which the Chinese government started to become more involved in the economy of society. The strengthening of labour protection in China was partly a process of modern state building where labour protection was gradually incorporated into the political life of the state.

References

Literature

Anderson, Adelaide Mary. 1928. *Humanity and labour in China*. London: Student Christian Movement.

Barnett, Robert W. 1941. *Economic Shanghai: Hostage to politics*. New York: Institute of Pacific Relations.

Bergere, Marie-Claire. 2009. *Shanghai: China's gateway to modernity*. Trans. Janet Lloyd. Stanford: Stanford University Press.

Chan, C.S. 1929. Social legislation in China under the Nationalist Government. *International Labour Review* 19: 60–75.

[Chen, Zongchen] 陈宗城. 1933. [Foreign settlements and the problem of implementation of factory law in foreign-owned factories] 租界与外厂之施行工厂法问题 (zū jiè yǔ wài chǎng zhī shī xíng gōng chǎng fǎ wèn tí). [*Oriental Magazine*] 东方杂志 13: 85–92.

Chen, Yifeng. 2014. The international labour organisation and labour governance in China 1919–1949. In *China and ILO fundamental principles and rights at work*, ed. Roger Blanpain, vol. eds. Ulla Liukkunen and Chen Yifeng. Bulletin of Comparative Labour Relations 86: 19–54. Alphen aan den Rijn: Kluwer Law International.

[Cheng, Haifeng] 程海峰. 1934. [Factory inspection in China] 中国工厂检查 (zhōng guó gōng chǎng jiǎn chá). [*Labour Monthly*] 劳工月刊 13: 1–31.

Coble, Parks M. 1980. *The Shanghai capitalists and the Nationalist Government, 1927–1937*. Cambridge, MA: Harvard University Press.

Djang, T.K. 1944. Factory inspection in China. *International Labour Review* 50: 284–299.

Feetham, Richard. 1931. *Report of the Hon. Richard Feetham to the Shanghai Municipal Council*. Shanghai: North-China Daily News and Herald.

Fishel, Wesley R. 1952. *The end of extraterritoriality in China*. Berkeley: University of California Press.

Henriot, Christian. 1993. *Shanghai 1927–1937: Municipal power, locality and modernization*. Trans. Noel Castelino. Berkeley: University of California Press.

Henry, P. 1927. Some aspects of the labour problem in China. *International Labour Review* 15: 24–50.

Hinder, Eleanor M. 1944. *Life and labour in Shanghai: A decade of the labour and social administration in the international settlement*. New York: Institute of Pacific Relations.

Jarman, Robert L. (ed.). 2008a. *Shanghai: Political & economic reports 1842–1943* 14: 1925–1926. Archive Editions.

Jarman, Robert L. (ed.). 2008b. *Shanghai: Political & economic reports 1842–1943* 14: 1928–1930. Archive Editions.

Jarman, Robert L. (ed.). 2008c. *Shanghai: Political & economic reports 1842–1943* 17: 1931–1935. Archive Editions.

Johnstone, William Crane. 1937. *The Shanghai problem*. Stanford: Stanford University Press.

Keeton, G.W. 1969. *The development of extraterritoriality in China*. New York: Howard Fertig.

Kotenev, A.M. 1927. *Shanghai: Its municipality and the Chinese*. Shanghai: North China Daily News & Herald.

Kotenev, A.M. 1925. *Shanghai: Its mixed court and council*. Shanghai: North China Daily News & Herald.

Lieu, D.K. 1936. *The growth and industrialization of Shanghai*. Shanghai: China Institute of Pacific Relations.

[Ma, Changlin] 马长林. 2002. [The struggle over the power of factory inspection in Shanghai – A prolonged contestation in the 1920s] 上海租界内工厂检查权的争夺—20世纪30年代一场旷日持久的交涉 (shàng hǎi zū jiè nèi gōng chǎng jiǎn chá quán de zhēng duó – 20 shì jì 30 nián dài yī chǎng kuàng rì chí jiǔ de jiāo shè). [*Academic Monthly*] 学术月刊 2002(5): 63–70.

Pone, C. 1932. Towards the establishment of a factory inspectorate in China. *International Labour Review* 25: 591–604.

Porter, Robin. 1994. *Industrial reformers in Republican China*. New York: M. E. Sharpe.
Ruskola, Teemu. 2013. *Legal orientalism: China, the United States and modern law*. Cambridge, MA: Harvard University Press.
[Shi, Meiding] 史梅定 ed. 2001. [*Chronicle of settlements in Shanghai*] 上海租界志 (shàng hǎi zū jiè zhì). [Shanghai: Shanghai Academy of Social Sciences Publishing Housc] 上海:上海社会科学院出版.
Stephens, Thomas B. 1992. *Order and discipline in China: The Shanghai mixed court 1911–1927*. Seattle: University of Washington Press.
[Tang, Qihua] 唐启华. 2010. [*Treaty revision campaign of the Beijing Government, 1912–1928: Out of the shadow of the "Abrogation of unequal treaties"*] 被不平等条约遮蔽的北洋修约史 (bèi bù píng děng tiáo yuē zhē bì de běi yáng xiū yuē shǐ), [Beijing: Social Science Academic Press (China)] 北京:社会科学文献出版社.
[Tian, Tong] 田彤. 2008. [The International Labour Organisation and the Nanjing Nationalist Government (1927–1937): From the perspective of improving the relationship between workers and employers] 国际劳工组织与南京国民政府(1927–1937)— 从改善劳资关系角度着眼 (guó jì láo gōng zǔ zhī yǔ nán jīng guó mín zhèng fǔ (1927–1937) — cóng gǎi shàn láo zī guān xì jiǎo dù zhuó yǎn). [*Zhejiang Social Sciences*] 浙江社会科学 2008(1): 101–106.
(Unsigned article). 1924. Labour conditions and labour regulation in China. *International Labour Review* 10: 1005–1028.
Wagner, Augusta. 1938. *Labor legislation in China*. Peking: Yenching University.
Wakeman, Frederic. 1995. *Policing Shanghai 1927–1937*. Berkeley: University of California Press.
Willoughby, Westel W. 1922. *China at the conference: A report*. Baltimore: The Johns Hopkins Press.
Willoughby, Westel W. 1927. *Foreign rights and interests in China*. Baltimore: The Johns Hopkins Press.
Woodhead, H. G. W. (ed.). 1921–2. *The China year book 1921–2*. Tientsin: Tientsin Press, Limited.
Woodhead, H. G. W. (ed.). 1924–5. *The China year book 1924–5*. Tientsin: Tientsin Press, Limited.
Woodhead, H. G. W. (ed.). 1925–6. *The China year book 1925–6*. Tientsin: Tientsin Press, Limited.
Woodhead, H. G. W. (ed.). 1926–7. *The China year book 1926–7*. Tientsin: Tientsin Press Limited.
Woodhead, H.G.W. (ed.). 1929. *Extraterritoriality in China: The case against abolition*. Tientsin: Tientsin Press.
Woodhead, H.G.W. (ed.). 1932. *The China year book 1932*. Shanghai: The North-China Daily News & Herald.
Woodhead, H.G.W. (ed.). 1939. *The China year book 1939*. Shanghai: The North-China Daily News & Herald.
[Xu, Dingxin] 徐鼎新 and [Xiaoming Qian] 钱小明. 1991. [*History of Shanghai general chamber of commerce 1902–1929*] 上海总商会史1902–1929 (shàng hǎi zǒng shāng huì shǐ 1902–1929). [Shanghai Academy of Social Sciences Publishing House] 上海社会科学出版社.
Yuen, Koo Ping (ed.). 1935. *China's labour laws 1929–1935*. Shanghai: The Commercial Press.
[Zhu, Maocheng] 朱懋澄. 1933. [Implementation of factory law and factory inspection] 工厂法的施行与工厂检查 (gōng chǎng fǎ de shī xíng yǔ gōng chǎng jiǎn chá). [*Education and the Public*] 教育与民众 8: 741–748.

Documents and Official Publications

ILO Documents

[China Office of the International Labour Organisation] 国际劳工组织中国分局 (guó jì láo gōng zǔ zhī zhōng guó fēn jú biān). 1948. [*International Labour Organisation and China*] 国际劳工组织与中国 (guó jì láo gōng zǔ zhī yǔ zhōng guó), Shanghai.

Commission on International Labour Legislation. 1920. Report Presented to the Peace Conference Geneva: International Labour Office.
International Labour Office. 1937. *The World textile industry: Economic and social problems*. Geneva: ILO.
Minutes of the 20th Session of the Governing Body of the International Labour Office, Geneva, October 1923.
Minutes of the 52nd Session of the Governing Body of the International Labour Office, Geneva, April 1931.
Minutes of the 56th Session of the Governing Body of the International Labour Office, Geneva, January 1932.
Minutes of the 79th Session of the Governing Body of the International Labour Office, Geneva, May 1937.
Record of proceedings of the International Labour Conference: First Annual Meeting (29 October – November 1919), Washington, DC, USA, 1920.
Record of Proceedings of the International Labour Conference, 12th session, Geneva, 1929.
Record of proceedings of the International Labour Conference, 13th session, Geneva, 1929.
Record of proceedings of the International Labour Conference, 17th session, Geneva, 1933.
Record of proceedings of the International Labour Conference, 23rd session, Geneva, 1937.

Other International Law Sources

Supplementary Treaty of Commerce and Navigation between Japan and China, 8 October 1903.
Treaty of Amity, Commerce, and Navigation between Mexico and China, 14 December 1899.
Treaty of Bogue concluded between the British Empire and China, 8 October 1843.
Treaty of Friendship, Commerce, and Navigation between Peru and China, 26 June 1874.
Treaty between the United Kingdom and China Respecting Commercial Relations, 5 September 1902.
Treaty between the United States and China for the Extension of the Commercial Relations Between Them, 8 October 1903.

Chinese Regulation

[Factory Law] 工厂法 (gōng chǎng fǎ), Nationalist Government, adopted 21 December 1929.
[Factory Inspection Law] 工厂检查法 (gōng chǎng jiǎn chá fǎ), Nationalist Government, adopted 10 February 1931.
[Labour Union Law] 工会法 (gōng huì fǎ), Nationalist Government, adopted and effective 21 October 1929.
[Law Governing the Settlement of Disputes between Employers and Employees] 劳资争议处理法 (láo zī zhēng yì chǔ lǐ fǎ), Nationalist Government, adopted and effective 9 June 1928.
[Provisional Factory Regulations] 暂行工厂通则 (zàn xíng gōng chǎng tōng zé), Ministry of Agriculture and Commerce, Beijing Government, adopted and effective 29 March1923.

Publications of Shanghai Municipal Council

Municipal Gazette of the Shanghai Municipal Council: 25 January 1923; 5 April 1923; 19 July 1924; 30 October 1942.
Shanghai Municipal Council. 1928. *Handbook of licence conditions 1928*. Shanghai: Kelly and Walsh.

Shanghai Municipal Council. 1934. *Report for the year 1933*. Shanghai: Kelly and Walsh.
Shanghai Municipal Council. 1935. *Regulation of industrial conditions, reprinted from the 1934 annual report*. Shanghai: The North-China Daily News & Herald.
Shanghai Municipal Council. 1936. *Regulation of industrial conditions, reprinted from the 1935 annual report*. Shanghai: The North-China Daily News & Herald.
Shanghai Municipal Council. 1937. *Regulation of industrial conditions, reprinted from the 1936 annual report*. Shanghai: The North-China Daily News & Herald.
Shanghai Municipal Council. 1939. *Regulation of industrial conditions, reprinted from the 1938 annual report*. Shanghai: The North-China Daily News & Herald.

Archive

Letter from Adelaide Anderson to Thomas Tchou, dated 25 April 1930. Available in Archive on Adelaide Anderson, with the Women's Library of the London School of Economics and Political Science, under catalogue 7AMA/D/04 "Factory Inspectorate in China – Correspondence 1929–1936".
Letter from Adelaide Anderson to Eleanor M. Hinder, dated 22 January 1932. Available in Archive on Adelaide Anderson, with the Women's Library of the London School of Economics and Political Science, under catalogue 7AMA/D/04 "Factory Inspectorate in China – Correspondence 1929–1936".
Letter from Camille Pone to Adelaide Anderson, dated 1 December 1932. Available in Archive on Adelaide Anderson, with the Women's Library of the London School of Economics and Political Science, under catalogue 7AMA/D/04 "Factory Inspectorate in China – Correspondence 1929–1936".
Letter from Eleanor M. Hinder, dated 20 April 1933. Available in Archive on Adelaide Anderson, with the Women's Library of the London School of Economics and Political Science, under catalogue 7AMA/D/04 "Factory Inspectorate in China – Correspondence 1929–1936".
Letter from Thomas Tchou to Adelaide Anderson, dated 26 March, 1930. Available in Archive on Adelaide Anderson, with the Women's Library of the London School of Economics and Political Science, under catalogue 7AMA/D/04 "Factory Inspectorate in China – Correspondence 1929–1936".

Other Sources

[A Full Story of the Newly Promulgated Provisional Factory Regulations] 新订工厂暂行法规之始末 (xīn dìng gōng chǎng zàn háng fǎ guī zhī shǐ mò). [*Morning Post*] 晨报, 25 March 1923.
Child Labour Commission. 1924. Report of child labour commission 1923. *Municipal Gazette* Vol. XVII, No. 927.19 July 1924.
Chinese Government. 1920. Questions for readjustment submitted by China to the peace conference. *Chinese Social and Political Sciences Review* 5: 116–161.
Commission on Extraterritoriality in China. 1926. *Report of the commission on extraterritoriality in China, Peking, 16 September 1926*. Washington: Government Printing Office.
[Draft Agreement Respecting the Implementation of Factory Law in the International Settlement] 上海公共租界内施行工厂法之协定草案 (shàng hǎi gōng gòng zū jiè nèi shī xíng gōng chǎng fǎ zhī xié dìng cǎo àn). 1935. *Labour Monthly* 5(7): 7–8.
Great Britain Foreign Office. 1925. *Papers respecting labour conditions in China*. London: H.M Stationery Office.

[Ministry of Industry Compilation Committee of the Chinese Labour Yearbook] 实业部中国劳动年鉴编纂委员会 (shí yè bù zhōng guó láo dòng nián jiàn biān zuǎn wěi yuán huì). 1933. [Chinese Labour Yearbook of the Twenty-first Year] 二十一年中国劳动年鉴 (èr shí yī nián zhōng guó láo dòng nián jiàn).

Song, Mayling. 1924. *Industrialism and the Chinese women*, North China Daily News, 14 July 1924.

Chapter 5
Implementation Mechanisms for Chinese Labour Law: Institutions, Practices, and Challenges

Zengyi Xie

5.1 Introduction

China has already established a primary legal framework of labour law. Up to now, it has promulgated and implemented a series of laws on the protection of employees, including the Labour Law,[1] the Labour Contract Law,[2] the Employment Promotion Law,[3] the Law on Occupational Diseases Prevention and Control,[4] the Occupational Safety Law,[5] the Trade Union Law,[6] the Labour Dispute Mediation and Arbitration Law,[7] and the Social Insurance Law (2010).[8] As far as legislation is concerned, a system of laws on the protection of employees has basically been

[1] [Labour Law of the People's Republic of China] 中华人民共和国劳动法 (zhōng huá rén mín gòng hé guó láo dòng fǎ), 1994.

[2] [Labour Contract Law of the People's Republic of China] 中华人民共和国劳动合同法 (zhōng huá rén mín gòng hé guó láo dòng hé tóng fǎ), 2007.

[3] [Employment Promotion Law of the People's Republic of China] 中华人民共和国就业促进法 (zhōng huá rén mín gòng hé guó jiù yè cù jìn fǎ), 2007.

[4] [Occupational Disease Prevention and Control Law of the People's Republic of China] 中华人民共和国职业病防治法 (zhōng huá rén mín gòng hé guó zhí yè bìng fáng zhì fǎ), 2001.

[5] [Occupational Safety Law of the People's Republic of China] 中华人民共和国安全生产法 (zhōng huá rén mín gòng hé guó ān quán shēng chǎn fǎ), 2002.

[6] [Trade Union Law of the People's Republic of China] 中华人民共和国工会法 (zhōng huá rén mín gòng hé guó gōng huì fǎ), 1992.

[7] [Labour Dispute Mediation and Arbitration Law of the People's Republic of China] 中华人民共和国劳动争议调解仲裁法 (zhōng huá rén mín gòng hé guó láo dòng zhēng yì tiáo jiě zhòng cái fǎ), 2007.

[8] [Social Insurance Law of the People's Republic of China] 中华人民共和国社会保险法 (zhōng huá rén mín gòng hé guó shè huì bǎo xiǎn fǎ), 2010.

Z. Xie (✉)
Institute of Law, Chinese Academy of Social Sciences, Beijing, People's Republic of China
e-mail: xiezengyi@cass.org.cn

U. Liukkunen, Y. Chen (eds.), *Fundamental Labour Rights in China — Legal Implementation and Cultural Logic*, Ius Gentium: Comparative Perspectives on Law and Justice 49, DOI 10.1007/978-3-319-23156-3_5

established. In particular, promulgation of the Labour Contract Law, the Labour Dispute Mediation and Arbitration Law and the Employment Promotion Law have strengthened the protection of employees both in terms of substantive rights and in terms of procedures. Most observers agree that employees' rights are extensively increased by the new development in Chinese labour law.[9] Over the course of China's economic and legal reforms, however, it has often been observed that creating a vast body of legislation is far easier than ensuring its effective implementation.[10] In the future, implementation of these laws will be increasingly emphasized, as China continues to construct a legal system for employee protection. At a general level, the overall implementation of Chinese labour law consists of administrative law enforcement mechanisms and judicial procedures. The former mainly includes labour inspection, while the latter mainly includes labour mediation,[11] labour arbitration and labour litigation. To sum up, labour inspection, labour mediation, labour arbitration and labour litigation are the main mechanisms for implementation of Chinese labour law as well as the main systems for resolution of labour disputes. Generally speaking, Chinese labour laws provide for public enforcement by labour authorities and other agencies as well as through private dispute resolution, and expressly authorize a range of civil, administrative, and even criminal penalties for violations of labour laws.[12]

In recent years, with the improvement of legislation, China has further strengthened implementation of labour law. However, the implementation of labour law in China is still unsatisfactory: labour law violations are often found; unified standards are lacking as is coordination between different implementation mechanisms; and the "arbitration before trial" mode of dispute resolution has always been controversial.

Given the nature of the labour relationship and the general disadvantaged status of employees as a group compared with the employer when labour violations or labour disputes happen, the key to the implementation mechanism of labour law is to provide a timely, easy and cheap way through which an employee might obtain a sufficient remedy, and so that disputes between employee and employer could be settled efficiently. This article will carry out a detailed analysis of implementation, the problems this involves and how to improve it.

---

[9] Garcia 2009, at p. 247.

[10] Harper Ho 2009, at p. 37.

[11] In China, mediation may be carried out by various types of organizations, including e.g. specific mediation commissions, arbitration organs and courts.

[12] Harper Ho 2009, at p. 45.

5.2 Labour Inspection

5.2.1 Content and Method of Labour Inspection

Labour inspection functions and the powers of labour administrative departments are provided for by the Labour Law, the Labour Contract Law and other relevant laws and regulations. The Labour Law provided for the first time for labour inspection.[13] The Regulations on Labour Security Supervision, promulgated by the State Council in 2004, contain more detailed provisions on these functions and powers and their exercise, as well as on matters of labour inspection.[14] In addition, the Regulations also provide a procedure for labour inspection, namely by conducting a routine inspection tour, examining written materials submitted by the employer as required, accepting information or complaints and by other means.[15] According to the Regulations, labour inspection is conducted by the labour authorities at the county or city level.[16] The Labour Contract Law further clarifies the wide range of matters covered by labour inspection, including working rules, conclusion and termination of labour contracts, labour dispatch, working hours, rest and vacation, minimum wages, social security, and so on.[17]

In reality, labour inspection plays an important role in labour protection in China. Compared with labour arbitration or litigation, labour inspection has unique advantages: it is a better deterrent against violations by employers because labour administrative organs can exercise coercive State power, and its procedures are speedier, more efficient and cheaper for employees. This is especially important because of the large number of migrant workers in China.[18] Limited by their lack of knowledge and economic capacity, some migrant workers are unable to uphold their own rights through lengthy arbitration or litigation procedures. Thus labour inspection plays a crucial role in protecting migrant workers' lawful rights and interests, especially in helping them obtain payment of their wages in arrears.

---

[13] "The administrative departments of labour under the people's governments at or above the county level shall, in accordance with the law, supervise and inspect the implementation of laws, rules and regulations on labour by the employing unit, and have the power to stop any acts that run counter to laws, rules and regulations on labour and order the rectification thereof." [Labour Law of the People's Republic of China] 中华人民共和国劳动法 (zhōng huá rén mín gòng hé guó láo dòng fǎ), 1994, Article 85.

[14] See [Regulations on Labour and Social Security Supervision] 劳动保障监察条例 (láo dòng bǎo zhàng jiān chá tiáo lì), 2004, Article 11.

[15] Ibid., Article 14.

[16] Ibid., Article 13.

[17] [Labour Contract Law of the People's Republic of China] 中华人民共和国劳动合同法 (zhōng huá rén mín gòng hé guó láo dòng hé tóng fǎ), 2007, Article 74.

[18] In 2012, the total number of migrant workers had reached 262.61 billion, 9.83 million more than the previous year. See [Statistical Communiqué of the People's Republic of China on the Development of Human Resource and Social Security Undertakings in 2012] 2012年度人力资源和社会保障事业发展统计劇报 (2012 nián dù rén lì zī yuán hé shè huì bǎo zhàng shì yè fā zhǎn tǒng jì gōng bào), 2013.

In practice, labour inspection has achieved positive results. For example, in 2012, labour inspection organs throughout the country carried out 2.076 million on-site inspections and 2.131 million written examinations of employers, investigated and dealt with 412,000 cases of violation of labour law, and, through labour inspection, ordered employers to sign labour contracts with 8.055 million employees, and pay a total of 20.08 billion yuan wages or other benefits in arrears to 6.225 million employees, and ordered 125,000 employers to pay 5.22 billion yuan social insurance fees for their employees.[19] Thus it can be seen that labour inspection plays an important role in protecting employees' basic rights.

5.2.2 *Challenges Faced by Labour Inspection*

5.2.2.1 Matters Involving Labour Inspection

As noted above, labour inspection in China has a very broad scope, covering almost all aspects of recruitment and employment. Although a broad coverage of labour inspection is to the advantage of employees, too broad a coverage is not good for effective implementation. This can be seen from the International Labour Organization's (ILO) Labour Inspection Convention No. 81, which provides that: "The functions of the system of Labour inspection shall be: (a) to secure the enforcement of the legal provisions relating to conditions of work and the protection of workers while engaged in their work, such as provisions relating to hours, wages, safety, health, the employment of children and young persons, and other connected matters, in so far as such provisions are enforceable by labour inspectors…".[20] In accordance with that Convention, matters of labour inspection are limited basically to fundamental working conditions and do not include matters such as entering into employment contracts, working rules, termination of employment contracts, and the like. Therefore the scope of labour inspection should not be expanded indefinitely, but should be limited mainly to working hours, wages, safety, health, employment of children and young persons, and other matters relating to the basic human rights and personal interests of employees.

Two main reasons explain why the scope of labour inspection in China should be limited and not too broad. Firstly, because of the limited number of administrative personnel as compared to the number of employers and employees, wide coverage of labour inspection is apparently more than administrative organs can cope with. Secondly, laws in many countries have provided for other procedures through which employees can also settle labour disputes with their employers.[21] Thirdly, some cases are beyond the capacity of the labour administrative agency. For example, in cases of employment termination, both employer and employee are required to

[19] Ibid.

[20] Labour Inspection Convention No. 81, Article 3(1).

[21] [Xie] 谢增毅 2010, at p. 114.

produce evidence so as to determine whether termination of a labour contract is justifiable. In addition, these complicated cases also involve difficult calculation of economic compensation and damages, which are better dealt with by judicial organs than labour administrative organs. Moreover, cases of employment termination are very large in number, whether in China or abroad. Letting labour administrative departments handle these cases would greatly increase their workload. For example, among the labour disputes dealt with by the Labour Dispute Arbitration Commission of Beijing in 2012, 31 % were related to employment termination.[22] Given that, China should appropriately reduce the coverage of labour inspection. For example, cases of termination of labour contracts should not be handled through labour inspection. Other types of case where it is difficult to judge whether the employer has violated the law or not and the remedy to the injured party is complex should not be handled by labour inspectors. These kinds of cases should be handled by arbitration commissions or courts, which offer more formal procedures for disputants.

5.2.2.2 Shortage of Labour Inspection Personnel

At the end of 2012, there were 3,291 labour inspection organs and 25,000 full-time labour inspectors in labour departments at various levels throughout the country.[23] The number of labour inspectors was woefully inadequate compared with the huge numbers of enterprises, individually-owned businesses, and their employees. Statistics show that, by the end of 2013, there were 15.2784 million enterprises and 44.3629 million individually-owned businesses.[24] Overall throughout the country in 2012 there were 767.04 million working persons, including 371.02 million urban employed persons.[25] Therefore the numbers of labour inspection organs and personnel are apparently inadequate.

As a result of the limited numbers of labour inspection organs and personnel, labour inspection in China mainly takes the form of passive inspection, namely inspections carried out upon receipt of a complaint. The number of labour inspections carried out by labour inspection organs at their own initiative is relatively small, which might affect the effectiveness of labour inspection. For example, in 2010, labour inspection organs throughout the country dealt with 384,000 cases of labour law violations, of which 336,000 or 87.5 % were reported and complaint

[22] [First Civil Division of the Higher People's Court of Beijing Municipality] 北京市高级人民法院民一庭, 2013, at pp. 26–27.

[23] See [Statistical Communiqué of the People's Republic of China on the Development of Human Resource and Social Security Undertakings] 年度人力资源和社会保障事业发展统计制报 (nián dù rén lì zī yuán hé shè huì bǎo zhàng shì yè fā zhǎn tǒng jì gōng bào), 2010/2011/2012.

[24] [Development Report on the National Market Entities in 2013] 2013年全国市场主体发展报告 (2013 nián quán guó shì chǎng zhǔ tǐ fā zhǎn bào gào), 2013, at pp. 1–2.

[25] See [Statistical Communiqué of the People's Republic of China on the Development of Human Resource and Social Security Undertakings] 年度人力资源和社会保障事业发展统计制报 (nián dù rén lì zī yuán hé shè huì bǎo zhàng shì yè fā zhǎn tǒng jì gōng bào), 2010/2011/2012.

cases. The percentage in 2011 and 2012 was 91.3 % and 88.8 % respectively.[26] Because of excessive reliance by labour inspection on complaints by employees (about 90 % of cases), some employees whose rights are infringed upon but who are unable or find it difficult to file a complaint – for example, juvenile employees or employees with a low educational level – are often unable to obtain a remedy from labour administrative organs.

5.3 Labour Arbitration

5.3.1 The Origin of Labour Arbitration

According to the Labour Law, where a labour dispute occurs, the parties involved may apply for mediation; either party may also directly apply to a labour dispute arbitration commission for arbitration. A party who is dissatisfied with the arbitration award may file a lawsuit in a court.[27] Therefore labour arbitration is a procedural requisite of labour litigation, in that a party to a labour dispute may not bring a dispute to a court without first going through the arbitration procedure. This is an important feature of the labour dispute resolution mechanism in China and shows the significance of labour arbitration in the country. There is a historical reason for the establishment of a compulsory labour arbitration system. Before the establishment of the market economic system in the early 1990s, China operated a planned economic system under which most enterprises were owned by the state and, consequently, most labour disputes occurred in state-owned enterprises (SOEs). Before promulgation of the Labour Law, provisions on labour disputes were mainly contained in the Interim Provisions on the Settlement of Labour Disputes in State-Owned Enterprises (1987) and the Regulations on the Settlement of Labour Disputes in Enterprises (1993).[28] From these provisions it can be seen that the labour dispute settlement system at that time was mainly applicable to SOEs. Since employees in SOEs were regarded as the "masters" of their enterprises, and labour disputes between SOEs and their employees were different from those between private enterprises and their employees under the market economic system, China had established a labour arbitration system with a heavy administrative colour but a light antagonistic complexion, which was more peaceful and friendly. Later this system was implemented not only in SOEs, but also in all other enterprises.

[26] See ibid.

[27] [Labour Law of the People's Republic of China] 中华人民共和国劳动法 (zhōng huá rén mín gòng hé guó láo dòng fǎ), 1994, Article 79.

[28] [Shi] 史探径 2007, at p. 148.

5.3.2 *Main Characteristics of Labour Arbitration*

In 2007 China adopted the Labour Dispute Mediation and Arbitration Law, which in many respects improved the labour dispute system. The Law expands the scope of labour arbitration and lowers the key barriers to workers' access to formal labour dispute resolution processes.[29] Compared with court procedures, labour arbitration has the following characteristics. Firstly, labour arbitration commissions are tripartite organizations consisting of representatives of labour administrative departments, trade unions and enterprises.[30] Arbitrators are appointed by labour arbitration commissions. Although the arbitrators are independent in handling individual cases, the arbitration commissions, as organs, should follow the guidance of local labour agencies. Secondly, compared with labour litigation, labour arbitration is more convenient and speedy. The deadline to apply for arbitration of a labour dispute is 1 year,[31] which is relatively short. Moreover, generally, an arbitration tribunal must complete the handling of a case within 45 days from the date of acceptance of an application for arbitration,[32] which is also relatively short as compared with litigation. To facilitate the speedy settlement of disputes, a "single ruling" system is applied to some small-claim cases. In those cases, the arbitration award is final and the employer may not bring the dispute to a court after the arbitration.[33] Thirdly, special rules on the burden of proof apply in arbitration cases. The parties have the responsibility to give evidence for their own claims. However, where the evidence relevant to the matter under dispute is kept and controlled by the employer, the employer has to provide that evidence.[34] And fourthly, arbitration of labour disputes is free of charge and the funds for a labour dispute arbitration commission are provided by the government,[35] which is conducive to encouraging employees to uphold their lawful rights through legal procedures.

---

[29] Harper Ho 2009, at p. 77.

[30] [Labour Dispute Mediation and Arbitration Law of the People's Republic of China] 中华人民共和国劳动争议调解仲裁法 (zhōng huá rén mín gòng hé guó láo dòng zhēng yì tiào jiě zhòng cái fǎ), 2007, Articles 18 and 19.

[31] Ibid., Article 27.

[32] Ibid., Article 43.

[33] In order to prevent some employers from engaging in malicious litigation aimed at stalling for time and increasing workers' cost of upholding their rights and interests, the [Labour Dispute Mediation and Arbitration Law of the People's Republic of China] 中华人民共和国劳动争议调解仲裁法 (zhōng huá rén mín gòng hé guó láo dòng zhēng yì tiào jiě zhòng cái fǎ), 2007 provides for a system whereby the arbitral award is final in some small-claims cases. Ibid., Article 47.

[34] Ibid., Article 6.

[35] Ibid., Article 53.

5.3.3 Cases Handled by Labour Arbitration

For various reasons, the number of labour cases had been increasing rapidly during the period before adoption of the Labour Contract Law. According to statistics published by the former Ministry of Labour and Social Security, during the 12 years between 1995 and 2006, the number of labour dispute cases increased by 13.5 times and the number of collective labour dispute cases increased by 5.4 times.[36] In 2007, a total of 350,000 labour dispute cases was accepted by labour arbitration commissions throughout the country.[37] Since 2008, with implementation of the Labour Contract Law and other relevant laws and regulations, a drastic increase has occurred in the number of labour arbitration cases. In 2008, a total of 693,000 labour dispute cases were accepted by labour arbitration commissions at various levels throughout the country, 98.0 % higher than the previous year.[38] In the same year, a total of 286,000 labour dispute cases were accepted by courts, 93.93 % higher than 2007.[39] After 2008, the number of labour arbitration cases gradually stabilized (see Table 5.1).

The statistics in Table 5.1 demonstrate that the total number of labour arbitration cases has been fairly stable since 2009. Statistics also show that labour arbitration plays an important role in reducing the caseload of courts. Take Beijing as an example: in 2012, a total of 20,540 labour dispute cases were accepted by courts of first instance in the municipality,[40] while in the same year a total of 66,463 labour dispute cases were accepted by labour arbitration organs in the same area.[41] The number of court cases was only 31 % of arbitration cases. In 2011, total court cases at first instance numbered 18,054,[42] while a total of 59,465 cases were accepted by labour arbitration organs[43]; the proportion was about 30 %. Accordingly, a rough estimation shows that between two-thirds and 70 % of labour disputes were finally settled through arbitration and only 30 % to one-third of arbitration cases go to the court procedure. This therefore shows that labour dispute resolution in China is institutionalized by the government, with most labour disputes, contractual and statutory,

[36] [Xinhua Net] 新华网, 3 July 2007.

[37] See [Statistical Communiqué of the People's Republic of China on the Development of Human Resource and Social Security Undertakings in 2007] 2007年度人力资源和社会保障事业发展统计制报 (2007 nián dù rén lì zī yuán hé shè huì bǎo zhàng shì yè fā zhǎn tǒng jì gōng bào), 2008.

[38] See [Statistical Communiqué of the People's Republic of China on the Development of Human Resource and Social Security Undertakings in 2008] 2008年度人力资源和社会保障事业发展统计制报 (2008 nián dù rén lì zī yuán hé shè huì bǎo zhàng shì yè fā zhǎn tǒng jì gōng bào), 2009.

[39] [Wang] 王胜俊 2009.

[40] [First Civil Division of the Higher People's Court of Beijing Municipality] 北京市高级人民法院民一庭, 2013, at p. 18.

[41] Ibid., at p. 26.

[42] Ibid., at p. 13.

[43] Ibid., at p. 19.

Table 5.1 Labour dispute cases accepted by labour arbitration organs in China (2009–2012)

Year	Number of totalcases	Number of collective cases
2009	684,000	14,000
2010	601,000	9,000
2011	589,000	7,000
2012	641,000	7,000

See [Statistical Communiqué of the People's Republic of China on the Development of Human Resource and Social Security Undertakings] 年度人力资源和社会保障事业发展统计瞓报 (nián dù rén lì zī yuán hé shè huì bǎo zhàng shì yè fā zhǎn tǒng jì gōng bào), 2009/2010/2011/2012

resolved in the government-provided system, though a significant number of cases still reach and are resolved in the courts.[44]

5.3.4 Challenges Faced by Arbitration

Although labour arbitration organs play an important role in resolving labour disputes, many significant problems exist in these organs themselves. Firstly, although the tripartite principle has been provided for by the Labour Dispute Mediation and Arbitration Law, it is very difficult to implement. In practice, it is very rare for representatives of employees and enterprises to participate in the arbitration of labour disputes and almost all arbitrators come from labour administrative departments.[45] In contrast to labour tribunals or labour courts in the UK and Germany, which are composed of professional judges, representatives of employers and employees, labour arbitration organs in China are still far from "tripartite".[46] Secondly, labour arbitration organs are not professional enough. Almost all arbitrators in arbitration organs at the grassroots level are civil servants, some of whom have not received much legal education or professional training. Moreover, unlike those for judicial personnel, such as lawyers, judges, and prosecutors, the qualification for labour arbitrators is not high: there is no national qualifying examination, nor are there enough training and appraisal mechanisms for labour arbitrators.[47]

---

[44] Brown 2012, at p. 562.

[45] Wang 2013 b, at p. 80.

[46] See [Xie] 谢增毅 2008, at p. 108.

[47] Wang 2013 b, at p. 80.

5.4 Labour Litigation

According to the Labour Dispute Mediation and Arbitration Law, a party to a labour dispute who objects to an arbitral award may bring the dispute to a court for trial. However, there is no specialized labour court in China and labour disputes are tried by ordinary courts. Generally speaking, labour disputes are treated as a type of civil case to which the relevant provisions of the Civil Procedure Law (1991, amended 2012) are applicable.[48] The system whereby the second instance is final also applies to labour dispute cases. Although courts serve as appellate bodies for parties to labour disputes who are not satisfied with arbitral awards, they must carry out a full examination of both issues of fact and issues of law and parties who are dissatisfied with the judgment of the court of first instance may appeal to a court of second instance. In most courts, labour dispute cases are tried by the civil division of the court. In recent years, however, some courts have established a specific labour division to be responsible for the trial of labour dispute cases so as to raise the level of specialization of the trial. For example, by 2011, labour tribunals had been established under the First Intermediate People's Court of Beijing Municipality, the Second Intermediate People's Court of Beijing Municipality, and the people's courts of Fengtai, Daxing, Haidian, Dongcheng, and Chaoyang districts of Beijing Municipality.[49] The number of cases tried by these tribunals has also been growing steadily in recent years. Statistics show that the total number of labour dispute cases tried by courts in the whole country was 286,221 in 2008, 317,072 in 2009, and 327,407 in 2010.[50] From these statistics we can see that a large number of labour dispute cases are tried by courts every year. But overall, as these statistics illustrate, the number of labour dispute cases tried by courts of first and second instance is only about a half of the number of labour dispute cases settled by labour arbitration organs. In recent years, the Supreme People's Court has issued a series of judicial interpretations to explain some of the rules of labour law. Since implementation of the Labour Law, the Supreme People's Court has issued four judicial interpretations of the law, which clarify the meanings of relevant provisions in the law and contain some rules not provided for in the law.[51] Although there has been controversy about

[48] [Civil Procedure Law of the People's Republic of China] 中华人民共和国民事诉讼法 (zhōng huá rén mín gòng hé guó mín shì sù sòng fǎ), 1991 (as revised in 2013).

[49] [First Civil Division of the Higher People's Court of Beijing Municipality] 北京市高级人民法院民一庭, 2011, at p. 26.

[50] [Wang] 王蓓 2012, at p. 85.

[51] [Interpretation of the Supreme People's Court of Several Issues on the Application of Law in the Trial of Labour Dispute Cases] 最高人民法院关于审理劳动争议案件适用法律若干问题的解释 (zuì gāo rén mín fǎ yuàn guān yú shěn lǐ láo dòng zhēng yì àn jiàn shì yòng fǎ lǜ ruò gān wèn tí de jiě shì), 2001; [Second Interpretation of the Supreme People's Court of Several Issues on the Application of Law in the Trial of Labour Dispute Cases] 最高人民法院关于审理劳动争议案件适用法律若干问题的解释(二) (zuì gāo rén mín fǎ yuàn guān yú shěn lǐ láo dòng zhēng yì àn jiàn shì yòng fǎ lǜ ruò gān wèn tí de jiě shì (èr)), 2006; and [Third Interpretation of the Supreme People's Court of Several Issues on the Application of Law in the Trial of Labour Dispute Cases] 最高人民法院关于审理劳动争议案件适用法律若干问题的解释(三) (zuì gāo rén mín fǎ yuàn

the Supreme Court's interpretations, the interpretations in general are helpful for the local courts to apply the rules in handling labour cases.

Currently, labour litigation procedure in China is faced with the following three main challenges. Firstly, labour litigation is generally treated as a type of civil litigation and in practice judges tend to try labour dispute cases according to the thinking and rules of civil law, which can sometimes put employees in a disadvantaged position. Secondly, the procedure for labour litigation is complicated. In labour litigation, there are also two instances of which the second is final. Moreover, in labour cases courts must deal not only with issues of law, but also with issues of fact. In labour dispute cases, parties may have to go through complicated procedures of "one arbitration and two trials", which is not conducive to speedy settlement. Thirdly, because of lack of ability or applicable legal provisions, some courts are not active in accepting certain types of labour dispute cases, such as cases of discrimination in employment. As a result, some victims of labour law violations find it difficult to obtain a remedy from a court.[52]

5.5 Labour Dispute Mediation

Mediation plays an important role in the resolution of labour disputes in China. Firstly, mediation organs or specialized labour dispute mediation organs have been established throughout the country to mediate labour disputes. According to the Labour Dispute Mediation and Arbitration Law, where a labour dispute arises, the parties may apply for mediation to the following mediation organizations: (1) labour dispute mediation commissions within enterprises; (2) people's mediation institutions established at the grass-roots level; and (3) organizations with the function of labour dispute mediation established in towns, townships or neighbourhoods.[53] The number of labour dispute cases settled by mediation organizations (including those settled by arbitration organs through mediation outside the arbitration procedure) was 685,000 in 2010, 726,000 in 2011, and 762,000 in 2012.[54] This shows that the number of labour disputes settled through mediation is larger than the number of cases settled through arbitration.

---

guān yú shěn lǐ láo dòng zhēng yì àn jiàn shì yòng fǎ lǜ ruò gān wèn tí de jiě shì (sān)), 2010; [Fourth Interpretation of the Supreme People's Court on Certain Issues Concerning the Application of Law in the Trial of Labour Dispute Cases] 最高人民法院关于审理劳动争议案件适用法律若干问题的解释(四) (zuì gāo rén mín fǎ yuàn guān yú shěn lǐ láo dòng zhēng yì àn jiàn shì yòng fǎ lǜ ruò gān wèn tí de jiě shì (sì)), 2013.

[52] Xie 2014, at p. 161.

[53] [Labour Dispute Mediation and Arbitration Law of the People's Republic of China] 中华人民共和国劳动争议调解仲裁法 (zhōng huá rén mín gòng hé guó láo dòng zhēng yì tiáo jiě zhòng cái fǎ), 2007, Article 10.

[54] See [Statistical Communiqué of the People's Republic of China on the Development of Human Resource and Social Security Undertakings] 年度人力资源和社会保障事业发展统计赒报 (nián dù rén lì zī yuán hé shè huì bǎo zhàng shì yè fā zhǎn tǒng jì gōng bào), 2010/2011/2012.

Specialized mediation organizations are not the only organizations that mediate labour disputes. Arbitration organs and courts also try their best to settle labour disputes through mediation in labour arbitration or litigation cases. According to the Labour Dispute Mediation and Arbitration Law, before making an arbitration award, a labour arbitration organ must first try to settle the case through mediation.[55] In practice, over one third of the labour dispute cases accepted by arbitration organs have been settled through arbitral mediation in recent years (see Table 5.2).

These figures show that between 35 and 40 % of labour dispute cases accepted by labour arbitration organs are settled through mediation. The percentage is even higher in some areas. For example, among the cases dealt with by labour arbitration organs in Beijing Municipality in 2011 and 2012, the percentages of those settled through mediation were 52.8 %[56] and 51.2 %[57] respectively. Additionally, a large percentage of labour disputes tried by courts are settled through mediation (see Table 5.3).

Table 5.3 demonstrates that about one third of the labour litigation cases tried by courts are settled through mediation. The rate of utilization and the success rate of mediation in settlement of labour disputes are high, and mediation is used extensively in arbitration as well as in courts.[58] This is a very important feature of the Chinese labour dispute resolution system. Therefore, if we add labour dispute cases settled through mediation in the process of arbitration and litigation to those settled

Table 5.2 Percentages of mediation, arbitral award and other means used in cases accepted by arbitration organs (2008–2010)

Year	Mediation (%)	Arbitral award (%)	Other means (%)
2008	35.5	44.1	20.4
2009	36.5	42.2	21.4
2010	39.5	42.0	18.5

Quoted from [Cheng] 程延园 and [Wang] 王甫希 2012, at p. 14

Table 5.3 Number of court cases and cases settled by mediation (2008–2010)

Year	Total cases	Cases settled by mediation	Percentage
2008	286,221	93,368	32.6 %
2009	317,072	105,666	33.3 %
2010	327,407	140,412	42.9 %

[Wang] 王蓓 2012, at p. 87

[55] [Labour Dispute Mediation and Arbitration Law of the People's Republic of China] 中华人民共和国劳动争议调解仲裁法 (zhōng huá rén mín gòng hé guó láo dòng zhēng yì tiào jiě zhòng cái fǎ), 2007, Article 42.

[56] [First Civil Division of the Higher People's Court of Beijing Municipality] 北京市高级人民法院民一庭, 2012, at p. 21.

[57] [First Civil Division of the Higher People's Court of Beijing Municipality] 北京市高级人民法院民一庭, 2013, at p. 26.

[58] Brown 2012, at p. 564.

by specialized mediation organizations, we will find that, among the different dispute resolution mechanisms, mediation is the one that resolves the largest number of labour disputes. This is an important feature of the Chinese labour dispute resolution system, compared with other jurisdictions, and to some extent reflects the Chinese tradition of settling disputes through mediation.

Currently the main problem with labour dispute mediation in China is the building of mediation organs. As for labour dispute mediation commissions within enterprises, according to the Labour Law, establishing such organs is optional rather than compulsory.[59] The new Regulations on Consultation and Mediation for Labour Disputes in Enterprises issued by the Ministry of Human Resources and Social Security contain a further provision, namely that large and middle-sized enterprises should establish mediation commissions, while small and mini enterprises need not have such commissions.[60] Therefore, it is difficult for an employee to obtain a remedy through the internal mediation procedure in small and mini enterprises. As far as township and neighbourhood mediation organizations are concerned, the main problems faced by this kind of mediation organ are weak organization and lack of financial resources.[61] The law does not elaborate on matters such as who should establish these mediation organizations at township level, whether these mediation organizations should be established in every place at township level, whether they are independent or not and how to finance them, and so on.[62] Consequently, mediation commissions at township level vary considerably in different areas in terms of their sponsors, function and funding resources, and so on, which makes it difficult for all mediation commissions to work well. As far as people's mediation commissions are concerned, their level of specialization is relatively low because mediation by these commissions has broad coverage, namely all "civil disputes", including disputes on torts, labour disputes, disputes between neighbours, disputes concerning marriages, housing, contracts, land taking, farming, and so on.[63] Finally, the law

[59] [Labour Law of the People's Republic of China] 中华人民共和国劳动法 (zhōng huá rén mín gòng hé guó láo dòng fǎ), 1994, Article 80.

[60] [Regulations on Consultation and Mediation for Labour Disputes in Enterprises] 企业劳动争议协商调解规定 (qǐ yè láo dòng zhēng yì xié shāng tiáo jiě guī diìng), 2011, Articles 13 and 14.

[61] [Wang] 王蓓 2012, at p. 88.

[62] [Labour Dispute Mediation and Arbitration Law of the People's Republic of China] 中华人民共和国劳动争议调解仲裁法 (zhōng huá rén mín gòng hé guó láo dòng zhēng yì tiáo jiě zhòng cái fǎ), 2007, Article 10.

[63] [Mediation Law of the People's Republic of China] 中华人民共和国仲裁法 (zhōng huá rén mín gòng hé guó zhòng cái fǎ), 2010, Articles 2 and 3. In China, people's mediation commissions are established at the village or community level to provide voluntary and free mediation to parties in civil disputes. This mediation procedure is completely voluntary. As these mediation commissions are widely established at the grass-roots level, a large number of disputes are settled through them. According to the statistics of the Ministry of Justice of PRC, in 2013 people's mediation commissions nationwide accepted 9.40 million disputes and the success rate of mediation was over 90 %. See [General Report of the Work of Justice Administration of 2013] 二〇一三年司法行政工作综述 (2013 nián sī fǎ xíng zhèng gōng zuò zōng shù), 2014.

does not have a clear standard on the qualification of mediators[64]; consequently, many of them are not professional enough, whereas labour disputes are ever more complex.

5.6 Challenges and Debates

5.6.1 Lack of Unity of and Coordination Between Different Dispute Resolution Mechanisms

The foregoing analysis illustrates that China has established various mechanisms for implementation of the labour law and for resolution of disputes, including labour inspection, mediation, arbitration and litigation, thereby providing parties to labour disputes with many different ways of resolving them. These mechanisms make it more convenient for parties to labour disputes to settle them by providing alternative dispute resolution methods. But, on the other hand, they also involve problems. Firstly, parties to some labour disputes may have to go through lengthy and complicated dispute resolution procedures (see Fig. 5.1).

These complicated and lengthy procedures are contrary to the purpose of establishing multiple dispute resolution mechanisms, namely to resolve disputes in a simple and speedy way. In particular, some employers may try to use complicated

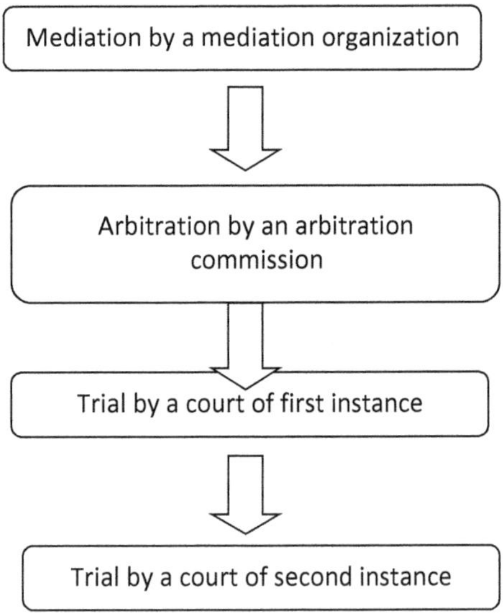

Fig. 5.1 Complete procedures for labour disputes (The procedures here are the possible complete procedures. This does not mean that every case has to go through all procedures)

[64] [Labour Dispute Mediation and Arbitration Law of the People's Republic of China] 中华人民共和国劳动争议调解仲裁法 (zhōng huá rén mín gòng hé guó láo dòng zhēng yì tiáo jiě zhòng cái fǎ), 2007, Article 11.

judicial procedures maliciously to harm the interests of employees. Secondly, different dispute resolution mechanisms may lead to different results. For example, disputes over labour remuneration, overtime pay or other financial compensation provided for in Article 85 of the Labour Contract Law can be settled not only through labour inspection procedures of labour administrative organs but also through labour arbitration or litigation procedures. However, an employee may be awarded different amounts of economic compensation or damages for the same dispute if choosing to settle the dispute through arbitration or administrative procedures.[65] And thirdly, there are overlaps between different procedures. For example, if a party to a labour arbitration case refuses to accept the arbitral award and brings the dispute to court, the court must re-examine both issues of fact and issues of law in the case. As a result, issues of fact and law in the same case may go through three different judicial procedures, which is a waste of judicial resources to some extent.

5.6.2 *Imperfection of the Collective Dispute Resolution System*

Currently, the majority of labour dispute cases in China are individual dispute cases. Collective labour dispute cases are in fact very few, while many so-called "collective labour dispute" cases are in essence "individual labour disputes" that involve many individuals, rather than genuine collective labour disputes resulting from the establishment of trade unions or the conclusion or implementation of collective agreements. Consequently, the procedure for dealing with collective labour disputes in China is relatively simple. According to the Labour Law, disputes resulting from implementation of collective contracts may be settled through arbitration or litigation. The unions can bring disputes to arbitration commissions or the courts as plaintiffs.[66] As for disputes resulting from conclusion of collective agreements, the Labour Law only provides that they "shall be handled through consultation by all the parties concerned brought together by the labour administrative department of a local government".[67] It does not elaborate on such issues as who the parties concerned are, how labour administrative departments should coordinate the consultation, and what procedures the consultation should follow. Therefore, the collective labour dispute resolution mechanism should become the focus of future reform of the labour dispute resolution mechanism in China.

[65] [Xie] 谢增毅 2011, at p. 191.

[66] [Trade Union Law of the People's Republic of China] 中华人民共和国工会法 (zhōng huá rén mín gòng hé guó gōng huì fǎ), 1992 (as revised in 2001), Article 20.

[67] [Labour Law of the People's Republic of China] 中华人民共和国劳动法 (zhōng huá rén mín gòng hé guó láo dòng fǎ), 1994, Article 84.

5.6.3 The Debate over the "One Arbitration and Two Trials" Mode

In China, the compulsory arbitration mode, or the "one arbitration and two trials" mode, for resolving labour disputes has always been controversial. The issue was heatedly debated during formulation of the Labour Dispute Mediation and Arbitration Law in 2007. The main argument against this mode is that, compared with ordinary civil procedures, which consist only of court procedure, the current labour dispute resolution mode, which consists of both arbitration and litigation, has too many links in the handling of cases and consequently prevents victims from obtaining a remedy in a timely manner. Therefore, critics of this mode call for abolition of the arbitration procedure, or adoption of an "either arbitration or trial" mode.[68] The debate continues to this day. Even now, some scholars oppose the "one arbitration and two trials" system and advocate abolition of the compulsory arbitration procedure before litigation. They maintain that there is no legal or jurisprudential basis for making labour arbitration a pre-procedure for labour litigation and the State should respect the autonomy of will of the parties to labour disputes and establish a judicial labour dispute settlement mechanism of "either arbitration or litigation and separation of trial from arbitration, with both being final".[69] A similar opinion is that the "one arbitration and two trials" mode runs counter to the principles of the economics of law and that China should restructure the labour dispute settlement system, abolish the "one arbitration and two trials" mode, and replace it with the "either arbitration or trial" mode.[70] Others hold that China should adopt the internationally accepted dual structure doctrine that distinguishes between disputes over interests and disputes over rights. The latter should be mediated or arbitrated by non-governmental mediation or arbitration organs, or tried by courts. With respect to disputes over interests, these should be dealt with by a tripartite negotiation mechanism that has the competence to make final decisions.[71]

The debate over the labour dispute resolution mode is centred on questions of how to understand the special nature of labour disputes and whether it is necessary to establish a special labour dispute resolution system which differs from ordinary civil disputes. As labour disputes have unique characteristics, it could be argued that a special dispute resolution mechanism should be established outside the ordinary civil dispute resolution procedure. Four main reasons favour this position.

Firstly, settling labour disputes through non-judicial procedures is conducive to reducing antagonism between employers and employees and maintaining a good labour relationship. The labour relationship is different from the ordinary civil law relationship and maintaining a good relationship of cooperation between employee and employer is of great importance. Bringing disputes directly to a court will easily

[68] See [Xie] 谢增毅 2008, at p. 104.
[69] [Qin] 秦国荣 2010, at p. 142.
[70] [Wang] 王蓓 2013a, at p. 120.
[71] [Zheng] 郑祝君 2012, at p. 94.

harm a friendly relationship and may intensify antagonism between employee and employer.

Secondly, a special dispute settlement mechanism could, to a certain degree, reduce the imbalance of strength and status between employer and employee in the labour relationship. During a labour dispute, the employee is often unable to carry out their normal work and is therefore faced with loss of wages, social insurance and other benefits, whereas losses suffered by the employer from the dispute are relatively small in most cases. Therefore, establishing free mediation services or summary arbitration procedures can speed up settlement of labour disputes, thereby reducing economic losses and improving the disadvantaged position of employees in the litigation procedure.

Thirdly, establishing special labour tribunals or other labour dispute resolution mechanisms reduces the caseload of courts. Since the labour relationship is a kind of extensive social relationship involving a large number of employees, the number of labour disputes is huge. Bringing all labour disputes directly to courts is not only to the disadvantage of employees, but also more than courts can handle. Fourthly, establishing a special labour dispute resolution mechanism is conducive to increasing the specialization of judges, arbitrators, and mediators.[72]

These four considerations suggest that establishment of a special labour dispute resolution system is necessary. The main approach to and basic principle for establishing a labour dispute resolution system in China should be to enable as many labour dispute cases as possible to be settled through low-cost and speedy mechanisms so as to prevent them from being brought directly to court. In that light, the "either arbitration or trial" mode proposed by some scholars is not an ideal one and the current system of "one arbitration and two trials" should be maintained rather than abolished. After over 20 years of implementation in practice, this system has already been widely accepted by society, is able to give full play to the role of mediation and arbitration, and allows parties to labour disputes to settle their disputes in a relatively amicable atmosphere, thereby reducing labour litigation.[73] Therefore, the current mode of "one arbitration and two trials" can be retained, but needs to be further reformed and improved

To reduce complexity and overlap, court procedure in the system may be reformed and streamlined in the future. A party to a labour arbitration case who is not satisfied with the arbitral award may be allowed to appeal the case to a court, but is allowed only to bring issues of law, not issues of fact, in the case to the court. Moreover, in courts, only labour cases involving important legal issues may be appealed to a higher-level court. Such a mechanism would uphold the litigation right of parties to labour disputes while, at the same time, avoiding lengthy procedures, thereby facilitating the timely conclusion of cases. As for cases of collective labour disputes, especially those involving disputes over interests, these are better settled through mediation procedures, rather than court procedures, which is also a common practice in many jurisdictions.

---

[72] See [Xie] 谢增毅 2008, at p. 98.

[73] [Xin] 信春鹰 2008, at pp. 16–17.

5.7 Conclusions

China has already established mechanisms for implementing the labour laws, namely an administrative law enforcement and labour dispute resolution approach consisting of labour inspection, mediation, arbitration and litigation. The key element and main objective of this system is to provide an easy, quick and cheap way through which the employee can easily obtain a remedy in a timely manner and disputes between employee and employer can be settled efficiently. In addition, in such procedures the government plays an important role. Except for court procedure, which is a judicial procedure, the government plays a leading role in other procedures, acting as a supervisor in labour inspection and basically sponsoring procedures for mediation and arbitration. This shows the government as a key player in the implementation mechanism for labour laws in China. As labour laws and regulations become ever more complex in China, the capacity of the relevant authorities and organizations is becoming increasingly important.

For historical and practical reasons, this system has some unique characteristics. Mediation, which plays a unique role in resolution of labour disputes, settles the largest number of labour disputes in the country. The system of "one arbitration and two trials" basically accords with the nature and demands of the labour dispute resolution mechanism and should be maintained and improved. In the future, court procedures for the trial of labour dispute cases need to be streamlined so as to facilitate the speedy resolution of disputes. This is of course not easy, but should be the direction of future reforms. Labour inspection is an important way of upholding employees' rights and interests and rectifying the unlawful behaviour of employers. But the scope of labour inspection needs to be narrowed and personnel should be strengthened both in numbers and training; additionally, labour inspection should be further coordinated with labour arbitration and litigation. Actually, private and public enforcement mechanisms will be most effective when they complement and reinforce each other.[74]

Currently, legislation for resolution of labour disputes mainly focuses on individual labour disputes while the procedure for resolution of collective labour disputes is relatively weak. Therefore, improving the procedure for resolution of collective labour disputes should become the focus of future reform of the system. Improvement of the collective labour dispute settlement system is a relatively long process that depends on strengthening the role of trade unions in labour protection and improving the collective bargaining system.

[74] Harper Ho 2009. at p.106.

References

Literature

Brown, Ronald C. 2012. Comparative alternative dispute resolution for individual labour disputes in Japan, China and the United States: Lessons from Asia? *St. John's Law Review* 86: 543–577.

[Cheng, Yanyuan] 程延园 and [Puxi Wang] 王甫希. 2012. [Labour relations in transition: Characteristics and trend of development of labour disputes in China] 变革中的劳动关系研究:中国劳动争议的特点与趋势 (biàn gé zhōng de láo dòng guān xì yán jiū: zhōng guó láo dòng zhēng yì de tè diǎn yǔ qū shì). [*Economic Theory and Business Management*] 经济理论与经济管理 8: 5–19.

Garcia, Monique. 2009. China's labour law evolution: Towards a new frontier. *ILSA of International and Comparative Law* 16: 235–256.

Harper Ho, Virginia E. 2009. From contracts to compliance? An early look at implementation under China's new labour legislation. *Columbia Journal of Asian Law* 23: 34–107.

[Qin, Guorong] 秦国荣. 2010. [Choice of legal mechanism of Chinese labour dispute resolution] 劳动争议解决的法律机制研究 (láo dòng zhēng yì jiě jué de fǎ lǜ jī zhì yán jiū) [*Jianghai Academic Journal*] 江海学刊 3: 142–148.

[Shi, Tanjing] 史探径. 2007. [*Social law*] 社会法 (shè huì fǎ). Beijing: [China Labour and Social Security Press] 中国劳动社会保障出版社.

[Wang, Shengjun] 王胜俊. 2009. *Report on the work of the Supreme People's Court in 2008.* Available at: http://www.gov.cn/test/2009-03/17/content_1261386.htm. Last accessed 19 June 2015).

[Wang, Bei] 王蓓. 2012. [Mediation of labour disputes: Empirical analysis and reform proposals] 劳动争议调解:实证分析与改革建言 (láo dòng zhēng yì tiáo jiě: shí zhèng fèn xī yǔ gǎi gé jiàn yán). [*Social Science Research*] 社会科学研究 6: 84–89.

[Wang, Bei] 王蓓. 2013a. [Reconstructing the individual labour disputes resolution mechanism by the "Either Trial or Arbitration" mode] 以"或审或裁"模式重构个别劳动争议处理机制 (yǐ "huò shěn huò cái" mó shì zhòng gòu gè bié láo dòng zhēng yì chù lǐ jī zhì) [*Legal Science*] 法学 4: 120-127.

[Wang, Bei] 王蓓. 2013b. [On the defects and improvement of China's labor dispute arbitration system] 我国劳动争议仲裁制度的缺陷与完善 (wǒ guó láo dòng zhēng yì zhòng cái zhì dù de quē xiàn yǔ wán shàn). [*Journal of Hebei University (Philosophy and Social Science)*] 河北大学学报 (哲学社会科学版) 3: 75–82.

[Xie, Zengyi] 谢增毅. 2008. [Settlement of labour disputes in China: Doctrines, institutions and challenges] 我国劳动争议处理的理念、制度与挑战 (wǒ guó láo dòng zhēng yì chǔ lǐ de lǐ niàn, zhì dù yǔ tiǎo zhàn). [*CASS Journal of Law*] 法学研究 5: 97–108.

[Xie, Zengyi] 谢增毅. 2010. [Studies on the power of labour administrative organs to order employers to undertake civil responsibilities] 劳动行政机关责令用人单位承担民事责任研究 (láo dòng xíng zhèng jī guān zé lìng yòng rén dān wèi chéng dān mín shì zé rèn yán jiū). [*Contemporary Law Review*] 当代法学 3: 111–117.

[Xie, Zengyi] 谢增毅. 2011. [*Labour law: comparison and reflections*] 劳动法的比较与反思 (láo dòng fǎ de bǐ jiào yǔ fǎn sī). Beijing: [Social Sciences Academic Press] 社会科学文献出版社.

Xie, Zengyi. 2014. New developments in anti-discrimination in the workplace in China: law and practice. In *China and ILO fundamental principles and rights at work*, ed. Roger Blanpain, vol. eds. Ulla Liukkunen and Chen Yifeng. Bulletin of Comparative Labour Relations 86: 143–162. Alphen aan den Rijn: Kluwer Law International.

[Xin, Chunying] 信春鹰 ed. 2008. [*An interpretation of the Labour Dispute Mediation and Arbitration Law of the People's Republic of China*] 中华人民共和国劳动争议调解仲裁法释义 (zhōng huá rén mín gòng hé guó láo dòng zhēng yì tiáo jiě zhòng cái fǎ shì yì). Beijing: [Law Press China] 法律出版社.

[Zheng, Zhujun] 郑祝君. 2012. [The dual structure of labour disputes and the reconstruction of the labour dispute resolution system in China] 我国劳动争议的二元结构与我国劳动争议处理制度的重构 (wǒ guó láo dòng zhēng yì de èr yuán jié gòu yǔ wǒ guó láo dòng zhēng yì chǔ lǐ zhì dù de chóng gòu). [*Legal Science*] 法学 1: 94–103.

Documents and Official Publications

ILO Documents

Convention concerning Labour Inspection in Industry and Commerce, adopted 11 July 1947, ILO C081. Entry into force 7 April 1950. (Labour Inspection Convention).

Chinese Regulation

Laws by the National People's Congress

[Civil Procedure Law of the People's Republic of China] 中华人民共和国民事诉讼法 (zhōng huá rén mín gòng hé guó mín shì sù sòng fǎ), National People's Congress, adopted and effective 9 April 1991. Revised and effective 31 August 2012.

[Trade Union Law of the People's Republic of China] 中华人民共和国工会法 (zhōng huá rén mín gòng hé guó gōng huì fǎ), National People's Congress, adopted and effective 3 April 1992. Revised and effective 27 October 2001.

Laws by the Standing Committee of the National People's Congress

[Arbitration Law of the People's Republic of China] 中华人民共和国仲裁法 (zhōng huá rén mín gòng hé guó zhòng cái fǎ), Standing Committee of the National People's Congress, adopted 31 August 1994, effective 1 September 1995.

[Employment Promotion Law of the People's Republic of China] 中华人民共和国就业促进法 (zhōng huá rén mín gòng hé guó jiù yè cù jìn fǎ), Standing Committee of the National People's Congress, adopted 30 August 2007, effective 1 January 2008. Revised and effective 24 April 2015.

[Labour Contract Law of the People's Republic of China] 中华人民共和国劳动合同法 (zhōng huá rén mín gòng hé guó láo dòng hé tóng fǎ), Standing Committee of the National People's Congress, adopted 29 June 2007, effective 1 January 2008. Revised 28 December 2012, effective 1 July 2013.

[Labour Law of the People's Republic of China] 中华人民共和国劳动法 (zhōng huá rén mín gòng hé guó láo dòng fǎ), Standing Committee of the National People's Congress, adopted 5 July 1994, effective 1 January 1995.

[Labour Dispute Mediation and Arbitration Law of the People's Republic of China] 中华人民共和国劳动争议调解仲裁法 (zhōng huá rén mín gòng hé guó láo dòng zhēng yì tiáo jiě zhòng cái fǎ), Standing Committee of the National People's Congress, adopted 29 December 2007, effective 1 May 2008.

[Occupational Disease Prevention and Control Law of the People's Republic of China] 中华人民共和国职业病防治法 (zhōng huá rén mín gòng hé guó zhí yè bìng fáng zhì fǎ), Standing Committee of the National People's Congress, adopted 27 October 2001, effective 1 May 2002. Revised and effective 31 December 2011.

[Occupational Safety Law of the People's Republic of China] 中华人民共和国安全生产法 (zhōng huá rén mín gòng hé guó ān quán shēng chǎn fǎ), Standing Committee of the National People's Congress, adopted 29 June 2002, effective 1 November 2002. Revised 31 August 2014, effective 1 December 2014.

[Social Insurance Law of the People's Republic of China] 中华人民共和国社会保险法 (zhōng huá rén mín gòng hé guó shè huì bǎo xiǎn fǎ), Standing Committee of the National People's Congress, adopted 28 October 2010, effective 1 July 2011.

Regulations by the State Council

[Regulations on Labour and Social Security Supervision] 劳动保障监察条例 (láo dòng bǎo zhàng jiān chá tiáo lì), State Council, adopted 26 October 2004, effective 1 November 2004.

Administrative Regulations

[Regulations on Consultation and Mediation for Labour Disputes in Enterprises] 企业劳动争议协商调解规定 (qǐ yè láo dòng zhēng yì xié shāng tiáo jiě guī dìng), Ministry of Human Resources and Social Security, adopted 30 November 2011, effective 1 January 2012.

Other Chinese Official Documents

[Interpretation of the Supreme People's Court of Several Issues on the Application of Law in the Trial of Labour Dispute Cases] 最高人民法院关于审理劳动争议案件适用法律若干问题的解释 (zuì gāo rén mín fǎ yuàn guān yú shěn lǐ láo dòng zhēng yì àn jiàn shì yòng fǎ lǜ ruò gān wèn tí de jiě shì), adopted 22 March 2001, effective 30 April 2001.

[Second Interpretation of the Supreme People's Court of Several Issues on the Application of Law in the Trial of Labour Dispute Cases] 最高人民法院关于审理劳动争议案件适用法律若干问题的解释(二) (zuì gāo rén mín fǎ yuàn guān yú shěn lǐ láo dòng zhēng yì àn jiàn shì yòng fǎ lǜ ruò gān wèn tí de jiě shì (èr)), adopted 10 July 2006, effective 1 October 2006.

[Third Interpretation of the Supreme People's Court of Several Issues on the Application of Law in the Trial of Labour Dispute Cases] 最高人民法院关于审理劳动争议案件适用法律若干问题的解释(三) (zuì gāo rén mín fǎ yuàn guān yú shěn lǐ láo dòng zhēng yì àn jiàn shì yòng fǎ lǜ ruò gān wèn tí de jiě shì (sān)), adopted 12 July 2010, effective 14 September 2010.

[Fourth Interpretation of the Supreme People's Court on Certain Issues Concerning the Application of Law in the Trial of Labour Dispute Cases] 最高人民法院关于审理劳动争议案件适用法律若干问题的解释(四) (zuì gāo rén mín fǎ yuàn guān yú shěn lǐ láo dòng zhēng yì àn jiàn shì yòng fǎ lǜ ruò gān wèn tí de jiě shì (sì)), adopted 31 December 2012, effective 1 February 2013.

Other Sources

[Development Report on the National Market Entities in 2013] 2013年全国市场主体发展报告 (2013 nián quán guó shì chǎng zhǔ tǐ fā zhǎn bào gào). 2014. [State Administration for Industry and Commerce] 国家工商行政管理总局. Available at: http://www.saic.gov.cn/zwgk/tjzl/zhtj/bgt/201401/P020140114489778954994.pdf. Last accessed 19 June 2015.

[First Civil Division of the Higher People's Court of Beijing Municipality] 北京市高级人民法院民一庭. [The Trial of Labour Dispute Cases by the Higher People's Court of Beijing

Municipality Between 2010 and 2011: Current Situation, Problems and Countermeasures] 北京市法院2010至2011年度劳动争议案件的审理情况、问题和对策意见 (běi jīng shì fǎ yuàn 2010 zhì 2011 nián dù láo dòng zhēng yì àn jiàn de shěn lǐ qíng kuàng, wèn tí hé duì cè yì jiàn). 2011. [*Labour and Social Security Law Journal*] 劳动与社会保障.

[First Civil Division of the Higher People's Court of Beijing Municipality] 北京市高级人民法院民一庭. [The Trial of Labour Dispute Cases by the Higher People's Court of Beijing Municipality Between 2011 and 2012: Current Situation, Problems and Countermeasures] 北京市法院2011至2012年度劳动争议案件的审理情况、问题和对策意见 (běi jīng shì fǎ yuàn 2011 zhì 2012 nián dù láo dòng zhēng yì àn jiàn de shěn lǐ qíng kuàng, wèn tí hé duì cè yì jiàn). 2012 [*Labour and Social Security Law Journal*] 劳动与社会保障.

[First Civil Division of the Higher People's Court of Beijing Municipality] 北京市高级人民法院民一庭. [The Trial of Labour Dispute Cases by the Higher People's Court of Beijing Municipality Between 2012 and 2013: Current Situation, Problems and Countermeasures] 北京市法院2012至2013年度劳动争议案件的审理情况、问题和对策意见 (běi jīng shì fǎ yuàn 2012 zhì 2013 nián dù láo dòng zhēng yì àn jiàn de shěn lǐ qíng kuàng, wèn tí hé duì cè yì jiàn). 2013. [*Labour and Social Security Law Journal*] 劳动与社会保障.

[General Report of the Work of Justice Administration of 2013] 二〇一三年司法行政工作综述 (2013 nián sī fǎ háng zhèng gōng zuò zōng shù). 2014. [Ministry of Justice, People's Republic of China] 中华人民共和国司法部. Available at: http://www.moj.gov.cn/index/content/2014-01/20/content_5215516.htm?node=7345. Last accessed 19 June 2015.

[Statistical Communiqué of the People's Republic of China on the Development of Human Resource and Social Security Undertakings in 2007] 2007年度人力资源和社会保障事业发展统计劁报 (2007 nián dù rén lì zī yuán hé shè huì bǎo zhàng shì yè fā zhǎn tǒng jì gōng bào). 2008. [Ministry of Human Resources and Social Security] 人力资源和社会保障部.

[Statistical Communiqué of the People's Republic of China on the Development of Human Resource and Social Security Undertakings in 2008] 2008年度人力资源和社会保障事业发展统计劁报 (2008 nián dù rén lì zī yuán hé shè huì bǎo zhàng shì yè fā zhǎn tǒng jì gōng bào). 2009. [Ministry of Human Resources and Social Security] 人力资源和社会保障部.

[Statistical Communiqué of the People's Republic of China on the Development of Human Resource and Social Security Undertakings in 2009] 2009年度人力资源和社会保障事业发展统计劁报 (2009 nián dù rén lì zī yuán hé shè huì bǎo zhàng shì yè fā zhǎn tǒng jì gōng bào). 2010. [Ministry of Human Resources and Social Security] 人力资源和社会保障部.

[Statistical Communiqué of the People's Republic of China on the Development of Human Resource and Social Security Undertakings in 2010] 2010年度人力资源和社会保障事业发展统计劁报 (2010 nián dù rén lì zī yuán hé shè huì bǎo zhàng shì yè fā zhǎn tǒng jì gōng bào). 2011. [Ministry of Human Resources and Social Security] 人力资源和社会保障部.

[Statistical Communiqué of the People's Republic of China on the Development of Human Resource and Social Security Undertakings in 2011] 2011年度人力资源和社会保障事业发展统计劁报 (2011 nián dù rén lì zī yuán hé shè huì bǎo zhàng shì yè fā zhǎn tǒng jì gōng bào). 2012. [Ministry of Human Resources and Social Security] 人力资源和社会保障部.

[Statistical Communiqué of the People's Republic of China on the Development of Human Resource and Social Security Undertakings in 2012] 2012年度人力资源和社会保障事业发展统计劁报 (2012 nián dù rén lì zī yuán hé shè huì bǎo zhàng shì yè fā zhǎn tǒng jì gōng bào). 2013. [Ministry of Human Resources and Social Security] 人力资源和社会保障部.

[Xinhua Net] 新华网. 2007. [*Understanding of the labour contract law by the Chairman of the Legal Committee of NPC*] 全国人大法律委员会主任委员解读劳动合同法 (quán guó rén dà fǎ lǜ wěi yuán huì zhǔ rèn wěi yuán jiě dú láo dòng hé tóng fǎ). Available at: http://www.xinhuanet.com/zhibo/20070723/wz.htm. Last accessed 19 June 2015.

Chapter 6
ILO and Child Labour Regulation in China – Prospects and Complexities

Ulla Liukkunen

6.1 Introduction

Child labour has been banned internationally. Child labour may lead to lifelong physical and psychological damage. There is evidence of a strong link between household poverty and child labour. And child labour perpetuates poverty through generations by keeping poor children out of school and reducing their prospects for upward social mobility.[1] The abolition of child labour was among the major objectives of the International Labour Organization (ILO) when it was founded in 1919.[2] Recently, however, the ILO has admitted that global deadlines to end the worst forms of child labour will not be met.[3] Although an increasing number of countries have committed to the principle of abolition of child labour, there has been a lack of a driving force which would turn political will as expressed in a significant number of ratifications of the ILO core Conventions on child labour into effective enforcement of this principle. Consequently, throughout the world changes that have taken place at the level of implementation of the child labour ban have been modest. All in all, both international and state level action against child labour have so far lacked the dynamics that would link children's rights with efforts to develop social systems and eliminate poverty.

[1] See ILO website on International Labour Standards on Child labour.

[2] However, in the early years of the ILO tackling child labour was not a priority of the Organization. See Droux 2013, at pp. 262–267.

[3] The ILO Director General affirmed in 2013 that the ILO will not meet its global target for ending the worst forms of child labour in 2016 because global progress in combating this issue has been too slow. See ILO Press Release, 8 October 2013.

U. Liukkunen (✉)
Faculty of Law, University of Helsinki, Helsinki, Finland
e-mail: ulla.liukkunen@helsinki.fi

U. Liukkunen, Y. Chen (eds.), *Fundamental Labour Rights in China — Legal Implementation and Cultural Logic*, Ius Gentium: Comparative Perspectives on Law and Justice 49, DOI 10.1007/978-3-319-23156-3_6

The existence of child labour is generally linked to problems of developing countries but it is an issue which touches all countries. Although the harmful effects of child labour are well known, the means that should be used in order to eliminate child labour are extremely complicated. The underlying reasons why children are made to work deserve careful attention when effective means are sought to combat this phenomenon. If we assess the child labour question without seeking to trace and influence these reasons, the objective of eliminating child labour will remain a distant prospect. However, finding an effective way to implement the child labour ban set out in the international labour standards of the ILO is a complex task. We need to look beyond the pure labour law framework to identify and understand the requirements for effectively abolishing child labour. In order for the human rights dimension of the child labour ban to be taken seriously, it is important to take into account the particular social and socio-political contexts in which countries in different phases of development are striving towards securing children's rights.

In the following analysis, the question of eliminating child labour and making regulation of this issue more efficient will be examined in the Chinese legal context. In so doing, attention is paid to the international legal framework which has shaped child labour standards in China. Since the 1990s China has made significant progress in developing a legal framework concerning this issue but the problem of child labour is serious in both the formal and informal sectors. It is generally known that implementation of legal rules in China may often lack efficiency. This in turn, affects the position of what is meant to be binding labour law regulation as a part of the legal system. However, the gap between written legislation and legal reality in China is often highlighted in simplistic ways so that little attention is paid to the socio-economic and historical context of this giant country with approximately 767 million workers.[4]

In terms of legal protection, ILO standards on child labour are generally considered as primary international tools for combating child labour. The ILO has had an influence on the development of Chinese labour legislation even beyond the core Conventions on child labour, the Minimum Age Convention No. 138 and the Worst Forms of Child Labour Convention No. 182, both of which the country has ratified.[5] Out of the eight ILO Conventions defined as core, or fundamental, Conventions in the Declaration of Fundamental Principles and Rights at Work (1998 Declaration), China has also ratified the Equal Remuneration Convention No. 100 and the Discrimination (Employment and Occupation) Convention No. 111. However, if we use fundamental labour rights as defined by the ILO 1998 Declaration as a yardstick when assessing the stage of development of Chinese labour law, we are immediately

[4] See Liukkunen 2014, at p. 169, where it is emphasized that in China "[i]mplementation of labour standards involves several different components that cannot be readily understood without familiarity with Chinese legal categories and concepts and their socio-economic context".

[5] China ratified the Minimum Age Convention No. 138 on 28 April 1999 and the Worst Forms of Child Labour Convention No. 182 on 8 August 2002. See also Cooney et al. 2013, at pp. 144–145, where it is pointed out that the influence of the ILO in China is apparent in issues which directly relate to workplace standards.

faced with the problem of lack of ratification of four of the core Conventions – the Forced Labour Convention No. 29, the Freedom of Association and Protection of the Right to Organise Convention No. 87, the Right to Organise and Collective Bargaining Convention No. 98, and the Abolition of Forced Labour Convention No. 105. Put differently, as fundamental labour rights are interrelated, recognition of each of them contributes to strengthening the others.[6] Thus, international labour standards on child labour should be viewed as part of a larger entity of core labour standards. The efficiency of implementation of the ILO core Conventions on child labour gains support from progress in promotion of other fundamental labour rights. As simple as it might sound, improving the societal and labour market position of adults contributes to improving the position of children.

Although the focus of this article is on labour law, it should be emphasized that merely focusing on the question whether a country has ratified the related international conventions and amended its national legislation accordingly is not enough when assessing the relevance of legislative measures that a country has used in order to prevent child labour. On the one hand, the question of effective implementation of international child labour standards requires a broad enough perspective which encompasses not only the level of legislation but also the level of legal culture. On the other hand, a perspective solely focusing on law remains limited because the roots of the child labour problem lie deeper. Therefore, a broader societal framework for the child labour issue should be borne in mind.

From the legal perspective, it is necessary to examine the regulatory framework on child labour from the view of whether it meets the conditions set out by the related ILO core Conventions and whether it is effective enough. In China the development of the labour law system has progressed with great speed if measured against the level of legislative work but the legal infrastructure has not evolved, nor indeed can it do so, at the same speed. The present complex transition has not fully reached the deepest levels of legal culture.[7] This is linked to problems of bringing about effective abolition of child labour and is concretized most strikingly in legal rules not being implemented efficiently and then exploited by domestic and foreign businesses.

While attention is drawn in the following to both public and private regulation and their enforcement in the Chinese context, it should be emphasized that these remarks do not attempt to be exhaustive. The objective is merely to offer some observations on the topic. As this article is written by a Western labour law scholar, the viewpoints it may offer on the evolving Chinese legal system remain limited.

[6] At the international level, the ILO 1998 Declaration has contributed to acknowledgement of the linkage between the four fundamental labour rights.

[7] See also Tapiola at Chap. 3 in this volume.

6.2 International Regulatory Framework

At the international level, core human rights treaties enshrine cross-cutting provisions to prevent and combat child labour. The ILO is a tripartite United Nations agency whose conventions provide the main instruments in the fight against child labour. The member states of the Organization are able to determine independently the action they deem necessary in implementing the provisions of the conventions they have ratified. The convention provisions are typically general in nature. They allow for a margin of appreciation that is sometimes difficult to define, and which the ILO supervisory bodies may then work to clarify in their praxis. For example, the Minimum Age Convention No. 138 allows states to determine the minimum age of working children but it cannot be lower than that for the completion of compulsory schooling and in any case no lower than 15 years.[8] In addition, the Convention allows the competent national authority to exclude some types of employment or work from the material scope of the Convention.[9] Light work can be allowed for young people between 13 and 15 years.[10] On the other hand, by virtue of the Worst Forms of Child Labour Convention No. 182, young persons from the age of 16 may be allowed to carry out dangerous work on certain conditions. Defining what constitutes hazardous work is left to the states.[11]

A state that ratifies an ILO Convention agrees to the monitoring by ILO supervisory bodies of Convention implementation and compliance. The regular ILO supervisory system concerning implementation of ratified Conventions is based on the activities of the Committee of Experts on the Application of Conventions and Recommendations (CEACR) that consist of direct requests and observations. The latter are included in annual reports to the General Conference of the ILO.[12] The International Labour Conference's Tripartite Committee on the Application of Conventions and Recommendations is another body of the regular system of supervision. Traditional supervisory mechanisms contain both regular and special ones. The ILO 1998 Declaration is complemented by a particular follow-up mechanism comprising global reports to be prepared on one fundamental right every year and annual follow-up concerning ILO core Conventions that have not been ratified.

It is expected that the way the ILO carries out its monitoring and support activities will have an influence on individual state behaviour. ILO Conventions have been viewed as being authoritative although advancing globalisation has brought about increased criticism of ILO capacity to meet its goals. The Organization is

---

[8] Minimum Age Convention No. 138, Article 2(3).

[9] Ibid., Article 4(1).

[10] Ibid., Article 7(1).

[11] Ibid., Article 3(3); see also the Worst Forms of Child Labour Convention No. 182, Article 4(1). On the other hand, defining hazardous work has been on the agenda of the international community since the early years of the twentieth century. See Lead Poisoning (Women and Children) Recommendation, 1919.

[12] By virtue of Article 22 of the Constitution of the ILO member states agree to make an annual report to the International Labour Office on the measures they have taken to give effect to the provisions of ratified Conventions.

struggling to increase ratifications of its Conventions to a sufficient level and, increasingly, to advance more efficient implementation of ratified Conventions. It could be asked whether the ILO's regulatory approach concerning child labour, which has notably sharpened with the Worst Forms of Child Labour Convention No. 182, together with the existing supervisory mechanisms, actually is able to guarantee enforcement of the child labour ban and whether all necessary action is really being taken to enforce this ban. For in many of the substantial number of countries that have ratified the ILO child labour Conventions, child labour is still a problem, and indeed is one that continues to flourish globally. Therefore, we need to consider whether the existing activities of the ILO and related policy work could be strengthened and whether a wider perspective would benefit the Organization's supervisory mechanisms in evaluating state action against child labour. This could involve greater and more systematic use of assessment by other international organs dealing with child labour, such as the UN Committee on the Rights of the Child supervising implementation of the Convention on the Rights of the Child, or the Committee on Economic, Social and Cultural Rights supervising implementation of the Covenant on Economic, Social and Cultural Rights.[13] In addition, the technical assistance provided to member states by the ILO could be further intensified because of the extent and persistence of the child labour problem.[14]

With its increasing interference in the field of soft law, the ILO could also adopt a more consistent policy on regulation concerning corporate social responsibility (CSR). On a more general level, the question is also about the need for the ILO to find a sustainable way to strengthen its role as a global human rights actor. The policy work of the Organization has not yet reached the forefront of tackling the adverse consequences of globalization. Even though the ILO has emphasized the significance of fundamental labour rights and adopted declarations with the aim of taking a more modern approach to the promotion of labour rights in the framework of the global shift that is taking place in the labour market, the ILO's role as a promoter of workers' human rights has remained somewhat modest. It can also be argued that ILO policies to enhance workers' human rights protection as a part of company CSR strategies have remained not only modest but also obscure. Unsuccessful efforts to abolish child labour in certain countries that have committed to combating it and that are attracting foreign direct investment highlight the fact that the ILO should also tackle the speeding development of private norm-giving in its search for solutions to effectively weed out child labour.

Regardless of its international acceptance, a typical problem when monitoring state compliance with international human rights treaties and conventions is the

[13] See also UN Committee on Economic, Social and Cultural Rights, Concluding Observations, 2014 and UN Committee on the Rights of the Child, Concluding Observations, 2013. The Concluding Observations of both Committees to China express concern for child labour in China.

[14] See, however, the work of the ILO within its International Programme on the Elimination of Child Labour (IPEC), the largest single operational programme of the ILO, which aims to strengthen the capacity of countries to deal with child labour and to promote an international movement to address the problem. See further ILO website, 'About the International Programme on the Elimination of Child Labour (IPEC)'.

slowness of monitoring organs and the lack of effective follow-up mechanisms. As the focus of the ILO is shifting increasingly from achieving ratifications by member states to implementation of the child labour ban, the Organization should pay appropriate attention to all the factors known to hinder effective implementation of the child labour ban. One of the problems with ILO supervisory mechanisms lies in the persuasive nature of supervision. It is possible that despite frequent critical observations by ILO supervisory bodies, the national legislation of a country which has ratified the ILO core Conventions on child labour still does not correspond to the standards of the Conventions.

In the case of China, ILO CEACR supervisory documents have pointed out certain defects in child labour legislation but the national legislature has not so far taken the initiative to reform existing legislation accordingly.[15] However, China has significantly increased its efforts in tackling the child labour issue through legislative reforms and by adopting specific policy measures that address the broader societal framework of the problem. It has also utilized supportive technical activities of the ILO.

6.3 Regulatory Framework in China

China ratified the Minimum Age Convention No. 138 in 1999 and the Worst Forms of Child Labour Convention No. 182 in 2002, as well as the UN Convention on the Rights of the Child in 1992. In addition, China ratified the International Covenant on Economic Social and Cultural Rights in 2001. However, other international instruments also contain labour standards that require attention in terms of combating child labour. In particular, a number of other ILO Conventions, which also regulate work by children and young persons, have not been ratified by China.[16] Among them is the Forced Labour Convention No. 29. It is also worth noting that Article 3(1)(a) of the Labour Inspection Convention No. 81, not ratified by China, specifically mentions that one of the functions of labour inspection is to secure enforcement of legal provisions relating to conditions of work and protection of workers including children and young persons.[17] In addition, Article 9 of the Private Employment Agencies Convention No. 181 requires that measures be taken in order

[15] See Sect. 6.3 below.

[16] See generally Trebilcock and Raimondi 2008, at pp. 24–29.

[17] Both Labour Inspection Conventions of the ILO, that is, Labour Inspection Convention No. 81 and Labour Inspection (Agriculture) Convention No. 129 are relevant to combating child labour. These Conventions are regarded as belonging to the Governance Conventions together with the Employment Policy Convention No. 122 and Tripartite Consultation (International Labour Standards) Convention No. 144 by virtue of the ILO Declaration on Social Justice for a Fair Globalization (2008). China has implemented Conventions No. 122 (Employment Policy) and No. 144 (Tripartite Consultation) among the Governance Conventions.

to ensure that child labour is not used or supplied by private employment agencies. The Decent Work for Domestic Workers Convention No. 189 is also noteworthy.[18]

The Labour Law of 1994, the Law on the Protection of Minors of 1991, and the Provisions on the Prohibition of Using Child Labour of 2002 constitute the major national-level legal instruments regulating child labour in China.[19] A prohibition on recruiting juveniles under the age of 16 is included in the Labour Law, which further provides that "art, sports and special-skill units that plan to recruit juveniles under the age of 16 shall go through review and approval procedures according to relevant State regulations and guarantee the right of the employed to receive compulsory education".[20] According to the Law on the Protection of Minors enacted by the National People's Congress in 1991, minors under the age of 16 may not be hired, except where otherwise prescribed by the state.[21] The Law on the Protection of Minors also regulates protection of young workers between 16 and 18. Anyone hiring young workers who have reached the age of 16 but not 18 have to observe state regulations regarding types of job, working hours, intensity of labour and protective measures, and may not assign these minors any over-strenuous work, jobs exposed to toxic or hazardous substances, or other jobs that imperil their physical or mental health, or any dangerous operations.[22]

The Provisions on the Prohibition of Using Child Labour of 2002 supplement and specify the general child labour prohibition in the Labour Law and the Law on the Protection of Minors. Moreover, the scope of application of the Provisions is broader than that of the Labour Law, as the Provisions also apply to workers of public entities. The Provisions prohibit recruitment of children and their use as agency (dispatched) workers.[23] By virtue of Article 13 of the Provisions on the Prohibition of Using Child Labour of 2002, arts and sports entities may employ professional artistic workers and athletes under 16 years old with the consent of the parents or other custodians of minors. However, as the CEACR has pointed out, the Minimum Age Convention No. 138 requires that permits granted in individual cases to participate in artistic performances must be granted by a competent authority

---

[18] See Domestic Workers Convention No. 189, Articles 3(2)(c) and 4, and Preamble.

[19] See [Labour Law of the People's Republic of China] 中华人民共和国劳动法 (zhōng huá rén mín gòng hé guó láo dòng fǎ), 1994; [Law on Protection of Minors] 中华人民共和国未成年人保护法 (zhōng huá rén mín gòng hé guó wèi chéng nián rén bǎo hù fǎ), 1991; [Provisions on the Prohibition of Using Child Labour] 禁止使用童工规定 (jìn zhǐ shǐ yòng tóng gōng guī dìng), State Council, 2002. The Provisions on the Prohibition of Using Child Labour of 2002 followed the earlier Provisions on the Prohibition of Using Child Labour of 1991, which are now expired.

[20] [Labour Law of the People's Republic of China] 中华人民共和国劳动法 (zhōng huá rén mín gòng hé guó láo dòng fǎ), 1994, Article 15.

[21] [Law on Protection of Minors] 中华人民共和国未成年人保护法 (zhōng huá rén mín gòng hé guó wèi chéng nián rén bǎo hù fǎ), 1991, Article 38.

[22] Ibid.

[23] [Provisions on the Prohibition of Using Child Labour] 禁止使用童工规定 (jìn zhǐ shǐ yòng tóng gōng guī dìng), 2002, Article 7.

after consultation with the organizations of employers and workers concerned.[24] Hence, Article 13 of the Provisions on the Prohibition of Using Child Labour does not fulfil the requirements set in the Minimum Age Convention No. 138 and the Provisions should be changed.

Another problem relates to lack of regulation of under-age apprentices in certain sectors. In general the minimum age for apprenticeship is 16. According to Article 1 of the Regulations on Strengthening and Improving Apprentices and Training Work, issued by the National Labour Bureau of China in 1981, candidates for an apprenticeship should be morally upright unmarried young women and men, having completed middle school, healthy, aged between 16 and 20.[25] Lowering ages for educational requirements is possible in special circumstances, yet subject to the approval of labour bureaux at the provincial level. As there is thus no comprehensive minimum age for apprentices in Chinese legislation, the use of apprenticeships has opened a path to child labour. In its comments on application of the Minimum Age Convention No. 138, the ILO CEACR has emphasized that the government should ensure that no child under 14 years works as an apprentice. Another problem with apprenticeships, noted by the International Trade Union Confederation (ITUC), is that they are also used to employ children in factories, which enables the use of child labour. The legislation specifies neither the conditions for apprenticeships nor work-study programmes. Moreover, work-study programmes – programmes where children engage in work through their schools – have resulted in child work, sometimes involving excessive working hours or dangerous circumstances.[26] Work-study programmes have also resulted in hazardous work.[27]

Under the Provisions on the Prohibition of Using Child Labour, employers are obliged to examine the identity documents of workers and keep a record.[28] If an employer fails to keep employment registration files or forges them, the administrative departments of public security may impose a fine of 10,000 yuan.[29] The administrative departments of labour security of people's governments at and above the county level are to be responsible for supervising and inspecting implementation of the Provisions on the Prohibition of Using Child Labour. According to the Provisions, labour unions, the Communist Youth League, women's associations and other mass organizations have an obligation to safeguard the legal rights and interests of minors according to law.[30]

[24] See ILO CEACR Direct Request, Minimum Age Convention – China, 2008.

[25] [Regulations on Strengthening and Improving the Training Work of Apprentices] 关于加强和改进学徒培训工作的规定 (guān yú jiā qiáng hé gǎi jìn xué tú péi xùn gōng zuò de guī dìng), 1981, Article 1.

[26] See ILO CEACR Direct Request, Minimum Age Convention – China, 2010a; see also Brown 2012, at p. 490.

[27] See the observations of the ITUC reported by ILO CEACR Observation, Minimum Age Convention – China, 2010.

[28] [Provisions on the Prohibition of Using Child Labour] 禁止使用童工规定 (jìn zhǐ shǐ yòng tóng gōng guī dìng), 2002, Article 4.

[29] Ibid., Article 8.

[30] Ibid., Article 5.

If an employer uses child labour, the administrative department of labour security may impose a fine of 5,000 yuan for each child worker for each month.[31] An employer who uses child labour in work places with toxic materials could be fined 50,000–300,000 yuan by virtue of the Regulations on Labour Protection in Working Places with Toxic Materials,[32] or 5,000 yuan for each child worker for each month, whichever fine is higher.[33] If the use of child labour in operation with toxic materials causes severe occupational poisoning hazard or causes any occupational poisoning accident, the employer will be investigated for criminal liability.[34] An employer who fails to send children back to their parents or other custodians within the prescribed time limit, despite being ordered to do so by the administrative departments of public security, may be fined 10,000 yuan for each child labourer for each month, starting from the day of the order for correction.[35] Additionally, the Department of Industry and Commerce Administration may revoke the employer's business licence or the Department of Civil Affairs may cancel the employer's registration as a civilian operated non-enterprise entity.[36] If the employer is a government agency or institutional entity, administrative sanctions or disciplinary sanctions by way of demotion or dismissal are given to the personnel directly responsible.[37] Administrative departments of public security bureaux may also order the employer to send child workers back to their original place of domicile to their parents or other custodians within a prescribed time limit, and to bear all the expenses for transportation and accommodation thereby incurred.[38]

There is further responsibility if a child worker is ill, injured or dies. The employer is responsible for sending the child to a medical institution for treatment, and must bear all the medical and living expenses during the period of medical treatment.[39] If the child is disabled or dies, the administrative departments of public security bureaux revoke the employer's business license. The employer must also pay lump-sum compensation to the lineal relatives of a disabled or dead child worker.[40]

---

[31] Ibid., Article 6.

[32] [Regulations on Labour Protection in Working Places with Toxic Materials] 使用有毒物品作业场所劳动保护条例 (shǐ yòng yǒu dú wù pǐn zuò yè chǎng suǒ láo dòng bǎo hù tiáo lì), 2002, Article 63.

[33] [Provisions on the Prohibition of Using Child Labour] 禁止使用童工规定 (jìn zhǐ shǐ yòng tóng gōng guī dìng), 2002, Article 6.

[34] [Regulations on Labour Protection in Working Places with Toxic Materials] 使用有毒物品作业场所劳动保护条例 (shǐ yòng yǒu dú wù pǐn zuò yè chǎng suǒ láo dòng bǎo hù tiáo lì), 2002, Article 63.

[35] [Provisions on the Prohibition of Using Child Labour] 禁止使用童工规定 (jìn zhǐ shǐ yòng tóng gōng guī ding), 2002, Article 6.

[36] Ibid.

[37] Ibid.

[38] Ibid.

[39] Ibid., Article 10. The amount of compensation is calculated under the relevant provisions of state employment-related injury insurance.

[40] Ibid.

In certain situations, criminal liability attaches to illegal use of child labour. For example, criminal responsibility may follow under the provisions of the Criminal Law[41] for anyone who abducts child labour, coerces child labour to work, uses child labour to work high above the ground, or in a radioactive, highly toxic, inflammable or explosive environment, or uses child labour under 16 years old, or causes death or serious disability to child labour.[42]

Although the sanction system is multi-dimensional, many observers have noted the need to evaluate its effectiveness.[43] The system should better correspond to the severity of violations of legal rules prohibiting child labour. In addition, the system does not function well in practice and more consistent use of the sanction system should thus be ensured. Given repeated reports that children are found in hazardous work and in positions comprising the worst forms of child labour, a more systematic approach to blatant exploitation may be warranted. Indeed, the ILO CEACR has noted the modest use of the sanction system available, for example, in the case where forced child labour was used in the Shanxi brick kilns in 2007.[44] The ITUC has claimed that many of the worst forms of child labour exist in China, involving not only work in brick kilns but in glass-making workshops, fireworks workshops and footwear factories.[45] For example, the prohibition of hazardous work has been violated so that children under 18 have had to do such work even within the school system.[46]

6.4 The Challenge of Efficient Implementation

The most pressing question concerning the elimination of child labour in China is to ensure efficient implementation of existing legal rules. In concrete cases of exploitation it is often pointed out that the problem lies in failure to enforce laws and regulations.[47] As statistics on the use of child labour are absent, the extent and forms of child labour are difficult to assess so that planning measures against child labour are consequently inadequate. In order to systematically improve implementation of existing rules and to develop a related labour inspection system, an important precondition would therefore be collection of representative child labour data which would be disaggregated by the sex, age and urban/rural status of the child.

[41] [Criminal Law of the People's Republic of China] 中华人民共和国刑法 (zhōng huá rén mín gòng hé guó xíng fǎ), 1979 (as revised in 2011), Article 244.

[42] [Provisions on the Prohibition of Using Child Labour] 禁止使用童工规定 (jìn zhǐ shǐ yòng tóng gōng guī dìng), 2002, Article 11.

[43] See e.g., Brown 2012, at p. 489.

[44] See ILO CEACR Direct Request, Worst Forms of Child Labour Convention – China, 2010b; see also Brown 2012, at p. 489.

[45] See ibid.

[46] See e.g., ILO CEACR Observation, Worst Forms of Child Labour Convention – China, 2006b.

[47] See e.g., Yunnan Province Women's Federation et al. 2002, at p. 23.

Generally speaking, local authorities that exercise a relatively high degree of power and autonomy have tended not to adopt systematic policies which would proactively tackle the child labour issue. Instead, local practices, which in many cases are influenced by the need to attract investments, have contributed to the inefficiency of existing regulation of child labour. Consequently at the national level there is a need to increase policy coordination and to adopt a comprehensive plan to monitor and enforce labour laws, with a view to eliminating local variations in reacting to child labour.[48]

A close link exists between child labour, forced labour and human trafficking – a link that should be much better recognized by the authorities.[49] For example, a study concerning the trafficking of children and women in Yunnan Province noted that in areas severely affected by trafficking, local authorities had failed to take effective action or establish adequate prevention mechanisms. There were even cases of village leaders aiding traffickers.[50] According to the ILO Forced Labour Convention No. 29, forced or compulsory labour is "all work or service which is exacted from any person under the menace of any penalty and for which the said person has not offered voluntarily". The Convention on the Worst Forms of Child Labour No. 182 complements this definition by classifying trafficking as among forms of slavery, or practices similar to slavery. Therefore it should be eliminated as a matter of urgency regardless of the level of development of the country.[51] Although the Law on the Protection of Minors prohibits trafficking in minors,[52] the connection between child trafficking and child labour is inadequately understood, and this continues to be a major problem even internationally. Yet there is evidence that labour trafficking is a very common phenomenon and that children are particularly vulnerable, thus being at significant risk of trafficking. However, China's National Plan of Action against

[48] The current approach remains fragmented and disorganized. See Harpur 2011, at p. 3.

[49] The Protocol of 2014 to the ILO Forced Labour Convention No. 29 notes the linkage between forced labour and trafficking. Importantly, the Palermo Protocol (Protocol to prevent, suppress and punish trafficking in persons, especially women and children, supplementing the United Nations Convention against transnational organized crime) which supplements the UN Convention against Transnational Organized Crime also concerns protecting victims of trafficking in persons, especially women and children.

[50] See Yunnan Province Women's Federation et al. 2002, at p. 21. The ITUC has made similar observations. See ILO CEACR Observation, Worst Forms of Child Labour Convention – China, 2010.

[51] See Belser et al. 2005. According to the International Confederation of Free Trade Unions, China is a source, transit and destination country for international human trafficking in women and children. Combating trafficking in labour poses exceptional challenges also because its cross-border dimension requires co-operation between authorities in different countries. See ILO CEACR Observation, Worst Forms of Child Labour Convention – China, 2010.

[52] See [Law on Protection of Minors] 中华人民共和国未成年人保护法 (zhōng huá rén mín gòng hé guó wèi chéng nián rén bǎo hù fǎ), 1991 (as revised in 2012), Article 41.

Trafficking (2013–2020) also governs measures related to child trafficking and shows that China is seeking means to address the problem.[53]

6.4.1 The Role of Local Regulation

So far, in the international debate on the child labour issue in China, little has been said about the role that local regulation plays in the Chinese legislative system. Little, too, has been discussed about the role that local regulation can play in eliminating child labour. As regulatory power at the local level may be used in order to further specify national-level labour regulation, it can be argued that assessing the Chinese regulatory framework from a multi-level perspective has been largely overlooked in the Western debate, which in turn has led to a distorted picture of the legal system in China.[54] Overall, only the problem of inconsistency between national and local level regulation and their policy goals has gained attention.[55] When local people's congresses and governments regulate in contradiction to national law, this can also weaken the overall legal framework of fundamental labour rights in China.[56]

However, local legislative power has sometimes been used to establish more precise regulation to advance workers' protection.[57] Indeed, some local-level regulatory developments have further specified national-level legislation on child labour. The Zhejiang Provincial Implementing Measures on the Provisions on the Prohibition of Using Child Labour of 2008 (Zhejiang Provincial regulation) offers an example of local regulation which promotes elimination of child labour and also specifies a definition of prohibited use of child labour.[58] The Zhejiang Provincial regulation also specifies protection of child workers so that there is an obligation to pay them a minimum amount if working children are found and dismissed.[59] According to the regulation, if a literature, art or sports unit recruits juveniles by virtue of related state provisions, effective measures have to be taken to protect their physical and psychological health.[60] The Zhejiang Provincial regulation also emphasizes the administrative accountability of provincial authorities in relation to

[53] [China's National Plan of Action against Trafficking (2013–2020)] 中国反对拐卖人口行动计划(2013-2020年) (zhōng guó fǎn duì guǎi mài rén kǒu xíng dòng jì huà (2013–2020)), 2013.

[54] See also Casale and Zhu 2013, at p. 10.

[55] See Peerenboom 2002, at p. 256.

[56] See ibid. and Liukkunen 2014, at p. 169.

[57] For experience of innovative local regulation in the field of anti-discrimination legislation see Paavilainen 2014.

[58] [Zhejiang Provincial Implementing Measures on the Provisions on the Prohibition of Using Child Labour] 浙江省实施《禁止使用童工规定》办法 (zhè jiāng shěng shí shī "jìn zhǐ shǐ yòng tóng gōng guī dìng" bàn fǎ), 2008, Article 5.

[59] Ibid., Article 17.

[60] Ibid., Article 6.

eliminating child labour.[61] It would seem that regulatory developments at the local level could at their best offer regulatory solutions that address elimination of child labour in a more nuanced way compared to national-level legislation.

That said, a major challenge for China is to ensure effective implementation of the existing national-level regulatory framework concerning child labour. Local economic competition between Chinese provinces and cities increasingly seems to hamper the realization of fundamental labour rights, with a flexible interpretation of labour legislation becoming one way of attracting foreign investment to the area. In addition to regulatory competition, local governments may compete for investment through prioritizing economic considerations over social ones when carrying out their labour related administrative tasks.[62] Together with ongoing economic and societal transition, the challenges that China faces due to its multi-level regulatory and administrative system seem to be growing.

6.4.2 The Role of Local Authorities

Overall, while the ineffectiveness of legislation has been largely identified as constituting one of the main weaknesses of the Chinese legal system, the particular problems of enforcing the child labour ban have received limited attention. Although steps have been taken by the Chinese government in order to strengthen the role of labour legislation, there are features of the legal system that enable advocating economic objectives at the cost of social development and children's rights. This is one of the questions where related exploitation has turned out to have serious consequences. The use of legislative and administrative power at the local level for business purposes at the cost of labour protection is one factor that can be presented as a serious obstacle to efficient promotion of fundamental labour rights in China. Moreover, the problem of extensive collusion between private businesses and local officials has contributed to this development.[63] Access to justice is also hampered by the weakness of the judiciary; for example, although local courts work under the budgetary power of local people's congresses, in practice local governments can provide them with additional financial resources, which affect their position.[64]

At the local level, the labour inspectorate is not able to conduct efficient supervision of child labour. As already noted, lack of representative statistics significantly hinders the planning of labour inspectorate activities. Moreover, problems arise because the number of inspectors is insufficient and because of corruption. Some of the most striking problems have related to the way labour inspections are carried out. The ILO CEACR has noted the problem of actually discovering child labour

---

[61] Ibid., Articles 3 and 4.

[62] See Liukkunen 2014, at p. 168.

[63] See ILO CEACR Observation, Worst Forms of Child Labour Convention – China, 2010.

[64] See Peerenboom 2002, at pp. 13–15 and Cooney, Biddulph, and Zhu 2013, at p. 392. For local courts' dependence on local administrative organs see Balme 2010, at p. 156.

related to the shortage of labour inspectors and collusion between enterprises and local authorities. According to the CEACR, it is common practice that factory owners are informed before inspections are carried out so that child workers can be hidden or given the day off.[65]

Traditionally, labour inspectors have been important partners in efforts to eradicate child labour.[66] In 2012, there were only 25,000 labour inspectors nationally. Although their number has been growing, they are still insufficient to take care of the responsibilities set in labour legislation. Again, while significant labour administration and labour inspection reforms have taken place in China, the labour administration and inspection system has not been capable of guaranteeing compliance with regulation of child labour.[67]

However, recent reforms of the labour administration and labour inspection system in China may offer new opportunities to put more effort into eliminating child labour. These reforms may enable a more systematic approach to labour inspection, which has not developed at the same speed as national-level labour legislation in general. The Labour Law and the Regulations on Labour and Social Security Supervision provide the legal framework for labour inspection.[68] In 2004, China reformed its Regulations on Labour Security Supervision with provisions which aim to ensure that violations of the Labour Law would be dealt with adequately.[69] The ILO Decent Work Country Programme in the People's Republic of China 2013–2015 includes strengthening the inspection and enforcement of labour law as one of its key objectives.[70] These efforts could bring China one step forward in a process that may bring development towards ratification of the ILO Labour Inspection Convention No. 81 and a more robust labour protection infrastructure.

6.4.3 Economic Dynamics, Legislative Reforms and Child Labour

With China's rapid labour-based economic development the framework to prevent the use of child labour is complex. The media have reported on an increasing number of cases which demonstrate not only the typical circumstances under which

---

65 ILO CEACR Observation, Minimum Age Convention – China, 2010.

66 See e.g., Herbert 2012.

67 For more details of these reforms, see Casale and Zhu 2013. The authors point out for example (at p. 38) that in 2009 the Chinese government introduced a national-level pilot project entitled "Twin Networks Management" in 60 cities nationwide with the aim of establishing an efficient labour inspection system to provide quality services to all employers and workers. The project was based on the experience of Shanghai and Chengdu. Three years later, the project was expanded to all Chinese cities.

68 [Regulations on Labour and Social Security Supervision] 劳动保障监察条例 (láo dòng bǎo zhàng jiān chá tiáo lì), 2004.

69 See also Cooney 2007, at pp. 1061–1062.

70 See ILO Decent Work Country Programme in the People's Republic of China 2013–2015.

children work but also the labour market reality, which enables the use of child labour so that even legislative reforms in the field of labour law may contribute to the phenomenon. The following case may serve as an example:

> At the beginning of March 2012, an agency recruited a 14 year old boy, Liufu Zong, to work in an electronics company in Dongguan, Guangdong province. The boy was from a very poor family living in a poor rural area. He had dropped out of school when he was 12 in order to help his father support the family.
>
> According to media reports, Liufu Zong worked on a production line six days a week about 10 or more hours per day. Two months later, he suddenly died. His death was believed to be a result of exhaustion caused by the working conditions. The electronics company, which eventually agreed to pay compensation to the family, argued that it did not know the real age of the boy and thought he was over eighteen. His real age was not revealed because the employment agency which had sent the boy to the factory used an identity card which showed his age as over 18.[71]

First of all, this concrete case illustrates some typical features of the child labour issue in the Chinese context. The case gained public attention and was followed by demands for better protection of children and young workers. The case, like several others reported by the Chinese media, captures some of the key characteristics of the child labour problem and its roots: extreme poverty, lack of education and poor working conditions. In rural areas, poverty combined with school expenses is an equation that many families are unable to solve. Their livelihood depends on their children working. Even though Chinese legislation guarantees nine years compulsory free education, fees are often required and poor families cannot afford them.[72] According to media reports, working conditions of child workers may be much worse than those of adults. Sometimes children have been found doing forced labour.

Second, this case illustrates how the emergence of employment agencies, regulated by the Labour Contract Law of 2007, and subjected to insufficient monitoring, has in practice offered a new pathway to the use of child labour.[73] When businesses actively seek ways to reduce labour costs they may consider Chinese labour legislation as not necessarily fully binding on them.[74] The employment agency (labour dispatch) system has also been extensively used in multinational companies' (MNCs') operations in China. As agency (dispatch) workers are employees of the

---

[71] See e.g., China Daily (USA), 2013.

[72] [Compulsory Education Law of the People's Republic of China] 中华人民共和国义务教育法 (zhōng huá rén mín gòng hé guó yì wù jiào yù fǎ), 1986, Article 2: no tuition or miscellaneous fee may be charged in the implementation of compulsory education.

[73] [Labour Contract Law of the People's Republic of China] 中华人民共和国劳动合同法 (zhōng huá rén mín gòng hé guó láo dòng hé tóng fǎ), 2007.

[74] Following enactment of the [Labour Contract Law of the People's Republic of China] 中华人民共和国劳动合同法 (zhōng huá rén mín gòng hé guó láo dòng hé tóng fǎ), 2007, scholars have noted some early evidence of a sharp increase in the number of agency workers. See Gallagher et al. 2011, at p. 3. See also generally ILO CEACR Observation, Minimum Age Convention – China, 2006a, which points out that although the vast majority of Chinese enterprises do not use child labour some employers have used children as the solution for reducing production overheads.

employment agencies this has enabled companies to avoid their normal responsibilities. This they have done eagerly.[75]

The Standing Committee of the National People's Congress has recently drawn up changes to the Labour Contract Law in order to limit the use of employment agencies that have caused worker exploitation.[76] However, the difficulties of ensuring effective implementation of the reformed regulation have remained and the reformed legislation has not yet met its objective of restricting misuse of agency workers. It appears that any corrective legislative action taken as part of reforms may fall short in effectiveness due to the ongoing weak status of legislation. In their own way, developments in recent years also show that different labour law reforms in a society going through profound transformation may have complicated consequences for labour market realities and the realization of labour rights. Unintended consequences of legal reforms in the field of labour law can also be seen as one reason for the growth of informal employment in China.[77]

It is generally very difficult to predict the effects of wide-scale legislative reforms in a developing country like China.[78] This also has to do with national-level laws not always being very clear or specific. They may be intentionally broad because they need to be simultaneously applicable to very different regional contexts. At the same time as a labour law system based on private legal relationships is being built in China, related labour law reforms are *de facto* being adjusted to the new economy. This has also had consequences for the use of child labour. And while public attention largely focuses on the formal labour market, the informal economy keeps on growing with a child labour problem that is extremely difficult to grasp.

Economic growth and supportive government policies may create complicated tensions in local governmental institutions. While reform policies have increased the importance of local regional governance, the increased authority of local authorities has also had negative effects, such as reduced conformity of local level regulation with national level mandatory labour legislation. It can also be argued that state policy strongly promoting economic growth leads to interlinking policy settings at the local level so that pressure for growth and investment makes better labour protection difficult if not impossible.[79] As provinces and cities are competing over investment, a great deal of national-level legislation is ignored at the local level. Both historical and cultural attitudes towards legal phenomena affect the role of legal institutions and legal rules.[80] Instilling in local authorities the importance of

[75] See also FIDH 2013, at p. 24.

[76] [Decision on the Revision of the Labour Contract Law of the People's Republic of China] 关于修改《中华人民共和国劳动合同法》的决定 (guān yú xiū gǎi zhōng huá rén mín gòng hé guó láo dòng hé tóng fǎ de jué dìng), 2012.

[77] See generally Gallagher et al. 2011, at pp. 2–3.

[78] On experimenting with legal reforms in China, see Woo and Gallagher 2011b, at p. 380.

[79] See Liukkunen 2014, at p. 169.

[80] See Woo and Gallagher 2011a, at p. 6. The authors emphasize that legal rules cannot be understood as "self-enforcing" but there is a need to internalize them by those to whom they are targeted. Hilary K. Josephs, on the other hand, has emphasized the need for strengthening local institutions comprehensively. See Josephs 2009, at p. 394.

compliance with mandatory labour legislation, so that the binding nature of legislation would affect their cooperation with businesses, is not easy.

6.5 Societal Factors Contributing to Child Labour

ILO monitoring mechanisms are sometimes claimed to be too technical and narrow. Yet they have also sought to pay attention to the underlying causes of child labour. The CEACR has noted that in China the State Council has provided more funds for rural compulsory schooling and stressed the importance of guaranteeing funding for compulsory education, which is one of the most effective means of combating child labour. Also emphasized is the need for accessible compulsory education for children of migrant workers.[81]

For several years, the Chinese government seems to have handled the child labour issue mainly through drawing up regulation. More recently, however, the picture has been changing. Above all, the linkage between the education system and child labour has increasingly received attention. The education system is based on a nine year compulsory education programme. However, implementation of the right to education has remained insufficient as a significant number of children remain outside the education system. This is because compulsory public education is often not free in practice and therefore a large number of children are excluded from school as many families cannot afford it. This is one of the factors maintaining a situation where families in poor areas have no choice but to have their children work. It would thus be very important to develop the existing public education system so that it would be accessible and affordable to all children.

The government has also paid increasing attention to problems caused by massive internal migration. Hundreds of millions of migrant workers have moved to cities from the countryside and contributed greatly to national economic growth. Their children have faced adverse consequences because of the national household registration (*hukou*) system when some families are not registered or their household registration does not grant them access to local services.[82] Hence there are migrant children who remain without an acknowledged status that would guarantee their entry into the local school system and access to social services. Even though efforts have been made to improve the situation of children of migrant workers, they remain at risk of ending up as child labour.[83] A remarkable number of children in rural areas live without household registration. In particular, children left by their parents in rural areas ("left-behind children") are often in a vulnerable position. Particular problems are also faced by disabled children and children of ethnic

[81] See ILO CEACR Observation, Minimum Age Convention – China, 2008 and ILO CEACR Observation, Minimum Age Convention – China, 2010.

[82] See also Herd et al. 2010, at pp. 23–24.

[83] See also ILO CEACR Observation, Minimum Age Convention – China, 2010.

minorities. In addition, state policy which favours the male gender has contributed to the vulnerability of girls. These factors illustrate the strong correlation between problems of child labour and discrimination or exclusion.

Remarkable progress has been recently made by developing supportive multi-annual action programmes, such as the third National Programme of Action for Child Development in China (2011–2020), the Ten Year Poverty Reduction Programme, the National Human Rights Action Plan of China (2012–2015) and the twelth Five-Year Social Economic Plan (2011–2015).[84] However, increased planning of important social and labour policy measures would greatly benefit from planning concrete implementation of those measures. As has been emphasized, lack of available representative data means that activities related to elimination of child labour cannot be fully planned and implemented. The absence of reliable data also makes it difficult to systematically assess the efficiency of supervision of the child labour ban.

6.6 Corporate Social Responsibility and Child Labour

Globalization and the increasing power of MNCs have put business behaviour increasingly in the spotlight when seeking elimination of child labour. Although international labour standards and related public regulation of states play a central role in promoting and protecting fundamental labour rights, increasing private regulation of these rights also needs attention. Because multinationals may adopt their own regulation on fundamental labour rights, the question of promoting these rights can be extended to the role that MNCs play in this. In the light of the fact that China continues to be globally the top country to attract foreign MNC investment, it is apparent that special attention should be devoted to multinationals' attitudes towards promoting fundamental labour rights when assessing implementation of the child labour ban in China.[85]

We have been witnessing a development where international policy guidance on MNCs' approaches to human rights has intensified as a way to advance responsible business behaviour in the absence of any international legally binding instrument. However, a recent UN Human Rights Council Resolution provides for establishment of an intergovernmental working group mandated with elaborating an international legally binding instrument to regulate the activities of transnational corporations

[84] [National Programme of Action for Child Development in China (2011–2020)] 中国儿童发展纲要 (2011 – 2020年) (zhōng guó ér tóng fā zhǎn gāng yào (2011 – 2020nián)), 2011; [Ten Year Poverty Reduction Programme] 中国的十年减贫战略 (2011–2020) (zhōng guó de shí nián jiǎn pín zhàn luè (2011–2020)); [National Human Rights Action Plan of China (2012–2015)] 国家人权行动计划 (2012 – 2015年) (guó jiā rén quán xíng dòng jì huá (2012 – 2015nián)), 2012; [12th Five-Year Plan for National Economic and Social Development of the People's Republic of China] 国民经济和社会发展第十二个五年规划纲要 (guó mín jīng jì hé shè huì fā zhǎn dì shí èr gè wǔ nián guī huà gāng yào), 2011.

[85] See e.g., China Development Forum 2013.

and other business enterprises.[86] All the major public international guidelines that seek to steer multinationals' behaviour recognize the status of ILO fundamental labour rights.[87] For example, according to the UN Guiding Principles on Business and Human Rights, companies should perform due diligence in accordance with internationally recognized labour standards.[88] The major public guidelines do not, however, form a consistent entity but can be considered merely as a collection of public codes of conduct amongst which companies are able to pick and choose the individual standards that best suit them and their context. When it comes to the responsibility of MNCs in relation to their suppliers, public international guidelines steering CSR norm-setting by multinationals are even much less developed and widen the opportunity for "*regime shopping*" by multinationals.[89]

With advancing globalization, production processes as well as supply chains and networks have become highly complex.[90] They may involve a large number of subcontractors at different levels simultaneously in China and abroad. A key development is that industrial processes are also commonly subcontracted.[91] This has a significant impact on how well the codes of conduct of MNCs and related monitoring of their production chains are able to cover all the phases of production. Another problem with CSR is that auditing does not involve all industrial processes and has become more difficult with increasingly scattered supply chains.

The ineffectiveness of private regulation in complex subcontracting chains has been proven over and over again. Because state monitoring mechanisms are insufficient and because it is easy for multinationals to "outsource" labour rights concerning their suppliers' workers, companies are able to maintain a normative regime that appears to be coherent without much real effort as to ensuring respect for fundamental labour rights. One of the most crucial questions to examine concerning MNCs operating in China is whether they truly extend their social responsibility to all their suppliers or whether they are merely trying to seek a competitive advantage from inefficient Chinese labour regulation and, in so doing, seek to benefit from local level regulatory differences and shortages of regulation or its implementation.[92] Evaluating a company's CSR strategy should involve looking into whether that strategy extends to its suppliers and whether implementation and enforcement of that strategy is being adapted to local circumstances. Private codes of conduct could successfully complement state regulation in the elimination of child labour if certain conditions are met. One of the central issues is that codes of conduct should cover the entire supply chain and that they should be monitored properly so that

[86] UN Human Rights Council, Resolution 26/9, 2014.

[87] See for example the ILO Tripartite Declaration of Principles concerning Multinational Enterprises and Social Policy, 1977 (amended in 2000 and 2006), and the OECD Guidelines for Multinational Enterprises, 1976 (amended in 2000 and 2011).

[88] See UN Economic and Social Council, Guiding Principles on Business and Human Rights, 2011.

[89] See also Abdul-Garafu 2009, at p. 61.

[90] See FIDH 2013, at p. 19; see also Banks 2006, at p. 90.

[91] See FIDH 2013, at p. 19.

[92] See also Lam 2009, at p. 237.

some form of reliable external monitoring takes place.[93] Generally, social audits can be useful in arranging necessary corrective action in the working conditions of suppliers.[94] Several studies have shown that it is difficult to make suppliers comply with the labour rights clauses of private codes of conduct, but explanations of ineffectiveness rarely grasp suppliers' real circumstances.[95] Even when the codes of MNCs aim to improve situations involving work by children, in the case of violations costs often have to be paid by the supplier, who might not be able to afford them.[96] If multinationals also contribute financially to improving the situation the changes are often more profound and permanent in nature.

There are multinationals that seek to pay heed to local circumstances in eliminating child labour. They may have adopted codes of conduct with wider content in the sense that in addition to abolition of child labour they include regulation on dealing with cases where children are found working in supply factories.[97] So it would seem that despite the shortcomings of company CSR strategies, multinationals can promote greater commitment and concrete action to guarantee fundamental labour rights in global terms. Although they cannot replace the primary responsibility – which lies with states, and related mandatory state regulation and its adequate implementation – MNCs can significantly advance the realization of fundamental labour rights and thus also the elimination of child labour.[98] Here, labour market organizations and civil society also need to step in strongly. Demands for fair trade leave no room for child labour. And these demands draw attention to the responsibility that MNCs should carry for their entire value chain.

A common observation is that along with the increasing power of multinationals the bargaining power of the workers' side has been diminishing. International framework agreements concluded on labour rights between MNCs and global union federations have, however, been viewed as an emerging counterforce in this situation.[99] Such agreements have gained an increasingly important role in promotion of fundamental labour rights, abolition of child labour included, and in strengthening social dialogue in the operations of multinationals.[100]

---

[93] See also Kolk and van Dulder 2002.

[94] See FIDH 2013, at p. 27.

[95] See for example Egels-Zandén 2007.

[96] See Kolk and van Dulder 2002, at pp. 266–267. For a case study demonstrating the problems of suppliers to improve their labour standards see Yu 2008.

[97] See Kolk and van Dulder 2002, at p. 298.

[98] The UN Committee on the Rights of the Child has emphasized state responsibility regarding the impact of business on children's rights by stating in its General Comment No. 16 (2013) that "the Host States have the primary responsibility to respect, protect and fulfill children's rights in their jurisdiction. They must ensure that all business enterprises, including transnational corporations operating within their borders, are adequately regulated within a legal and institutional framework that ensures that they do not adversely impact on the rights of the child and/or aid and abet violations in foreign jurisdictions".

[99] See also Schömann 2012.

[100] See Liukkunen 2014, at pp. 176–178.

Although international framework agreements do not form a homogeneous entity and great differences occur in their implementation and efficiency, starting from dispute resolution systems that might be applicable, fundamental labour rights almost always form an integral part of these agreements. Some agreements even reach to promotion of fundamental labour rights of the employees of MNCs' suppliers. International framework agreements are instruments under development and as yet still few, but promisingly they offer the possibility of promoting elimination of child labour within a globally operating company and even beyond. These agreements can contribute to the creation of effective private regulation that reaches the entire global supply chain. Some agreements also contain broader clauses on supporting children if child labour has been used.[101]

6.7 Conclusion

The role of law is changing in China, and the child labour issue should be viewed in the framework of the developing legal system and complex labour market transition. The way the Chinese legal system has developed has also had an impact on the effectiveness of child labour regulation. In the imperial era and during Mao's rule, law was viewed as a secondary or minor tool for organizing and governing Chinese society.[102] This legacy affects the status of legislation and the entire legal system but developments have been diverse. Even though law finally became a governance instrument at the end of the 1970s, it has only been that for a relatively short period – a period that has been characterized by various developmental phases. In a society where the legal order has not played a central role for very long, we cannot expect it to take a giant leap to become a key regulatory system in the full sense of the word.[103] The development of the Chinese legal system is also characterized by tensions that originate from different social, economic and political interests. Therefore in order to answer the question how child labour regulation could be made more effective we need to look at the wider context.

The wider framework affects how we should view the status of legislation. Ratification of the ILO core Conventions on child labour and adoption of the required legislation are really only to be seen as the first step, albeit a very important one, a trigger for a long process at the end of which lies the legal state aimed at by the Conventions. In China, national laws often establish broad rules which may later be clarified by rule-making by people's congresses and administrative authorities at the local level.[104] This also enables complementary and more precise regulatory approaches at the local level. The current legal framework on child labour consists of several laws and regulations and in some provinces local regulation complements

[101] See ibid.

[102] See generally Peerenboom 2002.

[103] See also Liu 2011, at pp. 234–236 and 264.

[104] See Wang 2011, at pp. 24 and 36.

them significantly. Overall, China has developed its legislation to meet the requirements of the ILO core Conventions on child labour. Yet, some issues would deserve more attention in order to bring the legislation fully into line with the content of the Conventions. For example, existing legislative child labour bans do not comprehensively concern apprenticeship, something that may be widely exploited.

Promoting respect for and protection of the human rights of workers has little impact unless enforcement of those rights is seen as an essential element in their being materialized. However, developing a more efficient labour law regime in terms of the child labour issue is a gradual process which should also involve an assessment of legal and administrative reforms and their interrelations. Children who have become engaged in agency work provide an example of how those in the weakest position may end up paying for reforms related to streamlining the labour market. In addition, some groups are in a particularly vulnerable position in China. For example, the fact that social rights often do not necessarily extend to the children of migrant workers due to the *hukou* system is a huge problem, directly linked to children becoming workers.

In order to understand the context of recent and ongoing legislative changes, we need to scrutinize various economic, social and political factors at play. It is crucial to recognize actors who can exercise an influence in turning the letter of the law into social reality. Institutions and practices that affect the shape that legal reality assumes are culturally loaded.[105] As we have seen, the manner in which a legislative child labour ban can be translated into social reality depends on a number of societal factors. In a country where a local government is able to reduce the effectiveness of national regulation, and where companies are able to exploit this reduced effectiveness, the legal infrastructure requires strengthening. Long-term efforts are needed in order to develop a more unified legal order and a stronger status for fundamental labour rights.

We should not underestimate the impact that ILO international labour standards have had in China. Significant efforts to secure the rights of children have been set forth by means of ratified ILO Conventions. Raising awareness of children's human rights is a step in the development of recognizing and securing the human rights of workers more widely. A related need is to better recognize the links between the individual fundamental labour rights themselves.

If the child labour issue remains unsolved, the consequences are felt by the most vulnerable individuals in society. Decisive development of labour law regulation has been among the demands constantly being made by the international child labour movement. As the ILO core Conventions on child labour have been increasingly ratified, demands have shifted to more effective implementation and enforcement of these Conventions. In the case of China, the question of proper enforcement of child labour regulation draws attention to key actors and their interplay. Securing child welfare requires state focus on sustainable economic and social development, and in advancing both of these they should not be separated in decision-making. Implementation of the child labour ban lacks efficiency and could be improved by

[105] See also Brown 2010, at p. 5.

further developing the resources and means of the labour inspectorate. At the same time, the interplay between local authorities and businesses that contributes to exploitation of children should be eliminated. Essentially much of the basic work for combating child labour rests in the hands of local authorities.

Although challenges remain in bringing Chinese legislation and practice into full conformity with the ILO core Conventions on child labour, recent reforms show prospects for further development. In the field of private regulation, we can also identify some developments that could play an important role in the fight against child labour. Yet, the larger picture is that MNCs have not been fully committed to efficient elimination of child labour. Although the Chinese legal system faces challenges which will take time to tackle – as they relate to further strengthening the entire legal infrastructure – it is clear that banning child labour in the country is the work of society as a whole.

References

Literature

Abdul-Garafu, Abdulai. 2009. Are multinational corporations compatible with sustainable development? The experience of development countries. In *Multinational enterprises and the challenge of sustainable development*, ed. John R. McIntyre, Silvester Ivanaj, and Vera Ivanaj, 50–72. Cheltenham: Edward Elgar.

Balme, Stéphanie. 2010. Local courts in Western China. In *Judicial independence in China: Lessons for global rule of law promotion*, ed. Randall Peerenboom, 154–179. Cambridge: Cambridge University Press.

Banks, Kevin. 2006. The impact of globalization on labour standards. In *Globalization and the future of labour law*, ed. D.R. Craig John and S. Micheal Lynk, 77–107. Cambridge: Cambridge University Press.

Belser, Patrick, Michaelle de Cock, and Farhad Mehran. 2005. *ILO minimum estimate of forced labour in the world.* Geneva: International Labour Office.

Brown, Ronald C. 2010. *Understanding labor and employment law in China.* Cambridge: Cambridge University Press.

Brown, Ronald C. 2012. *East Asian labor and employment law. International and comparative context.* Cambridge: Cambridge University Press.

Cooney, Sean. 2007. Making Chinese labour law work: The prospects for regulatory innovation in the People's Republic of China. *Fordham International Law Journal* 30: 1050–1097.

Cooney, Sean, Sarah Biddulph, and Ying Zhu. 2013. *Law and fair work in China.* London: Routledge.

Droux, Joëlle. 2013. From inter-agency concurrences to transnational collaborations: The ILO contribution to child welfare issues during the interwar years. In *Globalizing social rights. The International Labour Organization and beyond*, ed. Sandrine Kott and Joëlle Droux, 262–267. London: Palgrave Macmillan.

Egels-Zandén, Niklas. 2007. Suppliers' compliance with MNCs' codes of conduct: Behind the scenes at Chinese toy suppliers. *Journal of Business Ethics* 75: 45–62.

Gallagher, Mary E., Ching Kwan Lee, and Sarosh Kuruvilla. 2011. Introduction and argument. In *From iron rice bowl to informalization. Markets, workers, and the state in a changing China*, ed. Sarosh Kuruvilla, Ching Kwan Lee, and Mary E. Gallagher, 1–16. Ithaca/London: ILR Press.

Harpur, Paul D. 2011. New governance and the role of public and private monitoring of labor conditions: Sweatshops and China social compliance for textile and apparel industry. *Rutgers Law Record* 38: 49–73.

Josephs, Hilary K. 2009. Measuring progress under China's labor law: Goals, processes, outcomes. *Comparative Labor Law & Policy Journal* 30: 373–394.

Kolk, Ans, and Rob van Dulder. 2002. The effectiveness of self-regulation: Corporate codes of conduct and child labour. *European Management Journal* 20(3): 260–271.

Lam, Maria Lai-Ling. 2009. Sustainable development and corporate social responsibility of multinational enterprises in China. In *Multinational enterprises and the challenge of sustainable development*, ed. John R. McIntyre, Silvester Ivanaj, and Vera Ivanaj, 230–244. Cheltenham: Edward Elgar.

Liu, Sida. 2011. With or without the law: The changing meaning of ordinary legal work in China, 1979–2003. In *Chinese justice. Civil dispute resolution in contemporary China*, ed. Margaret Y.K. Woo and Mary E. Gallagher, 234–268. Cambridge: Cambridge University Press.

Liukkunen, Ulla. 2014. Transnational labour law and fundamental labour rights: Making Chinese workers matter? In *China and ILO fundamental principles and rights at work*, ed. Roger Blanpain, vol. eds. Ulla Liukkunen and Chen Yifeng. Bulletin of Comparative Labour Relations 86: 163–180. Alphen aan den Rijn: Kluwer Law International.

Paavilainen, Marja. 2014. Employment discrimination legislation and practice in China in the context of ILO discrimination convention No. 111: Successes, challenges and dynamics of change. In *China and ILO fundamental principles and rights at work*, ed. Roger Blanpain, vol. eds. Ulla Liukkunen and Chen Yifeng. Bulletin of Comparative Labour Relations 86: 125–142. Alphen aan den Rijn: Kluwer Law International.

Peerenboom, Randall. 2002. *China's long march toward rule of law*. Cambridge: Cambridge University Press.

Schömann, Isabelle. 2012. Transnational collective bargaining: In search of a legal framework. In *Transnational collective bargaining at company level: A new component of European industrial relations?* ed. Isabelle Schömann, Romuald Jagodzinski, Guido Boni, Stefan Clauwaert, Vera Glassner, and Teun Jaspers, 219–232. Bruxelles: European Trade Union Institute.

Tapiola, Kari. 2016. Economic, legal, social and political transition in China. In *Fundamental labour rights in China – Legal implementation and cultural logic*, ed. Ulla Liukkunen and Chen Yifeng, 67–82. Dordrecht: Springer.

Trebilcock, Anne and Raimondi Guido. 2008. The ILO's legal activities towards the eradication of child labour: An overview. In *Child labour in a globalized world. A legal analysis of ILO action*, eds. Giuseppe Nesi, Luca Nogler, and Marco Pertile, 17–38. Ashgate. Available at: http://www.ashgate.com/pdf/SamplePages/Child_Labour_in_a_Globalized_World_Cont.pdf. Last accessed 19 June 2015.

Wang, Jiangyu. 2011. China: Legal reform in an emerging socialist market economy. In *Law and legal institutions of Asia: Traditions, adaptations and innovations*, ed. Ann Black and Gary Bell, 24–61. Cambridge: Cambridge University Press.

Woo, Margaret Y.K., and Mary E. Gallagher. 2011a. Introduction. In *Chinese justice. Civil dispute resolution in contemporary China*, ed. Margaret Y.K. Woo and Mary E. Gallagher, 1–24. Cambridge: Cambridge University Press.

Woo, Margaret Y.K., and Mary E. Gallagher. 2011b. Conclusion: Chinese justice from the bottom up. In *Chinese justice. Civil dispute resolution in contemporary China*, ed. Margaret Y.K. Woo and Mary E. Gallagher, 380–402. Cambridge: Cambridge University Press.

Yu, Xiaomin. 2008. Impacts of corporate code of conduct on labour standards: A case study of Reebok's athletic footwear supplier factory in China. *Journal of Business Ethics* 81: 513–529.

Documents and Official Publications

ILO Documents

Constitution of the International Labour Organisation, adopted 1 April 1919. Entry into force 28 June 1919.
Convention concerning Forced or Compulsory Labour, adopted 28 June 1930, ILO C029. Entry into force 1 May 1932. (Forced Labour Convention).
Convention concerning Labour Inspection in Industry and Commerce, adopted 11 July 1947, ILO C081. Entry into force 7 April 1950. (Labour Inspection Convention).
Convention concerning Freedom of Association and Protection of the Right to Organise, adopted 9 July 1948, ILO C087. Entry into force 4 July 1950. (Freedom of Association and Protection of the Right to Organise Convention).
Convention concerning the Application of the Principles of the Right to Organise and to Bargain Collectively, adopted 1 July 1949, ILO C098. Entry into force 18 July 1951. (Right to Organise and Collective Bargaining Convention).
Convention concerning the Abolition of Forced Labour, adopted 25 June 1957, ILO C105. Entry into force 17 January 1959. (Abolition of Forced Labour Convention).
Convention concerning Employment Policy, adopted 9 July 1964, ILO C122. Entry into force 15 July 1966. (Employment Policy Convention).
Convention concerning Labour Inspection in Agriculture, adopted 25 June 1969, ILO C129. Entry into force 19 January 1972. (Labour Inspection (Agriculture) Convention).
Convention concerning Minimum Age for Admission to Employment, adopted 26 June 1973, ILO C138. Entry into force 19 June 1976. (Minimum Age Convention).
Convention concerning Tripartite Consultations to Promote the Implementation of International Labour Standards, adopted 16 May 1978, ILO C144. Entry into force 16 May 1978 (Tripartite Consultation (International Labour Standards) Convention).
Convention concerning Private Employment Agencies, adopted 19 June 1997, ILO C181. Entry into force 10 May 2000. (Private Employment Agencies Convention).
Convention concerning the Prohibition and Immediate Action for the Elimination of the Worst Forms of Child Labour, adopted 17 June 1999, ILO C182. Entry into force 19 November 2000. (Worst Forms of Child Labour Convention).
Convention concerning Decent Work for Domestic Workers, adopted 16 June 2011, ILO C189. Entry into force 5 September 2013. (Domestic Workers Convention).
Declaration on Fundamental Principles and Rights at Work, adopted by the International Labour Conference at its 86th Session, Geneva, 18 June 1998. (1998 Declaration).
Declaration on Social Justice for a Fair Globalization, adopted by the International Labour Conference at its 97th Session, Geneva, 10 June 2008.
Protocol of 2014 to the ILO Forced Labour Convention, 1930, adopted 11 June 2014, ILO P029.
Recommendation concerning the Protection of Women and Children against Lead Poisoning, adopted 28 November 1919, ILO R004. (Lead Poisoning (Women and Children) Recommendation).
Tripartite Declaration of Principles Concerning Multinational Enterprises and Social Policy, adopted by the Governing Body of the ILO at its 204th Session, Geneva, 16 November 1977.

ILO Committee of Experts on the Application of Conventions and Recommendations (CEACR)

ILO CEACR. Observation, adopted 2006a, published 96th ILC session (2007), Minimum Age Convention – China. Available at: http://www.ilo.org/dyn/normlex/en/f?p=1000:13100:0::NO:13100:P13100_COMMENT_ID,P11110_COUNTRY_ID,P11110_COUNTRY_NAME,P11110_COMMENT_YEAR:2272940,103404. Last accessed 19 June 2015.

ILO CEACR. Observation, adopted 2006b, published 96th ILC session (2007), Worst Forms of Child Labour Convention – China. Available at: http://www.ilo.org/dyn/normlex/en/f?p=1000:13100:0::NO:13100:P13100_COMMENT_ID:2272957. Last accessed 19 June 2015.
ILO CEACR. Observation, adopted 2008, published 98th ILC session (2009), Minimum Age Convention – China. Available at: http://www.ilo.org/dyn/normlex/en/f?p=1000:13100:0::NO:13100:P13100_COMMENT_ID:2295104. Last accessed 19 June 2015.
ILO CEACR. Direct Request, adopted 2008, published 98th ILC session (2009), Minimum Age Convention – China. Available at: http://www.ilo.org/dyn/normlex/en/f?p=1000:13100:0::NO:13100:P13100_COMMENT_ID:2295111. Last accessed 19 June 2015.
ILO CEACR. Observation, adopted 2010, published 100th ILC session (2011), Minimum Age Convention – China. Available at: http://www.ilo.org/dyn/normlex/en/f?p=1000:13100:0::NO:13100:P13100_COMMENT_ID:2334999. Last accessed 19 June 2015.
ILO CEACR. Direct Request, adopted 2010a, published 100th ILC session (2011), Minimum Age Convention – China. Available at: http://www.ilo.org/dyn/normlex/en/f?p=NORMLEXPUB:13100:0::NO:13100:P13100_COMMENT_ID:2335006. Last accessed 19 June 2015.
ILO CEACR. Direct Request, adopted 2010b, published 100th ILC session (2011), Worst Forms of Child Labour Convention – China. Available at: http://www.ilo.org/dyn/normlex/en/f?p=NORMLEXPUB:13100:0::NO:13100:P13100_COMMENT_ID:2335071:NO. Last accessed 19 June 2015.

Other ILO Documentation

Decent Work Country Programme in the People's Republic of China 2013 – 2015. Available at: http://www.ilo.org/public/english/bureau/program/dwcp/download/china.pdf. Last accessed 19 June 2015.
ILO Director-General calls on countries to boost efforts to fight child labour. ILO Press Release, 8 October 2013. Available at: http://www.ilo.org/global/about-the-ilo/newsroom/news/WCMS_223479/lang--en/index.htm. Last accessed 19 June 2015.
ILO website on International Labour Standards on Child Labour. Available at: http://www.ilo.org/global/standards/subjects-covered-by-international-labour-standards/child-labour/lang--it/index.htm#P13_2757. Last accessed 19 June 2015.
ILO website on International Programme on the Elimination of Child Labour (IPEC). Available at: http://www.ilo.org/ipec/programme/lang--en/index.htm. Last accessed 19 June 2015.

Other International Law Sources

Convention on the Rights of the Child, adopted 20 November 1989, 1577 U.N.T.S. 3. Entry into force 2 September 1990.
Organisation for Economic Co-operation and Development. 2008. *Guidelines for Multinational Enterprises*. Paris: OECD. Available at: http://www.oecd.org/corporate/mne/1922428.pdf. Last accessed 19 June 2015.
UN Committee on Economic, Social and Cultural Rights, Concluding Observations on the Combined Third and Fourth Periodic Reports of China, adopted by the Committee at its 64th session (16 September–4 October 2013).
UN Committee on the Rights of the Child. General comment No. 16 (2013) on State Obligations regarding the Impact of the Business Sector on Children's Rights, U.N. Doc. CRC/C/GC/16, 15 March 2013.
UN Economic and Social Council. 2011. *Guiding Principles on Business and Human Rights: Implementing the United Nations 'Protect, Respect and Remedy' Framework*. New York and Geneva: United Nations. Available at: http://www.ohchr.org/Documents/Publications/GuidingPrinciplesBusinessHR_EN.pdf. Last accessed 19 June 2015.

UN General Assembly. Protocol to Prevent, Suppress and Punish Trafficking in Persons, Especially Women and Children, Supplementing the United Nations Convention against Transnational Organized Crime. GA Res. 55/25, U.N.Doc. A/RES/55/25, 15 November 2000. (Palermo Protocol).
UN Human Rights Council. Resolution on Elaboration of an international legally binding instrument on Transnational Corporations and other Business Enterprises with respect to Human Rights. U.N. Doc. A/HRC/26/L.22, 26 June 2014.

Chinese Regulation

Laws by the Standing Committee of the National People's Congress

[Compulsory Education Law of the People's Republic of China] 中华人民共和国义务教育法 (zhōng huá rén mín gòng hé guó yì wù jiào yù fǎ), Standing Committee of the National People's Congress, adopted 12 April 1986, effective 1 July 1986. Revised 29 June 2006, effective 1 September 2006.
[Criminal Law of the People's Republic of China] 中华人民共和国刑法 (zhōng huá rén mín gòng hé guó xíng fǎ), Standing Committee of National People's Congress, adopted 6 July 1979, effective 1 January 1980. Revised 25 February 2011, effective 1 May 2011.
[Decision on the Revision of the Labour Contract Law of the People's Republic of China] 关于修改《中华人民共和国劳动合同法》的决定 (guān yú xiū gǎi zhōng huá rén mín gòng hé guó láo dòng hé tóng fǎ de jué dìng), Standing Committee of National People's Congress, adopted 28 December 2012, effective 1 July 2013.
[Labour Contract Law of the People's Republic of China] 中华人民共和国劳动合同法 (zhōng huá rén mín gòng hé guó láo dòng hé tóng fǎ), Standing Committee of the National People's Congress, adopted 29 June 2007, effective 1 January 2008. Revised 28 December 2012, effective 1 July 2013.
[Labour Law of the People's Republic of China] 中华人民共和国劳动法 (zhōng huá rén mín gòng hé guó láo dòng fǎ), Standing Committee of the National People's Congress, adopted 5 July 1994, effective 1 January 1995.
[Law on the Protection of Minors] 中华人民共和国未成年人保护法 (zhōng huá rén mín gòng hé guó wèi chéng nián rén bǎo hù fǎ), Standing Committee of the National People's Congress, adopted 4 September 1991, effective 1 January 1992. Revised 26 October 2012, effective 1 January 2013. Revised 26 October 2012, effective 1 January 2013.

Regulations by the State Council

[Provisions on the Prohibition of Using Child Labour] 禁止使用童工规定 (jìn zhǐ shǐ yòng tóng gōng guī dìng), State Council, adopted and effective 15 April 1991. Abolished 1 December 2002.
[Provisions on the Prohibition of Using Child Labour] 禁止使用童工规定 (jìn zhǐ shǐ yòng tóng gōng guī ding), State Council, adopted 1 October 2002, effective 1 December 2002.
[Regulations on Labour and Social Security Supervision] 劳动保障监察条例 (láo dòng bǎo zhàng jiān chá tiáo lì), State Council, adopted 26 October 2004, effective 1 November 2004.
[Regulations on Labour Protection in Working Places with Toxic Materials] 使用有毒物品作业场所劳动保护条例 (shǐ yòng yǒu dú wù pǐn zuò yè chǎng suǒ láo dòng bǎo hù tiáo lì), State Council, adopted 30 April 2002, effective 2 May 2002.

Administrative Regulations

[Regulations on Strengthening and Improving the Training Work of Apprentices] 关于加强和改进学徒培训工作的规定 (guān yú jiā qiáng hé gǎi jìn xué tú péi xùn gōng zuò de guī ding), National Labour Bureau of China, adopted 21 May 1981.

Local Regulations

[Zhejiang Provincial Implementing Measures on the Provisions on the Prohibition of Using Child Labour] 浙江省实施《禁止使用童工规定》办法 (zhè jiāng shěng shí shī "jìn zhǐ shǐ yòng tóng gōng guī dìng" bàn fǎ), People's Government of Zhengjiang Province, adopted 30 June 2008, effective 1 August 2008.

Other Chinese Official Documents

[China's National Plan of Action against Trafficking (2013–2020)] 中国反对拐卖人口行动计划 (2013–2020年) (zhōng guó fǎn duì guǎi mài rén kǒu xíng dòng jì huá (2013–2020)), State Council, adopted and effective 2 March 2013.

[National Human Rights Action Plan (2012–2015)] 国家人权行动计划 (2012–2015年) (guó jiā rén quán háng dòng jì huá (2012–2015nián)), State Council, 11 June 2012.

[National Programme of Action for Child Development in China (2011–2020)] 中国儿童发展纲要 (2011–2020年) (zhōng guó ér tóng fā zhǎn gāng yào (2011–2020nián)), State Council, adopted and effective 31 July 2011.

[Ten Year Poverty Reduction Programme] 中国的十年减贫战略(2011–2020) (zhōng guó de shí nián jiǎn pín zhàn luè (2011–2020)).

[12th Five-Year Plan for National Economic and Social Development of the People's Republic of China] 国民经济和社会发展第十二个五年规划纲要 (guó mín jīng jì hé shè huì fā zhǎn dì shí èr gè wǔ nián guī huá gāng yào), National People's Congress, adopted and effective 14 March 2011.

Other Sources

Casale, Giuseppe, and Changyou Zhu. 2013. Labour administrative reforms in China. Geneva: International Labour Office. Available at: http://www.ilo.org/wcmsp5/groups/public/---ed_dialogue/---lab_admin/documents/publication/wcms_224430.pdf. Last accessed 19 June 2015.

China Development Forum. 2013. Choosing China: Insights from multinationals on the investment environment. 2013 China development forum survey report. Available at: http://www.pwccn.com/webmedia/doc/634994768834001054_cn_dev_rpt_2013.pdf. Last accessed 1 2015.

FIDH. 2013. China's workers are calling for change. What role should brands play? Available at: https://www.fidh.org/IMG/pdf/rapport_chinese_workers-uk-hd3.pdf. Last accessed 19 June 2015.

Herbert, Ann. 2012. Opening speech at the conference on the application of child labour conventions, 6 September 2012. Available at: http://www.ilo.org/beijing/information-resources/public-information/speeches/WCMS_190026/lang--en/index.htm. Last accessed 19 June 2015.

Herd, Richard, Vincent Koen and Anders Reutersward. 2010. *China's labour market in transition: Job creation, migration and regulation*. Economic department working papers No. 749. Paris: OECD.

Yunnan Province Women's Federation, in collaboration with Yunnan Provincial Bureau of Statistics, Bureau of Statistics, Education Commission, and Justice Bureau of Jiangcheng and Menghai Counties. 2002. Yunnan province, China: Situation of trafficking in children and women: A rapid assessment. International Labour Organization. Available at: http://www.ilo.org/wcmsp5/groups/public/---asia/---ro-bangkok/documents/publication/wcms_bk_pb_12_en.pdf. Last accessed 19 June 2015.

Zheng, Caixiong and Zhao, Yinan. 2013. Family plans lawsuit in teen worker's death. China Daily USA, June 4. Available at http://usa.chinadaily.com.cn/china/2013-06/04/content_16562476.htm. Last accessed 19 June 2015.

Chapter 7
China – U.S. Implementation of ILO Standards by BITs and Pieces (FTAs)

Ronald C. Brown

7.1 Introduction

Implementing the International Labour Organization's (ILO) standards can be complex and requires analysis in different dimensions. For example, China has issued a new Social Security Insurance Law; its coverage and benefit levels are impressive and surpass many other countries' laws and clearly seem to meet the requirements of ILO Social Security (Minimum Standards) Convention No. 102. China has not yet ratified the Convention and in discussions with the Chinese, they say there are numbers of serious deficiencies already needing reform in its application and enforcement to the intended beneficiaries.[1] It seems, due to national characteristics, the law is filled with exceptions and variations within provinces and localities. Examples affecting both application and enforcement include the practice of using broad language in national legislation, leaving the specific detailed regulations with the local governments, and designating funding of some programmes to be implemented at the regional and local levels to allow for economic differences. Thus, it is elemental that when and how ILO labour standards are implemented is complex and requires multi-level analysis. This paper approaches that issue from assessing whether and how international obligations may affect implementation of ILO core labour standards.

I would like to credit my research assistant Scott Prange for his research assistance.

[1] The discussion, with Chinese scholars and Chinese Government Labour officials, took place during an academic conference on new Social Security Law at Peking University in December 2012. See Brown 2015.

R.C. Brown (✉)
William S. Richardson School of Law, University of Hawai'i Mānoa,
2515 Dole Street, 96822-2350 Honolulu, HI, USA
e-mail: ronaldc@hawaii.edu

U. Liukkunen, Y. Chen (eds.), *Fundamental Labour Rights in China — Legal Implementation and Cultural Logic*, Ius Gentium: Comparative Perspectives on Law and Justice 49, DOI 10.1007/978-3-319-23156-3_7

Distinguishing between the levels of obligation generated from commitment to the ILO Declaration versus a core Convention is important as the international instruments of Bilateral Investment Treaties (BITs) and Free Trade Agreements (FTAs) may use either or both. Discussion below explores the nature of the obligations as they may differ. The international vehicles employing labour obligations are found in BITs and FTAs and can be found in U.S. instruments, but are usually absent in China's FTAs. Currently, the U.S. and China are negotiating a BIT in which the U.S. Model BIT contains obligations relating to the ILO core labour standards. The theme of this paper is to discuss the impact of these international standards on China's current labour laws, if implemented, or their influence, if not implemented, as well as to assess the current gap between domestic laws and international standards. Also, briefly presented is a description of current labour legislation in the U.S. and in China and the existing gaps in the requirements of the ILO core labour standards were they to be implemented. This can provide a relevant assessment of possible areas of dispute as well as for reform.

The below organization explores and discusses: (1) comparative obligations of the ILO Declaration and the Conventions and cultural logic, (2) international influences and obligations arising from Bilateral Investment Treaties, Free Trade Agreements, and ILO standards, (3) aligning U.S. and Chinese law with ILO Labour Conventions: how far is the implementing gap? and, (4) conclusion and recommendations.

7.2 Comparative Obligations of the ILO Declaration and Conventions Within Cultural Logic

While the focus of this paper is on implementation of ILO "fundamental labour rights", it is also useful to understand the nature of the obligations flowing from the ILO Declaration versus the ILO Conventions and the common obstacles facing implementation of all laws and ILO obligations in the U.S. and in China, with its decentralized approach to legislation which may result in wide variations in interpretations and enforcement at local levels.

In the ILO Declaration on Fundamental Principles and Rights at Work (1998 Declaration), the ILO governing body declares that

> "all Members, even if they have not ratified the Conventions in question, have an obligation arising from the very fact of membership in the Organization to respect, to promote and to realize, in good faith and in accordance with the Constitution, the principles concerning the fundamental rights which are the subject of those Conventions, namely:
>
> (a) freedom of association and the effective recognition of the right to collective bargaining;
> (b) elimination of all forms of forced or compulsory labour;

(c) effective abolition of child labour; and
(d) elimination of discrimination in respect of employment and occupation."[2]

These rights are enshrined in eight ILO Fundamental Conventions, referred to in the 1998 Declaration as the Fundamental Conventions. They include: (1) Freedom of Association and Protection of the Right to Organize Convention No. 87[3]; (2) Right to Organize and Collective Bargaining Convention No. 98[4]; (3) Forced Labour Convention No. 29[5]; (4) Abolition of Forced Labour Convention No. 105[6]; (5) Minimum Age Convention No. 138[7]; (6) the Worst Forms of Child Labour Convention No. 182[8]; (7) Discrimination (Employment and Occupation) Convention No. 111[9]; and (8) Equal Remuneration Convention No. 100.[10]

7.2.1 Differentiating Obligations Under the ILO Declaration and Conventions

Intended to advance the international labour rights regime, the 1998 Declaration was promulgated by the International Labour Conference (ILC), concerned that existing ILO Conventions had not yet widely been ratified by its members.[11] The 1998 Declaration was radical in that it utilized an international set of core labour rights to be universally adopted regardless of whether individual signatories had

[2] ILO, Declaration, 1998, Article 2.

[3] Protects the right of workers and employers to establish and join organizations according to their own choices without prior authorization, and lays down a series of guarantees for the free functioning of organizations without any interference by the public authorities.

[4] Guarantees workers the right to enjoy adequate protection against anti-union discrimination, prohibits mutual interference between workers' and employers' organizations, and provides for measures to promote collective bargaining.

[5] Requires member states to suppress the use of forced or compulsory labour in all its forms as soon as possible, with certain exceptions, such as military service, properly supervised convict labour etc.

[6] Requires each member state to take effective measures to secure the immediate and complete abolition of forced or compulsory labour as a means of political coercion or education, punishment for political dissenters, economic development, labour discipline, punishment for participation in strikes, or discrimination.

[7] Aims at the abolition of child labour and requires member states to specify a minimum age for admission to employment not less than the age of completion of compulsory schooling.

[8] Requires members to take immediate and effective measures to secure the prohibition and elimination of the worst forms of child labour such as slavery, prostitution, drug trafficking etc.

[9] Calls for a national policy to eliminate discrimination in access to employment, training, and working conditions on the basis of race, colour, sex, religion, political opinion, national extraction or social origin and to promote equality of opportunity and treatment with regard to employment and occupation.

[10] Calls for equal pay for men and women for work of equal value without discrimination based on sex.

[11] ILO, Declaration, 1998.

endorsed corresponding ILO Conventions, apoliticizing specific labour rights, but to promote universal adoption, its drafters simply alluded to aspirational labour rights with vague language rather than institutionalizing substantive ones.[12]

As the 1998 Declaration applies universally, and the underlying ILO Conventions do not, both arguably may be integral to or both may be separate from the ILO Conventions, depending on individual signatories. Within the context of China, though, the 1998 Declaration must be bifurcated from the ILO Conventions, because while China, as an ILO member is bound by the Declaration, it has not ratified the entire battery of conventions, which may hint at underlying cultural logic.[13] On the world scene, that is, adhering to international norms like those in the Declaration, even if only aspirationally, may be how China would like to cultivate its image as a country, but at home, it is hesitant, through its regime of labour and employment laws, to enshroud some of the substantive standards as embodied in the ILO Conventions such as the freedom of association allowing more than one labour union, because doing so, it is thought by some, could affect the balance of governing powers. The problem is, with this distinction, the extent of China's 1998 Declaration obligation is ambiguous, because the Declaration's meaning, given its vague language, is largely informed by the actual ILO Conventions.

To this end, the ILO Constitution seems to be enshrouded by the 1998 Declaration but both clearly serve as the legal basis for the Conventions.[14] Turning to the Declaration's drafters, the ILC does not elucidate how the Declaration is distinct from the ILO Conventions and underlying labour rights. While both the 1998 Declaration and the ILO Conventions are related, they noted, both are sufficiently independent. The governments of the U.S., Chile, Sweden, France, and Brazil state that "the Declaration referred to adherence to principles and values and not to specific Conventions".[15] The Canadian government, whose ambassador chaired the drafting committee, likewise, stated that the ILO 1998 Declaration "should be based on the principles of the Constitution, reflected in the Conventions, but not on specific provisions of conventions".[16] Reflecting this point, the ILO legal advisor remarked: "the Declaration contemplated the implementation, not of specific provisions of Conventions, but rather of the principles of those Conventions".[17]

Because of this, the relationship between the 1998 Declaration and the ILO Conventions is contentious. According to the Declaration, its principles inform the ILO Conventions that form the basis for ILO fundamental core labour rights, but none of the ILC members can edify how.[18]

However, the 1998 Declaration is thought to strongly inform ILO Conventions, in some circles. A former ILO legal advisor, Francis Maupain, argues that the 1998

[12] Alston 2004.

[13] See Spieler 2003, at p. 99.

[14] ILC, Consideration of a possible Declaration, 1998.

[15] ILC, Report of the Committee, 1998, para. 217.

[16] Ibid., para. 22.

[17] Ibid., para. 72.

[18] ILC, Consideration of a possible Declaration, 1998.

Declaration and the ILO Conventions provide a fuller understanding of underlying labour rights, noting "there is no danger that the principles and their content will be liberated from the anchor of the relevant conventions and painstakingly constructed jurisprudence in relation to these rights *for the simple reasons that they are the anchors*".[19] Though there are four core labour standards, they include and cover eight ILO Conventions.[20] According to an AFL – CIO (American Federation of Labor – Congress of Industrial Organizations) policy statement, the 1998 Declaration's "core labour standards are based on international human rights law" and the relevant ILO Conventions "give content to these core standards".[21]

Within this framework, to be clear, while China is a signatory to the 1998 Declaration, it has ratified only four of the ILO Conventions, which embody the fundamental rights the former address: (1) Minimum Age Convention No. 138, (2) the Worst Forms of Child labour Convention No. 182, (3) the Discrimination (Employment and Occupation) Convention No. 111 and (4) the Equal Remuneration Convention No. 100.[22]

The legal implication of obligations emanating from a 1998 Declaration versus the Conventions is in the specificity contained in the latter and accompanying guides as to its proper application and interpretation versus the generalities contained in the Declaration allowing an easier measure of compliance with ILO standards and enforcement of specific obligations. Thus, as can be seen from the above analysis, different obligatory consequences appear to be flowing from the 1998 Declaration versus the Conventions, but perhaps it is a difference in degree rather than a difference in kind.

7.2.2 *Obligations Within Cultural Logic*

Whatever the resulting obligation and its resulting legal implementation, it must take place within the cultural logic of a country. The mutual assumption of particular cultural ideas provides human groups with common premises for predictably convergent inferential processes.

> This process of people collectively using effectively identical assumptions in interpreting each other's actions – i.e. hypothesizing as to each other's motivations and intentions – may be termed *cultural logic*. This logic relies on the establishment of stereotypes and other kinds of precedents, catalogued in individuals' personal libraries, as models and scenarios which may serve as reference in inferring and attributing motivations behind people's actions, and behind other mysterious phenomena.[23]

---

[19] Maupain 2005, at p. 450.

[20] Human Rights Watch 2007.

[21] AFL – CIO 2000.

[22] The ratification dates can be found on the ILO Normlex website.

[23] Enfield 2000.

In this case, its implementation must pass through the "Chinese characteristics" of law and law enforcement.[24] Government laws and regulations are decentralized in that national legislation generally sets forth broad standards, but leaves the local detailed implementing regulations to the provincial and local authorities. Thus, there can be wide variances in obligations regarding coverage, funding, and enforcement.

Likewise, there appear to be some similarities between China and the United States (U.S.) in their publically embracing the ILO 1998 Declaration and all of its laudable aims, while at the same time failing to ratify important fundamental labour rights, perhaps to protect national sovereignty over politically sensitive issues; perhaps feeling current national labour legislation is adequate and best meets the needs of its citizenry; or, that its current socio- political situation would not permit the required reforms to be acceptable. Or perhaps optimistically, it is a technique of cultural logic that bolsters the central government's ability to deflect domestic criticism of reforms to elevate standards by providing the political cover of – "the 'Emperor' is making us do this". It is interesting to see in the FTAs and BITs that the U.S. may state its commitment to ILO fundamental labour rights, but it redefines its obligations by footnotes to be obligated only as to the 1998 Declaration.[25] China, more forthrightly in its FTAs has not committed to ILO fundamental labour rights or the 1998 Declaration. This may illustrate a common cultural logic of the U.S. and China. Therefore, it is perhaps significant if the U.S. and China were to conclude their current negotiations of a BIT that included obligations to fulfill/implement the appropriate ILO standards as provided in the BIT. Thus, truly implementing an ILO obligation, whether it arises from the Declaration or a Convention, is complex and always has layers, and dimensions within layers.

7.3 International Influences and Obligations Arising from Bilateral Investment Treaties (BITs) and Free Trade Agreements (FTAs) and ILO Standards

7.3.1 China – U.S. Bilateral Trade and Investment Treaty (BIT) and ILO Standards

Currently, China and the U.S. are negotiating a bilateral investment treaty (BIT), which likely will further U.S. and Chinese commitments to the 1998 Declaration, while evading any meaningful commitment to ILO Conventions, bolstering the claim that each is committed to the former and not necessarily the latter and supporting an emerging cultural logic that portrays each as being good global citizens, but at the same time does not cause political "blowback" from those that might

[24] Brown 1997.

[25] KORUS 2011, Article 13.3 (a)–(f), at n. 17.

oppose implementation of "global labour standards", and giving the respective governments some "wiggle room" to negotiate future implementation of ILO standards.

As part of the U.S. – China Strategic Economic Dialogue (SED), an annual bilateral meeting, on June 18, 2008, China and the U.S. agreed to negotiations on a BIT.[26] The decision to launch these negotiations followed 17 months of exploratory talks by both countries, which laid the groundwork for the BIT. If realized, the China – U.S. BIT would cover, in both countries across all sectors, all bilateral investment. Although the U.S. has agreed with other countries to enter into BITs that cover all sectors and all types of investment and which have included labour standard provisions, this is the first time China may include a labour standards provision.[27] Last year, U.S. direct investment in China stood at $51 billion, while Chinese direct investment in the U.S. was $5.15 billion.[28]

It was a U.S. Administration priority to enhance labour and environmental standards in the model BIT so as to provide greater possible labour protections for workers. As a result, the 2012 Model BIT expands obligations in the area of labour in four important ways[29]:

1. The 2012 Model BIT includes an obligation on Parties to not waive or derogate from their domestic labour laws as an encouragement for investment, where such derogations would be "inconsistent" with non-derogable rights and not derogations in general.[30]
2. A new obligation to "effectively enforce" domestic laws. The 2012 model BIT also contains an obligation on Parties not to fail to effectively enforce their domestic labour and environmental laws as an encouragement for investment.

---

[26] The first Strategic Economic Dialogue between the U.S. and China was launched in September 2006. The second to the sixth Strategic Economic Dialogues were held in December 2006, May 2007, December 2007, June 2008, and December 2008, respectively. When President Barack Obama and President Hu Jintao first met in April 2009, the Strategic Economic Dialogue was renamed as the Strategic and Economic Dialogue to encompass strategic issues. The first Strategic and Economic Dialogue was held from 28 to 29 July 2009, in Washington, D.C.

[27] Bourassa 2013. Noting that following SED, the two countries held the U.S. – China Investment Forum on 16 June 2008, where both sides agreed on a technical framework and work plan for the BIT. Yet, the U.S. vowed that the timeline for concluding the agreement would be determined by the quality of progress made on some related issues with China.

[28] Talley and Mauldin 2013.

[29] Office of the Spokeperson of the U.S. Department of State, 2012. At the U.S. – China SED in July 2013, representatives from the U.S. and Chinese governments announced that the two countries had entered into sustained negotiations on the BIT, moving from its technical framework to talks on the actual text.

[30] U.S. Model BIT 2012, Article 13(2). "These obligations align with firmer commitments in recent U.S. free trade agreements (FTAs) and depart from the aspirational language of the 2004 Model and the BITs of other states, which merely require that parties 'should not' derogate from existing labor legislation or 'shall strive to ensure' not to do so. The obligations in question are not limited to investments from the other party, but equally apply to the weakening of labor standards in favor of investments of third states (Article 2(1)(c))", see Prislan and Zandvliet 2013.

3. Parties reaffirm their commitments under the ILO Declaration and recognize the importance of multilateral environmental agreements.[31]
4. The 2012 Model BIT subjects the articles on labour and environment to more detailed and extensive consultation procedures, but the labour provisions otherwise remain outside the treaty's dispute resolution provisions.[32] Although the 2012 Model BIT dictates how the U.S. and its partner will enforce the agreement to deal with investment disputes, it is less clear how the U.S. and its partner would enforce its employment/ labour provisions. The Article pertaining to these provisions simply states that the U.S. and its partners, when they have a dispute that falls under it, should notify the other in writing with a request for consultations, with the other responding within 30 days, and with both agreeing to work towards a mutually satisfying resolution.[33] Unlike model FTA language, the U.S. BIT does not wed investment sanctions with its employment and labour provisions nor does it seem to have any meaningful enforcement mechanism for them.[34]

In sum, under the 2012 Model BIT, the U.S. and its BIT partner commit to their respective obligations as ILO members and to their commitment to the ILO 1998 Declaration and its Follow-up.[35] Moreover, the U.S. and its BIT partner agree to affirm domestic laws and not to waver from them with respect to worker protections via sustained or reoccurring action or inaction.[36]

To clarify, the Model BIT specifies which domestic U.S. and partner laws would pertain to worker rights, reflecting the ILO fundamental labour rights as those related to (1) freedom of association, (2) effective recognition of the right to collective bargaining, (3) elimination of all forms of compulsory labour, (3) effective abolition of all forms of child labour and the worst forms of child labour, (4) elimination of discrimination in respect to employment and occupation, and (5) acceptable conditions of work with respect to minimum wages, hours of work, and occupational safety and health.[37] While the Model BIT now comprises all four "fundamental labour rights" listed as such in the ILO 1998 Declaration, as well as the right to acceptable conditions of work, which is otherwise not found in the Declaration, the final U.S. commitment in the proposed China – U.S. BIT is only to

---

[31] U.S. Model BIT 2012.

[32] U.S. Model BIT 2012, Article 13(4). On the other hand, it can be argued that investors might pursue claims relating to the non-enforcement of labour obligations as they arise under other standards for which arbitration is available, see Prislan and Zandvliet 2013.

[33] U.S. Model BIT 2012, Article 13(4).

[34] The U.S. Model FTA Social Dimension provision, illustrated in KORUS, also sets out a level of transnational administrative oversight and coordination, mechanisms of implementation, and enforcement mechanisms, some more meaningful than others. The typical U.S. enforcement mechanism weds trade and labour issues and authorizes State to State or stakeholder arbitration with penalties, see KORUS 2011.

[35] U.S. Model BIT 2012, Article 13(1).

[36] Ibid., Article 13(2).

[37] Ibid., Article 13(3) (a)–(f).

the 1998 Declaration. Further, under the Model BIT, however, the U.S. has restricted its commitment to conforming only to U.S. Congressional acts and regulations, pursuant to such an act, via an exculpatory footnote.[38]

The U.S. also has expressed interest in having a set of enforcement procedures to effectively monitor China's compliance with the national treatment obligations. For example, in tangent to the 2012 Model BIT dispute provisions, the U.S. has suggested that it is necessary to draft the BIT with specific presumptions, evidentiary burdens, or standards to allow inferences of discrimination when the Chinese public record is unclear.[39]

In regard to the U.S. – China BIT, the 2012 Model BIT is serving as the framework for negotiations. With regard to the 2012 U.S. Model BIT, the U.S. aims to bind other countries to preventing businesses from compromising worker protections under the banner of investment. However, within the Model BIT, it is clear that neither China nor the U.S., while committing to the more aspirational 1998 Declaration, seeks to commit to more substantive norms within the ILO conventions.[40]

7.3.2 Enforcing International and Domestic Obligations Under ILO Declaration or Conventions?

7.3.2.1 BIT

As discussed above, the 2012 U.S. Model BIT, if accepted by China, commits to the 1998 Declaration and further states that when a dispute falls under it, one should notify the other by writing a request for consultations, with the other responding within 30 days, and with both agreeing to work towards a mutually satisfying resolution.[41] Unlike model FTA language, the U.S. BIT does not wed investment sanctions with its employment and labour provisions nor does it allow for arbitration or

[38] Ibid., n. 17.

[39] Kong 2010, at p. 7.

[40] U.S. Model BIT 2012, Preamble. Noting that the parties have committed to the improvement of labour standards in the preamble paragraph, which expresses the goal to achieve the treaty objectives "in a manner consistent with … the promotion of internationally recognized labor rights." However, the AFL-CIO disagrees that the BIT with China has value and has come out against it. It is argued, "[t]he current U.S. approach to BITs is unacceptably flawed, and if the U.S. pursues a BIT with China now, it is likely to cause further harm to U.S.-based producers and America's working families", see Drake 2013. Scott Flaherty, who notes that the AFL-CIO's position is that the U.S. should not pursue a potential investment pact with China "because of China's poor track record on labor rights and a dispute settlement system that may allow state-owned Chinese companies to challenge U.S. laws."; see also Flaherty 2013.

[41] U.S. Model BIT 2012, Article 13(4).

seem to have any meaningful enforcement mechanism for them, rather more of a dialogue is provided. The specific obligations of the BIT were discussed earlier.[42]

So, it can be seen the U.S. 2012 Model BIT obligates the parties to the 1998 Declaration, not the Conventions, except as they may inform interpretation of the Declaration and it further provides that resolution of issues and enforcement will proceed with mutual consultations. Again, China accepting this provision may reflect a Chinese cultural logic of avoiding confrontation in dispute resolution and giving the appearance of being a good global citizen embracing international labour standards, but does not explain the U.S. position, other than maybe the 2012 Model BIT provides the same appearance of good global citizenship without specific commitments. It is an estimate of what they can best get.

7.3.2.2 Free Trade Agreement's Social Dimension Provisions[43]

While China and the U.S. are now negotiating a BIT and not a FTA, the social dimension provisions of the FTA are broader and more protective of labour interests and are usefully examined to show that model commitments and enforcement mechanisms are currently used by the U.S. and the European Union (EU) and are available to be employed also in BITs.

> "Since the beginning of the 1990's, the need to create a minimum social foundation for the development of trade – one that guarantees certain safeguards against social dumping – has resulted in the signing of an increasing number of Free Trade Agreements (FTAs) which include a 'social dimension' provision (labour and environment), either in the agreement itself or in a parallel agreement (e.g. NAFTA). Not only do such labour clauses list minimum

[42] Ibid., Article 13. The BIT provides the following obligations regarding labour:

The Parties reaffirm their respective obligations as members of the ILO their commitments under the ILO Declaration on Fundamental Principles and Rights at Work and its Follow-Up. The Parties recognize that it is inappropriate to encourage investment by weakening or reducing the protections afforded in domestic labor laws. Accordingly, each Party shall ensure that it does not waive or otherwise derogate from or offer to waive or otherwise derogate from its labor laws where the waiver or derogation would be inconsistent with the labor rights referred to in subparagraphs (a) through (e) of paragraph 3, or fail to effectively enforce its labor laws through a sustained or recurring course of action or inaction, as an encouragement for the establishment, acquisition, expansion, or retention of an investment in its territory. For purposes of this Article, "labor laws" means each Party's statutes or regulations, or provisions thereof, that are directly related to the following: (a) freedom of association; (b) the effective recognition of the right to collective bargaining; (c) The elimination of all forms of forced or compulsory labor; (d) the effective abolition of child labor and a prohibition on the worst forms of child labor; (e) the elimination of discrimination in respect of employment and occupation; and (f) acceptable conditions of work with respect to minimum wages, hours of work, and occupational safety and health. A Party may make a written request for consultations with the other Party regarding any matter arising under this Article. The other Party shall respond to a request for consultations within 30 days of receipt of such request. Thereafter, the Parties shall consult and endeavor to reach a mutually satisfactory resolution. The Parties confirm that each Party may, as appropriate, provide opportunities for public participation regarding any matter arising under this Article.

[43] See generally Compa and Meyer 2010.

commitments for the protection of human rights at work and refer to specific international labour rights adopted by the ILO, but they also provide for conflict resolution systems as well as funds and parallel labour cooperation/consultation. Indeed, a growing number of bilateral FTAs – particularly those signed by Canada, the U.S. and the EU – contain social and labour provisions along those lines".[44]

The case for a social dimension is based on the fact that transnational integration has benefits and costs. The benefits are usually spread widely across the population (more choice; lower prices to consumers) and take time to be felt through more efficient use of resources, economies of scale, higher productivity; new ventures and new job openings. The costs, on the other hand, can be highly concentrated such as closure of plants or lines of production, redundancies in concentrated geographic areas, and accelerated pace of production, pressure on wages and working conditions.[45]

Typical concerns related to designing the social dimension include addressing the effects on employment (changes related to FTA?), uneven bargaining power between capital and labour allowing "capital flight" to a more labour-advantage country, and harnessing regulatory competition to rein in "races to the bottom".

Generally, the social dimension provisions address a number of areas. These include a level of commitment to international labour rights. The U.S. normally commits to the ILO fundamental labour rights but by footnote, limits the definition of that commitment to the ILO 1998 Declaration, as for example in the U.S. South-Korea FTA (KORUS).[46] The provision also sets out a level of transnational administrative oversight and coordination, mechanisms for implementation, and enforcement mechanisms, some more meaningful than others. The typical U.S. enforcement mechanism weds trade and labour issues and authorizes state to state or stakeholder arbitration with penalties. This is in contrast to the European Union's FTAs which while committing to ILO fundamental labour rights do not wed trade and labour provisions and have a weaker enforcement mechanism.[47]

Under KORUS and the U.S. – Peru FTA (PFTA), labour standards are limited to the ILO 1998 Declaration and do not encompass the four ILO fundamental labour

[44] See ILO website on Free Trade Agreements and Labor Rights.

[45] van Liemt 2004, at p. 18.

[46] It provides, *"[T]he obligations set out in Article 19.2, as they relate to the ILO, refer only to the ILO Declaration."* [*emphasis added*], see KORUS 2011, Article 19(2)(1) and n. 1. The ILO core Conventions themselves are not expressly referenced in Article 19.2. The ILO recognizes eight fundamental labour conventions, seven of which existed at the time that the 1998 Declaration was adopted. These conventions are as follows: the Forced Labour Convention, the Freedom of Association and Protection of the Right to Organise Convention, the Right to Organise and Collective Bargaining Convention, the Equal Remuneration Convention, the Abolition of Forced Labour Convention, the Discrimination (Employment and Occupation) Convention, the Minimum Age Convention, and the Worst Forms of Child Labour Convention.

[47] ILO, European Free Trade Agreements, 2013; CBC News 2013; Cooper et al. 2011, at p. 19. The EU just concluded a new FTA with Canada (CETA), which may embrace additional ILO standards and have a more meaningful enforcement mechanism. The EU and the U.S. are in current negotiations for a new U.S. – EU FTA.

rights. While some stakeholders argue that the Declaration incorporates ILO Conventions and obligates the parties to abide by fundamental labour rights, others do not share this position largely because of the addition of a footnote to both FTA's, specifically excluding them and limiting it to only the ILO 1998 Declaration.[48]

On the other hand, some FTAs do make stronger commitments to ILO fundamental labour rights. For example, the EU in its FTA with South Korea, under Article 13.4, in accordance with the ILO and the ILO 1998 Declaration and its Follow-Up, parties "commit to respecting, promoting and realizing, in their laws and practice, principles concerning fundamental rights, namely: (1) freedom of association and effective right to collective bargain, (2) elimination of all forms of compulsory labour, (3) the effective abolition of child labour, and (4) the elimination of discrimination in respect of employment and occupation".[49]

Likewise, it appears that in the EU and Canada FTA (CETA), signed in 2014 the parties have agreed to ensure that their national laws conform to ILO fundamental labour rights.[50] However, unlike the EU – South Korea FTA, where both parties agreed to labour norms without seeking meaningful enforcement provisions, Canada appears to have conditioned its acceptance of the identified labour norms on the inclusion of language that expressly provides for effective enforcement mechanisms, to include up to possibly monetary punitive awards. To this end, there appears to be a bifurcated system proposed under CETA, under which parties, including third parties, may bring complaints that labour norms have been violated.[51]

The first dispute resolution mechanism, like under the EU – South Korea FTA, seems to be ministerial, in which either party may consult the other, should a dispute arise over labour norms. Under this mechanism, ministerial consultation occurs when either party notifies the other, and if the dispute is not resolved, the ministerial consultation moves to advisory groups composed of an expert review panel, whose members have been identified by the parties.[52] Upon 120 days of an advisory group/ expert review panel being assembled, it should issue to the parties an initial report, which is non-binding, but includes a finding of facts, the applicability of relevant provisions, and the rationale for any findings or recommendations.[53] Should the parties agree to the panel's initial report, they may notify the advisory group/panel of experts that they will develop an action plan to resolve the issue, within 90 days. But, should the parties not agree to the panel's report, they may ask it to reconvene

[48] U.S. – Korean FTA Implementation Act 2011, Article 19.2.1, n. 1. Noting that the ILO core conventions themselves are not expressly referenced. The ILO recognizes eight fundamental labour conventions, seven of which existed at the time that the 1998 Declaration was adopted. These conventions are listed *supra* n. 46.

[49] EU – South Korea FTA 2011, Article 13.4.

[50] EU – Canada Comprehensive Economic and Trade Agreement (Leaked Draft and unconfirmed) 2011; Media Advisory, 2014; EU Secret Deals 2014.

[51] EU – Canada Comprehensive Economic and Trade Agreement (Leaked Draft and unconfirmed) 2011, Dispute Settlement Provisions and Procedures, Section 33, Article 14, at 463 et seq.

[52] EU – South Korea FTA 2011, Article 11.

[53] Ibid., Article 13.

within 30 days, after which the panel must reconsider the complaint, and issue a final report within 60 days.[54] If after the advisory group/expert panel's final report, the parties are not able to agree to an action plan or do not execute an agreed-to action plan, the non-offending party may ask the panel to institute monetary awards.[55] Within 90 days, the panel, when considering why the parties have not implemented the action plan, considering both mitigating and aggravating factors, may award the monetary cost of implementing the action plan up to $15 million.[56]

The second mechanism, which is not found at all in the EU – South Korea FTA, but which both the EU and Canada appeared to have agreed to, per the latter's proposal, sets forth the following governmental, legal, and administrative frameworks for enforcing the labour norms within each respective party's domestic laws: (1) each party's government should take timely action to establish an administrative regime of inspection elements that gives due consideration to any interested party's complaint of an alleged contravention of labour norms,[57] (2) each party's government should through its legal regime provide for the commencement of proceedings which will lead to appropriate sanctions or remedies, (3) each party should ensure, vis-à-vis these legal proceedings, that there is due process, equitable treatment, and that injunctive relief is available, (4) each party to these proceedings receives appellate review, if required, after receiving the panel's final report.

Of course, it must be emphasized, the final language and obligations of CETA are not yet approved as of the date of this paper. Also, this analysis is not necessarily useful or applicable to China unless or until China enters into an FTA, but it does provide an alternate avenue at the international level to further implementation of fundamental labour rights.

7.3.3 *China: BITs, FTAs, and ILO Standards*

Currently, China and the EU, including its member countries, have neither a bilateral free trade nor an investment agreement.[58] However, China has entered into an agreement with one EU country, Germany, on totalizing social security issues, related to overlapping systems, dealing specifically with pensions, and is in negotiations with several others, including France, Sweden, Belgium, Finland, Denmark and Spain.[59] The agreement, however, includes no mention of either the ILO Declaration or the ILO Conventions.

---

[54] Ibid., Article 14.

[55] Ibid.

[56] Ibid., Annex III.

[57] Ibid., Annex III, Article 4.1.

[58] China FTA Network 2014.

[59] China Internet Information Center 2012.

Likewise, China and ASEAN have a bilateral free trade and investment agreement,[60] but the China – ASEAN FTA deals primarily with trade and tariffs and does not touch upon social dimensions of trade so as to include employment and labour provisions.[61]

In addition, China has concluded a free trade agreement with one ASEAN nation, Singapore.[62] The China – Singapore Free Trade Agreement (CSFTA) was the first comprehensive bilateral FTA that China has signed with another Asian country, covering customs procedures, economic cooperation, dispute settlement, rules of origin, sanitary measures, technical barriers to trade, trade in goods and services, and trade remedies, among others. The CSFTA entered into force on 1 January 2009. However, like the China – ASEAN FTA, the China – Singapore FTA deals mostly with trade and tariffs and does not envelop social dimensions such as employment and labour provisions and so does not touch social security regimes.[63]

China is also pursuing FTAs with other Asian neighbours, including Japan and South Korea. Currently, China and Japan have neither a bilateral free trade nor an investment agreement.[64] However, China is working with both Japan and South Korea on a joint study concerning the feasibility of pursuing such an agreement. Likewise, currently, China and South Korea have neither a bilateral free trade nor an investment agreement.[65] However, China has entered into an agreement with South Korea, on social security issues, related to overlapping systems, dealing specifically with pensions but it does not include a social dimension provision.[66]

It appears that China's only international obligation under a FTA or BIT relating to ILO fundamental labour rights will be the currently negotiated BIT agreement with the U.S., if and when concluded. It may be, as some argue, that China and the U.S. are much alike in that they may want the appearance of compliance with international labour rights without the enforceable obligations of ratified specific conventions, which returns to the earlier discussion on the inherent problem between the ILO 1998 Declaration and the ILO Conventions. That is, the Declaration is aspirational – it does not contain fundamental labour rights, *per se*: it simply declares that signatory countries should try to protect workers' rights according to the four fundamental labour rights, but does not lay out what that would look like, whereas the Conventions do. Within the U.S. 2012 Model FTA and the 2012 Model BIT there is a commitment by the parties to abide by their obligations as the ILO 1998 Declaration signatories, but that does not entail any substantive obligations in terms of aligning domestic law with ILO standards. Rather, the commitment is basically to affirm domestic laws that are already in place that implicate those five

[60] China FTA Network 2014.

[61] China – ASEAN FTA 2002.

[62] China – Singapore FTA 2008.

[63] China – Singapore FTA 2008.

[64] China FTA Network 2014.

[65] Ibid.; Zhang 2014.

[66] The agreement allows credits in each country so as to avoid double payments of social security costs, see Wang and Wei 2009.

labour concerns. There is no commitment by the parties to adopt or ratify any ILO Conventions which would lay out substantive standards.

The following section provides some preliminary discussion on what it would take to align U.S. and Chinese law with ILO Conventions along the five fundamental labour rights areas. That, of course, would be a purely theoretical goal since the model U.S. FTA and BIT do not really call for it.

7.4 Aligning U.S. and Chinese Law with ILO Labour Conventions: How Far Is the Implementing Gap?

In implementing ILO Conventions, an important question is: what is the gap, if any, between the standards of the fundamental labour Conventions and the current laws and practices covered by the Conventions so as to measure the changes or influences of international obligations on the resultant domestic labour legislation? And, an additional question arises as to how the labour provision obligations of a BIT or FTA would affect existing labour laws and the gap between these and ILO fundamental labour rights. This is discussed briefly below in general terms.

The U.S. 2012 Model BIT labour provisions provide it is inappropriate to encourage investment by weakening or reducing the protections in domestic labour laws where this would be inconsistent with the labour rights referred to in a later section containing the following[67]:

(a) Freedom of association;
(b) The effective recognition of the right to collective bargaining;
(c) The elimination of all forms of forced or compulsory labor;
(d) The effective abolition of child labor and a prohibition on the worst forms of child labor;
(e) The elimination of discrimination in respect of employment and occupation; and
(f) Acceptable conditions of work with respect to minimum wages, hours of work, and occupational safety and health.

So, as stated earlier, the U.S. 2012 Model BIT, while obligating the parties to the 1998 Declaration, though not the Conventions, the contents of the fundamental labour provisions are used to inform the interpretation and obligation of the 1998 Declaration. However, it is also clear the theme of embracing the "standards" of the 1998 Declaration, rather than the specific Conventions, provides room on the one hand to maintain current national labour laws while on the other hand espousing aspiration for accepting the more specific fundamental labour rights contained in the Conventions. This cultural logic perhaps is thought to have international political advantage.

[67] U.S. Model BIT 2012, Article 13(3).

The discussion below begins a description of the current gap between ILO fundamental labour rights and current labour laws in the U.S. and China that would need to be maintained under the BIT. This can show the contrast of what further needs to be accomplished in reforming the labour laws to allow for meaningful ratification and implementation of ILO fundamental labour rights.

7.4.1 ILO Conventions Nos. 87 and 98: Freedom of Association and Effective Recognition of the Right to Collectively Bargain

7.4.1.1 The Conventions

In contrast to the ILO Declaration, the ILO Freedom of Association and Protection of the Right to Organise Convention No. 87 and the Right to Organise and Collective Bargaining Convention No. 98 provide a substantive right, in the context of the employer-employee dynamic, for workers to organize and collectively bargain. On 1 July 1949, the International Labour Commission adopted these Conventions, which reflected emerging practice across the industrialized world at the time concerning governance of employer-employee relationships.[68] It is particularly significant because it establishes a firewall between employer and employee, ensuring equity in the relationship, recognizing an individual right exercised collectively, the right of workers to organize and be represented by trade unions in negotiating conditions of employment collectively; in tangent to an individual right conferred on workers, protection against acts of anti-union discrimination[69]; and a collective right attributed to trade union organizations, protection against acts of interference.[70] Under the Conventions, the ILO carved out an exception for some employer-employee relationships, exempting some falling within the public sector for administrative employees of the state.[71] Moreover, despite their endorsement of these rights, Conventions No. 87 and No. 98 do not extend to a corollary right to strike.

7.4.1.2 The Conventions and U.S. Praxis

The U.S. has not ratified Convention No. 87 or Convention No. 98,[72] likely because they do not conform to domestic law. Unlike Conventions No. 87 and No. 98, all of which yield a uniform framework giving substance to the right to organize and

[68] Milman-Silva 2009.

[69] Right to Organise and Collective Bargaining Convention No. 98, Article 1(1).

[70] Ibid., Article 2(2).

[71] Ibid., Article 6.

[72] The ratification dates can be found on the ILO Normlex website.

collectively bargain, in the U.S., a patchwork of federal and/or state and municipal laws dictate the substance of these rights.

In the U.S., under the Constitution, the right to organize and collectively bargain has not been held to be a fundamental constitutional right by the Supreme Court,[73] but under federal statute, namely the National Labor Relations Act (NLRA) it is expressly provided.[74] To this end, under the NRLA, private employers must engage in collective bargaining with the labour union and/or employees in good faith, and may not simply refuse to do so, but parties are not compelled to reach an agreement.[75] Since federal labour law generally preempts state labour law, where jurisdiction is over conduct that is either protected or prohibited; state labour law provisions are thus limited in their application. Generally, if a labour issue does not fall under the National Labor Relations Board's (NLRB) jurisdictional standards and those over which the NLRB declines or cedes jurisdiction, then state labour law may have precedence.[76]

However, as a general rule, in the U.S., under the constitution and federal law, public employees are not entitled to collective bargaining in the sense that private employees are, although a state may provide such a right by statute.[77] Public employees are not entitled to collective bargaining under common law[78]; they only enjoy rights specifically granted by statute.[79]

First, while Conventions No. 87 and No. 98 extend to all people the right to organize and collectively bargain, without only exempting state administrative public workers, U.S. law, while extending these rights to most people, excludes most public workers. To conform to the Conventions, the NLRA would need to be broadened in scope to include both private and most public workers, providing both some parity for rights.

---

[73] Contra, Coastal Florida Police Benev. Ass'n, Inc. v. Williams, 838 So. 2d 543 (Fla. 2003).

[74] 29 U.S.C.A. §§ 141 et seq. (1935).

[75] 356 U.S. 432, 349 (1958). Holding "the duty to bargain is limited to those subjects, and within that area neither party is legally obligated to yield … As to other matters, however, each party is free to bargain or not to bargain, and to agree or not to agree within the statutory phrase, and permissive (or non-mandatory) subjects of bargaining, which fall within the aspect of the relationship between employer and the employees."

[76] Bethlehem Steel Co. v. New York State Labor Relations Bd., 330 U.S. 767, 67 S. Ct. 1026, (1950). Stating that where the National Labor Board has consistently supervised labor relations in any given industry, it then has exclusive jurisdiction over any employer in that industry even if the Board has not yet exercised its powers over the particular employer.

[77] See State v. Florida Police Benev. Ass'n, Inc., 613 So. 2d 415 (Fla. 1992); See also Branch v. City of Myrtle Beach, 340 S.C. 405, 532 S.E.2d 289 (2000).

[78] State v. Delaware State Educational Ass'n, 326 A.2d 868 (Del. Ch. 1974). Holding that Public employees are not entitled to collective bargaining under common law.

[79] State, Dept. of Admin. v. Public Employees Relations Bd., 257 Kan. 275, 894 P.2d 777, 100 Ed. Law Rep. 336 (1995); Cal. – City of Hayward v. United Public Employees, 54 Cal. App. 3d 761, 126 Cal. Rptr. 710 (1st Dist. 1976). Holding that public employees enjoy rights specifically granted by statute. Michigan State AFL-CIO v. Employment Relations Com'n, 453 Mich. 362, 551 N.W.2d 165, 111 Ed. Law Rep. 490 (1996).

Second, in tangent to this issue, given U.S. Constitutional divisions of power between the federal and state governments, the federal government is unable to extend to state employees guarantees of rights to organize and collectively bargain; rather the state regulates its own workers' rights as such. To conform to ILO Conventions No. 87 and No. 98, the NRLA would have to be reformed in a way that ensures both federal and state employees are secured with such rights. This explains the footnote limitation in the 2012 Model BIT of committing to conform only federal Congressional acts and regulations to its obligations, but not the states.[80]

7.4.1.3 The Conventions and China Praxis

Like the U.S., China has not ratified ILO Conventions No. 87 and No. 98, likely because they also conflict with its domestic law.[81] Although the Chinese Constitution provides that citizens of the People's Republic of China shall enjoy freedom of assembly and of association[82] and the Chinese Trade Union Law of 2001 further emphasizes that all labourers shall have the right to participate in and form trade union organizations pursuant to the law, public or private, regardless of their nationality, race, sex, occupation, religious belief or education, and no organization or individual may hinder them from doing so or restrict them, Article 11 of the Trade Union Law nevertheless restricts workers' right to freedom of association in China.[83] Specifically, it provides that any establishment of a basic level trade union, local all-level federation of trade unions or a national or local specific industry trade union must be reported to the trade union organization at the next highest level for approval, so workers are not free to choose a union of their choice.[84] Clearly, this provision is inconsistent with the principle of association embodied in ILO Conventions No. 87 and No. 98, which provide that workers shall have the right to establish and to join an organization of their own choosing without previous authorization.[85]

However, Chinese labour law does seem to align with ILO Conventions No. 87 and No. 98, with respect to workers' rights to collectively bargain. Under Chinese labour law, the workers of an enterprise may sign a collective contract with the

[80] U.S. Model BIT 2012, Article 13(3) and n. 17.

[81] The ratification dates can be found on the ILO Normlex website.

[82] [Constitution of the People's Republic of China] 中华人民共和国宪法 (zhōng huá rén mín gòng hé guó xiàn fǎ), 1982, Article 35.

[83] [Trade Union Law of the People's Republic of China] 中华人民共和国工会法 (zhōng huá rén mín gòng hé guó gōng huì fǎ), 1992, Article 9.

[84] International Trade Union Confederation 2012.

[85] Qiu 2006. Noting in China, the unions consist of the All-China Federation of Trade Unions (ACFTU), local all-level federation of trade unions, sectoral unions and basic-level unions. [Trade Union Law of the People's Republic of China] 中华人民共和国工会法 (zhōng huá rén mín gòng hé guó gōng huì fǎ), 1992 (as revised in 2001), Article 9.

management regarding issues of pay, working hours, rest and vacation, safety and health, insurance and welfare.[86]

7.4.2 *ILO Conventions Nos. 29 and 105 Concerning the Elimination of All Forms of Forced and Compulsory Labour*

7.4.2.1 The Conventions

ILO Forced Labour Convention No. 29 and Abolition of Forced Labour Convention No. 105 define “forced and compulsory labour” as “all work or service, which is exacted from any person under the menace of any penalty and for which the said person has not offered himself voluntarily.” Meanwhile, it also provides several exceptions to “forced labour”, including military service, normal civic obligations, prison labour, emergencies, and minor communal services.[87] The Conventions further provide that member states shall take effective measures to secure the immediate and complete abolition of forced or compulsory labour in its most deplorable forms.[88]

7.4.2.2 The Conventions and U.S. Praxis

The U.S. has ratified these Conventions,[89] both of which align strongly with U.S. praxis, which prohibits all forms of forced or compulsory labour. The Thirteenth Amendment of the U.S. Constitution is the principal constitutional provision concerning forced or compulsory labour in the U.S., and it specifically outlaws slavery

---

[86] Brown 2006; see also [Rules on Collective Contracts] 集体合同规定 (jí tǐ hé tóng guī dìng), 2003, Article 1; See [Labour Contract Law of the People’s Republic of China] 中华人民共和国劳动合同法 (zhōng huá rén mín gòng hé guó láo dòng hé tóng fǎ), 2007, Article 33 para. 1. Stating the Regulation on Collective Contract of PRC. established by the Ministry of Labour and Social Security further specifies every aspect of a collective contract, such as its negotiation procedure, its content, its approval, examination and dispute settlement. With all of these inclusions, it seems that Chinese labour law has recognized workers’ right to collective bargaining.

[87] Forced Labour Convention No. 29, 1930. Requiring signatories to prevent the following forms of forced or compulsory labour: (a) as a means of political coercion or education or as a punishment for holding or expressing political views or views ideologically opposed to the established political, social or economic system; (b) as a method of mobilizing and using labour for purposes of economic development; (c) as a means of labour discipline; (d) as a punishment for having participated in strikes; (e) as a means of racial, social, national or religious discrimination.

[88] Forced Labour Convention No. 29, 1930 and Abolition of Forced Labour Convention No. 105, 1957.

[89] The ratification dates can be found on the ILO Normlex website.

and involuntary servitude, except as punishment for a person duly convicted of a crime.[90]

Additional protection of rights is afforded by the "equal protection clause" of the Fourteenth Amendment, which provides that no state shall "deny to any person within its jurisdiction the equal protection of the law". Thus, no agency of a state nor the officers or agents by whom its powers are exerted may deny the protection of the Thirteenth Amendment to any person within its jurisdiction, based on that person's race, colour, or nationality.[91]

Beyond the constitutional protections described above, the U.S. has specific federal legislation which requires "every employer" to pay "each of his employees" a minimum wage that is judiciously enforced by the federal government.[92]

7.4.2.3 The Conventions and China Praxis

Unlike the U.S., China has not ratified these Conventions,[93] and they only align with Chinese Labour Law in some respects, so that China would have to adopt additional protections to fully comply.

Under Chinese Labour Law and criminal law, forced and compulsory labour are illegal.[94] And, Chinese labour Law and criminal law both support this proposition by prohibiting employers from retaining workers or withholding their compensation after contract expiration.[95] However, Chinese law, in this respect, is anaemic in that

[90] See Clyatt v. U.S., 197 U.S. 207 (1905); See also U.S. v. Gaskin, 320 U.S. 527 (1944). Clarifying that the provisions of 42 U.S.C. § 1994 abolish peonage and prohibit anyone from holding or arresting a person and returning that person to peonage, or causing or aiding in the arresting or returning of a person to peonage. The provisions of 18 U.S.C. §§ 1581–1588 provide criminal penalties in connection with these and related practices. See Civil Rights Cases, 109 U.S. 3, 20 (1883). Noting The Thirteenth Amendment is self-executing and thus ancillary legislation is not required to abolish slavery.

[91] See Yick Wo v. Hopkins, 118 U.S. 356, 369 (1886); See also Levy v. Louisiana, 391 U.S. 68, 70 (1968); See also, Graham v. Richardson, 403 U.S. 365, 371 (1971).

[92] 29 U.S.C. and § 206. 29 U.S.C. § 216 stating any person who violates the requirements of the federal statute may be subject to damages, fines or imprisonment. 29 U.S.C. § 207 of the minimum wage law also allows for overtime pay. 29 U.S.C. § 207 of the minimum wage law also allows for overtime pay.

[93] The ratification dates can be found on the ILO Normlex website.

[94] ILO, The elimination of all forms of forced or compulsory labour, China.

[95] [Labour Law of the People's Republic of China] 中华人民共和国劳动法 (zhōng huá rén mín gòng hé guó láo dòng fǎ), 1994, Article 32. Noting that a worker may notify the employer of his decision to dissolve the labour contract at any time if the employer compels a worker to work by the use of force, threat or by means of illegally restricting personal freedom; [Criminal Law of the People's Republic of China] 中华人民共和国刑法 (zhōng huá rén mín gòng hé guó xíng fǎ), 1979 (as revised in 1995 and 2011), Articles 41 and 43. Stating in addition, if an employer compels workers to work by use of force, threat or by resorting to the means of restricting personal freedom or insults, punishes physically, beats, illegally searches or takes workers into custody, the public security organ shall detain the persons responsible for less than 15 days or levy a fine or give a warning and, if the case is serious enough to constitute a crime, criminal responsibility is attached.

it does not clearly define what types of forced and compulsory labour are barred, as stipulated under the Conventions, and in China it is argued that many types of such labour still exist, including debt bondage.[96]

More importantly, though, is a misalignment between the Conventions' exceptions for forced and compulsory labour for prison inmates and exceptions permitted under Chinese law. The definition of forced labour under ILO Forced Labour Convention No. 29 is subject to several exceptions, one of which is the prison labour exception, that is, any work or service exacted from any person as a consequence of a conviction in a court of law, provided that the said work or service is carried out under the supervision and control of a public authority and that the said person is not hired to or placed at the disposal of private individuals, companies or associations. On its face, the prison labour system in China is consistent with the exception. Prisoners working in labour reform enterprises have gone through judicial process and have been convicted by a court in accordance with relevant criminal provisions, and the work carried out by prisoners is under the supervision and control of the prison, which, at the same time, is subject to the supervision of a people's procuratorate. The state "Reeducation Through Labour System (RTL)" to reeducate offenders, appears to have ended on 28 December 2013.[97]

7.4.3 ILO Conventions Nos. 138 and 182: The Effective Abolition of Child Labour

7.4.3.1 The Conventions

The Conventions, which have been ratified by 169 countries and are the most widely-ratified international labour conventions, require each country to "take immediate and effective measures to secure the prohibition and elimination of the

---

According to the Chinese Criminal Code, where an employer, in violation of the laws and regulations on labour administration, compels its employees to work by restricting their personal freedom, if serious enough, the persons who are directly responsible for the offense shall be sentenced to fixed-term imprisonment of not more than three years or criminal detention and/or be fined.

[96] ILO, The elimination of all forms of forced or compulsory labour, China: "Bonded labour" or "debt bondage" is the practice when traffickers or recruiters unlawfully exploit an initial debt the worker assumed as part of the terms of employment. See discussion in Human Trafficking.org.

[97] "The bi-monthly session of the Standing Committee of the National People's Congress (NPC) adopted a resolution to abolish legal documents on '*laojiao*' (re-education through labor). The resolution nullifies a 1957 State Council decision on reeducation through labor, and a 1957 NPC Standing Committee resolution to adopt the State Council decision, likewise supplementary regulations from 1979. Reeducation through labor dealt with minor offenders whose crimes did not warrant full court proceedings. It allowed detention for up to four years without an open trial", see Zhu 2013. According to Human Rights Watch, two parallel mechanisms of extralegal punishment may still continue: one for drug offenders and another for prostitutes and their clients. As with re-education through labor, the police mete out custody and education sentences without trial and with little chance for appeal which appears similar to re-education through labor, see Jacobs 2014. See also Asia Catalyst 2013.

worst forms of child labour as a matter of urgency." Under the Conventions, "the worst forms of child labour" include "work which, by its nature or the circumstances in which it is carried out, is likely to harm the health, safety or morals of children." Exactly what constitutes such types of work is left to be determined by member states, in consultation with employer and worker organizations and in consideration of international standards, particularly ILO Recommendation No. 190 on the Worst Forms of Child Labour.[98]

7.4.3.2 The Conventions and U.S. Praxis

The U.S. has ratified these Conventions.[99] While generally, U.S. federal law aligns with the Conventions, protecting against most of the worst forms of child labour, it may need to be amended to deal with child labour to include all those under the age of 18, and those minors specifically working in agriculture, in terms of working time and conditions.

In the U.S., the federal Fair Labor Standards Act (FLSA) prohibits the employment of children in occupations that the Department of Labor (DOL) has deemed to be "particularly hazardous". However, although the Convention defines a child as "all persons under the age of 18," the FLSA restrictions on employment in particularly hazardous occupations do not apply to child farm workers aged 16 and above.[100]

Moreover, under the U.S. FLSA, two additional exemptions allow employment of children younger than 16 to work in jobs in agriculture that have been identified as being particularly hazardous for children.[101] First, children of any age can be employed to do particularly hazardous agricultural jobs on farms owned or operated by their parent or legal guardian. Second, the age 16 minimum for particularly hazardous employment does not apply to children enrolled in a vocational education-training programme or who have completed a specified training programme.

[98] ILO Recommendation No. 190, 1999. In determining the types of work referred to under Article 3(d) of the Convention [the "worst forms of child labour" definition], and in identifying where they exist, consideration should be given, as a minimum, to:

(a) work which exposes children to physical, emotional or sexual abuse;
(b) work underground, under water, at dangerous. heights or in confined spaces;
(c) work with dangerous machinery, equipment and tools, or which involves the manual handling or transport of heavy loads;
(d) work in an unhealthy environment which may, for example, expose children to hazardous substances, agents or processes, or to temperatures, noise levels, or vibrations damaging to their health;
(e) work under particularly difficult conditions such as work for long hours or during the night or work which does not allow for the possibility of returning home each day.

[99] The ratification dates can be found on the ILO Normlex website.

[100] Child Labor Bulletin 2007. The minimum age of 16 for particularly hazardous work under the FLSA is unique to agriculture; the minimum age for hazardous work in other sectors of the economy is 18.

[101] Ibid.

Moreover, although the ILO Worst Form of Child Labour Convention No. 182 calls for the list of hazardous occupations (HOs) to be "periodically examined and revised as necessary," the 11 HOs in agriculture have not been revised in more than 30 years.[102]

In addition, the ILO has recommended that children who "work for long hours" be included among the types of work that countries should consider when defining hazardous work under the Convention.[103] However, under the FLSA, the only restriction on children working in agriculture is that children cannot work during school hours.[104] Apart from this requirement, there is no limit on how early in the day children may begin work or how late in the day they may work, and not even any limit on the number of hours they may work during the day.

7.4.3.3 The Conventions and China Praxis

Like the U.S., China has ratified these Conventions,[105] and generally speaking, China's legislation prohibiting child labour is consistent with them. For example, Chinese labour law prohibits the employment of people below the age of 16, except in some extraordinary circumstances, such as in the areas of arts, sports and certain special arts and crafts. Even under these special cases, state approval is a precondition, and employers still must guarantee these employed minors' universal right to 9-year free and compulsory education. On its face, Chinese law not only complies with China's obligations under ILO Minimum Age Convention No. 138 and Worst Forms of Child Labour Convention No. 182, it also raises the standard, that is, the minimum age for employment is 16 instead of 15.[106] However, the Convention's protection for all children under the age of 18 could be contravened by the exception.

In total, there are also 14 articles under The Order of the State Council of the People's Republic of China No. 364: Provisions on the Prohibition of Using Child Labour. This mainly provides that the whole of society, that is, families, various civil societies, enterprises (both private and state-owned) and government (both central and local), shall fight against the practice of employing child labour, and

[102] Ibid.

[103] ILO Recommendation No. 190, 1999, para. 3.

[104] Non-agricultural work is usually dealt with by state law; see e.g., New York State Department of Labor. However, in agriculture, federal law prohibits minors under the age of 16 from being employed during school hours unless employed by their parent or a person standing in place of their parent; see Child Labor Bulletin 2007.

[105] The ratification dates can be found on the ILO Normlex website.

[106] [Provisions on the Prohibition of Using Child Labour] 禁止使用童工规定 (jìn zhǐ shǐ yòng tóng gōng guī dìng), 2002, Article 2.

more specifically requires the state and provinces to prohibit employers from engaging child labour, providing a stringent regime of punishment for those who do.[107]

Following the logic of The Order, the crime of abducting a child labourer is punished under the name of "crime of abducting children." According to the interpretation from the Chinese People's Supreme Court on the "crime of abducting children", "child" here is defined as a person under the age of 14.[108] However, in the case of child labour, the age is under 16.

7.4.4 *Conventions Nos. 100 and 111: The Elimination of Discrimination in Respect of Employment and Occupation*

7.4.4.1 The Conventions

According to ILO Equal Remuneration Convention No. 100, men and women workers are entitled to equal remuneration for work of equal value, which includes the ordinary, basic, or minimum wage or salary and any additional emoluments whatsoever payable directly or indirectly, whether in cash or in kind. The ILO Discrimination (Employment and Occupation) Convention No. 111 further requires member states to eliminate any discrimination on the basis of race, colour, sex, religion, political opinion, national extraction or social origin, which has the effect of nullifying or impairing equality of opportunity or treatment in employment or occupation.

---

[107] Ibid., Article 6(1); see also Morley 2009 at p. 120. Under the regulation, employers that employ child labor are to be fined 5000 yuan (RMB) for every child laborer. Moreover, Article 11 also specifically criminalizes employing child labourers to work in a dangerous environment. However, when reading this article carefully, one may find certain problems. Article 11 provides as follows:

"If anyone abducts a child laborer, coerces a child laborer to work, uses child labor to work high above the ground, in a well, in radioactive, highly toxic, flammable or explosive environment, or to engage in the work of fourth level physical labor intensity provided for by the state, uses child laborers under 14 years old, or causes death or serious disability to a child laborer, the criminal responsibilities shall be prosecuted pursuant to the provisions of the criminal law on the crime of abducting children, for the crime of coercing another person into labor or other crimes."

However, China has been accused of weakly enforcing these laws, and as a result, child labour is still widely reported, including in many hazardous industries such as construction. See China Labour Bulletin 2005.

[108] [Notice of the Supreme People's Court, the Supreme People's Procuratoral, the Ministry of Public Security and the Ministry of Justice on Issuing the Opinion Legally Punishing the Crimes of Abducting and Trafficking Women and Children] 最高人民法院、最高人民检察院、公安部、司法部印发《关于依法惩治拐卖妇女儿童犯罪的意见》(zuì gāo rén mín fǎ yuàn, zuì gāo rén mín jiǎn chá yuàn, gōng ān bù, sī fǎ bù yìn fā "guān yú yī fǎ chéng zhì guǎi mài fù nǚ ér tóng fàn zuì de yì jiàn"), 2010.

7.4.4.2 The Conventions and U.S. Praxis

The U.S. has not adopted these conventions.[109] However, in many respects, U.S. law aligns with the ILO Conventions.[110] For example, in line with the Conventions, Title VII of the U.S. Civil Rights Act of 1964, as amended, protects applicants and employees from discrimination in hiring, promotion, discharge, pay, fringe benefits, job training, classification, referral, and other aspects of employment, on the basis of race, colour, religion, sex (including pregnancy), or national origin. Religious discrimination includes failing to reasonably accommodate an employee's religious practices where the accommodation does not impose undue hardship. Additionally, Title I and Title V of the Americans with Disabilities Act of 1990, as amended, protect qualified individuals from discrimination on the basis of disability in hiring, promotion, discharge, pay, fringe benefits, job training, classification, referral, and other aspects of employment. Disability discrimination includes not making reasonable accommodation for the known physical or mental limitations of an otherwise qualified individual with a disability who is an applicant or employee, barring undue hardship. The Age Discrimination in Employment Act of 1967, as amended, also protects applicants and employees 40 years of age or older from discrimination based on age in hiring, promotion, discharge, pay, fringe benefits, job training, classification, referral, and other aspects of employment. Moreover, in addition to sex discrimination prohibited by Title VII of the Civil Rights Act, as amended, the Equal Pay Act of 1963, as amended, prohibits sex discrimination in the payment of wages to women and men performing substantially equal work, in jobs that require equal skill, effort, and time. It should be noted that, in the U.S., despite legal protections, there is still a gender gap in terms of pay.

Finally, unlike the Conventions, U.S. labour law does not provide for protection based on political opinion or social origin. However, the former is protected by the U.S. Constitution against government discrimination and in a few state jurisdictions against private entities by common-law remedies. Social origin, *per se*, is usually not covered except that anti-discrimination laws do protect against discrimination based on ethnicity and national origin.

7.4.4.3 The Conventions and China Praxis

Unlike the U.S., China has ratified the Equal Renumeration Convention No. 100 and Discrimination (Employment and Occupation) Convention No. 111.[111] In line with the Conventions, Chinese labour law explicitly provides that workers shall not be discriminated against in aspects of nationality, race, sex and religious beliefs

[109] The ratification dates can be found on the ILO Normlex website.

[110] Hawai'i Rev. Stat. Chapter 378. In addition to federal laws, state laws often provide additional and more liberal coverage. For example, Hawai'i covers sexual identity and reaches below 40 to any age.

[111] The ratification dates can be found on the ILO Normlex website.

with regard to employment. The law also emphasizes that women enjoy equal rights of employment to men and also provides special protection to female workers.[112] Moreover, the Protection of Women's Rights and Interests Law provides special protection for the welfare of female workers and reemphasizes the principle of non-discrimination in terms of occupation and employment.[113] However, compared with the ILO Conventions, Chinese labour law is silent on the issues of discrimination with regard to colour, political opinion and social origin.[114]

7.5 Conclusion and Recommendations

China, not unlike the U.S., is resistant to ratifying all of the ILO fundamental labour rights Conventions, though it has ratified more. Whether any of the emerging international obligations such as BITs or FTAs will saturate China's cultural logic any more than past ILO obligations remains to be seen. Perhaps it can at least be used for political cover in furthering domestic labour reforms. Many of the FTAs and BITs provide for additional obligations and bilateral enforcement mechanisms, as well as an additional set of review on compliance with ILO core labour standards. However, in fairness, each country is already a signatory to the ILO 1998 Declaration and does have many of the laws in place that are required to implement some of the fundamental labour rights, e.g., equal pay, collective bargaining, etc. Some ILO obligations, such as pluralistic unions, exist only in the U.S. and not in China; but neither country can claim that it is in complete accord with the core labour standard Conventions and therefore, each resists assenting to a BIT or FTA which would create those obligations outside the ILO ratification process.

In recent years, new treaty obligations, under social dimension provisions of FTAs and BITs, have directly bound signatory countries to ILO labour standards and their implementation. China has yet to embrace these treaty obligations under FTA social dimension provisions or BIT obligations, but is in current negotiations with the U.S. on a BIT, which includes such promises, though perhaps lacking in clarity of obligation or in having a meaningful enforcement mechanism. So far neither China nor the U.S. has committed to be obligated to more than the ILO 1998 Declaration in these international agreements, but it is also clear the BIT imposes

[112] [Labour Law of the People's Republic of China] 中华人民共和国劳动法 (zhōng huá rén mín gòng hé guó láo dòng fǎ), 1994, Chapter 7, Articles 58–64.

[113] [Law on the Protection of Rights and Interests of Women] 中华人民共和国妇女权益保障法 (zhōng huá rén mín gòng hé guó fù nǚ quán yì bǎo zhàng fǎ), 1992. Despite Chinese law, however, groups like Human Rights Watch and the IFTUC, have alleged that, in China, there is still widespread discrimination against women in the workplace, and that there is a significant gender pay gap. Moreover, these same groups allege that, in China, there is still rampant discrimination in the workplace against migrant workers, and between workers based on their urban or rural orientation; *supra*, IFTUC.

[114] This raises the issue of the equal treatment of migrant workers and ethnic minorities. See Brown 2006. Also see Zhu and Dai, 2002.

additional, more specific obligations on the parties, such as not to derogate from existing labour laws, etc. This leaves adoption and compliance to the usual ratification process and its socio-political considerations, thus side-stepping the "quick-fix" solution of committing to the more specific core labour standards and conventions of the ILO obligations in an international instrument.[115] Thus, even though the obligations are not as specific as could be, this approach of using an international treaty, such as an FTA or a BIT, gives labour rights groups one additional avenue of obligation and redress versus the slower, more cumbersome review by the ILO on issues of ILO labour rights compliance.

References

Literature

Alston, Philip. 2004. 'Core labor standards' and the transformation of the international labor rights regime. *European Journal of International Law* 15: 457–521.

Brown, Ronald C. 1997. *Understanding Chinese courts and legal process: Law with Chinese characteristics*. Boston: Kluwer Law International.

Brown, Ronald C. 2006. China's employment discrimination laws during economic transition. *Columbia Journal of Asian Law* 19: 361–427.

Brown, Ronald C. 2015. Measuring China's social insurance law under international standards of International Labour Organization and influences of social dimension provisions of free trade agreements and bilateral investment treaties. *Hong Kong Law Journal* 45:651.

Compa, Lance and Henning Meyer. 2010. *A social dimension for Transatlantic economic relations* [Electronic version]. London: The Global Policy Institute. Available via link at: http://digitalcommons.ilr.cornell.edu/reports/35/. Last accessed 19 June 2015.

Cooper, William H., Remy Jurenas, Michaela D. Platzer, and Mark E. Manyin. 2011. *The EU – South Korea Free Trade Agreement and its implications for the United States*. Congressional Research Service. Available at: https://www.hsdl.org/?abstract&did=719346. Last accessed 19 June 2015.

Enfield, Nick. 2000. The theory of cultural logic: How individuals combine social intelligence with semiotics to create and maintain cultural meaning. *Cultural Dynamics* 12: 35–64. Available at: http://cdy.sagepub.com/content/12/1/35.short. Last accessed 19 June 2015.

Maupain, Francis. 2005. Revitalization not retreat: The real potential of the 1998 ILO Declaration for the Universal Protection of Workers' Rights. *The European Journal of International Law* 16: 439–465.

Milman-Sivan, Faina. 2009. Freedom of association as a core labor right and the ILO: Toward a normative framework. *Law and Ethics of Human Rights* 3: 110–153.

Morley, Andrea. 2009. The challenges of change: Causes and consequences of child labor in China. In *Human rights and human welfare: Topical research digest – Human rights in China digest*, 118–129. Available at: https://www.du.edu/korbel/hrhw/researchdigest/china/ChildLaborChina.pdf. Last accessed 19 June 2015.

Qiu, Yang. 2006. ILO fundamental conventions and Chinese labor law: From a comparative perspective. *Chinese Law & Policy Review* 2: 14–83.

[115] While ratification of ILO Conventions does bring with it reporting and inspection responsibilities, FTAs and BITs can also bring their own enforcement mechanisms to bear on the standards of "un-ratified" conventions. Unfortunately, enforcement under the latter has not yet shown itself to be a model for compelling compliance.

Spieler, Emily A. 2003. Risks and rights: The case for occupational safety and health as a core worker right. In *Workers' rights as human rights*, ed. James A. Gross, 78–117. New York: Cornell University Press.
Talley, Ian and William Mauldin. 2013. U.S., China to pursue investment treaty. *The Wall Street Journal*. Available with subscription at: http://online.wsj.com/news/articles/SB10001424127887324425204578599913527965812. Last accessed 19 June 2015.
Wang, Yanzhong and Anan Wei. 2009. Issues of China's social security internationalization development. Konrad-Adenauer-Stiftung. Available at: http://www.kas.de/wf/doc/kas_18073-1522-2-30.pdf?091111045913. Last accessed 19 June 2015.
[Zhu, Yan] 朱艳 and [Liangtie Dai] 戴良铁. 2002. [Comparative study on discrimination with regard to employment] 就业歧视的比较研究 (jiù yè qí shì de bǐ jiào yán jiū). [*Economic Problem Investigation*] 经济问题探索 12: 21-23.

Documents and Official Publications

ILO Documents

Constitution of the International Labour Organisation, adopted 1 April 1919. Entry into force 28 June 1919.
Convention concerning Forced or Compulsory Labour, adopted 28 June 1930, ILO C029. Entry into force 1 May 1932. (Forced Labour Convention).
Convention concerning Freedom of Association and Protection of the Right to Organise, adopted 9 July 1948, ILO C087. Entry into force 4 July 1950. (Freedom of Association and Protection of the Right to Organise Convention).
Convention concerning the Application of the Principles of the Right to Organise and to Bargain Collectively, adopted 1 July 1949, ILO C098. Entry into force 18 July 1951. (Right to Organise and Collective Bargaining Convention).
Convention concerning Minimum Standards of Social Security, adopted 28 June 1952, ILO C102. Entry into force 27 April 1955. (Social Security (Minimum Standards) Convention).
Convention concerning the Abolition of Forced Labour, adopted 25 June 1957, ILO C105. Entry into force 17 January 1959. (Abolition of Forced Labour Convention).
Convention concerning Discrimination in Respect of Employment and Occupation, adopted 25 June 1958, ILO C111. Entry into force 15 June 1960. (Discrimination (Employment and Occupation) Convention).
Convention concerning Minimum Age for Admission to Employment, adopted 26 June 1973, ILO C138. Entry into force 19 June 1976. (Minimum Age Convention).
Convention concerning the Prohibition and Immediate Action for the Elimination of the Worst Forms of Child Labour, adopted 17 June 1999, ILO C182. Entry into force 19 November 2000. (Worst Forms of Child Labour Convention).
Declaration on Fundamental Principles and Rights at Work, adopted 18 June 1998 (Annex revised 15 June 2010). (1998 Declaration).
Equal Remuneration Convention, adopted 29 June 1951, ILO C100. Entry into force 23 May 1953.
Recommendation concerning the Prohibition and Immediate Action for the Elimination of the Worst Forms of Child Labour, adopted 17 June 1999, ILO R190. (Worst Forms of Child Labour Recommendation. No. 190).

Other ILO Documentation

Free Trade Agreements and Labour Rights. At http://www.ilo.org/global/standards/informationresources-and-publications/free-trade-agreements-and-labour-rights/lang--en/index.htm

International Labour Conference (ILC). *Report VII: Consideration of a possible Declaration of principles of the International Labour Organization concerning fundamental rights and its appropriate follow-up mechanism.* 1998. Geneva: International Labour Office.
International Labour Conference (ILC). 1998. *Report of the Committee on the Declaration of Principles*. Geneva: International Labour Office. Available at: http://www.ilo.org/public/english/standards/relm/ilc/ilc86/com-decl.htm. Last accessed 19 June 2015.
ILO website on European Free Trade Agreements. Available at: http://www.ilo.org/global/standards/information-resources-and-publications/free-trade-agreements-and-labour-rights/WCMS_115822/lang--en/index.htm. Last accessed 19 June 2015.
ILO website on Free Trade Agreements and Labor Rights. Available at: http://ilo.org/global/standards/information-resources-and-publications/free-trade-agreements-and-labour-rights/lang--en/index.htm. Last accessed 19 June 2015.
ILO. *The elimination of all forms of forced or compulsory labour*. Available at: http://www.ilo.org/public/english/standards/relm/gb/docs/gb277/pdf/d2-elim.pdf. Last accessed 19 June 2015.
Normlex. Information System on International Labour Standards. International Labour Organization (ILO). Available at: http://www.ilo.org/dyn/normlex/en/f?p=NORMLEXPUB:1:0::NO. Last accessed 19 June 2015.

Other International Law Sources

Agreement on Trade in Goods of the Framework Agreement on Comprehensive Economic Co-Operation between the People's Republic of China and the Association of Southeast Asian Nations. 4 November 2002. (China – ASEAN FTA). Available at: http://fta.mofcom.gov.cn/dongmeng/annex/xieyi2004en.pdf. Last accessed 19 June 2015.
China FTA Network website. 2014. Ministry of Commerce, People's Republic of China. Available at: http://fta.mofcom.gov.cn/english/fta_qianshu.shtml. Last accessed 19 June 2015.
Free trade Agreement between the European Union and its Member States, of the one part, and the Republic of Korea, of the other part. 14 May 2011. (EU – South Korea Free Trade Agreement). Available at: http://eur-lex.europa.eu/legal-content/EN/ALL/?uri=OJ:L:2011:127:TOC. Last accessed 19 June 2015.
Free trade Agreement between United States of America and the Republic of Korea. 30 June 2007. (KORUS FTA). Available at: http://www.ustr.gov/trade-agreements/free-trade-agreements/korus-fta/final-text. Last accessed 19 June 2015.
Sino – Singaporean Free Trade Agreement between the Governments of the People's Republic of China and the Republic of Singapore. 23 October 2008. (China – Singapore Free Trade Agreement). Available at: http://fta.mofcom.gov.cn/topic/ensingapore.shtml. Last accessed 19 June 2015.

Chinese Regulation

Laws by the National People's Congress

[Constitution of the People's Republic of China] 中华人民共和国宪法 (zhōng huá rén mín gòng hé guó xiàn fǎ), National People's Congress, adopted and effective 4 December 1982. Available at: http://english.people.com.cn/constitution/constitution.html. Last accessed 19 June 2015.
[Criminal Law of the People's Republic of China] 中华人民共和国刑法 (zhōng huá rén mín gòng hé guó xíng fǎ), National People's Congress, adopted 6 July 1979, effective 1 January 1980. Revised 25 February 2011, effective 1 May 2011.
[Law on the Protection of Rights and Interests of Women] 中华人民共和国妇女权益保障法 (zhōng huá rén mín gòng hé guó fù nǚ quán yì bǎo zhàng fǎ), National People's Congress, adopted 3 April 1992, effective 1 October 1992. Revised and effective 18 August 2005.

[Trade Union Law of the People's Republic of China] 中华人民共和国工会法 (zhōng huá rén mín gòng hé guó gōng huì fǎ), National People's Congress, adopted and effective 3 April 1992. Revised and effective 27 October 2001.

Laws by the Standing Committee of the National People's Congress

[Decision of the Standing Committee on the National People's Congress on Repealing Legislation on Reeducaiton through Labour] 全国人大常委会关于废止有关劳动教养法律规定的决定 (quán guó rén dà cháng wěi huì guān yú fèi zhǐ yǒu guān láo dòng jiào yǎng fǎ lǜ guī dìng de jué dìng), Standing Committee of the National People's Congress, adopted and effective on 28 December 2013.

[Labour Law of the People's Republic of China] 中华人民共和国劳动法 (zhōng huá rén mín gòng hé guó láo dòng fǎ), Standing Committee of the National People's Congress, adopted 5 July 1994, effective 1 January 1995.

Regulations by the State Council

[Decision of the State Council on Issues Concerning Reeducation through Labour] 国务院关于劳动教养问题的决定 (guó wù yuàn guān yú láo dòng jiào yǎng wèn tí de jué dìng), State Council, adopted and effective 3 August 1957.

[Provisions on the Prohibition of Using Child Labour] 禁止使用童工规定 (jìn zhǐ shǐ yòng tóng gōng guī ding), State Council, adopted 1 October 2002, effective 1 December 2002.

[Supplementary Provisions of the State Council for Rehabilitation through Labour] 国务院关于劳动教养的补充规定 (guó wù yuàn guān yú láo dòng jiào yǎng de bǔ chōng guī dìng), State Council, adopted and effective 29 November 1979.

Administrative Regulations

[Rules on Collective Contracts] 集体合同规定 (jí tǐ hé tóng guī dìng), Ministry of Labour and Social Security, adopted 30 December 2003, effective 1 May 2004.

Other Chinese Official Documents

[Notice of the Supreme People's Court, the Supreme People's Procuratoral, the Ministry of Public Security and the Ministry of Justice on Issuing the Opinion legally Punishing the Crimes of Abducting and Trafficking in Women and Children] 最高人民法院、最高人民检察院、剬安部、司法部印发《关于依法惩治拐卖妇女儿童犯罪的意见》 (zuì gāo rén mín fǎ yuàn, zuì gāo rén mín jiǎn chá yuàn, gōng ān bù, sī fǎ bù yǐn fā guān yú yī fǎ chéng zhì guǎi mài fù nǚ ér tóng fàn zuì de yì jiàn), 2010

U.S. Regulation

The Constitution of the United States.

Statutory Law

Age Discrimination in Employment Act. Public Law No. 90–202. (1967)
Americans with Disabilities Act. Public Law No. 101–336. (1990).
Civil Rights Act. Public Law No. 88–352 (1964).
Crimes and Criminal Procedure. U.S. Code Title 18. Public Law No. 114–19 (2011).
Equal Pay Act. Public Law No. 88–38 (1963).
Fair Labour Standards Act. 29 U.S. Code Chapter 8. Public Law No. 114–19. (1938).
Hawai'i Revised Statute Chapter 378 (Employment Practices) § 378–61 (2013).
National Labor Relations Act. 29 U.S. Code Chapter 27. Public Law No. 114–19. (1935).
U.S. – Korean Free Trade Agreement Implementation Act, Public Law No. 112–41 (2011).

Case Law

Bethlehem Steel Co. v. New York State Labor Relations Board, 330 U.S. 767 (1950).
Branch v. City of Myrtle Beach, 340 S.C. 405, 532 S.E.2d 289 (2000).
City of Hayward v. United Public Employees, 54 Cal. App. 3d 761, 126 Cal. Rptr. 710 (1st Dist. 1976).
Civil Rights Cases, 109 U.S. 3, 20 (1883).
Clyatt v. U.S., 197 U.S. 207 (1905).
Coastal Florida Police Benev. Ass'n, Inc. v. Williams, 838 So. 2d 543 (Fla. 2003).
Graham v. Richardson, 403 U.S. 365, 371 (1971).
Labor Board v. Borg-Warner Corp., 356 U.S. 342 (1958).
Levy v. Louisiana, 391 U.S. 68, 70 (1968).
Michigan State AFL-CIO v. Employment Relations Commission, 453 Mich. 362, 551 N.W.2d 165 (1996).
State Department of Administration v. Public Employees Relations Board, 257 Kan. 275, 894 P.2d 777 (1995).
State v. Delaware State Education Association, 326 A.2d 868 (Del. Ch. 1974).
State v. Florida Police Benevolent Association, Inc., 613 So. 2d 415 (Fla. 1992).
U.S. v. Gaskin, 320 U.S. 527 (1944).
Yick Wo v. Hopkins, 118 U.S. 356, 369 (1886).

Other Official Documents

Child Labor Requirements In Agricultural Occupations Under the Fair Labor Standards Act (Child Labor Bulletin 102). 2007. U.S. Department of Labor. Employment Standards Administration. Available at: http://www.dol.gov/whd/regs/compliance/childlabor102.pdf. Last accessed 19 June 2015.
Model Bilateral Investment Treaty: Fact Sheet. 2012. U.S. Department of State, Government of the United States. Available at: http://www.state.gov/r/pa/prs/ps/2012/04/188199.htm. Last accessed 19 June 2015.
Labor Standards: Hours of Work. New York State Department of Labor. Available at http://labor.ny.gov/workerprotection/laborstandards/workprot/hrswork.shtm. Last accessed 19 June 2015.

Other Sources

AFL – CIO. 2000. Statement by Executive Council. Voice@Work: The ILO Declaration on Fundamental Principles and Rights at Work. The American Federation of Labor and Congress of Industrial Organizations. Available at: http://www.aflcio.org/About/Exec-Council/EC-Statements/Voice-Work-The-ILO-Declaration-on-Fundamental-Principles-and-Rights-at--Work. Last accessed 19 June 2015.

Asia Catalyst. 2013. Custody and education: Arbitrary detention for female sex workers in China. Available at: http://asiacatalyst.org/blog/AsiaCatalyst_CustodyEducation2013-12-EN.pdf. Last accessed 19 June 2015.

Bourassa, Betsy. 2013. Treasury notes: U.S. and China breakthrough announcement on the Bilateral Investment Treaty Negotiations. U.S. Department of the Treasury. Available at: http://www.treasury.gov/connect/blog/Pages/U.S.-and-China-Breakthrough-Announcement-.aspx. Last accessed 19 June 2015.

CBC News. 2013. Summary of Canada – EU free trade deal tabled. Available at: http://www.cbc.ca/news/politics/summary-of-canada-eu-free-trade-deal-tabled-1.2286695. Last accessed 19 June 2015.

China Labour Bulletin. 2005. As China's economy grows, so does China's child labour problem. Available at: http://www.clb.org.hk/en/content/chinas-economy-grows-so-does-chinas-child-labour-problem. Last accessed 19 June 2015.

China.org.cn. 2012. Insurance for foreigners to be simplified. Available at: http://www.china.org.cn/china/2012-06/05/content_25565469.htm. Last accessed 19 June 2015.

Drake, Celeste. 2013. A BIT with China is the wrong solution to the wrong problem. AFL-CIO Now. Available at: http://www.aflcio.org/Blog/Political-Action-Legislation/A-BIT-with-China-Is-the-Wrong-Solution-to-the-Wrong-Problem. Last accessed 19 June 2015.

EU – Canada Comprehensive Economic and Trade Agreement (Leaked Draft and unconfirmed), 2011. Available at http://www.laquadrature.net/wiki/images/6/69/CETA_draft_jan_2011.pdf. Last accessed 19 June 2015.

EU Secret Deals. 2014. EU-secretdeals.info – New website reveals texts from Europe's US and Canadian trade negotiations (TTIP, CETA), published on bilaterals.org, available at http://www.bilaterals.org/?eu-secretdeals-info-new-website. Last accessed 19 June 2015.

Flaherty, Scott. 2013. AFL – CIO criticizes U.S. investment talks with China. AFL-CIO Now. Available upon registration at: http://www.law360.com/articles/488728/afl-cio-criticizes-us-investment-talks-with-china. Last accessed 19 June 2015.

Human Rights Watch. 2007. Understanding the ILO Declaration. *The 2007 US trade policy template: Opportunities and risks for workers' rights* 2: 3–7. Available at: http://www.hrw.org/legacy/backgrounder/usa/trade0607/trade0607web.pdf. Last accessed 15 Jan 2014.

Human Trafficking.org. China. *The center for gender equity at the academy of educational development.* Available at: http://www.humantrafficking.org/countries/china. Last accessed 19 June 2015.

Human Trafficking.org. China. *China national plan of action on combating trafficking in women and children (2008–2012)*. Available at http://www.humantrafficking.org/countries/china. Last accessed 19 June 2015.

International Trade Union Confederation (ITUC). 2012. Internationally recognised core labour standards in the People's Republic of China: Report for the WTO General Council review.

Jacobs, Andrew. 2014. For prostitutes jailed in China, forced labor with no recourse. *The New York Times*. Available at: http://www.nytimes.com/2014/01/02/world/asia/for-prostitutes-in-china-jail-with-no-recourse.html?_r=0. Last accessed 19 June 2015.

Kong, Qingjiang. 2010. *US – China Bilateral Investment Treaty Negotiations*. EAI Background Brief No. 507. Available at: http://www.eai.nus.edu.sg/BB507.pdf. Last accessed 19 June 2015.

Prislan, Vid and Ruben Zandvliet. 2013. Labor provisions in bilateral investment treaties: Does the new US model BIT provide a template for the future? *Perspectives on topical foreign direct investment issues by the Vale Columbia Center on Sustainable International Investment* 92: 1–3. Available at: http://ccsi.columbia.edu/files/2014/01/FDI_92.pdf. Last accessed 19 June 2015.

Trade Policies of the People's Republic of China. Available at: http://www.ituc-csi.org/IMG/pdf/final_china_tpr_2012_7_june_doc.pdf. Last accessed 19 June 2015.

van Liemt, Gijsbert. 2004. The social dimension of trade in ASEAN: A preliminary analysis of the issues involved. International Labour Organization. Draft version available at: http://www.ilo.org/wcmsp5/groups/public/---dgreports/---integration/documents/publication/wcms_079125.pdf. Last accessed 19 June 2015.

Zhang, Pengfei. 2014. S. Korea, China to hold 12th FTA negotiations next week. *China Central Television*. Available at: http://english.cntv.cn/2014/07/10/ARTI1404969435794317.shtml. Last accessed 19 June 2015.

Zhu, Ningzhu. 2013. China abolishes reeducation through labor. Xinhua. Available at: http://news.xinhuanet.com/english/china/2013-12/28/c_133003042.htm. Last accessed 19 June 2015.

Chapter 8
Combating Sexual Harassment at Work in China: Legislation, Practice and Social Context

Ninglan Xue

8.1 Introduction

Elimination of employment and occupation discrimination is one of the fundamental labour rights of the International Labour Organization (ILO). The ILO aims at safeguarding human rights in the workplace, promoting equal opportunities and equal treatment in employment. China has ratified the two core Conventions of the ILO on discrimination: the Equal Remuneration Convention No. 100, in 1990 and the Discrimination (Employment and Occupation) Convention No. 111, in 2006. Therefore, she has the obligation to adopt legislative and other relevant measures to implement those conventions domestically.

Article 1 of the Discrimination (Employment and Occupation) Convention No. 111 sets out the definition of discrimination in employment and occupation. Unsurprisingly, "gender" is one of the prohibited grounds of discrimination. Although the Convention No. 111 does not mention sexual harassment, it is generally agreed that sexual harassment in the workplace should be covered under the definition of discrimination. The Committee of Experts on the Application of Conventions and Recommendations (CEACR) has carried out a survey, within which sexual harassment was addressed as gender-based discrimination.[1] In 1996, the Special Survey on Equality in Employment and Occupation in respect of Discrimination (Employment and Occupation) Convention No. 111 confirmed that sexual harassment outrages personal dignity, equality and weakens workers' interest in the workplace. By weakening the foundation where working relationships are built and reducing the productivity thereof, sexual harassment has led to considerable

[1] See ILO CEACR 1988.

N. Xue (✉)
Institute of Law, Chinese Academy of Social Sciences, No. 15 Shatan Beijie, Dongcheng District, 100720 Beijing, People's Republic of China
e-mail: xuenl@cass.org.cn

U. Liukkunen, Y. Chen (eds.), *Fundamental Labour Rights in China — Legal Implementation and Cultural Logic*, Ius Gentium: Comparative Perspectives on Law and Justice 49, DOI 10.1007/978-3-319-23156-3_8

damage in the operation of enterprises. The Committee asserted that sexual harassment should enter the scope of application of the Convention.[2]

In China, gender discrimination is manifested in various aspects of employment and occupation. For example, gender discrimination can be found in the process of recruitment and promotion, unequal remuneration, difference in retirement age. In short, sexual harassment constitutes a serious form of gender discrimination in the workplace. Basically, it was only at the beginning of the twenty-first century when the topic of 'sexual harassment in the workplace' raised public concerns, and was prohibited in China.

"Sexual harassment" is not a native concept to China, but appeared in the 1970s in the United States. For the very first time American feminist jurist Catherine MacKinnon proposed the concept of sexual harassment in her landmark book "Sexual Harassment of Working Women: A Case of Sex Discrimination". She pointed out that sexual harassment is a form of discrimination which is an actionable matter under United States law. She also made a further distinction by dividing sexual harassment in the workplace into "exchange-type sexual harassment" and "hostile-type work environment sexual harassment". All of these had a profound impact on U.S. legislation and its judicial system.[3] The expression 'sexual harassment' started to be used by Chinese around the UN Fourth World Conference on Women in 1995. However, this does not mean that prior to the Conference no incidence of sexual harassment occurred in Chinese society. Indeed, in terms of this kind of unwelcome and sex-related conduct, Chinese people historically have had their own native expression, 'shua liumang' (literally 'to play the rogue'), which refers to harassing people by indecent means.[4] In 1999, the new version of the Chinese "dictionary" started to include the term "sexual harassment" and stated that:

---

[2] See ILO CEACR 1996.

[3] Weisberg 1996, at pp. 725–732. Chinese scholars have also pointed out that the concept of sexual harassment and its two categories were actually proposed by two American scholars: Lin Farley and Catherine Mackinnon. Lin Farley's 1978 masterpiece is the book "Sexual Shakedown: the Sexual Harassment of Women on the Job", published a year before MacKinnon's book. See Zhao 2006, at p. 23.

[4] In modern Chinese, the word "rogue" (流氓) has two meanings: one refers to individuals who are jobless or commit criminal offences and other misdemeanours, the other means molesting women and other bad behaviour. See CASS Institute of Linguistics Dictionary, 1981, at p. 717. In this paper, so-called "bullying" refers to the abovementioned indecent behaviour towards others. [Criminal Law of The People's Republic of China] 中华人民共和国刑法 (zhōng huá rén mín gòng hé guó xíng fǎ), 1979 and, [Regulations on the People's Republic of China on Administrative Penalties for Public Security] 中华人民共和国治安管理处罚条例 (zhōng huá rén mín gòng hé guó zhì ān guǎn lǐ chǔ fá tiáo lì), 1986 both had provisions for insulting women as hooliganism, breach of which resulted in criminal and administrative sanctions. In 1997, the revised Criminal Law of China abolished hooliganism; it is now an offence to act "indecently towards" or to "insult…a woman by force" (Article 237; see also Article 241). In 2006 [Public Security Administration Punishments Law of the People's Republic of China] 中华人民共和国治安管理处罚法 (zhōng huá rén mín gòng hé guó zhì ān guǎn lǐ chǔ fá fǎ) imposed administrative penalty measures for many acts, such as sending obscene, abusive, threatening or other kinds of information, interfering with the normal life of others; molesting others or intentional nudity in public places and other aggravated assaults (Article 42).

sexual harassment in the 1970s emerged in the United States and the term refers to a situation where, in the presence of unequal power relations, individuals in a higher social status force disadvantaged individuals to meet the former's sexual demands through abusing their power, and as a consequence, the latter may feel disturbed. According to the Chinese vocabulary, such behaviour is a manifestation of gender discrimination.[5]

In 1994, a group of Chinese sociology scholars conducted a survey on 169 women and 40 men from four different regions including Beijing. Based on non-random samples, the survey reveals that "sexual harassment against women, which plagues many countries around the world, also exists in China".[6] Women are the major victims of sexual harassment in the workplace. This is because they often serve at a lower level of all kinds of social organizational structures. In most political, economic, cultural and educational contexts, women are often treated as those who are led and managed while men are often in higher positions and paid more generously than women. In addition, traditional gender culture views women as subordinate to men. These patriarchal norms and values concerning the role of gender are still present in most family cultures of the world, and are even expanded to broader social relations other than family relations. As a result, male sexual harassment against women, especially in the workplace, has become a mainstream phenomenon. In 1992, the UN Committee on the Elimination of Discrimination against Women delivered its 19th General Recommendation, which illustrated the nature of and damage by sexual harassment in the workplace. According to the General Recommendation (Articles 6, 17 and 18), sexual harassment in the workplace is a kind of differential treatment based on sex, and forms direct gender discrimination in the workplace; it will hamper women in their full enjoyment of the right to a healthy working environment and the right to equal employment.

8.2 Chinese Legislation on Combating Sexual Harassment in the Workplace

Mostly inspired by international conventions and practice, since the 2000s, China started to develop its legal system to address the need to prevent and intervene in sexual harassment at work in China. Sexual harassment incidents which occur during the process of fulfilling a labour contract and job-seeking not only violate workers' basic civil rights, but also jeopardize realization of their labour rights. The Chinese Constitution extensively safeguards citizens' freedom of the person, the right to work, equal pay for equal work, and other rights. Besides, a series of laws

[5] [Ci Hai 1999 edition compact edition] 辞海 1999 年版缩印本 2000, at p. 1194.

[6] The survey found that 142 out of 169 women claimed that they had suffered various forms of sexual harassment, accounting for 84.02 % of the total. 107 individuals said they had suffered sexual harassment more than twice, accounting for 63.31 % and 152 individuals contended that they were aware that many females around them had been sexually harassed at one time or another. Tang 1995, at p. 31.

prohibits discrimination in employment and occupation. The legal framework of anti-sexual harassment is based on the Chinese Constitution[7] and the Law on the Protection of Rights and Interests of Women (Women's Law),[8] while the General Principles of the Civil Law[9] and Labour Law[10] form the core of the regulatory system. The Chinese Constitution, in its Article 38, states that the personal dignity of citizens of the People's Republic of China is inviolable. Insult, libel, false charge or frame-up directed against citizens by any means is prohibited. This is the foundation for other laws to regulate sexual harassment. Articles 98, 101 and 120 of the General Principles of the Civil Law contain provisions on the rights to life and health of citizens, reputation, honour and human dignity protected by law, prohibit the use of insults, libel or other means to damage the reputation of citizens. In the field of labour law, measures prohibiting discrimination are mainly enshrined in the Labour Law, the Labour Contract Law and the Employment Promotion Law.[11] For instance, Article 12 of the Labour Law stipulates that workers shall not be discriminated against in employment due to their nationality, race, sex, or religious belief. The Labour Contract Law and the Employment Promotion Law, although not stating that employers are obliged to prevent sexual harassment in the workplace, set out rather concrete provisions on elimination of discrimination in employment. Amongst them, Article 3 of the Employment Promotion Law states that workers enjoy the right to employment on an equal footing and to choice of jobs on their own initiative in accordance with law. In seeking employment, workers shall not be subject to discrimination because of their ethnic backgrounds, race, gender, religious beliefs, and so on. Article 27 of the Employment Promotion law specifically addresses protection of women's equal labour rights works as the principle opposing sexual harassment in the workplace.[12] Article 17 of the Labour Contract Law lists the compulsory terms of labour contracts, including item No. 8 which is about labour protection, working conditions and protection against occupational hazards and Article 52, which allows enterprise workers and employers to create special collective contracts that include labour safety and hygiene, female workers' rights protection and other conditions, which is evidence for individual economic

---

[7] [Constitution of the People's Republic of China] 中华人民共和国宪法 (zhōng huá rén mín gòng hé guó xiàn fǎ), 1982 (as revised in 2004).

[8] [Law on the Protection of Rights and Interests of Women of the People's Republic of China] 中华人民共和国妇女权益保障法 (zhōng huá rén mín gòng hé guó fù nǚ quán yì bǎo zhàng fǎ), 1992 (as revised in 2005).

[9] [General Principles of the Civil Law of the People's Republic of China] 中华人民共和国民法通则 (zhōng huá rén mín gòng hé guó mín fǎ tōng zé), 1986.

[10] [Labour Law of the People's Republic of China] 中华人民共和国劳动法 (zhōng huá rén mín gòng hé guó láo dòng fǎ), 1994.

[11] [Labour Contract Law of the People's Republic of China] 中华人民共和国劳动合同法 (zhōng huá rén mín gòng hé guó láo dòng hé tóng fǎ), 2007; [Employment Promotion Law of the People's Republic of China] 中华人民共和国就业促进法 (zhōng huá rén mín gòng hé guó jiù yè cù jìn fǎ, 2007. These two laws came into force simultaneously on 1 January 2008.

[12] [Employment Promotion Law of the People's Republic of China] 中华人民共和国就业促进法 (zhōng huá rén mín gòng hé guó jiù yè cù jìn fǎ), 2007, Article 27 provides that "the State shall guarantee that women and men enjoy equal labour rights."

organizations, private non-enterprise units and other employers including obligations and responsibilities while signing labour contracts.

Since the new millennium, China has witnessed a significant breakthrough in combating sexual harassment in two aspects, i.e., the express prohibition of sexual harassment against women by an amendment to the Law on the Protection of Rights of Interests of Women in 2005 and the unequivocal pronouncement of the employer's obligation to prevent and prohibit sexual harassment in workplace by the State Council in an administrative regulation in 2012.

8.2.1 Express Prohibition of Sexual Harassment Against Women by Amendment to the Law on the Protection of Rights and Interests of Women (Women's Law)

In 2003, two high-profile lawsuits on sexual harassment were lodged in Beijing[13] and Wuhan.[14] These received extensive media coverage, triggering widespread public concern. In turn, this to some extent accelerated the legislature into incorporating a ban on sexual harassment against women in the Women's Law when amending it in 2005.

After amendment, both substantive and procedural provisions against sexual harassment are contained in the Women's Law. Article 40 stipulates that sexual harassment against women is banned. Victims are entitled to complain to the entity or the relevant organs. This Article is in the Chapter on rights of the person (Chapter VI) and implies that direct objection to sexual harassment is one of those

[13] The plaintiff worked in a computer company and was sexually harassed many times by a male department manager. She therefore resigned. Being unemployed for a year and a half, she had been applying for job opportunities in many other computer network companies, but all her applications were rejected. When she was informed that it was the former department manager who used his influence in the industry to interfere with her re-employment, she filed a defamation suit with a district court in Beijing. However, the court held that the plaintiff had provided insufficient evidence, and could not prove that the defendant's conduct could constitute a violation of her reputation. Therefore, the judge did not rule for the plaintiff. See Zhang and Fan 2003.

[14] The plaintiff was a female teacher. She alleged that, from the beginning of the second half of 2000, the defendant, the deputy director of her department, harassed her during a work discussion. During a trip organized by the school in 2001, the defendant invited her to his room at 11:00 pm to discuss work. Her private parts were touched and she was forced to kiss. Thereafter, as long as no one else was in the office, the defendant brazenly harassed her, touched her hands and shoulders, hugged her round the waist, and also sent her indecent text messages. A district court in Wuhan found that the plaintiff had established the facts as to harassment by the defendant and ordered the defendant to apologise to the plaintiff and pay compensation for mental suffering by way of damages in the sum of 2,000 Chinese yuan. The defendant appealed to the Intermediate People's Court. In October 2003, the appeal court upheld the ruling of an apology by the defendant to the plaintiff, but found that the defendant's conduct did not cause serious harmful consequences for the plaintiff, and therefore revoked the First Instance court's verdict on compensation. See Hou and Li 2003.

rights. Article 58 provides a channel for victims of sexual harassment to resort to legal remedy:

> If anyone commits sexual harassment …against women to violate this law, and if such act constitutes a violation of the public security administration, the victim may require the public security bureau to impose on the violator an administrative punishment or may initiate a civil action in the people's court.[15]

8.2.2 Exerting Obligation for Employers to Prevent Sexual Harassment by Special Rules on the Labour Protection of Female Employees

On 28 April 2012, the State Council of China adopted the Special Rules on the Labour Protection of Female Employees (Special Rules) which replaced the 1988 version.[16] The Special Rules is a regulation providing special labour protection for women. It not only emphasizes special protection from the physical and physiological perspectives, but also extends to providing protection in mental and psychological aspects. Article 11 of the Special Rules stipulates that employers must prevent and prohibit sexual harassment of female employees in their workplace. Accordingly, each employer has the obligation to prevent and stop sexual harassment against female employees within its unit. This provision reflects a significant transformation of values in the field of labour legislation in China. It shows that labour law not only protects female workers from risks of the material environment but also from risks of the social environment. It further illustrates that sexual harassment in the workplace is not purely an offence as between the perpetrator and the victim, but also a kind of employment discrimination closely related to the right to work, human dignity as well as labour safety. Employers shoulder an obligation to provide a safe and friendly environment, and equal treatment to all their employees.

The recent amendment to the Women's Law is a major step towards better prevention of sexual harassment. In the past, the public generally considered sexual harassment as a private matter between two individuals, namely a moral issue or a behavioural issue, but not a legal issue. At present, however, the law explicitly prohibits sexual harassment. It has been transformed from a moral issue into a legal matter with higher regard in modern ideology. Other laws have still not recognized the definition of sexual harassment and hold no jurisdiction on this kind of offence. This affects the public perception of sexual harassment and may lead to a lack of objective criteria on the part of courts. Indeed, a real understanding of the concept

---

[15] [Law on the Protection of Rights and Interests of Women] 中华人民共和国妇女权益保障法 (zhōng huá rén mín gòng hé guó fù nǚ quán yì bǎo zhàng fǎ), 2005, Article 58.

[16] The new [Special Rules on the Labour Protection of Female Employees] 女职工劳动保护特别规定 (nǚ zhí gōng láo dòng bǎo hù tè bié guī dìng), 2012, were reviewed and passed by the No. 200 standing meeting of the State Council on 28 April 2012, and came into force on the same day.

of sexual harassment is the only way to guarantee an unbiased ruling in the case, which inevitably affects correct enforcement of the law. Furthermore, poor remedy mechanisms hamper the incentive of victims to seek authoritative intervention.

The current regulatory framework on sexual harassment is a dual system, which comprises "workplace doctrine" and "rights doctrine". On the one hand, "workplace doctrine" places protection of the worker at its centre, mainly through regulation of sexual harassment. On the other hand, "rights doctrine" focuses on protecting the private rights of individuals, which are primarily regulated by civil law, so that the perpetrator is held responsible. It is the sanction system that helps to achieve relief for victims to defend their related human rights, such as dignity.[17] At present, China's prevention of and intervention in sexual harassment is not perfect. The weakness of the current legal framework is mainly reflected in that (1) civil legislation, especially the Civil Procedure Law[18] in sexual harassment infringement disputes, fails to allocate the burden of proof appropriately, as well as evidence gathering by the judge; and (2) labour legislation, where sexual harassment relief mechanisms have not been established. Obligations of the employer in preventing sexual harassment should be reflected in national labour laws and not merely limited to the section on female worker protection. There has also not so far been a provision dealing with sanctions on employers who fail to fulfil their obligations[19] or an applicable non-litigation settlement mechanism.

8.3 Analysis of a Typical Case

Since 2000, several sexual harassment cases have been reported, which have stirred extensive public discussion. Most of the cases occurred between bosses and their subordinates and consisted of *quid pro quo* sexual harassment. No case involves hostile work environment harassment. At the end of 2005, shortly after the amendment to the Women's Law coming into force, a court in Chongqing heard a case filed by a female primary school teacher against her principal for sexual harassment.

---

[17] See Yang and Zhang 2005, at p. 16.

[18] [Civil Procedure Law of the People's Republic of China] 中华人民共和国民事诉讼法 (zhōng huá rén mín gòng hé guó mín shì sù sòng fǎ), 1991 (as second revised in 2012).

[19] The author believes that employers neglect to fulfil the obligation to prevent sexual harassment, and their failure may bring consequences which include: sharing liability with perpetrators toward the victim; whereas employees have, as a result of sexual harassment, been transferred, or paid reduced benefits, dismissed or resigned, employers bear responsibility for corrective remedies; when the harm expands due to the fault of sexual harassment incidents, employers bear the responsibility to pay punitive damages to the victims. See Tang et al. 2012, at p. 170.

8.3.1 The Case

Since Ms. Wen became a teacher in a primary school in Chongqing in 1999, her principal Mr. Hu had harassed her in several ways, such as taking her to the office alone, and harassing her verbally and physically, sending many pornographic text messages. The behaviour of Mr. Hu seriously disturbed Ms. Wen's normal life, affected her marriage, and led to her suffering from neurasthenia.

On 8 August 2005, Ms. Wen brought a case before the court on the ground of infringement by Mr. Hu of her human dignity, and requested the court to order the defendant to apologize and to pay compensation for her mental damage. In February 2006, the court delivered the judgment of first instance, but did not support the plaintiff's claim and dismissed the action. According to the court, the plaintiff had not provided sufficient evidence to prove her claim. The appeal court took a similar view.[20] According to the appeal court, sending a short message was two-way conduct, and Ms. Wen did not refuse or show antipathy in her message. Therefore, the facts were not sufficient to support her claim. The appeal court dismissed her appeal and affirmed the original judgment.

8.3.2 Analysis

This case raises the question of how to identify sexual harassment in the judicial process. In the absence of a definition of sexual harassment in Chinese law, useful reference can be made by resorting to the Convention on Elimination of All Forms of Discrimination against Women (CEDAW) ratified by China and General Recommendation No. 19 delivered by the CEDAW Committee, as a ground for identifying the legal nature of the conduct of the defendant.[21] In this particular case, the conduct of Mr. Hu met the basic criteria of sexual harassment defined in international human rights instruments. Firstly, the conduct of Mr. Hu was against the will of Ms. Wen; was unwelcome and unacceptable, and therefore constituted an offence. Secondly, the conduct of Mr. Hu was of a sexual nature, for the purpose of meeting his physiological and psychological sexual needs. Thirdly, the status of Mr. Hu as principal forms power control over and oppression of Ms. Wen, which

[20] See Beijing Youth Daily 2006.

[21] As to whether the convention can be directly applicable in respective courts in various countries, provisions of countries differ from each other. In China, how to apply the international conventions ratified by China, including CEDAW, has not been clearly defined. It is usually transformed into national law in order to be applicable. The Chinese Constitution does not clearly offer a mechanism for applying the Convention, but nor does it prohibit the court from applying the Convention directly. As for a general recommendation, strictly speaking, States parties are not legally bound, but more and more countries and courts have invoked the general recommendations in adjudicating cases. Yet, under this trend, it is outdated to emphasize that general recommendations are not law.

facilitated his harassment. In sum, the conduct of Mr. Hu was typical sexual harassment in the workplace.

As to Ms. Wen, the absence of an express refusal of Mr. Hu's text message cannot be seen as her deliberately welcoming his long-time sexual harassment. Considering the unequal power status, and the plaintiff's need to keep her job, to maintain her marriage, and to survive in an unfavourable environment, she had to forbear. In the process of identifying sexual harassment, the court should consider unequal status in employment between the perpetrator and the victim, as well as the social and public environment in which the victim lives. Once the victim has explicitly expressed an objection against sexual harassment during the process, it is sufficient to prove the victim's unwillingness. However, if the nature of the victim's behaviour remains ambiguous (ài mèi), or if a victim tries to use the acts of the perpetrator to gain some advantage (yíng hé), it is unlikely that a legal case of sexual harassment could be established.

Internationally, relevant regulatory documents on the definition of sexual harassment often indicate "unwelcome" and "offence" as the two fundamental characteristics of sexual harassment.[22] To make these subjective characteristics into objective standards, American courts use the 'Reasonable Women Standard', which has great reference value for China. This standard is based on the viewpoint of the victim, using the objective standard of a "reasonable person" to measure the subjective feelings of the victim. The victim should be a reasonable person from the legal perspective. This approach does not consider the intention or motive of the perpetrator and therefore can restrict the harasser to blaming the victim for accepting harassment. In the Chinese context, the standard of "reasonable woman" can be extended to the standard of "reasonable victim".[23] "Reasonable victim" is an objective standard based on gender distinction. When the victim is a woman, the standard will be the

[22] For example, in 1980 the U.S. Equal Employment Opportunity Committee defined sexual harassment in its Guidance on Workplace Sexual Harassment as: unwelcome sexual advances and favours, and other verbal or physical harassment of a sexual nature. In 1990, the Council of the European Union, in its decision on protecting workplace dignity for both men and women, addressed sexual harassment as "an act of a sexual nature against the will of the party, or a sexually based act that has an unfair impact upon male and female employees in the workplace". Jiao 2002, at p. 20.

For example, see the conception by the Committee of Experts on the Application of Conventions and Recommendations: "The terms 'sexual harassment' or 'unsolicited sexual attention' include any insult or inappropriate remark, joke, insinuation and comment on a person's dress, physique, age, family situation, etc; a condescending or paternalistic attitude with sexual implications undermining dignity; any unwelcome invitation or request, implicit or explicit, whether or not accompanied by threats; any lascivious look or other gesture associated with sexuality; and any unnecessary physical contact such as touching, caresses, pinching or assault. In order to constitute sexual harassment in employment, an act of this type must, in addition, be justly perceived as a condition of employment or precondition for employment, or influence decisions taken in this field, and/or affect job performance. Sexual harassment may also arise from situations which are generally hostile to one sex or the other." ILO CEACR 1996, at para. 39.

[23] In the case of *Ellison v. Brady*, the Ninth Circuit Court of the United States Court of Appeals firstly used the "reasonable woman standard", see Neville 2004 in Dong (trans), at p. 255.

judgment of a reasonable woman; when the victim is a man (although very rarely), then the standard should be the judgment of a reasonable man.

8.4 Social and Cultural Environment for Implementation of Legislation Against Sexual Harassment

For a long time, "sex" was a forbidden topic in open discussion in China. Nowdays, sexual harassment is an issue still carefully avoided in public conversation. Although there are some improvements in legislation, a social attitude against sexual harassment has not yet formed. The current author took an active part in a research project of "Anti-sexual Harassment Research in the Workplace" and interviewed several female victims, family members of the victims, lawyers and judges in 2007.[24] This qualitative study attempts to understand institutional and cultural factors behind this social problem, and the impact of these factors on women's awareness and self-esteem through the experience of sexual harassment amongst female victims at work, as well as their personal attitudes toward sexual harassment. Based on comprehensive interviews, the project has noted that workplace sexual harassment is closely connected with the current social and cultural context.[25]

8.4.1 Double Standards for Men and Women on Sex-Related Issues in Informal Public Opinion

Currently, on the formal platform, the mainstream voice calls for laws or other institutional arrangements to combat sexual harassment. However, according to public opinion on the informal platform, for a victim sexual harassment is still an unmentionable topic. Amongst views on sexual harassment, Chinese people use sayings such as "it takes two to tango". Some people believe that sexual harassment could not occur if there is no acquiescence or acceptance by women. This has the effect on informal opinion of "blame the victims", and attributing sexual assault to women's "luring" and "indecent" acts. In some cases, many believe that women have an ulterior motive. In other words, women have a "particular intention" and then behave seductively. Therefore, female victims have suffered censure. To "preserve their reputation", many women have to give up their complaint and choose to forbear.

[24] This interview was conducted in 2005 under the joint project – sexual harassment research in the workplace – led by the gender and law research centre of the Chinese Academy of Social Sciences and the anti-domestic violence net in the China Law Society. See Research project on Sexual Harassment in the Workplace, 2009, at pp. 23 and 28.

[25] Research project on Sexual Harassment in the Workplace, 2009, at pp. 23–28.

8.4.2 *Weight of Saying No: Relevance of Social Status*

Experience of female victims shows that, on the one hand, for women who face harassment, explicitly saying "no" can really curb the perpetrator from continuing and developing the harassing act; on the other hand, in some cases, to curb sexual harassment also needs other equally important factors and conditions. After interviews, the research project found that a woman's refusal was a necessary condition to prevent sexual harassment, but not a sufficient one. Other factors including identity, social status, and power influence, are of similar importance to women's attitudes. Most women who can curb sexual harassment have higher social status. Some are teachers in universities; some are managers in employing units. Those who have failed to curb sexual harassment have relatively lower social status. Some of them are laid off workers; some are domestic workers, or temporary workers, and the like. In power relations and interaction with harassers, these women are obviously in a vulnerable position; their refusal has little impact upon the harassers' conduct.

8.4.3 *Lack of Internalized Policy in Most Working Units*

When facing sexual harassment, supporting policy and an appropriate working environment are of great importance. An effective policy on the part of the employer has a positive effect in preventing sexual harassment. However, almost all the employers that were interviewed within the research project lacked prevention and supervisory mechanisms against sexual harassment, such as a clear prevention code to combat sexual harassment, continuing education and training programmes, grievance mechanisms within work units/organizations, and so on. Many employers neglected or ignored female victims' rights, dignity, interests and feelings, and lacked the consciousness of protecting women's personal rights and interests in the workplace. Female victims faced difficulties in accessing real equal protection from measures installed by employers.

Therefore, in order to effectively curb sexual harassment, in addition to legislative reforms, it is also necessary to establish appropriate law enforcement and monitoring mechanisms. In my opinion, when amending the existing Regulations on Labour Security Supervision,[26] provisions on employment discrimination could and should be incorporated as an integral part of labour inspection as a whole. The government could also pay attention to current practices in other countries and regions in order to establish a specific committee on combating discrimination,[27] fulfilling

[26] [Regulations on Labour and Social Security Supervision] 劳动保障监察条例 (láo dòng bǎo zhàng jiān chá tiáo lì), 2004.

[27] For instance, the Equal Opportunities Commission (EOC) Hong Kong, which was established in 1996 and specializes in anti-discrimination matters, is one of its specific statutory government bodies in the field of anti-discrimination.

statutory oversight responsibilities.[28] From the perspective of social and cultural dimensions, prejudice against sexual harassment victims should be shed, through advocacy, education and training measures. It is of great importance to build a healthy, safe and friendly working environment based on the idea of gender equality.

8.5 Conclusion

Sexual harassment stems from abuse of power which is exerted by the relatively mighty over the relatively vulnerable. 'Relatively' means not only a comparison of status or seniority, but also strength between the parties in sexual harassment. The reason why sexual harassment in the workplace is so difficult to avoid and resolve is the influence imposed by the powerful on the powerless, which creates difficulties for the powerless to refuse and resist. In many cases, the latter even need to pay the price for doing so.

Modernizing traditional concepts, custom and culture is a precondition for putting the law on the books into practice. In terms of building an advanced gender-friendly culture against sexual harassment in the workplace, there is much room in China for improvement, such as enhancing public awareness, setting up relevant policy and mechanisms within employers, providing training for employees, training judicial and law enforcement officers regarding the concept of gender, and the nature and harm of sexual harassment.

In recent years, China has taken a series of legislative measures to implement ILO fundamental labour rights, and to eliminate discrimination in employment and occupation. Nonetheless, relevant legislation in China still needs to be improved, for instance, to define sexual harassment in the workplace, to explicate the obligation and responsibility of employers in the prevention and punishment of sexual harassment.

Since 2006, some Chinese enterprises (such as China COSCO Group) and transnational corporations (such as GE China Company) have actively set out internal mechanisms for prevention of sexual harassment.[29] These set good examples for other employers to fulfil their legal obligations. For example, China COSCO Group (China Ocean Shipping Group Company) considers prevention of sexual harassment as an important aspect of fulfilling its corporate social responsibility. It has developed internal prevention of sexual harassment through regulations which are embedded in enterprise risk management fields as part of a human rights risks

[28] On 1 January 2013, the [Shenzhen Special Economic Zone to promote gender equality regulations] 深圳经济特区性别平等促进条例 (shēn zhèn jīng jì tè qū xìng bié píng děng cù jìn tiáo lì) came into effect, stipulating that it is urgent to establish gender equality promotion agencies in Shenzhen. One of the responsibilities of the agency is to receive complaints, deal with gender discrimination disputes, and assist complainants in the people's courts.

[29] Women's Studies Institute of China 2013, at section 7.

prevention system. Moreover, the trade union and the corporation have signed a special collective contract on protecting the rights and interests of female workers where employer obligations on sexual harassment prevention were involved as separate contract terms, strengthening the responsibility to protect the rights of female workers. The group has also established multiple complaint report channels (such as a petition department, human resources sector and trade union), for female workers to choose. Altogether, these companies' proactive actions have played a remarkably positive role in prompting other Chinese companies/employers to conscientiously fulfil their legal obligations on sexual harassment prevention, and in building internal cooperation between different departments against sexual harassment.

References

Literature

[Hou, Fangfeng] 侯方峰 and [Changzheng Li] 黎昌政. 2003. [*The defendant apologized, country's first sexual harassment case has settled*] 被告道歉 全国首例性骚扰案尘埃落定 (bèi gào dào qiàn quán guó shǒu lì xìng sāo rǎo àn chén āi luò dìng). Available at: http://www.chinacourt.org/article/detail/2003/10/id/88755.shtml. Last accessed 19 June 2015.

[Jiao, Xingkai] 焦兴铠. 2002. [*Fight against workplace sexual harassment*] 向工作场所性骚扰问题宣战 (xiàng gōng zuò chǎng suǒ xìng sāo rǎo wèn tí xuān zhàn). [Taiwan Yuanzhao Publishing House] 台北：台湾元照出版彲司.

Neville, Kathleen. 2004. *Internal affairs: The abuse of power, sexual harassment, and hypocrisy in the work place*, translated by [Dong, Yu-tao] 董煜韬. [Central Compilation and Translation Press] 北京：中央编译出版社.

[Tang, Can] 唐灿. 1995. [Sexual harassment existing in China – Case studies from 169 females] 性骚扰在中国的存在—169名女性的个例研究 (xìng sāo rǎo zài zhōng guó de cún zài—169 míng nǚ xìng de gè lì yán jīu). [*Collection of Women's Studies*] 妇女研究论丛.

[Tang, Can] 唐灿, [Jue Huang] 黄觉 and [Ninglan Xue] 薛宁兰. 2012. [*Towards the rule of law -investigation and research on sexual harassment in the workplace*] 走向法治—工作场所性骚扰的调查与研究 (zǒu xiàng fǎ zhì—gōng zuò chǎng suǒ xìng sāo rǎo de diào chá yǔ yán jīu). [Chinese People's Public Security University Press] 北京：中国人民公安大学出版社.

Weisberg, Kelly D. 1996. Sexual harassment: Introduction. In *Applications of feminist legal theory to women's lives: Sex, violence, work and reproduction*, ed. Kelly D. Weisberg, 725–739. Philadelphia: Temple University Press.

[Women's Studies Institute of China (WSIC)] 中国妇女研究会办公室编 ed. 2013. [*Research newsletter*] 研究信息简报 (yán jīu xìn xī jiǎn bào).

[Yang, Lixin] 杨立新 and [Guohong Zhang] 张国宏. 2005. [*Construction of a legal regulating system to protect private rights and fight against sexual harassment*] 论构建以私权利保护为中心的性骚扰法律规制体系 (lùn gòu jiàn yǐ sī quán lì bǎo hù wéi zhōng xīn de xìng sāo rǎo fǎ lǜ guī zhì tǐ xì, [Fujian Normal University Philosophy and Social Sciences] 福建师范大学学报(哲学社会科学版).

[Zhang, Bo] 张博and [Fan Jun] 范军. 2003. [*Beijing's first sexual harassment case*] 京城首例性骚扰案原告一审败诉 (jīng chéng shǒu lì xìng sāo rǎo àn yuán gào yī shěn bài sù). [chinacourt.org]中国法院网. Available at: http://old.chinacourt.org/public/detail.php?id=89247. Last accessed 19 June 2015.

[Zhao, He-Jun] 赵合俊. 2006. [Sexual harassment and rape – To 'gender-neutral'] 性骚扰与强奸—走向"性别中立" (xìng sāo rǎo yǔ qiáng jiān—zǒu xiàng "xìng bié zhōng lì"). [*Collection of Women's Studies*] 妇女研究论丛.

Documents and Official Publications

ILO Documents

Convention concerning the Abolition of Forced Labour, adopted 25 June 1957, ILO C105. Entry into force 17 January 1959. (Abolition of Forced Labour Convention).
Convention concerning Discrimination in Respect of Employment and Occupation, adopted 25 June 1958, ILO C111. Entry into force 15 June 1960. (Discrimination (Employment and Occupation) Convention).
Equal Remuneration Convention, adopted 29 June 1951, ILO C100. Entry into force 23 May 1953.

ILO Committee of Experts on the Application of Conventions and Recommendations (CEACR)

ILO CEACR. 1988. General Survey on Equality in Employment and Occupation. Available at: http://www.ilo.org/public/libdoc/ilo/P/09661/09661(1988-75-4B).pdf. Last accessed 19 June 2015.
ILO CEACR. 1996. *Special survey on equality in employment and occupation in respect of convention no. 111*. Available at: http://www.ilo.org/public/libdoc/ilo/P/09661/09661(1996-83-4B).pdf. Last accessed 19 June 2015.

Other International Law Sources

Convention on Elimination of All Forms of Discrimination against Women, adopted 18 December 1979, 1249 U.N.T.S 13. Entry into force 3 September 1981. (CEDAW)
UN Committee on the Elimination of Discrimination against Women. 1992. General Recommendation No. 19, adopted at the 11th session. Available at: http://www.un.org/womenwatch/daw/cedaw/recommendations/recomm.htm. Last accessed 19 June 2015.

Chinese Regulation

Laws by the National People's Congress

[Civil Procedure Law of the People's Republic of China] 中华人民共和国民事诉讼法 (zhōng huá rén mín gòng hé guó mín shì sù sòng fǎ), National People's Congress, adopted and effective 9 April 1991. Revised and effective 31 August 2012.
[Constitution of the People's Republic of China] 中华人民共和国宪法 (zhōng huá rén mín gòng hé guó xiàn fǎ), National People's Congress, adopted and effective 4 December 1982. Available at: http://english.people.com.cn/constitution/constitution.html. Last accessed 19 June 2015.
[General Principles of the Civil Law of the People's Republic of China] 中华人民共和国民法通则(zhōng huá rén mín gòng hé guó mín fǎ tōng zé), National People's Congress, adopted 12 April 1986, effective 1 January 1987. Revised and effective 27 August 2009.
[Law on the Protection of Rights and Interests of Women] 中华人民共和国妇女权益保障法 (zhōng huá rén mín gòng hé guó fù nǚ quán yì bǎo zhàng fǎ), National People's Congress, adopted 3 April 1992, effective 1 October 1992. Revised and effective 18 August 2005.

Laws by the Standing Committee of the National People's Congress

[Criminal Law of the People's Republic of China] 中华人民共和国刑法 (zhōng huá rén mín gòng hé guó xíng fǎ), Standing Committee of National People's Congress, adopted 6 July 1979, effective 1 January 1980. Revised 25 February 2011, effective 1 May 2011.

[Employment Promotion Law of the People's Republic of China] 中华人民共和国就业促进法 (zhōng huá rén mín gòng hé guó jiù yè cù jìn fǎ), Standing Committee of the National People's Congress, adopted 30 August 2007, effective 1 January 2008. Revised and effective 24 April 2015.

[Labour Contract Law of the People's Republic of China] 中华人民共和国劳动合同法 (zhōng huá rén mín gòng hé guó láo dòng hé tóng fǎ), Standing Committee of the National People's Congress, adopted 29 June 2007, effective 1 January 2008. Revised 28 December 2012, effective 1 July 2013.

[Public Security Administration Punishments Law of the People's Republic of China] 中华人民共和国治安管理处罚法 (zhōng huá rén mín gòng hé guó zhì ān guǎn lǐ chǔ fá fǎ), Standing Committee of the National People's Congress, adopted 28 August 2005, effective 1 March 2006. Revised 26 October 2012, effective 1 January 2013.

[Regulations on the People's Republic of China on Administrative Penalties for Public Security] 中华人民共和国治安管理处罚条例 (zhōng huá rén mín gòng hé guó zhì ān guǎn lǐ chǔ fá tiáo lì), Standing Committee of the National People's Congress, adopted 5 September 1986, effective 1 January 1987. Abolished 1 March 2006.

Regulations by the State Council

[Regulations on Labour and Social Security Supervision] 劳动保障监察条例 (láo dòng bǎo zhàng jiān chá tiáo lì), State Council, adopted 26 October 2004, effective 1 November 2004.

[Special Rules on the Labour Protection of Female Employees] 女职工劳动保护特别规定 (nǚ zhí gōng láo dòng bǎo hù tè bié guī dìng), State Council, adopted and effective 28 April 2012.

Local Regulations

[Shenzhen Special Economic Zone to Promote Gender Equality Regulations] 深圳经济特区性别平等促进条例 (shēn zhèn jīng jì tè qū xìng bié píng děng cù jìn tiáo lì), Shenzhen Municipal People's Congress, adopted 28 June 2012, effective 1 January 2013.

Other Sources

[Beijing Youth Daily] 北京青年报. 2006. [*The first case of sexual harassment: Female teacher appeals today*] 性骚扰第一案 败诉女教师今日上诉 (xìng sāo rǎo dì yī àn bài sù nǚ jiào shī jīn rì shàng sù), 20 February 2006.

[Ci Hai 1999 edition compact edition] 辞海 1999年版缩印本 (cí hǎi 1999 nián bǎn suō yìn běn). 2000. [Shanghai Dictionary Publishing House] 上海辞书出版社.

[CASS Institute of Linguistics Dictionary Editing Room] 中国社会科学院语言研究所词典编辑室. 1981. [*Modern Chinese Dictionary*] 现代汉语词典 (xiàn dài hàn yǔ cí diǎn). [The Commercial Press] 商务印书馆.

[Research project on Sexual Harassment in the Workplace] "工作场所中的性骚扰研究"课题组. 2009. [Sexual harassment at the workplace: Inequality in powers and identities shown in twenty cases] 工作场所中的性骚扰:多重权力和身份关系的不平等—对20个案例的调查和分析 (gōng zuò chǎng suǒ zhōng de xìng sāo rǎo: duō chóng quán lì hé shēn fèn guān xì de bù píng děng—duì 20 gè àn lì de diào chá hé fēn xī). [*Collection of Women's Studies*] 妇女研究论丛.

Chapter 9
Chinese Labour Law Development and *Hukou* Discrimination

Dong Yan

9.1 Introduction

Until 2014, China had ratified 25 Conventions adopted by the International Labour Organization (ILO), including four of the core Conventions.[1] In the meantime, China has been accelerating its work building a labour law framework for a market-oriented economy, especially since the 1990s. Many ILO standards have either already been reflected prior to their ratification or incorporated after their ratification in Chinese labour laws. A system of a "floor of labour rights" has thereby been established with the intention of complying with the requirements set out by ratified ILO rights.

In particular, China's ratification of the Discrimination (Employment and Occupation) Convention No. 111, in 2006, indicates her engagement to apply labour rights without discrimination in the workplace. However, it can be argued that what could be called *Hukou* discrimination against over 200 million rural migrant workers has become the biggest barrier for China to pave the way towards workplace equality. In a relevant response, Article 1 of Convention No. 111 articulates that "for the purpose of this Convention the term discrimination includes any distinction, exclusion or preference made on the basis of race, colour, sex, religion, political opinion, national extraction or social origin, which has the effect of nullifying or impairing equality of opportunity or treatment in employment or occupation".

[1] The core Conventions ratified by China are: the Equal Remuneration Convention No. 100 (ratified on 2 November 1990); the Discrimination (Employment and Occupation) Convention No. 111 (ratified on 12 January 2006); the Minimum Age Convention No. 138 (ratified on 28 April 1999); and the Worst Forms of Child Labour Convention No. 182 (ratified on 8 August 2002).

D. Yan (✉)
School of Law, Beijing Foreign Study University,
No. 2 Xisanhuan North Road, Beijing 100089, People's Republic of China
e-mail: yandong@bfsu.edul.cn

U. Liukkunen, Y. Chen (eds.), *Fundamental Labour Rights in China — Legal Implementation and Cultural Logic*, Ius Gentium: Comparative Perspectives on Law and Justice 49, DOI 10.1007/978-3-319-23156-3_9

Since, as is commonly suggested, rural migrant workers are often disfavoured due to their "social origin", namely "*Hukou* status", so-called *Hukou* discrimination in China falls into the sphere of the Convention.

This chapter aims to evaluate the impact of Chinese labour law development on *Hukou* discrimination by taking the concept of "social origin" in Convention No. 111 as a point of reference. The approach adopted for this work contains three main components. First, an introduction to explain the nature of the *Hukou* system, with the "social origin" of "rural migrant workers" being addressed by reference to their *Hukou* status; second, the phenomenon of *Hukou* discrimination prior to the 1994 Labour Lawis spelled out[2]; and third, the development of Chinese labour law is evaluated against its impact on *Hukou* discrimination. This chapter is concerned with the development of China's labour regulations as against *Hukou* discrimination, the impact of which has not previously been fully explored or precisely addressed so far. What is more, this article uses Convention No. 111 as the instrument and benchmark to evaluate that impact.

The nature of the *Hukou* system is demonstrated in the following by reference to the Regulations on Household Registration and other related institutions,[3] such as the rationing and job allocation systems and the conception of rural migrant workers is spelled out with particular emphasis on their "social origin", namely rural or non-local *Hukou* status. Second, this article seeks to illustrate *Hukou* discrimination against rural migrant workers prior to 1995, through material drawn from existing literature. Finally, I will analyse the assembled labour regulations, with the aim of testing the actual progress of labour regulations in dealing with discrimination based on *Hukou*-related "social origin". The results of that analysis offer some theoretical and policy implications in relation to implementing Convention No. 111 arising out of the operation of Chinese labour laws in modern-day China.

My preliminary findings indicate that the post-1995 labour regulations have made great progress in eliminating the rural-urban rights gap, as the rural *Hukou* status of migrant workers is no longer a barrier for them to access employment opportunities and associated rights. Notwithstanding, another form of "social origin" – non-local *Hukou* status – of rural migrant workers remains a ground for employment discrimination. Residency-based discrimination, instead of rural-urban divided discrimination, is the core factor triggering workplace inequality against rural migrant workers. In order to fulfil China's commitment to Convention No. 111, the legislature in China needs to throw more light upon the problem of residency-based discrimination created by the *Hukou* system, which has been underemphasised by many authors.

[2] [Labour Law of the People's Republic of China] 中华人民共和国劳动法 (zhōng huá rén mín gòng hé guó láo dòng fǎ), 1994.

[3] [Regulations on Household Registration] 中华人民共和国户口登记条例 (zhōng huá rén mín gòng hé guó hù kǒu dēng jì tiáo lì), 1958.

9.2 Background: The *Hukou* Status of Rural Migrant Workers

Before embarking upon analysing *Hukou* inequality in the workplace, it is necessary to address the background of two special terms – the "*Hukou* system" and "rural migrant workers" to describe the evolution of the *Hukou* system and to explain its relation to rural migrant workers and their "social origin" – *Hukou* status.

9.2.1 The Category of "Social Origin" Under the Hukou System

The *Hukou* system, as an instrument for rural-urban mobility control, refers to the system of residency registration which is required by the Regulations on Household Registration (RHR), issued by the Standing Committee of the National People's Congress (NPC).[4] Although the RHR has only 24 Articles, it carved out a complete administrative mechanism to deal with Household Registration. Its key effect, however, was to introduce the household registration book (*Hukoubu*) in order to erect "a hereditary, matrilineal system which divided China's agricultural and non-agricultural (rural/urban) populations, and effectively bound the peasantry to the land they tilled".[5]

Hukou registration is mandatory for all citizens of the People's Republic of China (PRC) aged 1 month and over.[6] The various police stations across the country – known as Public Security Bureaux (PSBs) – all have specific sections that deal with household registration. Failure to comply with these latter provisions in Article 7 will give rise to penal consequences for the individual concerned.[7] In essence, it is the Household Registration Book, rather than the RHR, that spells out a specific set of categories for personal information. The *Hukoubu* is a booklet resembling a passport,[8] the first page of which contains the terms and conditions for issuing and presenting *Hukou* documents.[9] A detailed classification of *Hukou* status appears on

---

[4] Ibid.

[5] Windrow and Guha 2005, at p. 3.

[6] [Regulation on Household Registration] 中华人民共和国户口登记条例 (zhōng huá rén mín gòng hé guó hù kǒu dēng jì tiáo lì), 1958, Article 7.

[7] Ibid., Article 20.

[8] The cover of the *Hukoubu* is plastic or laminated, of reddish brown colour, together with the national emblem printed in gold. The inside pages are not numbered, and contain full information on all household members, such as date of birth, birthplace and gender.

[9] The details of those conditions and terms are as follows: first, the *Hukoubu* is an identification document which indicates the citizen's identity and the relationship between family members. It is used and managed by PSBs for household inquiries. The householder or members of the household have to present this certificate to police for investigation and verification whenever needed. Second,

the second page of the *Hukoubu*. Here, *Hukou* registration is dual-classified, both by residential location ("*Hukou suozaidi*", literally referring to the place of *Hukou* registration) and by Hukou type ("*Hukou leibie*", literally referring to the type of *Hukou* registration – either "agricultural" or "non-agricultural").

The registered residential location is the place presumed to be where the registrant lives permanently. That permanent location will be the geographical area within which the citizen conducts the majority of their economic and political activities. Normally, the citizen's home address will be registered as the permanent location, although for some groups, such as college students, the address of the institution to which they are affiliated will, instead, be recognized as the place of registration.[10]

The classification into agricultural or non-agricultural *Hukou* registration tends to reflect the type of work, either farming or industrial, of the registrant. Normally, rural residents who work in farming activities, except those who work for state-owned farms, are registered as agricultural *Hukou*, which will then also apply to their family members. The rest of the population, mainly urban dwellers, are registered with a non-agricultural *Hukou*. Once the type of *Hukou* has initially been decided, it will remain fixed for the household and its successors, regardless of whether there might subsequently be any change in the actual work undertaken by members of the household. Indeed, the given registration, irrespective of whether it came from the original registration or was inherited, is very difficult to change, unless a special procedure – known as "*nongzhuanfei*" – can be satisfied.[11] The classification into "rural" and "urban" status is, in the words of Chan and Zhang, the citizen's "socio-economic eligibility".[12] Indeed, that division gradually came to be attached to entitlement to receive economic benefits, such as state-subsidized grain supply.

Prior to the 1980s a set of institutional frameworks existed to support implementation of the *Hukou* system. In rural areas, individual farmers were organised into collective production groups – People's Communes – which were responsible for managing farming work and for delivering welfare to their members.[13] The household members of a People's Commune were commonly registered as possessing rural *Hukou* status – and it may be noted that the RHR requires rural residents to

---

the householder has to keep the *Hukoubu* in proper condition and not to alter, transfer or lend the register privately and must report immediately to the PSB when the household register is lost or damaged. Third, the *Hukoubu* is the property of the issuing authority. Fourth, the householder has to report to the police station on any change in registered items. Fifth, if the whole household moves out of the registered region, it should apply for cancellation of household registration.

[10] See [Regulation on Household Registration] 中华人民共和国户口登记条例 (zhōng huá rén mín gòng hé guó hù kǒu dēng jì tiáo lì), 1958, Articles 3 and 10.

[11] [Agricultural to Non-agricultural] 农转非 (nóng zhuǎn fēi) refers to the process for those who hold agricultural Hukou status to transfer to non-agricultural Hukou registration.

[12] Chan and Zhang 1999, at p. 821.

[13] The People's Commune was a formal administrative body which organised farmers collectively during the period 1958–1985.

register collectively with their People's Commune.[14] The Commune was a unit of local administration that owned all of the assets and ran the entire agricultural production. The commune authority had power to allocate labour and other resources within its territory. In the course of their daily life, commune members were assigned working tasks, and were awarded "work points" for the work which they completed. Income distribution within a commune was based partly on work, and partly on the free supply of food.[15]

Urban dwellers and their families were closely tied to their own economic entities, namely work-units. Labour welfare and rights were guided by a set of strict administrative organisations, and were provided through work units.[16] After achieving control of the ownership of the majority of enterprises, China adopted a strait-jacketed job allocation mechanism, known as the "unified allocation" (*tongchou anpai*) labour system, to assign jobs for urban *Hukou* holders. Between the 1950s and the 1980s, urban dwellers who held urban *Hukou* registration, after completing their schooling, would wait for local officials to allocate them a job. The devolved local Labour Bureaux would find vacancies for unemployed urban dwellers, allegedly taking their preferences into account.[17] For these urban *Hukou* holders, most of whom were urban dwellers, a grain rationing system was applied to the provision of basic foodstuffs by the state through official retail outlets located inside enterprises or districts.

Any change of registration status, including geographical movement, had to be initiated by the organisations to which the individuals were attached, and approval had to be forthcoming from various authorities such as labour authorities, PSBs and grain bureaux. When farmers planned to move to an industrial work unit, an additional administrative procedure (*nongzhuanfei*) also had to be satisfied. Transferring from a rural to an urban registration category would usually occur in conjunction with a change of residence from rural to urban, and, therefore, was subject to a dual approval process to amend both registration aspects.[18] It should also be noted that industrial undertakings were largely concentrated within urban areas during the period of the planned economy, so that obtaining an industrial job, as the key pre-condition for *nongzhuanfei*, inevitably involved a move from the countryside to the cities. In such cases, registrants had to obtain permission in relation to two separate matters – change of residence and registration type – through a variety of state agencies, such as PSBs and grain rationing agencies, in both their home area and in the area of their intended destination.

---

[14] [Regulation on Household Registration] 中华人民共和国户口登记条例 (zhōng huá rén mín gong hé guó hù kǒu dēng jì tiáo lì), 1958, Article 4.

[15] [Luo] 罗平汉 2000, at p. 39.

[16] The state used administrative controls to intervene directly in the economy by owning the means of production, planning all production and distribution arrangements by setting prices as well as employment quotas and wages.

[17] Wang 2005, at p. 78.

[18] [Gao] 高涛 2013, at p. 22.

In the event of failure to comply with those administrative requirements established by the *Hukou* system and other institutions, individuals could lose their affiliation to their organisation, which served as the sole provider of their living subsistence. Although none of these institutions was explicitly set up to check on the migration of farmers to cities, over time they evolved to become effective interlocking institutions which immobilized farmers. Therefore, for Chinese citizens, *Hukou* status became their "social origin" as defined by Convention No. 111. According to the ILO website, social origin includes social class, socio-occupational category and caste.[19] Clearly, agricultural (rural) and non-agricultural (urban) *Hukou* status was designed to reflect the socio-occupational category of Chinese citizens. Since *Hukou* status is hard to amend, Chinese citizens have to carry it during most of their life and the same may apply even to their successors. Taking farmers for example, their social origins are very likely "agricultural" statuses.

9.2.2 Emergence of Rural Migrant Workers and Their "Social Origin"

Since 1977, when the reformist Deng Xiaoping gained political power, the prime concern of the Chinese government has been to promote economic development and greater participation in the global economy.[20] The widely held view was that market-oriented reforms would replace centrally planned mechanisms. In this context, labour allocation and the grain rationing system, which used to serve as the key to mobility control and the planned economy, become increasingly problematic in exposing the labour force to the market. In consequence, a series of reforms was set in train with a view to removing these two "albatrosses" from around the neck of the market.

In the field of employment reform, key developments were aimed at loosening the "fixed labour" system in both rural and urban areas, and the government issued new policies designed to improve the economic performance of agricultural collectives. In particular, the policy of Household Responsibility Reform (HRR), which had been applied in the agricultural sector during the 1980s, was extended to have effect nationwide. Key features of the HRR were decollectivization and liberalisation of labour. Indeed, by 1983, 98 % of rural households had been decollectivized.[21] As the reforms further shifted a majority of the land and labour from the People's Commune to individual households, members were no longer so heavily dependent upon their organisations. The cities, meanwhile, saw adoption of a number of reforms in 1980, which aimed to diversify employment channels beyond State or collective firms. The "fixed labour" system underwent a complete overhaul

[19] ILO website, Q&As on business, discrimination and equality, 2012.

[20] Lin et al. 1996.

[21] White 1993, at p. 100.

following introduction of the "contract labour system" in the early 1980s.[22] Since the 1994 Labour Law was enacted, the "fixed labour" system has been completely removed, and has given way to an emerging labour market.

The grain rationing system was brought to an end in cities and towns throughout the country in 1993. When the farmers had been allowed to sell their grain in the 1980s, urban residents were given the choice of topping up their barns through recourse to the markets, alongside the remaining grain rationing scheme which operated for them. Indeed, up until the 1990s, when agricultural products were no longer subject to shortages and were widely available on the market, grain rationing ceased to be an important State concern. Consequently, the State Council decided to put an end to grain rationing in 1993.[23]

The choice of migration for work was made available to Chinese citizens because of various institutional changes during the economic reform. Combining the abolition of grain rationing and the emergence of a commodity market, physical barriers against movement have been disappearing in the aftermath of the reform. Chinese citizens can travel freely in China so long as they are not involved in long-term settlement, and can access living subsistence through markets. Moreover, employment opportunities in urban areas are becoming available to migrants after expansion of industrial sectors, particularly the growth of non-SOEs.

Market force is also driving individuals, especially rural residents, to grasp employment opportunities in other more developed regions. This might be better explained by the "push and pull theory", with "some structural factors of uneven economic development in different areas (…) responsible for the migration of rural people from under-developed to more-developed areas and cities".[24] The large urban-rural and inland-coast gap provides a tremendous incentive to migrate toward urban areas.[25] The growth of various forms of enterprise has created demand for labour in those booming industrial areas which form a "pull" force to bring in workers from rural places.

Although physical mobility for work has become a widespread phenomenon, the *Hukou* registration of migrants does not always reflect actual occupational and residential changes. This is mainly for two reasons. First, geographical mobility for work is not always granted with a change of registered residential status. Procedurally, amending registered residency usually involves administrative approvals from both home and host PSBs. In particular, the PSBs in host cities very often require substantial qualifications from an applicant to establish a change of residential status.

Second, even if a rural migrant is working in an industrial sector, his or her rural *Hukou* can remain unchanged, due to the restrictions laid down by the remaining

[22] See Solinger 1999.

[23] [Circular on Accelerating the Reform of the Grain Circulation System] 国务院关于加快粮食流通体制改革的通知 (guó wù yuàn guān yú jiā kuài liáng shí liú tōng tǐ zhì gǎi gé de tōng zhī), 1993.

[24] Tan 2005, at p. 7.

[25] *Ibid.*

nongzhuanfei control. According to current *nongzhuanfei* policy, rural *Hukou* holders nowadays have greater chances to register urban status compared to the strict control prior to the 1980s. However, they are still not allowed to alter their registration until several loosely defined criteria, such as urban property ownership and permanent employment status, have been met. Therefore, many rural workers in the industrial sector have to remain with rural status unless their *nongzhuanfei* application has satisfied those pre-set conditions and been approved by local authorities.

In a state of internal migration, compared with local workers, rural migrant workers carry their social origin as non-local and rural *Hukou* status. The original *Hukou* status of rural migrants is normally the rural type, which indicates their agricultural profession. The residency of rural migrants registered under the *Hukou* system is the village address where they came from. In the course of migration, the abovementioned administrative barriers block rural migrants from having their registration type and place amended to reflect their new working status (industrial type rather than agricultural type) and residency (local rather than non-local resident).[26] Nonetheless, rural migrant workers may be defined as a group of non-local rural *Hukou* holders working inside the urban industrial sector.

9.3 Discrimination Based on the Social Origin of Rural Migrant Workers Prior to 1995

Rural migrant workers appear clearly to be subject to *Hukou*-related institutional inequality. This is because, when rural migrant workers move to a place outside their area of registration and undertake occupation as industrial workers, both their rural and non-local registration status will often provide an excuse to deny them rights to access employment opportunities and labour benefits offered by local state agencies.

9.3.1 Institutional Inequality in Access to Employment Opportunities

The economic reform from 1978 triggered a twin-track legal development for state-owned enterprises (SOEs) and non-SOEs respectively. After the economic reform had started, labour legislation was issued for SOEs, and legislation sought to push those enterprises from an administrative organ to a market-oriented entity by introducing various horizontal labour governance mechanisms. The regulation aimed particularly to force SOEs to respond to, or to run profitably within, the market

[26] [Gao] 高涛 2013, at pp. 20–22.

environment. However, SOEs were restrained from recruiting rural workers, as they had been during the period of the planned economy. The economic reforms reduced external administrative intervention in the labour management of SOEs, but still treated those enterprises as a means of reducing urban unemployment and discouraged them from recruiting from the rural labour pool. In 1982, the State Council produced a Circular on Prevention of Applying Unfair Methods to Recruit or Transfer Workers 1982 (1982 Circular),[27] which called for tight restrictions on recruitment from rural areas, in order to release the pressure on urban unemployment. According to the 1982 Circular, all SOEs and collectively-owned enterprises in urban areas were prohibited from recruiting rural residents (rural *Hukou* holders) apart from a few exceptional cases, which were subject to approval from the provincial government. The Interim Provisions on Recruitment for State-Run Enterprises 1986 (1986 Interim Provisions)[28] also sent somewhat ambiguous restrictive signals regarding the recruitment of rural residents. On the one hand, SOEs were granted recruitment autonomy, principally by Article 2 of the 1986 Interim Provisions; yet, on the other hand, Article 12 imposed an additional approval procedure for SOEs when seeking to hire workers from the countryside.

The development of private firms, catalysed by liberal economic policies, created a different form of employment relationship, resulting in policy conflicts with the labour system that had developed largely out of the experiences of SOEs.[29] Consequently, those employed outside SOEs outstripped the capacity of the government to respond.[30] The 1986 Interim Provisions on Implementing an Employment Contract System in State-run Enterprises[31] in particular indicated the conditions underpinning such "open recruitment" under supervision by the local labour authority. However, in order to attract foreign investment, many local authorities in the early 1990s loosened their control over recruitment in FIEs and imposed no administrative penalty when FIEs failed to seek approval before engaging in cross-regional recruitment.[32] In practice, the restriction on recruiting rural and non-local *Hukou*

[27] [Circular on Prevention of Applying Unfair Methods to Recruit or Transfer Workers] 国务院关于严禁在招收、调配职工工作中搞不正之风的通知 (guó wù yuàn guān yú yán jìn zài zhāo shōu, diào pèi zhí gōng gōng zuò zhōng gǎo bù zhèng zhī fēng de tōng zhī), 1993.

[28] [Interim Provisions on Recruitment for State-Run Enterprises] 国营企业招用工人暂行规定 (guó yíng qǐ yè zhāo yòng gōng rén zàn xíng guī dìng), 1986.

[29] See Chan 1995.

[30] Potter 2001, at p. 104.

[31] [Interim Provisions on Implementing the Employment Contract System in State-run Enterprises] 国营企业实行劳动合同制暂行规定 (guó yíng qǐ yè shí xíng láo dòng hé tóng zhì zàn xíng guī dìng), 1986.

[32] For example, both the [Changchun Measure of FIEs Labour] 长春外商投资企业劳动管理办法 (cháng chūn wài shāng tóu zī qǐ yè láo dòng guǎn lǐ bàn fǎ), 1993 and the [Tianjin Measure of FIEs Labour Management] 天津外商投资企业劳动管理办法 (tiān jīn wài shāng tóu zī qǐ yè láo dòng guǎn lǐ bàn fǎ), 1994 allowed their local FIEs to recruit workers cross-regionally without approval in advance.

holders was not fully implemented, owing to lack of incentives from the enforcement agencies and enterprises.[33]

As a result, labour legislation between 1978 and 1993 afforded a different level of accessibility for rural *Hukou* holders, depending upon the type of enterprise ownership. The straitjacket approach to employment governance under the planned economy began to be loosened, although it still retained a certain impact on employment relationships in SOEs during the post-Cultural Revolution period. The state seemed reluctant to loosen its administrative hold over both rural and non-local *Hukou* holders entering the state sector. Meanwhile, non-SOEs were covered by market-orientated regulations. The state also granted considerable autonomy to non-SOEs in respect of their recruitment of workers, and rural and non-local *Hukou* holders were made eligible for non-state employment. Although finding work for rural workers was not a state priority, enthusiasm amongst non-SOEs to recruit from the countryside was stimulated by the cheap labour costs associated with these workers.

9.3.2 Institutional Inequality in Access to Work-Related Welfare and Rights

Due to the fact that SOE employment was effectively inaccessible to rural and non-local *Hukou* holders, the wage protection and work-related benefits provided for SOE workers were also generally unavailable to them. Moreover, some unlawful charges, such as fees collected by local authorities when issuing travel documents and certificates, even targeted only migrant workers.

First, the extent of wage inequality suffered by rural migrant workers is not insignificant. Cook and Margaret have pointed out the institutional difference of the wage system between urban and rural workers, observing that:

> the workers in the urban public sector are protected by institutional wage determination and by the government commitment to provide them with employment. The wages of rural migrants are more market-determined and their reservation wages are weakened by lack of village opportunities, of information and of security.[34]

Evidence compiled from a variety of empirical studies supports the existence of wage inequality between rural and urban workers. For example, Meng and Zhang analysed and compared two sets of statistical data drawn, respectively, from the Shanghai Floating Population Survey, and the Shanghai Residents and Floating Population Survey – collected by the Institute of Population Studies at the Shanghai Academy of Social Sciences in 1995.[35] Their study indicated that a large part of the

---

[33] See Goodall and Warner 1997.

[34] Cook and Maurer-Fazio 1999, at p. 87.

[35] See Meng and Zhang 2001. Sampling area: Shanghai; Sample size: Shanghai floating Population survey: 6,609 observations; Shanghai Residents and Floating Population Survey: 3,000 observations; Ibid., at p. 488.

earnings gap is due to intra-occupational factors, which are unexplained from an economic perspective. Productivity differences were unlikely to be a major factor in contributing to the income gap between rural migrant and urban workers. Therefore, some other non-economic factors must have given rise to that gap.

Third, work-related benefits, in particular, were strongly influenced by this ownership-oriented approach. The work-related social insurance infrastructure remained exclusively within SOEs, as established under the planned economy, and, indeed, the Opinion from the Ministry of Labour of 1983 confirmed that the 1951 Regulations on Labour Insurance[36] was still applicable to SOEs (Article 6).[37] Meanwhile, the 1983 Opinion also pointed out that: "given the difference of economic conditions between SOEs and enterprises under other ownership forms, there shall accordingly be allowed some differentiations regarding the level of labour welfare".[38]

Therefore, work-related social insurance, such as unemployment insurance and work-related injury insurance, were generally unavailable to non-SOE workers, who were more likely rural migrant workers. Last but not least, the urban employment promotion strategy during the 1980s regarded the inflow of rural residents as the biggest barrier to curbing urban unemployment, and laid down restrictions for such movement. Thus, for instance, the term "reasonable control of rural labour migration" appeared in Article 6 of the Circular on Enforcing Adjustment of Job Vacancies of 1990 to put a hold on the unemployment issue.[39] It also articulated detailed mechanisms for control, such as providing for a temporary work permit and establishing an employment quota system.

9.4 Legislative Development Against Hukou Discrimination in the Workplace 1995–2013

The Labour Law was introduced in 1994 as a regulatory instrument which crossed ownership borders and came into force in 1995. The Labour Law omitted use of the terminology of SOEs and non-SOEs, so that, once an "employment relationship"

---

[36] [Opinion on Considering the Protection on Labour Insurance and Welfare of Workers in the Process of Economic Reform] 关于在经济改革中要注意保障企业职工的劳动保险、福利待遇的意见 (guān yú zài jīng jì gǎi gé zhōng yào zhù yì bǎo zhàng qǐ yè zhí gōng de láo dòng bǎo xiǎn, fú lì dài yù de yì jiàn), 1983. [Labour Insurance Regulations of the People's Republic of China] 中华人民共和国劳动保险条例 (zhōng huá rén mín gòng hé guó láo dòng bǎo xiǎn tiáo lì), 1951.

[37] Ibid.

[38] [Opinion on Considering the Protection on Labour Insurance and Welfare of Workers in the Process of Economic Reform] 关于在经济改革中要注意保障企业职工的劳动保险、福利待遇的意见 (guān yú zài jīng jì gǎi gé zhōng yào zhù yì bǎo zhàng qǐ yè zhí gōng de láo dòng bǎo xiǎn, fú lì dài yù de yì jiàn), 1983, Article 6.

[39] [Circular on Enforcing the Adjustment of Job Vacancies] 劳动部关于加强职工余缺调剂工作的通知 (láo dòng bù guān yú jiā qiáng zhí gōng yú quē tiáo jì gōng zuò de tōng zhī), 1990.

was formed, the employee and employer fell solely under the jurisdiction of the Labour Law. The boundary between state and non-SOE enterprises was no longer formally drawn within the labour legislative framework. It is thus worth exploring details of that symbolic legislation – the Labour Law – before undertaking further investigations in relation to Chinese labour regulations.

The Labour Law defines an "employee" and an "employer" on the basis of what is stated in Article 2:

> this law applies to enterprises and individually-owned economic organisations (hereinafter referred to as the "employer", or "employers", as the context may require from time to time) and employees who form an Employment relationship with them within the territory of the PRC. State organs, institutional organisations and social groups and employees who form a labour contract relationship with them shall conform to this law.

The Labour Law disregards the previous method of classification, and introduces, instead, a "one-off" test of the employment relationship to define its scope of application.

Once the existence of an employment relationship is confirmed, the Labour Law will be applied equally to all workers in the workplace, unless indicated otherwise. Enterprise ownership-based distribution of rights is no longer accepted as a legitimate justification, in the light of the equal treatment principle. Once an employment relationship has been identified, therefore, any legitimate rights will apply equally, without considering the ownership characteristics of the employer involved.

The labour laws issued since 1994 have generally followed a similar pattern to the Labour Law. Consequently, the form of the "employment relationship" has become a major concern for Chinese lawmakers. Since the ownership type of the enterprise has little, if any, material impact on the features of the employment relationship, post-1994 labour legislation generally applies to enterprises under all ownership types, unless specifically addressed otherwise. These new governing features of post-1994 labour laws appear across all aspects of the employment field.

The Labour Law has speeded up the process of withdrawing its intervention in SOEs. In particular, the autonomy of recruitment within SOEs has been promoted as a means of replacing the administrative allocation of labour to work posts.[40] The principle behind these laws is to allow any employer and any employee to choose each other. In this context, the authorities are thus not supposed to ban SOEs to recruit rural *Hukou* holders from the countryside.

A fresh set of legislative reforms was launched after 1994 with a view to resolving problems of inequality against rural migrant workers. In addition to the Labour Law, China's leadership launched proposals for laws to develop individual employment protection rights in four areas: (1) labour contracts; (2) employment promotion; (3) labour dispute conciliation and arbitration; (4) social insurance.

---

[40] The Ministry of Labour stressed the principle of equality and transparency at any stage of recruitment for all kinds of "employer unit". See [Circular on Illegal Charges for Recruiting Workers] 关于严禁用人单位录用职工非法收费的通知 (guān yú yán jìn yòng rén dān wèi lù yòng zhí gōng fēi fǎ shōu fèi de tōng zhī), 1995.

On 29 June 2007, the Labour Contract Law was enacted by the Standing Committee of the National People's Congress, and that measure came into force on 1 January 2008.[41] The Labour Contract Law applies generally to all employment relationships, including labour contracts between enterprises and their rural migrant workers. The Labour Contract Law seeks a balance between allowing parties to negotiate terms at their discretion, while at the same time not sacrificing protection in terms of the framework of rights laid down by the Labour Law. According to the Labour Contract Law, an employer and an employee may agree to stipulate matters in an employment contract, such as wages, terms of the contract, working hours, labour protection and training.[42] Meanwhile, Article 3 requires the following: "the conclusion of employment contracts shall comply with the principles of legality, fairness, equality, free will, negotiated consensus and good faith". In other words, employment contracts need to satisfy the minimum criteria set out by other regulations, such as minimum wage provisions and health and safety requirements.

The Labour Contract Law contains provisions that deal with non-compliance. Specific arrangements are also designed to ensure that workers, particularly rural migrant workers, may actualize their rights as provided by their labour contracts. Penalties can be imposed on the employer by the authorities in cases where, for example, wages are not paid on time, or they are below locally stipulated minimum levels, and where working conditions fail to satisfy the legal requirements.[43]

In a related development, the Standing Committee of the NPC took over the responsibility for drafting a Labour Dispute Mediation and Arbitration Law, which was approved on 29 December 2007 and brought into force on 1 May 2008.[44] Although the Labour Dispute Mediation and Arbitration Law does not modernise the whole procedure, some changes to the administrative part of the labour dispute resolution process certainly exert a positive effect on vulnerable workers, such as rural migrant workers. The Labour Dispute Mediation and Arbitration Law specifically stresses the need to promote and bring accessible justice to workers.[45] It also cuts costs for workers by providing a free service, and reduces "red tape" by introducing a non-appealable arbitration mechanism.[46] These measures have been particularly welcomed by rural migrant workers, who are often unable to afford the costs and time required to settle disputes in places where they do not reside.

[41] [Labour Contract Law of the People's Republic of China] 中华人民共和国劳动合同法 (zhōng huá rén mín gòng hé guó láo dòng hé tóng fǎ), 2007.

[42] Ibid., Article 7.

[43] Ibid., Articles 30–32.

[44] [Labour Dispute Mediation and Arbitration Law of the People's Republic of China] 中华人民共和国劳动争议调解仲裁法 (zhōng huá rén mín gòng hé guó láo dòng zhēng yì tiáo jiě zhòng cái fǎ), 2007.

[45] Ibid., Article 1.

[46] Ibid., Articles 47 and 53.

On 29 August 2007, the proposed Employment Promotion Law was approved, and came into force along with the Labour Contract Law on 1 January 2008.[47] The proposed measures contained in the Employment Promotion Law establish a context of anti-discrimination for rural migrant workers. Article 31 clearly points out that rural workers who move to urban areas to seek employment will enjoy equal labour rights with urban workers and will not be subjected to discriminatory restrictions. There are provisions on anti-discrimination measures to improve the position of migrant workers. Moreover, Article 22 stresses that "the state will implement comprehensive employment policies in both urban and rural areas aimed at guiding the orderly migration of surplus rural labour to areas of employment by establishing a sound and equitable employment system for both urban and rural workers".

On 28 October 2010, the Social Insurance Law was finally enacted by the NPC, and scheduled to come into force on 1 July 2011.[48] The Social Insurance Law combines five different types of social insurance scheme, which are designed to cover all Chinese workers and citizens, which inevitably includes rural migrant workers.[49] In particular, the Social Insurance Law also requires that necessary arrangements be made for the transferability of social insurance accounts. For instance, Article 19 stipulates how to calculate pension fund accumulation and the method of transfer between different pooling regions, which is particularly important for rural migrant workers.

In response to the pressing issue of rural migrant workers, the government has introduced a number of positive measures to promote protection of groups disadvantaged by their *Hukou* status. Promotion of the rights of rural migrant workers has been given top priority amongst recent reforms. Thus, over 20 pieces of law and regulation have been issued to facilitate the movement of migrants, addressing their vulnerability and improving their employability.

Many of these regulations are dedicated to curbing particular aspects of the problems triggered by *Hukou* status. The earlier excessive limitations and unreasonable fees imposed on migrants seeking either temporary or permanent employment in urban-based enterprises have been abolished. In 2003, the state decided to draw upon the public budget in order to cover the costs incurred by the management of migration, which had previously been directly chargeable to rural migrant workers. In 2005, the Ministry of Labour and Social Security (MoLSS) also dismantled the arrangements provided for in the Interim Provisions of Managing Trans-Provincial Employment of Rural Workers of 1994 which had restricted cross-province job-seeking.[50] In addition, on 27 August 2003, the Administrative Licence Law was

[47] [Employment Promotion Law of the People's Republic of China] 中华人民共和国就业促进法 (zhōng huá rén mín gòng hé guó jiù yè cù jìn fǎ), 2007.

[48] [Social Insurance Law of the People's Republic of China] 中华人民共和国社会保险法 (zhōng huá rén mín gòng hé guó shè huì bǎo xiǎn fǎ), 2010.

[49] See Article 2 of the [Social Insurance Law of the People's Republic of China] 中华人民共和国社会保险法 (zhōng huá rén mín gòng hé guó shè huì bǎo xiǎn fǎ), 2010. The five types of social insurance scheme addressed by the Social Insurance Law are basic pension, basic medical insurance, work-related injury insurance, unemployment insurance and maternity insurance.

[50] [Interim Provisions for Managing Trans-Provincial Employment of Rural Workers] 农村劳动力跨省流动就业管理暂行规定 (nóng cūn láo dòng lì kuà shěng liú dòng jiù yè guǎn lǐ zàn xíng guī dìng), 1994.

enacted, and came into force on 1 July 2004.[51] This Law prohibits local government from issuing "profession reservation provisions", which had previously barred non-local job seekers from accessing a range of jobs.[52]

The All-China Federation of Trade Unions (ACFTU) announced on 9 August 2003 that it would unionise as many rural migrant workers as possible. Consequently, in the first month of 2003, over 34 million workers joined local trade unions in cities and townships throughout the country. In 2006, the ACFTU set a target of unionising a further six million rural migrant workers.[53] Meanwhile, as Chan has observed, pressure has been building for lower-level union officers to be more responsive to the needs of rural migrant workers.[54]

In recent years, several special regulations have come into force to provide public-funded skills training to rural migrant workers. The major goal of these regulations has been to fill the occupational training gap left by previous policies for rural migrant workers. For instance, a special new project – the so-called "Spring-Breeze Movement" – was set up by way of a normative document to finance occupational training dedicated to rural migrant workers who are seeking their first employment.[55] In 2009, in order to combat the impact of pervading global economic turmoil, the Ministry of Human Resource and Social Security (MoHRSS) called upon local labour authorities to support occupational training, particularly for rural migrants, which is provided through the trade unions.[56]

9.5 Evaluation: Progress and Challenges

In terms of evaluating progress and challenges involving the legislative movements mentioned above, the Discrimination (Employment and Occupation) Convention No. 111 provides a sound reference point, calling for equal rights and workplace welfare for all workers. In fact, ILO rights offer two aspects to measure discrimination based on social origin. These can be borrowed to evaluate the developments of

[51] [Administrative License Law of the People's Republic of China] 中华人民共和国行政许可法 (zhōng huá rén mín gòng hé guó xíng zhèng xǔ kě fǎ), 2003.

[52] The purpose of "profession reservation provisions" issued by local authorities does not fit into any category of eligible situation for administrative permission listed in Article 12 of the [Administrative License Law of the People's Republic of China] 中华人民共和国行政许可法 (zhōng huá rén mín gòng hé guó xíng zhèng xǔ kě fǎ), 2003. Moreover, Article 13 stipulates that administrative permission shall not be set when matters can be solved through the market. In the case of labour mobility, the rule of the labour market is to override restrictions.

[53] For further details, see Chinese Central Government website, 2006.

[54] See Chan 2004.

[55] [Circular on Conducting the Spring-Breeze Movement to Perfect Employment Service for Rural Migrant Workers] 关于开展春风行动完善农民工就业服务的通知 (guān yú kāi zhǎn chūn fēng xíng dòng wán shàn nóng mín gōng jiù yè fú wù de tōng zhī), 2004.

[56] [Circular on Further Regulating Employment Skills Training for Rural Migrant Workers] 进一步规范农民工培训工作的通知 (jìn yī bù guī fàn nóng mín gōng péi xùn gōng zuò de tōng zhī), 2009.

labour law in combating *Hukou* discrimination. First, whether social origin, *Hukou* status in this context, is used to deny certain groups of people, rural migrant workers, access to various categories of job or limit them to certain types of activity. Second, whether discrimination based on social origin, *Hukou* status in this context, denies its victims, namely rural migrant workers, the possibility to move from one class or social category to another.[57]

The effects of the most recently-launched economic reforms are highly controversial in the world of work. On the one hand, the market economy allegedly promotes freer movement of labour and goods in China. In particular, market-oriented reforms contribute to easing severe restrictions on rural-to-urban migration. Economic reform has released millions of rural labourers from agricultural production; they are then absorbed by emerging urban industries. Market-oriented reforms discharge labour bureaux from "the responsibility of micro-managing labour allocation", which opens up access to industrial employment opportunities for the rural labour supply.[58] Moreover, apart from employment promotion, occupational health and safety inspection, dispute settlement, and work-related welfare – which are still under vertical administrative management – employers and employees are allowed to work out the rest of their terms and conditions themselves, subject to these being no lower than the statutory floor. This, arguably, also evens out institutional inequality as between rural and urban workers, since both of them are left to bargain with their employers on a contractual basis. The social origin registered under the *Hukou* system no longer formally "appears" as a legitimate excuse to discriminate against certain types of worker.

On the other hand, in the era of the market economy, implementation of Convention No. 111 still faces challenges when applied in practice. One phenomenon faced by the state is widely applied decentralisation in the field of labour and work-related welfare administrative management. Taking the Social Insurance Law as an example, this still defines local authorities as the key stakeholders for running such a scheme. Indeed, the medical insurance scheme even relies on city level authorities to run the medical insurance fund pool.

Decentralisation, however, in conjunction with self-contained local interests, creates a set of practical problems for rural migrant workers in accessing their rights. First, there have been many long-standing instances of local authorities acting in a less generous manner to "outsiders" than to local residents when distributing work-related welfare. Second, central regulations are often inadequately implemented – for a number of reasons, such as the incompetence and narrowly-defined interests of local authorities – while responsibility for implementation is delegated to provincial and lower levels of public authority.

[57] ILO website, Q&As on business, discrimination and equality, 2012.

[58] [Luo] 罗干 1995.

9.5.1 Institutional Exclusion Based on Local or Non-local Status

Local (mainly urban) officials and dwellers have shared the same worries regarding the social risks associated with massive farmer migration. Due to the rural-urban income gap, the relaxation of restrictions on movement turned into a "one-way labour traffic" to the cities. Central and metropolitan officials doubt the capacity of large and medium-sized cities to absorb the migrant workforce smoothly. Hence, most metropolitan officials appear hostile to the idea of massive "free", in many official documents referred to as "blind", migration.

As a result, when local authorities take over the distribution of work-related welfare, migrants are likely to be excluded, or made subject to additional conditions to access these benefits. Work-related welfare schemes – pension, work-related injury, and unemployment insurance – have only recently been made formally available to local residents, and some of these remain, practically speaking, inaccessible to non-local migrants. The unemployment insurance scheme, as provided for by the 1999 Regulations on Unemployment Insurance,[59] has placed all urban enterprises and institutional organisations and their employees within its jurisdiction. However, in practice, very few workers without local residency are actually able to be registered as unemployed, in order to enjoy those benefits, on account of the procedural issues referred to earlier.

While the responsibility for formulating a mechanism to deliver work-related welfare has been handed over to local authorities, the state has begun to be faced with an increasing number of cases where work-related welfare schemes fail to "toe the state's line". In turn, the decentralised work-related welfare system also raises the problem of inadequate portability of welfare for migrant workers who need to transport and access their benefits in different places. When workers move from one place to another, the danger is that they may lose their entitlement to access work-related welfare, as the authorities in the new location cannot transfer their previous contribution accordingly by reason of lack of systemic consistency and bridging instruments between regions.

However, these initiatives for institutional reform have proved to be both difficult and highly controversial. One of the most common concerns is that the Social Insurance Law does not specify the role of central and local agencies, as the current framework failed to do.[60] It is vital for state and local agencies to act together in running the nationwide work-related welfare system.

[59] [Regulations on Unemployment Insurance] 失业保险条例 (shī yè bǎo xiǎn tiáo lì), 1999.

[60] According to the [Social Insurance Law of the People's Republic of China] 中华人民共和国社会保险法 (zhōng huá rén mín gòng hé guó shè huì bǎo xiǎn fǎ), 2010, the central agency responsible for social insurance is the Ministry of Human Resource and Social Security, and local agencies are the local labour bureaus.

9.5.2 Weak Implementation for Non-locals

State regulations have proved slow and inadequate in being implemented by local enforcement agencies, such as labour arbitration committees and labour bureaux. The allocation of central and local responsibilities for labour regulations has not necessarily reflected the pattern of challenges involved in the modernisation of the labour market. Where the interests of local and central authorities are not fully consistent, a number of practical problems arise in the process of implementing regulations.

First, misinterpretation of labour laws by local authorities often occurs. There has been a battle to persuade the relevant institutions to apply the Labour Law to rural migrant workers, even though the Labour Law sets out no conditions for workers to enjoy labour rights. The Ministry of Labour (MoL) has shown no intention of excluding rural migrant workers, even though its position has often been interpreted otherwise.[61] In 1996, both the Ningxia and Fujian Provincial Labour Bureaux raised queries about "rota-based agricultural workers" with a view to obtaining further clarification of their worker status.[62] In 2003, a number of local judicial departments raised a query to the Supreme Court regarding similar issues.[63] Rather strangely, that query was again forwarded to the MoLSS.[64] In its responses, the Ministry has repeatedly had to remind those institutions to re-visit the Labour Law for answers.[65]

[61] See [Explanation on Various Provisions of Labour Law of the People's Republic of China] 关于《劳动法》若干条文的说明 (guān yú láo dòng fǎ ruò gān tiáo wén de shuō míng), 1994.

[62] Rota-based agricultural workers were recruited into the mining and construction industries during the 1980s. The idea was to boost the labour force for those industrial sectors which involve heavy physical activity. Due to the nature of this work, the workforce has to be physically strong, and renewed regularly for health protection purposes. Over the 1980s, the urban workforce was still fixed by the planned economy for life, which did not match the demand from these sectors. The State Council issued three directives to allow the mining, construction and transportation industry to recruit fixed-term farmers to fill their vacancies from 1984. The workers recruited under this scheme were called rota-based workers, which had to be replaced on a regular basis to "protect their health". The maximum term is 8 years.

[63] Actually the inquiry raised from local People's Courts to the No. 1 Civil Tribunal of the Supreme Court was whether the [Trial Measure on Work-related Injury Insurance] 工伤保险暂行办法 (gōng shāng bǎo xiǎn zàn xíng bàn fǎ) applies to rota-based agricultural workers. The core issue, therefore, is whether rota-based agricultural workers are qualified as "workers", insofar as they are defined by the Labour Law, regardless of their *Hukou* registration status.

[64] The direction of inquiry seems to be the wrong way around. According to the [Law on Legislation of the People's Republic of China] 中华人民共和国立法法 (zhōng huá rén mín gòng hé guó lì fǎ fǎ), 2000, the Supreme Court holds the power of judicial interpretation. It is perfectly enabled to resolve confusion under its own jurisdiction. The rota-based agricultural worker scheme was created by a State Council directive. Hence, the State Council or NPC Standing Committee which enacted the Labour Law should be the ideal candidate to seek authoritative advice or clarification. The MoLSS can provide a ministerial opinion but carries much less weight than the Supreme Court, the State Council and the NPC.

[65] The MoLSS articulated that, when an employment relationship is formed with agricultural workers (including rota-based agricultural workers), the Labour Law applies. The employment relation-

Second, very often the law itself is not to blame, but, rather, the law is not being implemented sufficiently firmly. A number of reasons explain why local law enforcement agencies might wish to adopt "soft" implementation of state regulations – whether to protect local economic and public interests, or even by reason of corruption on the part of local officials.[66] Given such possibilities, therefore, issues associated with migrant workers may often find themselves marginalised, where resolving the problems associated with them may compete with other aspects of local interest.

9.5.3 Limited Chance to Change Hukou *Status*

It remains difficult for rural migrant workers to change their *Hukou* status. Both residency and occupation registration are subject to control by local governments. The central government, on the one hand, has released a number of policies to untie control of rural-to-urban upgrade, namely *nongzhuanfei*.[67] On 24 July 2014, the State Council issued its Opinion on Further Reform of the Hukou System (2014 Opinion), which spells out a plan to abolish agricultural/non-agricultural registration nationwide.[68]

Central government, on the other hand, remains conservative in loosening control of changing registered residency. According to the 2014 Opinion, only towns and small cities welcome non-local *Hukou* holders to settle permanently.[69] Indeed, many other local governments are more cautious regarding the inflow of permanent residents, especially those in big cities. For instance, Beijing municipal government has released a decision to "strictly control the population in Beijing". Since there is a very slim chance for migrants to gain the same *Hukou* status as local residents in big cities, the possibility to change *Hukou*-related social origin is thus limited. *Hukou*-related social origin remains inerasable for rural migrant workers.

9.6 Conclusions

Creating equal protection for migrant workers, as required by the Discrimination (Employment and Occupation) Convention No. 111 and Chinese labour laws, is becoming, and will continue to be, increasingly difficult. In particular, compliance

ship-based approach is confirmed by the Labour Law, and wards off speculation arising from the worker's social status.

[66] See Zhao and Li 2006.

[67] According to one report, 13 provinces and municipalities have already cancelled the category of agricultural (rural)/ non-agricultural (urban) Hukou status since 2008. Cited from Sina news 2008.

[68] [68] [Opinion on Further Reform of the Hukou System] 国务院关于进一步推进户籍制度改革的意见 (guó wù yuàn guān yú jìn yī bù tuī jìn hù jí zhì dù gǎi gé de yì jiàn), 2014. Sohu news 2014.

[69] Ibid., Chapter 2, Article 4.

with Convention No. 111 involves not simply abolition of the rural-urban *Hukou* division or the *Hukou* system completely. “Rural” *Hukou* status, as the “social origin” of rural migrant workers, used to be a ground for discrimination against them in the workplace. Since 1995, when the Labour Law came into force, and especially after the new millennium, “rural origin” has been replaced by “non-local origin”, also defined as non-local *Hukou* status, as the key factor for rural migrant workers to be treated unfavourably.

Indeed, combating residency-related inequality remains within the scope of application of Convention No. 111. Eliminating residency-related inequality is not an uncomplicated or trouble-free project, especially when the need exists for detailed and thoughtful work in terms of opening up access to individual social security schemes for “outsiders”, where the challenge of constructing a coherent national framework remains problematic, and where there is a need for painstaking management of the relationship between central and local authorities. It is even more of a challenge when, as is currently required, the whole project has to be undertaken in light of the conditions of today’s market economy, where a delicate balance between social and economic interests needs to be maintained during the process of reform. At the end of the day, in order to put China’s endorsement of Convention No. 111 into practice, solutions are needed for the world of work in China. However, these solutions have to be based upon a careful understanding of the scale and nature of the inequality that currently operates against rural migrant workers.

References

Literature

Chan, Anita. 1995. The emerging patterns of industrial relations in China and the rise of two new labour movements. *China Information* 9(4): 36–59.

Chan, Anita. 2004. A new China? Some hope for optimism for Chinese labor. *New Labor Forum* 13(3): 16–75.

Chan, Kam Wing, and Li Zhang. 1999. The Hukou system and rural-urban migration in China: Processes and changes. *The China Quarterly* 160: 818–855.

Cook, Sarah, and Margaret Maurer-Fazio. 1999. Introduction. In *The workers’ state meets the market*, ed. Sarah Cook and Margaret Maurer-Fazio, 1–15. London: Frank Cass.

[Gao, Tao] 高涛. 2013. [Agriculture to non-agriculture] 农转非 (nóng zhuǎn fēi). [*Archives World*] 档案天地 10: 20–22.

Goodall, Keith, and Malcolm Warner. 1997. Human resources in Sino-Foreign joint ventures: Selected case studies in Shanghai, compared with Beijing. *International Journal of Human Resource Management* 8(5): 569–594.

Lin, Justin Yifu, Li Zhou, and Cai Fang. 1996. *The China miracle: Development strategy and economic reform*. Hong Kong: Chinese University Press.

[Luo, Pinghan] 罗平汉. 2000. [Analysis of supply mechanism in people’s commune] 人民公社供给制探析 (rén mín gōng shè gōng jǐ zhì tàn xī). [*Contemporary China History Study*] 当代中国史研究 (dāng dài zhōng guó shǐ yán jiū) 7(3): 38–46.

Meng, Xin, and Junsen Zhang. 2001. The two-tier labor market in urban China: Occupational segregation and wage differentials between urban residents and rural migrants in Shanghai. *Journal of Comparative Economics* 29(3): 485–540.
Potter, Pitman B. 2001. *The Chinese legal system: Globalization and local legal culture*. London/New York: Routledge.
Solinger, Dorothy. 1999. *Contesting citizenship in urban China*. Berkeley: University of California Press.
Tan Shen. 2005. *Rural workforce migration: A summary of some studies*. Available at: http://e-sociology.cass.cn/pub/english/PAPERS/P020050202558916718281.pdf. Last accessed 19 June 2015.
Wang, Fei-Ling. 2005. *Organizing through division and exclusion: China's Hukou system*. Stanford: Stanford University Press.
White, Gordon. 1993. *Riding the tiger: The politics of economic reform in post-Mao China*. Stanford: Stanford University Press.
Windrow, Hayden, and Anik Guha. 2005. The hukou system, migrant workers, & state power in the People's Republic of China. *Northwestern Journal of International Human Rights* 3(1): 1–18.
Zhao, Litao, and Jianying Li. 2006. *China transforming its hukou system: Path dependence and local interests*. EAI working paper No. 128. Singapore: East Asian Institute.

Documents and Official Publications

ILO Documents

Convention concerning Discrimination in Respect of Employment and Occupation, adopted 25 June 1958, ILO C111. Entry into force 15 June 1960. (Discrimination (Employment and Occupation) Convention).
Convention concerning Minimum Age for Admission to Employment, adopted 26 June 1973, ILO C138. Entry into force 19 June 1976. (Minimum Age Convention).
Convention concerning the Prohibition and Immediate Action for the Elimination of the Worst Forms of Child Labour, adopted 17 June 1999, ILO C182. Entry into force 19 November 2000. (Worst Forms of Child Labour Convention).
Equal Remuneration Convention, adopted 29 June 1951, ILO C100. Entry into force 23 May 1953.

Other ILO Documentation

ILO website on Q&As on Business, Discrimination and Equality. *International Labour Organization*, Available at: http://www.ilo.org/empent/areas/business-helpdesk/WCMS_DOC_ENT_HLP_BDE_FAQ_EN/lang--en/index.htm#Q2. Last accessed 19 June 2015.

Chinese Regulation

Laws by the National People's Congress

[Law on Legislation of the People's Republic of China] 中华人民共和国立法法 (zhōng huá rén mín gòng hé guó lì fǎ fǎ), National People's Congress, adopted 15 March 2000, effective 1 July 2000.

Laws by the Standing Committee of the National People's Congress

[Administrative License Law of the People's Republic of China] 中华人民共和国行政许可法 (zhōng huá rén mín gòng hé guó xíng zhèng xǔ kě fǎ), Standing Committee of the National People's Congress, adopted 27 August 2003, effective 1 July 2004.

[Employment Promotion Law of the People's Republic of China] 中华人民共和国就业促进法 (zhōng huá rén mín gòng hé guó jiù yè cù jìn fǎ), Standing Committee of the National People's Congress, adopted 30 August 2007, effective 1 January 2008. Revised and effective 24 April 2015.

[Labour Contract Law of the People's Republic of China] 中华人民共和国劳动合同法 (zhōng huá rén mín gòng hé guó láo dòng hé tóng fǎ), Standing Committee of the National People's Congress, adopted 29 June 2007, effective 1 January 2008. Revised 28 December 2012, effective 1 July 2013.

[Labour Dispute Mediation and Arbitration Law of the People's Republic of China] 中华人民共和国劳动争议调解仲裁法 (zhōng huá rén mín gòng hé guó láo dòng zhēng yì tiáo jiě zhòng cái fǎ), Standing Committee of the National People's Congress, adopted 29 December 2007, effective 1 May 2008.

[Labour Law of the People's Republic of China] 中华人民共和国劳动法 (zhōng huá rén mín gòng hé guó láo dòng fǎ), Standing Committee of the National People's Congress, adopted 5 July 1994, effective 1 January 1995.

[Regulations on Household Registration] 中华人民共和国户口登记条例 (zhōng huá rén mín gòng hé guó hù kǒu dēng jì tiáo lì), Standing Committee of the First National People's Congress, adopted and effective 9 January 1958.

[Social Insurance Law of the People's Republic of China] 中华人民共和国社会保险法 (zhōng huá rén mín gòng hé guó shè huì bǎo xiǎn fǎ), Standing Committee of the National People's Congress, adopted 28 October 2010, effective 1 July 2011.

Regulations by the State Council

[Circular on Accelerating the Reform of the Grain Circulation System] 国务院关于加快粮食流通体制改革的通知 (guó wù yuàn guān yú jiā kuài liáng shí liú tōng tǐ zhì gǎi gé de tōng zhī), State Council, adopted and effective 15 February 1993.

[Circular on Prevention of Applying Unfair Methods to Recruit or Transfer Workers] 国务院关于严禁在招收、调配职工工作中搞不正之风的通知 (guó wù yuàn guān yú yán jìn zài zhāo shōu, diào pèi zhí gōng gōng zuò zhōng gǎo bù zhèng zhī fēng de tōng zhī), State Council, adopted and effective 19 April 1982.

[Interim Provisions on Implementing the Labour Contract System in State-Run Enterprises] 国营企业实行劳动合同制暂行规定 (guó yíng qǐ yè shí xíng láo dòng hé tóng zhì zàn xíng guī dìng), State Council, adopted 12 July 1986, effective 1 October 1986.

[Labour Insurance Regulations of the People's Republic of China] 中华人民共和国劳动保险条例 (zhōng huá rén mín gòng hé guó láo dòng bǎo xiǎn tiáo lì), State Council, adopted and effective 26 February 1951.

[Opinion on Further Reform of the Hukou System] 国务院关于进一步推进户籍制度改革的意见 (guó wù yuàn guān yú jìn yī bù tuī jìn hù jí zhì dù gǎi gé de yì jiàn), State Council, adopted 25 July 2014, effective 30 July 2014.

[Regulations on Unemployment Insurance] 失业保险条例 (shī yè bǎo xiǎn tiáo lì), State Council, adopted and effective 22 January 1999.

Administrative Regulations

[Circular on Conducting the Spring-Breeze Movement to Perfect Employment Service for Rural Migrant Workers] 关于开展春风行动完善农民工就业服务的通知 (guān yú kāi zhǎn chūn fēng xíng dòng wán shàn nóng mín gōng jiù yè fú wù de tōng zhī), Ministry of Labour and Social Security, adopted and effective 16 December 2004.

[Circular on Enforcing the Adjustment of Job Vacancies], 劳动部关于加强职工余缺调剂工作的通知 (láo dòng bù guān yú jiā qiáng zhí gōng yú quē diào jì gōng zuò de tōng zhī), Ministry of Labour, adopted and effective 15 June 1990.

[Circular on Fully Applying the Labour Contract Mechanism] 劳动部关于全面实行劳动合同制的通知 (láo dòng bù guān yú quán miàn shí xíng láo dòng hé tóng zhì de tōng zhī), Ministry of Labour, adopted and effective 24 August 1994.

[Circular on Further Regulating Employment Skills Training for Rural Migrant Workers] 进一步规范农民工培训工作的通知 (jìn yī bù guī fàn nóng mín gōng péi xùn gōng zuò de tōng zhī), Ministry of Human Resource and Social Security, adopted and effective 5 May 2009.

[Circular on Illegal Charges for Recruiting Workers] 关于严禁用人单位录用职工非法收费的通知 (guān yú yán jìn yòng rén dān wèi lù yòng zhí gōng fēi fǎ shōu fèi de tōng zhī), Ministry of Labour, adopted and effective 9 June 1995.

[Explanation on Various Provisions of Labour Law of the PRC] 关于《劳动法》若干条文的说明 (guān yú "láo dòng fǎ" ruò gān tiáo wén de shuō míng), Ministry of Labour, adopted and effective 4 September 1994.

[Interim Provisions of Managing Trans-Provincial Employment of Rural Workers] 农村劳动力跨省流动就业管理暂行规定 (nóng cūn láo dòng lì kuà shěng liú dòng jiù yè guǎn lǐ zàn xíng guī dìng), Ministry of Labour, adopted and effective 17 November 1994.

[Opinion on Considering the Protection on Labour Insurance and Welfare of Workers in the Process of Economic Reform] 关于在经济改革中要注意保障企业职工的劳动保险、福利待遇的意见 (guān yú zài jīng jì gǎi gé zhōng yào zhù yì bǎo zhàng qǐ yè zhí gōng de láo dòng bǎo xiǎn, fú lì dài yù de yì jiàn), Ministry of Labour and Personnel, adopted and effective 17 August 1983.

[Provisions on Recruitment for State-Run Enterprises] 国营企业招用工人暂行规定 (guó yíng qǐ yè zhāo yòng gōng rén zàn xíng guī dìng), Ministry of Labour and Personnel, adopted and effective 1 October 1986.

[Trial Measure on Work-related Injury Insurance] 工伤保险暂行办法 (qǐ yè zhí gōng gōng shāng bǎo xiǎn zàn xíng bàn fǎ), Ministry of Labour, adopted 12 August 1996, effective 1 October 1996. Abolished 9 November 2007.

Local Regulations

[Changchun Measure of FIEs Labour] 长春外商投资企业劳动管理办法 (cháng chūn wài shāng tóu zī qǐ yè láo dòng guǎn lǐ bàn fǎ), Changchun City People's Government, adopted and effective 18 December 1993.

[Dalian Provincial Government Provisions on Rural Hukou Management] 大连市农村户口管理规定 (dà lián shì nóng cūn hù kǒu guǎn lǐ guī dìng), Dalian City People's Government, adopted 10 March 2003, effective 1 May 2003.

[Jiangsu Provincial Government Provisions on Huji Management in the Regions at County Level] 江苏省县以下地区户籍管理规定 (Jiāngsū shěng xiàn yǐxià dìqū hùjí guǎnlǐ guīdìng), Jiangsu Province People's Government, adopted 4 September 1998, effective 8 September 1998.

[Tianjin Measure of FIEs Labour Management] 天津外商投资企业劳动管理办法 (tiān jīn wài shāng tóu zī qǐ yè láo dòng guǎn lǐ bàn fǎ), Standing Committee of Tianjin Municipalities People's Congress, adopted and effective 14 July 1994.

Other Chinese Official Documents

[Trial Measure for Trade Union to Participate in Labour Dispute Settlement] 工会参与劳动争议处理试行办法 (gōng huì cān yǔ láo dòng zhēng yì chǔ lǐ shì xíng bàn fǎ), All China Federation of Trade Unions, adopted and effective 17 August 1995.

Other Sources

[Chinese Central Government] 中国中央政府. 2006. [ACFTU: Strive for 6 million this year to join trade unions] 全国总工会:今年力争发展600万农民工加入工会 (quán guó zǒng gōng huì jīn nián lì zhēng fā zhǎn 600 wàn nóng mín gōng jiā rù gōng huì). Available at: http://www.gov.cn/jrzg/2006-01/11/content_154089.htm. Last accessed 19 June 2015.

[Luo, Gan] 罗干. 1995. [Talks at the review meeting on organising the orderly flow of peasant migrants during the spring festival period] 1995 年春运 期间组织民工有序流动工作总结会上的讲话 (1995 nián chūn yùn qī jiān zǔ zhī mín gōng yǒu xù liú dòng gōng zuò zǒng jié huì shàng de jiǎng huà). [Beijing Labour Bureau] 北京市劳动局.

[Sina News] 新浪新闻. 2008. [13 provinces and municipals have abolished rural/urban Hukou registration] 十三省市取消城乡户口差别 城乡二元户籍制度打开缺口 (shí sān shěng shì qǔ xiāo chéng xiāng hù kǒu chā bié chéng xiāng èr yuán hù jí zhì dù dǎ kāi quē kǒu). 14 December 2008. Available at: http://finance.sina.com.cn/roll/20081214/20325633402.shtml. Last accessed 19 June 2015.

[Sohu News] 搜狐新闻. 2014. [China is going to abolish rural/urban *Hukou* registration and establish a residency registration system] 我国将取消城乡二元户口制 统一登记为居民户口 (wǒ guó jiāng qǔ xiāo chéng xiāng èr yuán hù kǒu zhì tǒng yī dēng jì wéi jū mín hù kǒu). 30 July 2014. Available at: http://www.guancha.cn/broken-news/2014_07_30_251759.shtml. Last accessed 19 June 2015.

Chapter 10
Reforming the Regulatory Mechanism for the Collective Labour Relationship in China: Diagnosis and Outlook

Jingyi Ye

10.1 Introduction

The year 2014 witnessed the 20th anniversary of the promulgation of the Labour Law of the People's Republic of China (Labour Law).[1] As the first piece of labour legislation after the reform and opening up, the Labour Law sets up the framework for today's labour relationship governance system in China. However, increasing tensions in labour relationships, especially in collective labour relationships, have brought special significance to examining the existing labour governance system, as well as exploring the desirable direction of future reform.

For the current research undertaking, what is particularly relevant is the International Labour Organization's (ILO's) 1998 Declaration on Fundamental Principles and Rights at Work (1998 Declaration), of which China voted in favour at its adoption. Its relevance to China is exacerbated by accelerating economic globalization and China's renewed commitment to labour protection and social justice. By the end of 2014, out of the 25 ILO Conventions ratified by China, 4 fall into

This article is part of the work in progress under the research project "Creating a Legal Framework for Harmonious Labour Relations in China" funded by the National Planning Office of Philosophy and Social Science of China (Approval No: 11&ZD031). The author thanks Dr. Wei Qian and Dr. Yan Tian for their valuable assistance. Of course, all errors remain the author's responsibility.

[1] [Labour Law of the People's Republic of China] 中华人民共和国劳动法 (zhōng huá rén mín gòng hé guó láo dòng fǎ), 1994.

J. Ye (✉)
Labour Law and Social Security Law Insitute, Peking University Law School,
Chen Ming Building, Beijing 100871, People's Republic of China
e-mail: yezipku@pku.edu.cn

U. Liukkunen, Y. Chen (eds.), *Fundamental Labour Rights in China — Legal Implementation and Cultural Logic*, Ius Gentium: Comparative Perspectives on Law and Justice 49, DOI 10.1007/978-3-319-23156-3_10

the category of fundamental labour Conventions.[2] However, the Freedom of Association and Protection of the Right to Organise Convention No. 87 and the Right to Organise and Collective Bargaining Convention No. 98 are not yet ratified. Recognition and protection of these fundamental labour rights is essential in enabling workers to claim their fair share in China's economic boom. With a view to improving China's regulation of collective labour relationships, the ILO Conventions concerned could be good sources of inspiration for further reform aims, even if immediate ratification of these two Conventions cannot be expected.

10.2 Labour Law and the Evolving Labour Governance System in China

Labour law in the contemporary sense, which originated from the industrial revolution in the West, aims to promote peaceful labour relationships, reflecting the concerted wisdom of human beings' reaction to the challenges arising from industrialisation, urbanisation and modernisation. The same applies to the enactment of China's Labour Law in 1994,[3] which was driven by China's transition to a market economy. The drafting of the Labour Law in 1994 took useful reference from those international labour Conventions which China had ratified as well as the valuable experience of foreign countries.[4] Twenty years of labour law practice in China reveals China's commitment to developing harmonious labour relationships and to assuring labour rights. This is vital for China's economy. To some extent, the Labour Law has played a crucial role in promoting China's economic transition.

The Labour Law is a revolutionary reform of the governance system of labour relationships in China. From 1949 to the late 1970s, under the planned economy, labour resources in China were distributed unitarily through state planning,[5] and regulation of labour relationships is coloured with administrative characteristics. The labour relationship governance system duplicates much of the administrative system. Legislation during this period consisted mainly of regulations and policy papers issued by the State Council, important examples of which include the Labour

[2] The core Conventions ratified by China are: the Equal Remuneration Convention No. 100 (ratified on 2 Nov 1990); the Discrimination (Employment and Occupation) Convention No. 111 (ratified on 12 Jan 2006); the Minimum Age Convention No. 138 (ratified on 28 Apr 1999); and the Worst Forms of Child Labour Convention No. 182 (ratified on 8 Aug 2002).

[3] [Labour Law of the People's Republic of China] 中华人民共和国劳动法 (zhōng huá rén mín gòng hé guó láo dòng fǎ), 1994.

[4] By March 1994, China had ratified 17 out of a total of 174 conventions so far adopted by the International Labour Organization. See [Li] 李伯明 1994.

[5] After its foundation, the People's Republic of China implemented a fixed-personnel policy. This means that labour resources were allocated by the state and all personnel were fixed in their positions.

Insurance Regulations of the People's Republic of China in 1951,[6] Regulations on Salary Reform in 1952[7] and Tentative Provisions on Retirement of Workers and Clerks in 1958.[8]

Since 1979, China has been carrying out a reform and opening up policy in pursuit of its modernisation project. With reform of the economic structure and establishment of a market economy, labour legislation has developed remarkably. At the beginning of the reform and opening up, reform of the labour relationship governance system started with foreign-funded enterprises[9] and the private economy. Experiments were taken to regulate labour relationships through labour contracts and labour dispute arbitration.[10] In the late 1980s, the reform was extended to state-owned enterprises (SOEs).[11] Especially since promulgation of the Labour Law, China has issued a series of labour laws and regulations and thus a multi-level labour governance system has been formed with the Labour Law as its core. Labour legislation has made several remarkable breakthroughs and a basic labour legal system has been founded, reshaping the labour relationship governance system and the relationship between employers, employees and the state in China. Meanwhile, in some sense this also paves the way for future reform of the labour governance system.

---

[6] [Labour Insurance Regulations of the People's Republic of China] 中华人民共和国劳动保险条例 (zhōng huá rén mín gòng hé guó láo dòng bǎo xiǎn tiáo lì), 1951. It was also the first regulation on social insurance of the People's Republic of China, and which set up the rules on injuries during and out of work, maternity leave and pensions. It was the predecessor of China's social security system and laid the foundation for the unification of labour and social security.

[7] [Regulations on Salary Reform] 国务院关于工资改革的规定 (guó wù yuàn guān yú gōng zī gǎi gé de guī dìng), 1956.

[8] [Tentative Provisions on Retirement of Workers and Clerks] 国务院关于工人, 职员退休处理的暂行规定 (guó wù yuàn guān yú gōng rén, zhí yuán tuì xiū chǔ lǐ de zàn xíng guī dìng), 1958.

[9] Foreign-funded enterprises in China are categorised into three types: Sino-foreign equity joint ventures, Sino-foreign cooperative joint ventures and foreign-owned enterprises.

[10] China came up with the reform and opening up policy in 1978 and the former Ministry of Labour and Personnel issued the Notification on Testing the System of Labour Contracts in 1983. Through pilot projects in local areas, the system of labour contracts was carried out in accordance with a market economy. At the same time, with development of reform of the economy and the labour system, the labour dispute arbitration mechanism was restored in 1986 after 30 years of suspension.

[11] The State Council issued four important regulations in 1986, namely [Tentative Provisions on the System of Labour Contracts in State Enterprises] 国营企业实行劳动合同制暂行规定 (guó yíng qǐ yè shí xíng láo dòng hé tóng zhì zàn xíng guī dìng), 1986; [Tentative Provisions on Employment in State-Owned Enterprises] 国营企业招用工人暂行规定 (guó yíng qǐ yè zhāo yòng gōng rén zàn xíng guī dìng), 1986; [Tentative Provisions on Dismissing Undisciplined Employees in State-Owned Enterprises] 国营企业辞退违纪职工暂行规定 (guó yíng qǐ yè cí tuì wéi jì zhí gōng zàn xíng guī dìng), 1986; and [Tentative Provisions on Unemployment Insurance in State-Owned Enterprises] 国营企业职工待业保险暂行规定 (guó yíng qǐ yè zhí gōng dài yè bǎo xiǎn zàn xíng guī dìng), 1986. The role of labour contracts in formation of the labour relationship was emphasised and thus free will between enterprises and employees was respected. Unlike the practice in the planned economy, the labour relationship was no longer formed under the administrative power.

Over the past 20 years, China has preserved a central role for the market in allocating labour resources, and for the law in regulating the labour market. Thus regulation of labour relationships through administrative means is replaced by the operation of a contractual system. Hence, a preliminary system of labour relationship governance has been established in the service of the socialist market economy. This system consists of the following elements: the labour contract mechanism is the core, autonomy of labour and capital being its infrastructure, with labour standards, collective contracts and labour dispute settlement being integral parts. Moreover, this system works in coordination with other social systems such as employment promotion and social security. At the beginning of the twenty-first century, the system is being further developed through promulgation of four statutes: the Employment Promotion Law (2007),[12] the Labour Contract Law (2007),[13] the Labour Dispute Mediation and Arbitration Law (2007)[14] and the Social Insurance Law (2010)[15] issued in succession, consolidating socialist labour legislation system with Chinese characteristics.

Secondly, generally speaking, the labour law system in China has more or less met the demand arising from rapid growth of the national economy and industrial upgrading. China's achievements in full employment, in steady improvement of employees' living standards and maintenance of harmonious labour relationships have received worldwide recognition. However, the Labour Law has its limitations owing to the economic and social structure at the time of its enactment. On the one hand, at the time of enacting, since the legislators failed to reach consensus, the Labour Law as it stands is silent on most issues concerning collective labour relationships. The mechanism of collective consultation, which is historically rooted in the practice of SOEs, is legally recognized at the expense of being passive towards other issues such as collective labour dispute settlement and representativeness of trade unions. On the other hand, in SOEs and public institutions, the system of fixed personnel and fixed positions is still practiced as a result of the constraints of state-administered financial allocation. This has caused the widespread practice in those sectors of informal employment through labour dispatching and other means, and also intensified the instability of labour relationships and discriminatory treatment within work units. Problems in employment also arise in matters such as arrears of salary and social insurance, employment discrimination and lack of remedies for work-related injuries. In short, the Labour Law and subsequent laws fail to regulate the labour market framework based on a set of uniform standards. In scenarios

[12] [Employment Promotion Law of the People's Republic of China] 中华人民共和国就业促进法 (zhōng huá rén mín gòng hé guó jiù yè cù jìn fǎ), 2007.

[13] [Labour Contract Law of the People's Republic of China] 中华人民共和国劳动合同法 (zhōng huá rén mín gòng hé guó láo dòng hé tóng fǎ), 2007.

[14] [Labour Dispute Mediation and Arbitration Law of the People's Republic of China] 中华人民共和国劳动争议调解仲裁法 (zhōng huá rén mín gòng hé guó láo dòng zhēng yì tiáo jiě zhòng cái fǎ), 2007.

[15] [Social Insurance Law of the People's Republic of China] 中华人民共和国社会保险法 (zhōng huá rén mín gòng hé guó shè huì bǎo xiǎn fǎ), 2010.

where state planning and a market system coexist, contractual governance and administrative governance also run side by side. Labour problems are extremely complicated and diversified in the process of development.

However, the Labour Law has its own drawbacks, particularly in that to a certain extent it has ignored regulation of collective labour relationships.[16] The Labour Contract Law of 2008, one of the most important labour statutes, in following the line of the Labour Law, focuses on regulation of individual labour relationships. Under this logic, both laws underline contractual autonomy between labour and capital through treating collective labour relationships as contractual. In adhering to contractual autonomy between capital and labour, the Labour Law fails systematically to tackle their conflicts of interest. These limitations are deeply rooted in social conditions at the time of legislation.

Against this background, an examination of the regulation of collective labour relationships is a rather timely and significant undertaking for Chinese labour law research.

10.3 Existing Regulatory Framework of Collective Labour Relationships in China: New Challenges and Opportunities

China has been undergoing a social upheaval since its economic transition. At present, the complexity of the international and domestic economic situation also finds its repercussions in labour laws and labour relationships. At the current stage, problematic labour relationships in China can be seen from the continuous increase in the number of labour disputes, especially collective labour unrest.[17] More specifically, China's economy has also been considerably affected by the global financial crisis since 2008, the consequence of which has intensified interest conflicts between employers and employees. This presents an enormous challenge for existing governance mechanisms in achieving and maintaining harmonious labour relationships. Governance of collective labour relationships has become a focal point in contemporary China. It is imperative to develop and improve mechanisms of collective labour relationship governance, as a supplement to proper management of individual labour relationships.

Currently, the status quo of China's labour relationships is complicated, with various conflicts intertwined and the overall situation being grim, as illustrated by an increasing number of collective labour conflicts, their expanding scale and their rising intensity. When turning to the regulatory framework for collective labour

[16] Jia and Wei 2014; [Zhu] 朱家甄 1994.

[17] This can be illustrated by statistics in [Li and Tian] 李林 and 田禾 2014. The report shows that over the past 13 years, among more than a hundred group events, labour disputes account for about 3 % of mass incidents involving over 100 persons, and that labour disputes accounting for 36.5 % of mass incidents with thousands of persons are the main cause of such incidents.

disputes, the existing mechanisms of labour governance are weak. This not only affects industrial peace and social stability, but even threatens the political security of the country. The main problems with China's collective labour relationship will be analysed as follows.

10.3.1 Rapid Rise of Collective Labour Disputes

10.3.1.1 Increase in Number of Collective Labour Disputes

According to the statistics of the Institute of Sociology, Chinese Academy of Social Sciences (CASS), about 30 % of China's mass incidents are due to problems involving labour disputes and environmental pollution.[18] Taking as an example Guangdong Province, a strong manufacturing centre for labour-intensive industries, in the first half of 2013, 126 collective labour conflicts involving over 30 individuals occurred in Guangzhou. Those involving group labour disputes accounted for 30 % among all labour dispute cases heard by Foshan Intermediate People's Court. Meanwhile, collective labour disputes are no longer confined within the private sector, but have also been frequently observed in SOEs. An investigation of Shenzhen Luohu District People's Court shows that among the cases heard in 2008 involving SOEs, collective labour disputes accounted for as much as 80 %, and "it is not rare at all to witness group disputes with dozens or even hundreds of people".[19] Besides, cases of collective labour disputes also occurred in sectors involving hospital care workers,[20] teachers and other employees. In some areas, collective labour disputes even occurred at the level of industrial sectors. For instance, a chain of group strikes occurred in the rattan industry in Shunde District of Foshan City in 2011.[21] Overall, the issue of collective labour disputes has become a widespread social problem in China.

10.3.1.2 Increase in Number of Workers Involved in Collective Labour Disputes

Cases of collective labour disputes before the Court show an ever-increasing number of workers involved every year. Taking Foshan as an instance again, in 2010 an average of 19 people were involved in each case, and in 2012 the number rose to 30.[22] In 2012, the Legal Aid Centre of Anji County People's Court, Zhejiang, dealt

---

[18] [Li and Tian] 李林 and 田禾 2014, at pp. 270–288.

[19] See [Ding] 丁建华 2010.

[20] For instance, in 2011, care workers of Shanghai Xinhua Hospital collectively protested since the hospital did not pay for their social insurance. See [Bao] 包璐影 2011.

[21] See [Gui] 桂良 2012.

[22] See [Liu] 刘晓燕 2013.

with 21 cases of group disputes, of which 7 cases involved over 100 migrant workers.[23] In addition, one must be aware of the fact that many labour disputes with thousands of labourers involved stay outside judicial procedure.

10.3.1.3 Radicalisation of Collective Labour Conflicts

Collective labour disputes may escalate into features of mass disturbances such as road blockages,[24] demonstrations, strikes, and sabotage in the workplace and so on, as well as incidents of group violence. For example, during the notorious "Jilin Tonghua Iron and Steel Incident", because of mass layoffs caused by the merger and acquisition of SOEs, the general manager was beaten to death by protesters while the police failed to intervene to rescue him.[25]

Generally speaking, core issues of collective labour disputes are related to wages, economic compensation (for extra work or termination of labour contracts) and payment of social insurance premiums.

10.3.2 Flawed Regulatory Framework for Collective Labour Relationships

According to the procedure for labour dispute settlement set up by the Labour Law and rules of democratic management in enterprises provided by other statutes such as the Trade Union Law,[26] there currently exist both direct and indirect mechanisms for collective labour dispute settlement. The direct mechanism refers to intervention by the state in disputes between employers and employees through mediation, arbitration, litigation, inspection and other means. The indirect mechanism includes methods of encouraging workers to establish trade unions, to participate in collective consultation and to exercise their right to democratic management in enterprises, so as to cultivate self-regulation of industrial relationships. The two mechanisms represent two different sets of dispute management, namely the *ex post facto* remedy and proactive prevention. Nevertheless, each of the two mechanisms proves impotent in facing major challenges of contemporary collective labour disputes, as a result of flawed legislation.

---

[23] See [Xia, Yang and Wang] 夏正芳, 杨晓蓉 and 王芬 2013.

[24] In 2009, about 1,000 staff from Baoding Cotton Mill "made a walking tour to Beijing" along the State Road, and about 1,000 workers from Wuhan Boiler Factory protested by blocking roads three times. See [Yang] 杨琳 2009.

[25] See [Zhou] 周正华 2009.

[26] [Trade Union Law of the People's Republic of China] 中华人民共和国工会法 (zhōng huá rén mín gòng hé guó gōng huì ǎ), 1992.

10.3.2.1 Problems of Direct Regulatory Mechanisms

Existing procedures for labour dispute settlement, first established in the Labour Law of 1994 and concretised by the Labour Contract Law and the Labour Dispute Mediation and Arbitration Law in 2007, have proved incapable of resolving collective labour disputes. Judicial policy dealing with collective labour disputes is concerned with local economic and industrial policies or community interests at the local level. Therefore, dispute settlement institutions, such as labour dispute arbitration committees and courts, often take an evasive attitude by breaking a collective dispute down into parallel individual ones.[27] In addition, the procedure for individual dispute settlement is time-consuming. It is difficult for workers in a collective labour dispute to obtain timely legal remedies, thus forcing them to seek self-remedy through illegal means. Some courts have found that labourers may "test the water" through filing an individual case first and the many others may decide their next move, hinging on the judgment.[28] The treatment of an individual dispute could even become the prologue to a collective dispute of potential escalation.

Secondly, claims from collective labour disputes have multiplied. While wages, the amount of economic compensation, and payment of social insurance premiums are still the main subjects of labour disputes, interest claims also occur in litigation from collective labour disputes. Meanwhile, workers have also begun to appeal for improvement of their remuneration and reallocation of labour interests, apart from complaining about employers' illegal acts such as wages in arrears and refusal to sign labour contracts.[29] Yet under current mechanisms, judicial and administrative bodies are confined to examining the legality of an enterprise's activities and have little discretion to cope with disputes over interests,[30] which is *per se* a matter of legitimacy. In cases where the activities of employers are found to be legal, it is difficult for existing laws to justify the intervention of judicial and administrative organs, leaving disputes over interests largely outside the realm of the law.

Thirdly, the limitations of the above-mentioned legal mechanisms in practice leads to a situation where local governments often choose to respond with emergency

---

[27] There is room for collective labour dispute litigation in the existing litigation system, where the understanding of "collective labour dispute", however, is different from that in the law on collective labour relationships. According to the latter, any labour dispute involving more than 10 individuals can be called a "collective labour dispute". Therefore, courts tend to apply relevant judicial rules on the basis of individual labour disputes. For example, in Guangdong, a case on arrears of wages involved over 200 workers, and the amount of overdue wages claim by individual workers was relatively small. Nonetheless, the court insisted on filing separately, which forced the parties and agents to prepare more than 200 copies of entrustment agreements, complaints, agent representations and so on. See [*Guangzhou Daily*] 广州日报 2014.

[28] [Liu] 刘晓燕 2013.

[29] [Qian] 钱培坚 2013.

[30] Labour disputes can be divided into disputes on rights and disputes over interests. Disputes on rights refer to disagreements as to proper implementation of employment contracts or collective agreements. However, disputes over interests often result from workers' claim for changes to labour conditions, typically such as demanding a raise in wages or holiday pay. It is observed that the number of disputes over interests in China has grown rapidly most recently.

administrative means to certain individual cases of collective labour disputes, which carries the risk of causing social unrest. In practice, executive branches of government and local judicial departments may work together and intervene through administrative channels, so as to force a compromise between employers and employees.[31] Some local governments come up with innovative practice where workers' rights to a remedy in case of being wronged are guaranteed by putting additional financial burdens on enterprises.[32] Both methods of administrative emergency intervention and this innovative practice are suspiciously *ultra vires* and contravene the principle of the rule of law. Moreover, new disputes may easily be fermented since an agreement reached under pressure from the government authorities might not accord with the genuine will of the parties. The settlements agreed in these individual cases are usually not generalizable on a larger scale.[33] Overall, these irregular administrative interventions are without legal basis, which has not only considerably undermined the authority of the law, but also often deviates from the parties' expectations as to social justice.

10.3.2.2 Problems of Indirect Regulatory Mechanism

In addition to a mechanism for direct intervention in collective labour relationships, the Trade Union Law and other subsequent relevant statutes conceives an indirect regulatory mechanism. However, the underdevelopment of an indirect regulatory mechanism makes it difficult to perform the role of prevention of and mediation in labour disputes.

In China, indirect regulation in collective labour relationships is mainly characterised by organisational guarantees from trade unions, promotion of collective bargaining, and democratic management of enterprises. Practice depicts a more sophisticated story. On the one hand, the mechanism for indirect regulation, where

[31] For instance, in January 2013, 1,300 workers at an electrical products factory in Bao'an District of Shenzhen City went on strike and required the employer to provide compensation for a buyout. Local street officials, as well as dozens of staff from labour boards, the emergency command, police stations, and community services and so on, entered the factory to placate the parties until the employer compromised and the workers returned to work. See [Huang and Zhan] 黄浩苑 and 詹奕嘉 2013.

[32] Jimei District of Xiamen City has established a "special fund for workers' pay talks", which means the government may advance wages that were illegally withheld by employers from workers, so as to meet the latter's urgent needs and to reduce the probability of the occurrence of collective labour conflicts. See [Yong] 永平 2012.

[33] For example, in October 2011, employees of another factory in Bao'an District of Shenzhen City went on strike since they disagreed with the employer's calculation of wages. They returned to work after the government put pressure on both parties, which made the government believe that the issue had been resolved. However, since the focus of the dispute was not settled, the workers slowed down their work efficiency by an observable drop to no less than 30 % of that in the normal state, indicating the continuance of conflict at any time. The factory finally solved the problem when the workers obtained assistance from lawyers and reached an agreement after negotiation with the employer. See [Wang] 王道军 2011.

the All-China Federation of Trade Unions (ACFTU) plays a key role, is premised on the win-win theory between labour and capital. As such, it fails to take up the issue of labour conflicts squarely and seriously. On the other hand, it took lengthy efforts to enforce and spread this indirect mechanism in China. For example, the current Trade Union Law was passed as early as 1992, and yet the establishment of trade unions in the private economic sector lags far behind. The situation had not improved by 2010, when the ACFTU oriented its focus on establishing trade unions in the private economic sector by issuing The Decision on Further Strengthening the Work of Trade Unions in Enterprises to Comprehensively Discharge Their Function.[34] The former Ministry of Labour and Social Security promulgated the Interim Measures for Collective Consultation on Wages in 2000,[35] but its full coverage had to wait until 2011. That year, the ACFTU formulated the Working Plan to Further Promote Collective Consultation on Wages from 2011 to 2013,[36] which pronounced that by the end of 2013 over 80 % of enterprises that had organised trade unions should build a system of collective consultation on wages. Up to October 2013, it was reported that nationwide 276 million workers had participated in collective consultation on wages.[37] Yet, according to another survey published on *Labour Daily* website in 2013, 27 % of respondents had no idea of collective consultation on wages, and 45 % confirmed that no such consultation was conducted in their companies.[38] As for democratic management of enterprises, it was only promulgation of Regulations on Democratic Management of Enterprises in 2012 that introduced the workers' congress to non-public enterprises and confirmed the rights of dispatched workers and migrant workers to participate.[39] As can be seen, the mechanism for indirect regulation in collective labour relationships is still a fresh concept in China, as the system is still immature and short of established practice. When enforced, the mechanism meets considerable resistance in reality.

With regard to trade unions, upon occurrence of a collective labour conflict, often these are unwilling, afraid or unable to represent the workers in negotiating with employers to settle a dispute. Trade unions are unwilling to do so since they traditionally regard themselves as welfare organisations for workers and lack both the awareness and the sense of identity as employees' representatives to participate in labour disputes. They are afraid to do so since their finances are highly dependent

[34] [The Decision on Further Strengthening the Work of Trade Unions in Enterprises to Comprehensively Discharge Their Function] 关于进一步加强企业工会工作充分发挥企业工会作用的决定 (guān yú jìn yī bù jiā qiáng qǐ yè gōng huì gōng zuò chōng fēn fā huī qǐ yè gōng huì zuò yòng de jué dìng), 2010.

[35] [Interim Measures for Collective Consultation on Wages] 工资集体协商试行办法 (gōng zī jí tǐ xié shāng shì xíng bàn fǎ), Ministry of Labour and Social Security, 2000.

[36] [Working Plan to Further Promote Collective Consultation on Wages from 2011 to 2013] 2011–2013 年深入推进工资集体协商工作规划 (2011–2013 nián shēn rù tuī jìn gōng zī jí xié shāng gōng zuò guī huà), 2011.

[37] See [Fan and Qi] 樊曦 and 齐中熙 2013.

[38] See [Tian and Ma] 田静 and 马思华 2013.

[39] [Regulations on Democratic Management of Enterprises] 企业民主管理规定 (qǐ yè mín zhǔ guǎn lǐ guī dìng), 2012.

on the employers' contribution and the law is still insufficient to protect union cadres from retaliation by employers. As a result, the trade unions for their own sake often avoid confrontation with employers. They are unable to do so since they are short of the necessary professional skills in negotiation, lack relevant legal knowledge to exercise collective labour rights of employees, and in particular, are inexperienced in bargaining with employers.[40] Consequently, workers in collective labour disputes tend to seek backup from other social organisations such as townspeople's associations, thus carrying dispute settlement off the legal track.

Concerning workers' congresses, the main problems lie not only in low coverage in the private economic sector and the lack of representativeness of dispatched and migrant workers, but also in various flaws in operation. Flaws are especially prominent when enterprises are in the process of shutting-down, closing-up, merger and acquisition, business restructuring, or business relocation. For example, according to statistics from Shenzhen Federation of Trade Unions, in 2011 the numbers of serious group petitions, collective labour disputes and mass incidents were respectively 212, 415 and 692, most of which were related to the above business transformation issues.[41] Boiled down, the following reasons could be accountable. First of all is failure to implement the rules on election of employee representatives provided by the Regulations on Democratic Management of Enterprises.[42] The number of cadre representatives often disproportionately outnumbers that of ordinary employees among the representatives. As a result, the expected function of congresses to check and balance has fallen into pure formalism. Secondly, the publicity of business affairs stipulated by the Regulations is not properly implemented. Enterprises fail to disclose to their employees crucial information such as business conditions and the progress of transformation, which can cause speculation, panic and misunderstanding among workers, and may foreshadow an outbreak of collective labour unrest. Furthermore, the legal rights of workers' congresses recognised in the Regulations are not fully respected. In some cases the employer's programme of employee relocation was not sent to the congress for examination and approval, which provoked collective conflicts.

In particular, China's economy has been seriously tested by the global financial crisis. China is under heavy pressure to ensure employment, while intensified collective conflicts of labour interests render maintenance of harmonious labour relationships a fairly challenging task. Typical problems occur such as increase in the number of labour disputes, the expanding range of disputed matters and insufficiency of labour rights protection. In view of this status quo, China needs innovation of theories, mechanisms and practice to improve the system of labour governance, in particular that regulatory mechanisms for collective labour relationships should be carefully redesigned.

---

[40] See [Zhang] 张辉 2010.

[41] See investigation report by [Huang and Zhan] 黄浩苑 and 詹奕嘉 2013.

[42] [Regulations on Democratic Management of Enterprises] 企业民主管理规定 (qǐ yè mín zhǔ guǎn lǐ guī dìng), 2012.

10.4 Future Legislation of Labour Governance: An Outlook

Labour legislation in China is now proceeding rapidly to satisfy the requirement of social and economic development. In the past 10 years, the path of China's modernisation has reached a crossroads: one that is heavily export-oriented, operating on low labour costs and low-standard human rights; or alternatively, one that is driven by domestic economic consumption, emphasising protection of labour rights, promotion of industrial upgrading and establishment of a harmonious society. China has demonstrated its resolve to opt for the latter path. Since 2005, China has made much progress in labour and social security legislation. Nevertheless, debates, sometimes heated, as to the choice of path have from time to time reopened in the process of legislation and legal enforcement. The path of Chinese labour and social security law development forms part and parcel of China's exploration for a modernization path suitable for its own national conditions.

The Chinese Communist Party (CCP) has also realised the importance of developing a constructive collective labour relationship. In the fourth plenary session of the eleventh central committee of the Communist Party of China, the CCP adopted the Decision of the CCP Central Committee on the Comprehensive Promotion of Several Major Issues of the Rule of Law,[43] in which "ensuring and improving the people's wellbeing, promoting the social governance system and innovating the legal system construction" is acknowledged to be a priority agenda for the CCP. Meanwhile, the Decision of the CCP Central Committee on Some Major Issues Concerning Comprehensively Deepening the Reform,[44] approved at the previous plenary session, made a thorough layout with regard to regulation of collective labour relationships. The Decision requires "improving the democratic management system in enterprises and public institutions with congresses of workers and employees as its basic form", "ensuring employees' democratic rights in participating in management and supervision",[45] "improving the system of collective consultation on wages in enterprises",[46] and "innovating the labour governance mechanism, opening up channels for workers to effectively make reasonable appeals".[47] As deepening the reform and promoting the rule of law are mutually enforcing, the two decisions of the CCP constitute sister chapters (in the words of President Xi Jinping).[48]

[43] [Decision of the CCP Central Committee on the Comprehensive Promotion of Several Major Issues of the Rule of Law] 中共中央关于全面推进依法治国若干重大问题的决定 (zhōng gòng zhōng yāng guān yú quán miàn tuī jìn yī fǎ zhì guó ruò gān zhòng dà wèn tí de jué dìng), 2014.

[44] [Decision of the CCP Central Committee on Some Major Issues concerning Comprehensively Deepening the Reform] 中共中央关于全面深化改革若干重大问题的决定 (zhōng gòng zhōng yāng guān yú quán miàn shēn huà gǎi gé ruò gān zhòng dà wèn tí de jué dìng), 2013.

[45] Ibid., Section 29.

[46] Ibid., Section 44.

[47] Ibid., Section 43.

[48] [People's Daily] 人民日报 2014.

Problems arising from the progress of development would desirably be settled by development itself. Elimination of collective labour conflicts could be achieved temporarily and in some localities on an *ad hoc* basis, yet to construct a harmonious collective labour relationship, the fundamental solution relies on institutional innovation. The new mechanism of labour governance should be characterised by industrial collective autonomy, indirect government intervention and safeguards by trade unions at upper levels. China needs to correct three mistaken views of the collective labour relationship, actively endorse local reforms and explore means for coordination of collective labour relationships with Chinese characteristics.

10.4.1 Correcting Three Mistaken Views

The institutional innovation of labour governance in China requires us to correct the "Financial Crisis Attribution Doctrine", the "Doctrine of Marginal Reparation to the Mechanism of Direct Intervention" and the "Doctrine of Disorder from Indirect Intervention".

First of all, the institutional innovation of labour governance requires us to reject the "Financial Crisis Attribution Doctrine". This doctrine attributes the current situation of collective labour conflicts to the global financial crisis since the summer of 2008. Following this logic, collective labour conflicts in China would be settled automatically as the financial crisis is gradually eliminated. According to this doctrine, the optimal solution to collective labour conflicts is better to wait patiently or to facilitate recovery of the economy rather than to innovate labour governance mechanisms. This opinion proves to be wrong because those who upheld this opinion fail to see the negative influence of collective labour conflicts upon economic recovery. Nor are they able to figure out why the collective labour relationship had even tended to be more strained in recent years when the Chinese economy was improving. More importantly, this opinion is blind to structural and chronic factors causing severe collective labour conflicts in China. In terms of the structural factor, large-scale manufacturing is prominent in China. This requires labour intensity and strict discipline and often results in collective action by workers. Concerning the chronic factor, one aspect refers to situations where the unlimited supply of labour is about to come to an end. Episodes of shortage of workers occur periodically in some cities. This signifies a reversal between labour supply and demand in some sectors, and may improve the bargaining power of workers in the long term. The other aspect of the chronic factor refers to generational changes of Chinese industrial workers. The new generation of migrant workers possesses a higher level of education and stronger rights consciousness. Hence they have more sophisticated material and spiritual needs, and thus, unlike their parents, are less obedient. With all these factors combined, tension in collective labour relationships is an inevitable aspect, rather than a temporary or incidental aspect, of China's social and economic development. What is imperative for China at this stage is to strengthen the guidance and regulation of collective labour relationships.

Secondly, the institutional innovation of labour governance rejects the "Doctrine of Marginal Reparation to the Mechanism of Direct Intervention". This doctrine considers that the existing direct intervention mechanism only requires marginal reparation because this mechanism, including mediation, arbitration, litigation and supervision, is sufficient in coping with collective labour conflicts in China. For example, the disconnection among different mechanisms can be repaired through coordination among arbitration tribunals, courts and labour inspectorates. From this view, the existing direct regulatory mechanism is still relevant and bound to continue its role in collective labour governance in the future. Nevertheless, as discussed above, the direct regulatory mechanism is designed for settlement of individual labour disputes and of little aid in settling collective labour disputes. Furthermore, the current parting and separating strategies of "breaking up collective labour disputes into several individual ones" cannot be a durable success, as workers exchange information and easily coordinate with each other. Moreover, the direct regulatory mechanism is mainly used to correct employers' illegal acts but is not as useful for settling disputes over interest within the legal scope. Still, human and financial resources available to government at various levels for tackling collective labour disputes have their own limit, since investment in them is already huge and cannot go much further. Consequently, marginal reparation to the existing direct intervention mechanism is incapable of coordinating collective labour relationships.

Finally, the "Doctrine of Disorder from Indirect Intervention" is untenable. According to this doctrine, empowering workers with more collective labour rights is equivalent to encouraging confrontation between employees and employers, which may escalate collective labour conflicts. Furthermore, concerns are expressed that this approach may cause politicisation of workers' claims and lead to political movements. In short, this doctrine is anxious about loss of control over industrial relationships because the state cannot intervene directly. This opinion is equally questionable. Firstly, regardless of whether the law provides workers with collective labour rights, with or without collective labour rights being recognized by the law, confrontation between labour and capital would naturally happen. Legal empowerment may give rise to legitimate confrontations, but also reduce illegal ones outside the law. Besides, a good prospect for legitimate confrontations squeezes the room manipulable for other organisations such as townspeople's associations. Secondly, loss of control over labour conflicts is rather owing to disempowerment. Lack of legitimate means of struggle means forcing workers to come up with other, illegal, means. Irrespective of collective labour rights, recognised or not, the possibility remains of politicisation of the workers' movement. What is wise for the state is regulation via empowerment, leading the workers' movement onto the economic track. In sum, the direction of future reform of the labour governance mechanism is that workers should be given more substantive collective labour rights such as the right to strike, so as to rule out other (illegal) means of labour confrontation.

10.4.2 *Exploring a Workable Labour Governance Mechanism with Chinese Characteristics*

The proposed mechanism for labour governance should be characterised by industrial collective autonomy, indirect government intervention and safeguards by trade unions at upper levels. Industrial collective autonomy refers to collective negotiations between employers and workers themselves on major labour issues and settling relevant collective labour disputes. Indirect government intervention connotes that governments grant collective autonomy for both sides so as to mitigate collective labour conflicts and pursue a win-win outcome. Safeguards by trade unions at upper levels mean that the trade unions should support and supervise the lawful exercise of collective labour rights by grass-roots trade unions.

The key to establishing this new labour governance mechanism lies in the creation of decent institutional incentives, by which workers, employers, government authorities and trade unions at various levels are induced to accept this mechanism. The aspiration is drawn from the Right to Organise and Collective Bargaining Convention No. 98. Article 5 of the Convention suggests that:

> measures appropriate to national conditions shall be taken, where necessary, to encourage and promote the full development and utilisation of machinery for voluntary negotiation between employers or employers' organisations and workers' organisations, with a view to the regulation of terms and conditions of employment by means of collective agreements.[49]

Thus what is involved is, through appropriate institutional design, to bring all concerned parties to conduct negotiation in good faith and in a reasonable, peaceful manner.

For acceptance by workers, it is essential to ensure representation of their will in collective consultation and collective action as well as their ability to force employers back to the negotiating table. As for employers, their stake in stability in production and workplace peace should overwhelm the price they pay for their compromise. On the government's side, the new mechanism must be capable of generating industrial peace and social stability at lower costs than those involved in the existing direct intervention mechanism. To steer the commitment of trade unions to this new mechanism, it should extricate them from impotence in intervening in collective industrial conflicts.

Immediate accomplishment of this new mechanism cannot be expected. Its design needs constant experimentation and improvement. At present, experiments are taking place mainly in Guangdong province and the Shenzhen Special Economic Zone. The draft Provisions of Shenzhen Special Economic Zone on Collective Consultation (Shenzhen Provisions),[50] and the Provisions of Guangdong Province on Collective Contract in Enterprises (Guangdong Provisions) adopted in September

---

[49] Right to Organise and Collective Bargaining Convention No. 98, 1949, Article 5.

[50] [Provisions of Shenzhen Special Economic Zone on Collective Consultation (Draft)] 深圳经济特区集体协商条例 (草案) (shēn zhèn jīng jì tè qū jí tǐ xié shāng tiáo lì (cǎo àn)), 2010.

2014,[51] have embodied many valuable innovative points, compared with the Interim Measures for Collective Consultation on Wages (National Measures) at central government level.[52]

Firstly, as for labourers, the Shenzhen Provisions and the Guangdong Provisions tackle the issue of representativeness of grass-roots trade unions and the lack of bargaining power of workers, by prescribing several specific measures. The National Measures provide that the capacity of representing labourers in collective consultations is monopolised by trade unions. As we have seen, some trade unions are unwilling, afraid or unable to negotiate, thus failing to discharge their duties as the representatives of workers. The first draft of the Shenzhen Provisions, while preserving the capacity of the chief representatives of chairmen of corporate trade unions, provides that other representatives must be elected by workers' congresses from among those who volunteer or are recommended jointly by other workers. In this way, with the leading role of trade unions in negotiations being guaranteed, workers are entrusted to have their own spokesmen. In the National Measures, no solution is provided for cases where workers want to launch a collective consultation but trade unions refuse to follow up. Whereas this scenario cannot be remedied under the National Measures, the Shenzhen Provisions stipulate that as long as more than one fifth of the workforce requires the trade union to initiate negotiations, the latter may not refuse to do so. The Shenzhen Provisions further provide that no kinship should exist between representatives from opposing sides so as to avoid undue considerations in collective negotiations. Further, the Shenzhen Provisions ban employers from fake negotiations, and penalties are provided for transgressors. With regard to refusal to negotiate or default in responding to negotiation offers without justification, a fine is provided in the Shenzhen Provisions and, similarly, the Guangdong Provisions provide a remedy through applying for mediation.

Secondly, as for employers, the two ordinances improve the institution of collective negotiations, which give incentives for employers' acceptance of the new collective labour governance mechanism. In the face of pressure by workers' collective action, employers are often motivated to settle disputes via collective negotiations as the maintenance of workplace peace and a stable workforce is still a better trade-off. Previously, due to lack of institutional guarantees collective negotiation could find itself in a "pie in the sky" situation. Owing to lack of organisation and legal recognition, the representatives elected spontaneously by workers fall short of ability to achieve a settlement. For example, one Hong Kong businessman complains, "We are negotiating with flocks of people all the time, just like bargaining in fairs, and the fertility of those negotiations is doubtful".[53] In the Shenzhen Provisions and the Guangdong Provisions the institution of collective negotiation is strengthened into a credible means of collective labour dispute settlement, dispelling the chaos

[51] [Provisions of Guangdong Province on Collective Contract in Enterprises] 广东省企业集体合同条例 (guǎng dōng shěng qǐ yè jí tǐ hé tóng tiáo lì), 2014.

[52] [Interim Measures for Collective Consultation on Wages] 工资集体协商试行办法 (gōng zī jí tǐ xié shāng shì xíng bàn fǎ), 2000.

[53] See [Long] 龙飞 2010.

brought about by spontaneous negotiations, and turning industrial collective autonomy into a mechanism truly attractive to employers.

Thirdly, as for governments, the Shenzhen Provisions design a new role for them. Governments can retreat from directly mediating in collective labour disputes to a lessened role which functions to facilitate collective negotiations. In the Shenzhen Provisions, governments are relieved from direct intervention in collective labour disputes. Even if governments may act as a mediator upon a request from employers and employees, they are no more than one of several parties involved in the labour mediation committee. Thereby, governments are able to shed various problems ensuing from direct administrative intervention, such as exorbitant cost, temporariness and fragility of imposed solutions, generating new disputes. Thus governments attain a much more detached and neutral role in collective labour disputes, which is more desirable for them.

Last but not least, the Shenzhen Provisions also redefine the role for trade unions at upper levels in that they also retreat from direct participation in collective labour disputes, functioning instead as organisers, supervisors and facilitators. Trade unions at upper levels are often unfamiliar with local situations and, when dealing with collective labour disputes, often find that direct mediatory work far exceeds their ability. For this reason, the Shenzhen Provisions relieve trade unions at upper levels from direct engagement in mediation of collective labour disputes. Instead, like governments, they may act as a member of the labour mediation committee only in accordance with an application from employers and employees. As conceived in the Shenzhen Provisions, trade unions at upper levels are not to directly participate in collective negotiations, their responsibilities being to organise elections of workers' representatives and provide the latter with guidance and training in case of need. Consequently, trade unions at upper levels are able to exercise their expertise in and oversight of labour dispute settlement.

In short, the shared legislative spirit of the Shenzhen Provisions and the Guangdong Provisions accords with the new mechanism of collective labour governance proposed by this article. Such a mechanism would be characterised by industrial collective autonomy, indirect government intervention and safeguards by trade unions at upper levels. The two ordinances adopt a series of incentives and restructure the complicated relationships among workers, employers, government and trade unions, which hopefully will induce their acceptance of the new mechanism. Legal reform in China often starts with local experiments and, should such experiments succeed, are to be followed by possible nationwide promotion. Given such a tradition, the legislative practice of Guangdong and Shenzhen are significant in accumulating valuable experience and exploring a model that can be applied nationwide. These local reforms are in accordance with projects on "promoting a social management system and innovating legal constructions" and "innovating labour governance mechanisms, facilitating channels for workers' claims" as put forward by the Communist Party of China in its respective fourth and third Plenary Session of the 18th Central Committee. The state should support those local experiments and promote them nationwide on the basis of lessons drawn from practice.

References

Literature

Jia, Junling and Wei Qian. 2014. The evolution and development of China's labour law 1994. In *Cross-currents in modern Chinese labour law*, ed. Alan C. Neal, 47–62. Alphen aan den Rijn: Kluwer Law International.

[Zhu, Jiazhen] 朱家甄. 1994. [Several important issues in the implementation of the labour law] 劳动部副部长朱家甄谈《劳动法》实施中的几个主要问题 (láo dòng bù fù bù zhǎng zhū jiā zhēn tán "láo dòng fǎ" shí shī zhōng de jǐ gè zhǔ yào wèn tí). [*China Labour Science*] 中国劳动科学.

Documents and Official Publications

ILO Documents

Convention concerning Freedom of Association and Protection of the Right to Organise, adopted 9 July 1948, ILO C087. Entry into force 4 July 1950. (Freedom of Association and Protection of the Right to Organise Convention).

Convention concerning the Application of the Principles of the Right to Organise and to Bargain Collectively, adopted 1 July 1949, ILO C098. Entry into force 18 July 1951. (Right to Organise and Collective Bargaining Convention).

Convention concerning Discrimination in Respect of Employment and Occupation, adopted 25 June 1958, ILO C111. Entry into force 15 June 1960. (Discrimination (Employment and Occupation) Convention).

Convention concerning Minimum Age for Admission to Employment, adopted 26 June 1973, ILO C138. Entry into force 19 June 1976. (Minimum Age Convention).

Convention concerning the Prohibition and Immediate Action for the Elimination of the Worst Forms of Child Labour, adopted 17 June 1999, ILO C182. Entry into force 19 November 2000. (Worst Forms of Child Labour Convention).

Declaration on Fundamental Principles and Rights at Work, adopted by the International Labour Conference at its 86th Session, Geneva, 18 June 1998 (1998 Declaration).

Equal Remuneration Convention, adopted 29 June 1951, ILO C100. Entry into force 23 May 1953.

Chinese Regulation

Laws by the National People's Congress

[Trade Union Law of the People's Republic of China] 中华人民共和国工会法 (zhōng huá rén mín gòng hé guó gōng huì fǎ), National People's Congress, adopted and effective 3 April 1992. Revised and effective 27 October 2001.

Laws by the Standing Committee of the National People's Congress

[Employment Promotion Law of the People's Republic of China] 中华人民共和国就业促进法 (zhōng huá rén mín gòng hé guó jiù yè cù jìn fǎ), Standing Committee of the National People's Congress, adopted 30 August 2007, effective 1 January 2008. Revised and effective 24 April 2015.

[Labour Contract Law of the People's Republic of China] 中华人民共和国劳动合同法 (zhōng huá rén mín gòng hé guó láo dòng hé tóng fǎ), Standing Committee of the National People's Congress, adopted 29 June 2007, effective 1 January 2008. Revised 28 December 2012, effective 1 July 2013.

[Labour Dispute Mediation and Arbitration Law of the People's Republic of China] 中华人民共和国劳动争议调解仲裁法 (zhōng huá rén mín gòng hé guó láo dòng zhēng yì tiáo jiě zhòng cái fǎ), Standing Committee of the National People's Congress, adopted 29 December 2007, effective 1 May 2008.

[Labour Law of the People's Republic of China] 中华人民共和国劳动法 (zhōng huá rén mín gòng hé guó láo dòng fǎ), Standing Committee of the National People's Congress, adopted 5 July 1994, effective 1 January 1995.

[Social Insurance Law of the People's Republic of China] 中华人民共和国社会保险法 (zhōng huá rén mín gòng hé guó shè huì bǎo xiǎn fǎ), Standing Committee of the National People's Congress, adopted 28 October 2010, effective 1 July 2011.

Regulations by the State Council

[Labour Insurance Regulations of the People's Republic of China] 中华人民共和国劳动保险条例 (zhōng huá rén mín gòng hé guó láo dòng bǎo xiǎn tiáo lì), Government Administration Council of the Central People's Government, adopted and effective 26 February 1951.

[Regulations on Salary Reform] 国务院关于工资改革的规定 (guó wù yuàn guān yú gōng zī gǎi gé de guī dìng), State Council of People's Republic of China, adopted and effective 4 July 1956.

[Tentative Provisions on Dismissing Undisciplined Employees in State-Owned Enterprises] 国营企业辞退违纪职工暂行规定 (guó yíng qǐ yè cí tuì wéi jì zhí gōng zàn xíng guī dìng), State Council, adopted 12 July 1986, effective 1 October 1986.

[Tentative Provisions on Employment in State-Owned Enterprises] 国营企业招用工人暂行规定 (guó yíng qǐ yè zhāo yòng gōng rén zàn xíng guī dìng), State Council, Ministry of Labour and Personnel, adopted and effective 2 July 1986.

[Tentative Provisions on Retirement of Workers and Clerks] 国务院关于工人、职员退休处理的暂行规定 (guó wù yuàn guān yú gōng rén, zhí yuán tuì xiū chǔ lǐ de zàn xíng guī dìng), State Council, adopted 16 November 1957, effective 6 February 1958.

[Tentative Provisions on the System of Labour Contracts in State Enterprises] 国营企业实行劳动合同制暂行规定 (guó yíng qǐ yè shí xíng láo dòng hé tóng zhì zàn xíng guī dìng), State Council, adopted and effective 7 December 1986.

[Tentative Provisions on Unemployment Insurance in State-Owned Enterprises] 国营企业职工待业保险暂行规定 (guó yíng qǐ yè zhí gōng dài yè bǎo xiǎn zàn xíng guī dìng), State Council, adopted 12 July 1986, effective 1 October 1986.

Administrative Regulations

[Interim Measures for Collective Consultation on Wages] 工资集体协商试行办法 (gōng zī jí tǐ xié shāng shì xíng bàn fǎ), Ministry of Labour and Social Security, adopted 10 October 2000, effective 10 October 2000.

Other Chinese Official Documents

[Decision of the CCP Central Committee on Some Major Issues Concerning Comprehensively Deepening the Reform] 中共中央关于全面深化改革若干重大问题的决定 (zhōng gòng zhōng yāng guān yú quán miàn shēn huà gǎi gé ruò gān zhòng dà wèn tí de jué dìng), adopted at the Third Plenary Session of the 18th Central Committee of the Communist Party of China on 12 November 2013.

[Decision of the CCP Central Committee on the Comprehensive Promotion of Several Major Issues of the Rule of Law] 中共中央关于全面推进依法治国若干重大问题的决定 (zhōng gòng zhōng yāng guān yú quán miàn tuī jìn yī fǎ zhì guó ruò gān zhòng dà wèn tí de jué dìng), adopted at the Fourth Plenary Session of the 18th Central Committee of the Communist Party of China on 23 October 2014.

[Decision on Further Strengthening the Work of Trade Unions in Enterprises to Comprehensively Discharge Their Function] 关于进一步加强企业工会工作充分发挥企业工会作用的决定 (guān yú jìn yī bù jiā qiáng qǐ yè gōng huì gōng zuò chōng fēn fā huī qǐ yè gōng huì zuò yòng de jué dìng), All-China Federation of Trade Union, adopted and effective 26 July 2010.

[Provisions of Guangdong Province on Collective Contract in Enterprises] 广东省企业集体合同条例 (guǎng dōng shěng qǐ yè jí tǐ hé tóng tiáo lì), Standing Committee of the Guangdong Province People's Congress, adopted 25 September 2014, effective 1 January 2015.

[Provisions of Shenzhen Special Economic Zone on Collective Consultation (Draft)] 深圳经济特区集体协商条例(草案) (shēn zhèn jīng jì tè qū jí tǐ xié shāng tiáo lì(cǎo àn)), Shenzhen Municipal People's Congress, adopted and effective 19 January 2010.

[Regulations on Democratic Management of Enterprises] 企业民主管理规定 (qǐ yè mín zhǔ guǎn lǐ guī dìng), All-China Federation of Trade Union, adopted and effective 13 February 2012.

[Working Plan to Further Promote Collective Consultation on Wages from 2011 to 2013] 2011–2013 年深入推进工资集体协商工作规划 (2011–2013 nián shēn rù tuī jìn gōng zī jí tǐ xié shāng gōng zuò guī huà), All-China Federation of Trade Union, adopted and effective 8 January 2011.

Other Sources

[Bao, Luying] 包璐影. 2011. [More than 500 Xinhua Hospital health caring workers 'struck' for explanation] 新华医院500多名护工"罢工"讨说法 (xīn huá yī yuàn 500 duō míng hù gōng "bà gōng" tǎo shuō fǎ), 8 November 2011. Available at: http://news.qq.com/a/20111108/000457.htm. Last accessed 19 June 2015.

[Ding, Jianhua] 丁建华. 2010. [Proper Labour Dispute at SOEs will Promote Harmonious Labor Relations] 妥处国企劳资纠纷 促进劳动关系和谐 (tuǒ chǔ guó qǐ láo zī jiū fēn cù jìn láo dòng guān xì hé xié). [Chinacourt.org] 中国法院网. Available at: http://www.chinacourt.org/article/detail/2010/04/id/404340.shtml. Last accessed 19 June 2015.

[Fan, Xi] 樊曦 and [Zhongxi Qi] 齐中熙. 2013. [Collective wage consultation has covered 150 million employees in China] 全国工资集体协商覆盖职工1.5亿人 (quán guó gōng zī jí tǐ xié shāng fù gài zhí gōng 1.5 yì rén). [*Henan Workers' Daily*] 河南工人日报, Available at: http://media.workercn.cn/sites/media/hngrrb/2013_10/18/GR0107.htm. Last accessed 19 June 2015.

[Gui, Liang] 桂良, 2012. [In recent years collective labour disputes have accounted for 30 per cent of all labour cases heard by Foshan Intermediate People's Court—the Court will be issuing more than 200 companies a "Reminder"] 近年来佛山中院受理劳动争议案群体性劳资纠纷占三成—佛山中院将向逾200家企业发放《提示》 (jìn nián lái fó shān zhōng yuàn shòu lǐ láo dòng zhēng yì àn qún tǐ xìng láo zī jīu fēn zhàn sān chéng—fó shān zhōng yuàn jiāng xiàng yú 200 jiā qǐ yè fā fàng "tí shì"). [*Information Times*] 信息时报. Available at: http://informationtimes.dayoo.com/html/2012-10/31/content_1990201.htm. Last accessed 19 June 2015.

[Huang, Haoyuan] 黄浩苑 and [Yijia Zhan] 詹奕嘉. 2013. [*Survey of labour disputes in some Pearl River Delta Enterprises in the transformation and updating process*] 珠三角部分企业转型升级过程中的劳资纠纷调查 (zhū sān jiǎo bù fèn qǐ yè zhuǎn xíng shēng jí guò chéng zhōng de láo zī jiū fēn diào chá). Available at: http://www.gd.xinhuanet.com/newscenter/2013-02/28/c_114841590_2.htm. Last accessed 19 June 2015.

[Labour rights] 劳动权益 (láo dòng quán yì). 2014. [*Guangzhou Daily*] 广州日报. Available at: http://gzdaily.dayoo.com/html/2014-04/26/content_2609561.htm. Last accessed 19 June 2015.

[Li, Boyong] 李伯明. 1994. [Explanation on the Draft Labour Law of the People's Republic of China (by the Minister of Labour Mr. Li Boyong to the 6th Session of the Standing Committee of the 8th National People's Congress)] 关于《中华人民共和国劳动法(草案)》的说明 (guān yú zhōng huá rén mín gòng hé guó láo dòng fǎ cǎo àn de shuō míng). Available at: http://www.npc.gov.cn/wxzl/gongbao/2001-01/02/content_5003185.htm. Last accessed 19 June 2015.

[Li, Lin] 李林 and [Tian He] 田禾 eds. 2014. [*Blue book of rule of law: Annual report on China's Rule of Law No. 12 (2014)*] 法治蓝皮书:中国法治发展报告 No. 12(2014) (fǎ zhì lán pí shū: zhōng guó fǎ zhì fā zhǎn bào gào No. 12 (2014)). [Social Science Academic Press] 中国社会科学院出版社.

[Liu, Xiaoyan] 刘晓燕. 2013. [Shock waves brought by mass cases: focus on labour disputes, No. 1] 群体性案件带来的冲击波 聚焦劳动争议案件系列报道之一(qún tǐ xìng àn jiàn dài lái de chōng jī bō jù jiāo láo dòng zhēng yì àn jiàn xì liè bào dào zhī yī). [*China Court*] 人民法院报. Available at: http://rmfyb.chinacourt.org/paper/html/2013-05/07/content_63101.htm. Last accessed 19 June 2015.

[Long, Fei] 龙飞. 2010. [Shenzhen provisions on collective wage consultation compromised in second review] 深圳工资集体协商条例二审"被妥协" (shēn zhèn gōng zī jí tǐ xié shāng tiáo lì èr shěn "bèi tuǒ xié"). [*China Business Journal*] 中国经营报. Available at: http://www.cb.com.cn/economy/2010_1023/158924.html. Last accessed 19 June 2015.

[Newspaper commentator] 本报评论员. 2014. [To facilitate the comprehensive deepening of reform with the rule of law: On the 4th Plenary Session of the 18th Central Committee of the CCP No. 4] 用法治为全面深化改革护航 (yòng fǎ zhì wèi quán miàn shēn huà gǎi gé hù háng). [*People's Daily*] 人民日报. Available at: http://news.xinhuanet.com/2014-10/27/c_1112998448.htm. Last accessed 19 June 2015.

[Qian, Peijian] 钱培坚. 2013. [Shanghai Minhang District's Trade Union branch is to reform and improve the system of labour conflict prevention and implement "tripartite examination" on major programmes of employee relocation] 上海闵行区总健全劳资矛盾预警防控体系—企业涉及重大劳动力调整方案须"三方联合会审" (shàng hǎi mǐn háng qū zǒng jiàn quán láo zī máo dùn yù jǐng fáng kòng tǐ xì qǐ yè shè jí zhòng dà láo dòng lì tiáo zhěng fāng àn xū "sān fāng lián hé huì shěn"). [*Workers' Daily*] 工人日报. Available at: http://www.shzgh.org/renda/node5902/node18796/u1a5999726.html. Last accessed 19 June 2015.

[Tian, Jing] 田静 and [Sihua Ma] 马思华. 2013. [27 per cent of respondents have no idea of collective wage consultation] 27% 受访者不清楚工资集体协商概念 (27% shòu fǎng zhě bù qīng chǔ gōng zī jí tǐ xié shāng gài niàn), 18 October 2013. Available at: http://www.labourdaily.cn/ldb/node13/node29885/u1ai166879.html. Last accessed 19 June 2015.

[Wang, Daojun] 王道军. 2011. [Foundries of Citizen Shenzhen Establish Labour Commission] 西铁城深圳代工厂设立劳资委员会(xī tiě chéng shēn zhèn dài gōng chǎng shè lì láo zī wěi yuán huì). [*Oriental Morning Post*] 东方早报. Available at: http://finance.sina.com.cn/stock/t/20111227/030511070353.shtml. Last accessed 19 June 2015.

[Xia, Zhengfang] 夏正芳, [Xiaorong Yang] 杨晓蓉 and [Fen Wang] 王芬. 2013. [Innovating new legal aid mechanisms to safeguard social equality and justice—Anji County Court investigation report on legal aid cases] 创新法律援助机制 维护社会公平正义 浙江省安吉县法院关于法律援助案件的调研报告(chuàng xīn fǎ lǜ yuán zhù jī zhì wéi hù shè huì gōng píng zhèng yì zhè jiāng shěng ān jí xiàn fǎ yuàn guān yú fà lǜ yuán zhù àn jiàn de diào yán bào gào). [*China Court*] 人民法院报. Available at: http://rmfyb.chinacourt.org/paper/html/2013-07/04/content_66254.htm?div=-1. Last accessed 19 June 2015.

[Yang, Lin] 杨琳. 2009. [Hardship of labour-management conflicts] 劳资矛盾忧患 (láo zī máo dùn yōu huàn). [*Outlook Weekly*] 瞭望.

[Yong, Ping] 永平. 2012. [Empirical mode of Jimei Court's efficient settlement on demand of unpaid salary has been acclaimed] 集美法院高效化解工人讨薪纠纷 经验模式广受好评 (jí měi fǎ yuàn gāo xiào huà jiě gōng rén tǎo xīn jiū fēn jīng yàn mó shì guǎng shòu hǎo píng).

Available at: http://news.china.com.cn/txt/2012-09/06/content_26451715.htm. Last accessed 19 June 2015.

[Zhang, Hui] 张辉. 2010. [To solve the gridlock of "doubled income"] 求解"收入倍增"困局 (qiú jiě "shōu rù bèi zēng" kùn jú), [*Outlook Weekly*] 瞭望 11. Available at: http://www.lwgcw.com/NewsShow.aspx?newsId=3808

[Zhou, Zhenghua] 周正华. 2009. [Full review of incident where the general manager of Jilin Tonghua Steel was killed by employees] 吉林通钢总经理被职工打死事件全纪录 (jí lín tōng gāng zǒng jīng lǐ bèi zhí gōng dǎ sǐ shì jiàn quán jì lù). [*China News Weekly*] 中国新闻周刊. Available at: http://news.sina.com.cn/c/sd/2009-08-05/101418369233.shtml. Last accessed 19 June 2015.

Postscript: Labour Rights in China's Changing Political Economy

Teemu Ruskola

The varied and wide-ranging contributions to this volume have presented the reader with a rich analysis of the changing status of fundamental labour rights in the People's Republic of China (PRC), and of the range of challenges to their implementation. Rather than trying to summarize the developments that have been analyzed in the preceding chapters, these last few pages will consider briefly some of their wider social, political, economic, and cultural implications.

It is of utmost symbolic as well as practical significance that the Labour Law of 1994,[1] which forms the foundation of China's current labour regime, is set out in universal terms, applying to all employment relationships without regard to the nature of the employer. It bears emphasizing that this is a major departure from the preceding regime, under which terms of employment varied radically depending on whether one worked in the state-run economy, the collective economy, or the private economy. At least in principle, labour is today a singular, abstract category, to be regulated in a consistent fashion across all sectors.

Indeed, it is no accident that promulgation of the Labour Law coincided with the so-called "corporatization" (*gongshihua*) of state-owned enterprises (SOEs), accomplished with the aid of the Company Law,[2] promulgated a year earlier.[3] While small and medium-sized SOEs have been privatized, the state continues to hold a controlling ownership in the largest SOEs even after their conversion to the legal form of corporations, which has allowed it to maintain a significant degree of con-

[1] [Labour Law of the People's Republic of China] 中华人民共和国劳动法 (zhōng huá rén mín gòng hé guó láo dòng fǎ), 1994.

[2] [Company Law of the People's Republic of China] 中华人民共和国公司法 (zhōng huá rén mín gòng hé guó gōng sī fǎ), 1993.

[3] See generally Ruskola 2000.

T. Ruskola (✉)
Emory University Law School, Atlanta, GA 30307, USA
e-mail: teemu.ruskola@emory.edu

U. Liukkunen, Y. Chen (eds.), *Fundamental Labour Rights in China — Legal Implementation and Cultural Logic*, Ius Gentium: Comparative Perspectives on Law and Justice 49, DOI 10.1007/978-3-319-23156-3 trol in critical sectors of the economy. However, even as the state has sought to preserve its control over capital inasmuch as possible, notwithstanding a formal change in the structure of its ownership, the 1994 Labour Law and subsequent legislation have unambiguously effected a revolution – or in Marxian terms, a counter-revolution – in the state's relationship to labour.

Historically, a work unit (*danwei*) in an SOE provided its members not only with life-time job security but also a cradle-to-grave system of welfare, including housing, childcare, schools, hospitals, and retirement benefits. This extended structure of welfare was a status privilege available only to the elite urban workforce; contracts were associated with workers performing marginal, degraded, and temporary labour. Corporatized SOEs, in contrast, have withdrawn the social contract of life-time employment – the vaunted "iron rice bowl" of Maoist socialism – and replaced it with individual employment contracts, subject to the vagaries of hiring and firing. The revolutionary aspect of the post-1994 labour and employment law regime lies thus precisely in the fact that it does not distinguish among SOEs, collective enterprises, and private enterprises, nor between Chinese and foreign enterprises, or urban and rural. In essentially one generation, employment has thus become a saleable commodity throughout the PRC economy.

Seen from this wider perspective, the developments in labour and employment law analyzed in this volume can be seen as part of a larger reconfiguration of legal, political, and economic subjectivity. The social as well as psychological significance of the universalization of the employment contract cannot be overstated. It is a key institution in establishing the worker as an economic subject who agrees to the terms of his or her employment – a technology of "manufacturing consent", to use sociologist Michael Burawoy's phrase.[4] Indeed, in comparison to the more or less coercive cultivation of socialist unity in SOEs, the employment contract has been aptly described as an "anti-solidarity machine", atomizing the workforce and turning each employee ultimately into an individual entrepreneur responsible for his or her own material needs.[5] Strikingly, the PRC has not ratified any of the International Labour Organization (ILO) core Conventions regarding collective bargaining.[6]

Furthermore, it is important to recognize that the construction of autonomous market actors, both on the level of the enterprise and of the individual, has resulted in tectonic shifts in the boundaries among the spheres of the state, the market, and the family. As we contemplate the future development of labour law in the PRC, whether in relation to ILO core labour rights or other international standards, we must therefore keep in mind its place in the larger political economy of which it is a part. With the breakdown of the labour regime associated with socialist SOEs, social welfare benefits that were previously delivered by the work unit must today be provided by other means – either through markets (like housing in the PRC today), or directly by the state (like education), or by the family (like childcare, for example). The consequences of restructuring the labour relationship have thus cas-

[4] Burawoy 1979.

[5] See Lee and Shen 2011.

[6] Namely, the Freedom of Association and Protection of the Right to Organise Convention No. 87 and the Right to Organise and Collective Bargaining Convention No. 98.

caded across numerous institutions, reconfiguring the entire social landscape. The abiding significance of Chinese labour rights reform can thus hardly be overstated.

In a sense, the smashing of the iron rice bowl and contractualization of all labour relations have brought about a new kind of equality among workers, albeit one based on a "leveling-down" of the distinction between the socialist "labour aristocracy" of SOEs and other workers, rural and otherwise. The consequences of this across-the-board commodification of labour are especially painful in a state whose official governing ideology is socialism. For the first time in China's history there exists today a large class of impoverished and radically powerless industrial workers – of rural as well as urban origin – yet there is no adequate political or analytic vocabulary to address their condition. When the economic reforms began in 1978, they were premised on the Party-State's announcement in 1978 that the class struggle had been won, allowing the nation to focus on economic development instead.[7] Paradoxically, today's massive class inequality has been made possible by the elimination of class from the official lexicon of the PRC. The erstwhile ideologically glorified – though politically subordinated – Chinese workers have thus been transformed into an army of servants of globalization.[8]

As the preceding chapters have shown, international labour rights provide a valuable vantage point for examining the ongoing transformation of labour relations in the PRC. We have seen that local cultural and political logics do not always yield to the universal aspirations of international standards, yet it remains important to analyze the challenges facing China in a global frame, in relation to workers elsewhere facing similar problems. One notable aspect of globalization not considered in this volume entails the accelerating export of Chinese capital abroad, followed by relocation of Chinese workers and the globalization of Chinese labour practices. Perhaps most notably, the status of Chinese workers and labour practices abroad has come under scrutiny in the context of Chinese investment in Africa.[9]

As we continue to address global and local challenges in the organization of work, in China and elsewhere, it is important to keep in mind both the potential and limits of the frameworks we bring to our analysis.[10] As I have noted elsewhere, all too often we take those frameworks as givens, seeking to fit Chinese facts into Western theories. A more fruitful comparative approach must consider the possibility that China – in this case, the way in which work is organized in China – can generate theory itself, new insights about labour, rather than being only a source of data to confirm or disprove theories of North Atlantic origin.[11]

In considering the limitations of the ILO's conception of fundamental labour rights, Liukkunen and Chen observe that it is a distinctly liberal one, positing the worker as a bearer of a set of rights.[12] Over the course of the second half of the

---

[7] See the Communiqué of the Third Plenary Session of the Eleventh Central Committee of the Chinese Communist Party, 1978.

[8] The phrase is Rhacel Parreñas's, though I use it in a broader sense. See Salazar Parreñas 2001.

[9] See e.g. Lee 2009.

[10] See generally Ruskola 2013.

[11] Ruskola 2013, at p. 221.

[12] See Liukkunen and Chen, Chap. 1 in this volume.

twentieth century, Chinese socialism failed to live up to its core principle – egalitarianism – by establishing a status hierarchy of workers, with privileges for some. Yet it is woefully evident that the abolition of that hierarchy and its replacement with a regime of formally equal workers entering into labour contracts with employers has not resulted in widely shared social equality; on the contrary. The increasing society-wide economic polarization that has accompanied the restructuring of labour relations in China remains perhaps the ultimate challenge for labour law, demanding new insights and new approaches that will be ultimately of global relevance, given the growth of economic inequality everywhere.

References

Literature

Burawoy, Michael. 1979. *Manufacturing consent: Changes in the labor process under monopoly capitalism*. Chicago: University of Chicago Press.

Lee, Ching-Kwan. 2009. Raw encounters: Chinese managers, African workers and the politics of casualization in Africa's Chinese enclaves. *China Quarterly* 199: 647–666.

Lee, Ching-Kwan, and Yuan Shen. 2011. An anti-solidarity machine? Labor Nongovernmental Organizations in China. In *From iron rice bowl to informalization: Markets, workers, and the state in a changing in China*, ed. Sarosh Kuruvilla, Ching-Kwan Lee, and Mary E. Gallagher, 175–187. Ithaca: Cornell University Press.

Liukkunen, Ulla, and Yifeng Chen. 2016. Developing fundamental labour rights in China – A new approach to implementation. In *Fundamental labour rights in China – Legal implementation and cultural logic*, ed. Ulla Liukkunen and Chen Yifeng, 1–18. The Netherlands: Springer.

Ruskola, Teemu. 2000. Conceptualizing corporations and kinship: Comparative law and development theory in a Chinese perspective. *Stanford Law Review* 52: 1599–1729.

Ruskola, Teemu. 2013. *Legal orientalism: China, the United States, and modern law*. Cambridge: Harvard University Press.

Salazar Parreñas, Rhacel. 2001. *Servants of globalization: Women, migration, and domestic work*. Stanford: Stanford University Press.

Documents and Official Publications

ILO Documents

Convention concerning Freedom of Association and Protection of the Right to Organise, adopted 9 July 1948, ILO C087. Entry into force 4 July 1950. (Freedom of Association and Protection of the Right to Organise Convention).

Convention concerning the Application of the Principles of the Right to Organise and to Bargain Collectively, adopted 1 July 1949, ILO C098. Entry into force 18 July 1951. (Right to Organise and Collective Bargaining Convention).

Chinese Regulation

[Company Law of the People's Republic of China] 中华人民共和国制司法 (zhōng huá rén mín gòng hé guó gōng sī fǎ), Standing Committee of the National People's Congress, 29 December 1993. Entry into force 25 December 1999.

[Labour Law of the People's Republic of China] 中华人民共和国劳动法 (zhōng huá rén mín gòng hé guó láo dòng fǎ), Standing Committee of the National People's Congress, adopted 5 July 1994, effective 1 January 1995.

Other Sources

Communiqué of the 3rd Plenary Session of the Eleventh Central Committee of the Communist Party of China, adopted 22 December 1978. [*Peking Review*] 29 December 1978.